Debt Advice Handbook Scotland

....

1st edition

Pauline Allan, Martin Barr, Danna Higgins, Estelle Kerr, Lorna Maisey, Ken McEwan, Ged Mulvey and Joanne Porter

Child Poverty Action Group

Child Poverty Action Group works on behalf of the more than one in four children in the UK growing up in poverty. It does not have to be like this. We use our understanding of what causes poverty and the impact it has on children's lives to campaign for policies that will prevent and solve poverty – for good. We provide training, advice and information to make sure hard-up families get the financial support they need. We also carry out high-profile legal work to establish and protect families' rights. If you are not already supporting us, please consider making a donation, or ask for details of our membership schemes, training courses and publications.

Published by Child Poverty Action Group
30 Micawber Street
London N1 7TB
Tel: 020 7837 7979
info@cpag.org.uk
cpag.org.uk

© Child Poverty Action Group 2024

This book is sold subject to the condition that it shall not, by way of trade or otherwise, be lent, resold, hired out or otherwise circulated without the publisher's prior consent in any form of binding or cover other than that in which it is published and without a similar condition including this condition being imposed on the subsequent purchaser.

A CIP record for this book is available from the British Library
ISBN: 978 1 915324 01 6

Child Poverty Action Group is a charity registered in England and Wales (registration number 294841) and in Scotland (registration number SC039339), and is a company limited by guarantee, registered in England (registration number 1993854). VAT number: 690 808117

Cover design by Colorido Studios
Internal design by Devious Designs
Typeset by DLxml, a division of RefineCatch Limited, Bungay, Suffolk
Content management system by Konnectsoft
Printed in the UK by CPI Group (UK) Ltd, Croydon CR0 4YY

The authors

This *Handbook* has been planned, developed and written by the members of the MATRICS team. Funded by the Scottish government, MATRICS (Money Advice Training, Resource, Information and Consultancy Service) is a partnership between Money Advice Scotland (MAS) and Citizens Advice Scotland (CAS).

Pauline Allan began her career as a social worker, moving into debt advice in the late 1990s. She was the manager of the Edinburgh City Council debt advice team and became coordinator of the MATRICS team in 2010.

Martin Barr has worked in various debt advice roles for over 30 years, primarily as a debt adviser, before joining MAS where he helped develop its first training programme. He currently works for CAS within the MATRICS team delivering the MATRICS learn programme.

Danna Higgins has worked in debt advice for 28 years. She was a frontline debt adviser in Edinburgh before joining the MATRICS team as a money advice consultant in 2016. She was involved in developing the MATRICS learn programme and delivers training and consultancy to debt advisers.

Estelle Kerr worked as a money adviser in Ross and Cromarty CAB, providing advice and financial education from 2013 to 2019. She became a housing adviser with Inverness, Badenoch and Strathspey CAB. She joined MAS in 2021 as a digital adviser before moving into the MATRICS team as a money advice consultant.

Lorna Maisey has worked in debt advice for nine years. She was a frontline debt adviser in West Lothian before joining the MATRICS team as a money advice consultant in 2022.

Ken McEwan has been involved in giving and training on debt advice since 1985. He has worked with MAS as a trainer since 2001 and is one of the original members of the MATRICS team.

Ged Mulvey has over 12 years of experience in debt advice. He has worked as a debt adviser for West Lothian Council and for Perennial, and is currently the training development lead at MAS. He has been a money advice consultant with MATRICS since 2018.

Joanne Porter is a welfare rights worker at CPAG in Scotland.

Acknowledgements

First of all, many thanks to the Scottish government for providing the funds to enable this new Scottish resource to be published free online. It is available at cpag.org.uk/handbooks and is updated regularly.

This *Handbook* is based on CPAG's *Debt Advice Handbook* which has been the standard text for debt advice in England and Wales for over 30 years. The authors of that book, most notably Mike Wolfe and Peter Madge, are gratefully acknowledged.

We are very grateful to Kim Banks, Carole Benzie, Kelly Gallagher, Natalia Mallon, Joe McMonagle, Tony Pearson and Christine Sinclair for checking and providing an adviser-level view of the text. Thanks also to Robyn Moffat-Wall for her advice on the economic abuse chapter and to Ian Horne from the Scottish Courts and Tribunal Service for his advice on the court fines chapter. Special thanks to John Cook and the individual teams at the Accountant in Bankruptcy for reviewing Chapter 6.

Last but not least, thanks to the team at CPAG. Thanks also to Katherine Dawson for producing the index and Kathleen Armstrong for proofreading the text.

This book is dedicated to all the hard-working debt advisers in Scotland.

The law covered in this book was correct on and includes regulations laid up to 1 July 2024.

Contents

The authors	iii
Acknowledgements	iv
How to use this *Handbook*	x
Abbreviations	xii

Chapter 1	**Debt advice: an outline**	1
1.	Professional debt advice	1
2.	The debt advice system	10
3.	Administration	12

Chapter 2	**Key skills**	16
1.	Interviewing	16
2.	Negotiating	17
3.	Letter writing	18
4.	Representing clients in court	21
5.	Changing policy	25
6.	Challenging poor debt collection	28
7.	Budgeting advice	33

Chapter 3	**The six stages of the debt advice process**	39
1.	Stage 1: find out the whole situation	39
2.	Stage 2: deal with emergencies	45
3.	Stage 3: check liabilities	49
4.	Stage 4: listing creditors and priority and non-priority debts	51
5.	Stage 5: create the initial Common Financial Statement	57
6.	Stage 6: maximise income and reduce expenditure	62

Chapter 4	**Household debt**	68
1.	Child support payments	68
2.	Spousal maintenance payments	72
3.	Gas and electricity charges	73
4.	Council tax	79
5.	Water charges	87

Chapter 5	**Consumer credit**	92
1.	Introduction	92
2.	The Consumer Credit Act 1974	93

3. Pre-contractual information	97
4. Key elements of consumer credit agreements	98
5. Withdrawal, cancellation and cooling-off periods	100
6. Unfair relationships	101
7. Arrears notices	103
8. Default notices	104
9. Voluntary termination of hire purchase and personal contract purchase agreements	104
10. Time orders	105
11. Section 75 credit card protection	107
12. Early repayment rules under the Consumer Credit Act	108
13. Credit reference agencies	108
14. The Financial Conduct Authority's role	112
15. Financial Ombudsman Service and Financial Services Compensation Scheme	112

Chapter 6 Statutory debt solutions in Scotland 115
1. Introduction 115
2. The Common Financial Tool 116
3. The Debt Arrangement Scheme 129
4. The Minimal Asset Process 150
5. Full Administration Bankruptcy 156
6. Creditor petitions for bankruptcy 165
7. Protected trust deeds 169
8. Common rules in bankruptcy 186
9. Statutory moratorium on diligence 199

Chapter 7 Money claims in the sheriff court 208
1. Introduction 208
2. Simple procedure 208
3. Ordinary cause 220
4. Summary warrant 230

Chapter 8 Housing debt 234
1. Social housing sector 234
2. Private rented sector 240
3. Mortgage arrears 250

Chapter 9 Diligence 271
1. Attachment and exceptional attachment 271
2. Earnings arrestment 281
3. Bank arrestment 284
4. Money attachment 292

5. Inhibition in execution	295
6. On the dependence	297
7. Adjudication for debt	298
8. Summary diligence	299

Chapter 10 Non-diligence debt recovery — 303
1. Introduction — 303
2. Direct earnings attachments — 303
3. Deduction from earnings orders — 308
4. Third-party deductions — 313

Chapter 11 Time to pay directions and orders — 321
1. Time to pay directions — 321
2. Time to pay orders — 325

Chapter 12 Prescription and limitation — 330
1. Introduction — 330
2. Short negative prescription (five years) — 331
3. Long negative prescription (20 years) — 333
4. Common debt types — 334
5. Dealing with a prescription case — 336

Chapter 13 Messengers-at-arms and sheriff officers — 340
1. Introduction — 340
2. What sheriff officers do — 341
3. Sheriff officers' powers to enforce debts from other parts of the UK — 344
4. Making a complaint about a sheriff officer — 344

Chapter 14 Business debts — 346
1. Introduction — 346
2. Types of small business — 348
3. Stages of debt advice — 354
4. Checklist — 374

Chapter 15 Debt and mental health — 375
1. Introduction — 375
2. Mental health conditions — 376
3. Issues for clients and advisers — 378
4. Data protection and sensitive personal data — 380
5. Debt and Mental Health Evidence Form — 380
6. Mental health and capacity to contract in Scotland — 382
7. Key requirements and guidance — 384

Chapter 16 Debt and vulnerability — 387
1. Introduction — 387
2. What is vulnerability? — 387
3. Client vulnerability — 389
4. Building useful relationships — 391
5. Clients with suicidal feelings — 392
6. Vulnerability and financial capability — 392
7. Safeguarding — 395
8. Actions and considerations — 395
9. Tools and support — 396

Chapter 17 Economic abuse — 399
1. Introduction — 399
2. What is economic abuse — 399
3. Who is affected by economic abuse — 400
4. Financial abuse versus economic abuse — 400
5. Identifying economic abuse — 401
6. The adviser's role — 402
7. Economic abuse and debt — 406
8. Financial Abuse Code — 410

Chapter 18 Debt when someone dies — 412
1. Liability for debts — 412
2. The executor — 413
3. The estate — 414
4. Checklist — 416

Chapter 19 Benefits and other payments — 418
1. Introduction — 418
2. How to use this chapter — 420
3. A–Z of benefits and tax credits — 422
4. A–Z of other financial help — 440

Chapter 20 Court fines — 448
1. Introduction — 448
2. The Crown Office and Procurator Fiscal Service — 448
3. Non-payment of court fines — 450
4. Debt solution — 452
5. Checklist for action — 452

Chapter 21 Student debt — 454
1. Advising students — 454
2. Tuition fees — 455

3. Student loans 455
4. Bursaries and grants 458
5. Educational trusts and endowments 461
6. Help with housing costs 461
7. Council tax 462
8. Overdrafts 463

Appendices
Appendix 1 Glossary 464
Appendix 2 Useful organisations 476
Appendix 3 Statement of Undertaking and Statement of Truth 480
Appendix 4 Abbreviations used in the notes 483

Index 484

How to use this *Handbook*

This *Handbook* has been planned, developed and written by the members of the MATRICS team. MATRICS provides second-tier support to the free-to-client money advice sector in Scotland. It provides training, consultancy support, information and resources to help ensure quality services for people with unmanageable debt throughout Scotland. MATRICS learn is a learning platform to train advisers on all aspects of debt and debt solutions. This *Handbook* is designed to complement and add to other learning opportunities. For more information, email consultancy@matrics.org.uk or call 0845 123 2326.

This *Handbook* is also produced:
- as a guide and training aid for new debt advisers;
- as a reference for those who undertake debt advice alongside other sorts of advice work or other professional disciplines – eg, social workers and housing officers;
- for specialist debt advisers as a first step in accessing primary legislation and regulations;
- for managers or purchasers of debt advice services to help understand and evaluate debt advice.

The subjects covered within debt advice are vast and could fill many volumes. In this *Handbook*, much detail has been deliberately excluded to keep it accessible and to make clear the structure of debt advice work.

Chapters 1 to 3 assist those interested in **debt advice**, outlining the processes and skills involved. They should be read by new debt advisers and those who have done some debt work and would like to think more about the structure behind their practical experience. These chapters can also be used by those who commission or manage debt advice as a means of clarifying the product with which they are dealing.

Chapter 4 deals with **household debt**, including council tax arrears.

New advisers should ensure they are familiar with the basic rules on **consumer credit** (explained in **Chapter 5**) and can identify each type of credit and other debts contained in other chapters because this is fundamental to using the rest of the *Handbook*.

If you are already familiar with the debt advice processes, you may wish to use **Chapter 6** to help you think about the best strategy for a particular debt. This might include **statutory debt solutions** such as the Debt Arrangement Scheme, bankruptcy or a protected trust deed.

Money claims in the sheriff court are covered in **Chapter 7**.

Housing debt, including private rented and social rented sectors, together with mortgage arrears are dealt with in **Chapter 8**.

Diligence is covered in **Chapter 9**. It includes sections on earnings arrestment, bank account arrestment, attachment and exceptional attachment.

Chapter 10 covers **debt recovery** through a deduction from earnings order, direct earnings attachment and third-party deductions.

Time to pay directions and orders are covered in **Chapter 11**.

Prescription is covered in **Chapter 12**. It covers both the five-year and the 20-year rules.

If the client is threatened with enforcement (sheriff officers and messengers-at-arms) action, refer to **Chapter 13**.

Specific debts are dealt with in **Chapter 14 (business debt), Chapter 18 (debt when someone dies)** and **Chapter 21 (student debt)**. An overview of **benefits and other payments** in Scotland is in **Chapter 19. Chapter 20** looks at **court fines**.

Chapters 15, 16 and 17 cover **mental health, vulnerability and economic abuse**.

Details of other useful reference material and organisations can be found in the **Appendices**.

Abbreviations

AA	attendance allowance	DMHEF	Debt and Mental Health Evidence Form
AFIP	armed forces independence payment	DPA 2018	Data Protection Act 2018
AiB	Accountant in Bankruptcy	DPP	Debt Payment Programme
ADP	adult disability payment	EA	earnings arrestment
ADR	alternative dispute resolution	EO	enforcement order
AFO	arrestment of funds order	ESA	employment and support allowance
APR	annual percentage rate		
BRO	Bankruptcy Restriction Order	EU	European Union
CA	carer's allowance	FAB	Full Administration Bankruptcy
CAB	Citizens Advicve Bureau	FCA	Financial Conduct Authority
CAO	conjoined arrestment order	FEO	fines enforcement officer
CAS	Citizens Advice Scotland	FOS	Financial Ombudsman Service
CCA 1974	Consumer Credit Act 1974	GDPR	General Data Protection Regulation
CCA 2006	Consumer Credit Act 2006		
CDP	child disability payment	HB	housing benefit
CFS	Common Financial Statement	HMRC	HM Revenue and Customs
CFT	Common Financial Tool	HP	hire purchase
CMA	Current maintenance arrestment	IIDB	industrial injuries disablement benefit
CMS	Child Maintenance Service	IS	income support
CONC	*Consumer Credit Sourcebook*	JSA	jobseeker's allowance
COPFS	Crown Office and Procurator Fiscal Service	LLP	limited liability partnership
		LSB	Lending Standards Board
CSA	Child Support Agency	MA	maternity allowance
CSP	carer support payment	MAP	Minimal Asset Process
CTC	child tax credit	MaPS	Money and Pensions Service
CTR	council tax reduction	MAS	Money Advice Scotland
DAIP	Debt Advice and Information Package	MATRICS	Money Advice Training, Resource, Information and Consultancy Service
DAS	Debt Arrangement Scheme		
DCO	debtor contribution order	MCOB	*The Mortgages and Home Finance: cConduct of bBusiness sSourcebook*
DEA	direct earnings attachment		
DEO	deduction from earnings order		
DLA	disability living allowance	MIG	mortgage indemnity guarantee
DHP	discretionary housing payment		

Abbreviations

NI	national insurance
PAYE	Pay As You Earn
PC	pension credit
PCP	personal contract purchase
PILON	pay in lieu of notice
PPI	payment protection insurance
PMB	protected minimum balance
PTD	protected trust deed
PIP	personal independence payment
SAP	statutory adoption pay
SCTS	Scottish Courts and Tribunals Service
SDA	severe disablement allowance
SLAB	Scottish Legal Aid Board
SLC	standard licence condition
SNS	Scottish National Standards
SNSAIP	Scottish National Standards for Information and Advice Providers
SMP	statutory maternity pay
SPBP	statutory parental bereavement pay
SPP	statutory paternity pay
SSP	statutory sick pay
SSPP	statutory shared parental pay
SSS	Social Security Scotland
STFCPB	short-term financial crisis payment break
SVO	seizure of vehicle order
TTPD	time to pay direction
TTPO	time to pay order
UC	universal credit
VAT	value added tax
WTC	working tax credit

Chapter 1

Debt advice: an outline

This chapter covers:
1. Professional debt advice (below)
2. The debt advice system (p10)
3. Administration (p12)

1. Professional debt advice

Debt advice is a set of tools and strategies used to help clients deal with financial difficulties. Debt advice provides help to clients by:
- explaining the implications of non-payment of each of their debts and, on this basis, deciding which are priorities;
- establishing whether or not they are liable for their debts, and assisting them to challenge their creditors if appropriate;
- enabling them to maximise their disposable income;
- assisting them to plan their budgets;
- providing impartial, independent and confidential advice to enable them to make an informed choice about the solutions available;
- helping them choose a strategy that will minimise the effects of their debt on their financial, social or personal wellbeing;
- preserving their home, essential goods and services, and liberty;
- assisting by advice or representation with the implementation of whatever strategy is chosen.

Debt advice is a professional activity

There is a package of attitudes, skills and strategies that are part of any debt advice service. This helps guarantee consistency and quality assurance.

Debt advice can be provided by specialists or professionals whose job primarily involves other activities – eg, housing officers, welfare rights officers or solicitors.

It can be provided by paid or voluntary workers.

In recent years, there has also been a growth in private debt management companies.

Chapter 1: Debt advice: an outline
1. Professional debt advice

Ensuring good practice

There are currently no individual qualifications for debt advisers in Scotland.

Previous qualifications such as the Scottish Vocational Qualification in advice and guidance and the Certificate of Money Advice Practice are not currently offered.

Therefore, individual advisers are not subject to a national quality control framework, as such, but their organisations are, through the Scottish National Standards for Information and Advice Providers (SNSAIP – often referred to as 'the Scottish National Standards' (SNS)).

For organisations

The *Scottish National Standards for Information and Advice Providers: a quality assurance framework 2009* is the accepted quality framework for agencies providing advice on housing, money, debt and welfare benefits issues in Scotland.[1] It is owned by the Scottish government and operated by the Scottish Legal Aid Board.

The standards are designed to help not-for-profit organisations to assess and improve the quality of their advice services, and their primary purpose is to encourage organisations to adopt a culture of continuous improvement for their advice work.

Accreditation also supports organisations to demonstrate to the public and funders that their advice service is well managed and provides good-quality advice.

> *Where can you find the standards?*
> You can find the SNS framework on the Scottish government's website.[2]
> The standards are in three sections.
> **Section 1** covers the six organisational standards. These are used to measure the performance of agencies through an audit process.
> **Section 2** covers the competencies that are based on which an agency's casework is peer-reviewed. **Note:** while the SNSIAP framework has not changed, the Scottish government has updated the competencies for advisers to ensure they reflect current legislation.[3]
> **Section 3** is a good practice guide. It was accurate at the time of publication in 2009, but you should now refer to the SNSIAP self-assessment guidance to help you prepare for audit and peer review.[4]

Before your agency can apply for accreditation, you must identify the types of advice your agency provides. There are three types of advice.

Active information, signposting and explanation (type I)

Type I work covers actions such as providing information either orally or in writing, signposting or referring the user to other available resources or services.

Chapter 1: Debt advice: an outline
1. Professional debt advice

It also includes the explanation of technical terms or clarifying an official document, such as a tenancy agreement or a possession order.

There is a distinction between the passive provision of information through the availability of leaflets (eg, in public places such as libraries) and the active provision of information by assisting the individual seeking help. These standards are aimed at 'active' providers.

Type I accreditation is a one-stage process made up of an audit against the organisational standards.

There is no procedure for auditing casework.

Casework (type II)

Type II work includes:
- a diagnostic interview where the problem and all relevant issues are identified;
- making a judgement as to whether the individual has a case that can be pursued.

Once it is established that the client has a case that can be pursued, actions that your agency may undertake include the following.
- Setting out a client's options or courses of action.
- Encouraging the client to take action on their own behalf.
- Providing practical aid with letters or forms.
- Negotiating with third parties on the client's behalf.
- Introducing the client by referral to another source of help.
- Support to clients in making their own case to their creditors.

Type II/III accreditation is a two-stage process which is made up of the peer review of case files, followed by an audit against the organisational standards. You cannot apply for audit until you have successfully completed the peer review process.[5]

Citizens Advice Bureaux (CABx) follow much the same accreditation process as other advice agencies offering type II/type III advice.[6] The only difference is there are fewer organisational standards CABx are required to self-assess against, as they have already undergone a Citizens Advice Scotland (CAS) audit.

Advocacy, representation and mediation at a tribunal or court action level (type III)

This work includes a range of further actions arising from the casework defined in type II. It may have been undertaken by the adviser preparing the tertiary work or may have come to the adviser by referral from another organisation or adviser.

The principal activities may include:
- advocacy and representation – where the adviser prepares a case for the user and represents or speaks on their behalf at a tribunal or court;
- mediation – where the adviser acts on behalf of the user by seeking to mediate between the user and a third party.

Type III work includes some activities that can only be undertaken by lawyers.

Chapter 1: Debt advice: an outline
1. Professional debt advice

The accreditation process for agencies offering type II advice and those offering type II and type III advice is the same.

How to apply and qualify for the standards

Step 1: get ready to self-assess against the organisational standards.
- Read the self-assessment guidance to help you identify what evidence the auditor will be looking for when you are audited.[7]

Step 2: complete your self-assessment.
- Complete the Self Assessment and Application Form.[8]
- You may find it helpful to use the three-page self-assessment summary to keep on track.[9]

Step 3: are you ready for accreditation?
- If no, use the self-assessment guidance[10] to identify what is missing and what you need to do to be ready for accreditation. If you are still unsure of what you need to do, contact the SNSIAP auditor.[11]
- If yes, move on to Step 4.

Step 4: apply for accreditation.
- When you are satisfied that you are ready to apply for accreditation, you should email SNSIAP to apply.[12] Your email must include:
  – name of your organisation; *and*
  – main contact details; *and*
  – the areas of advice you wish to be accredited in (housing and/or welfare benefits and/or money and debt); *and*
  – confirmation that you have completed the self-assessment and application form.

More detailed information on the process can be found at slab.org.uk/advice-agencies/scottish-national-standards-for-information-and-advice-partners/type-1-accreditation.

What happens next?

The first step is to have an internal audit of your policies and procedures.

The second step is to have a selection of your case files audited by peer reviewers. This is where individual advisers' cases can be subject to an external audit process.

Successful organisations are accredited at types I, II or III, depending on the level of service they offer. A list of accredited agencies can be found at slab.org.uk/advice-agencies/scottish-national-standards-for-information-and-advice-partners/list-of-agencies-already-accredited.

Citizens Advice Bureau accreditation

CABx follow much the same accreditation process as other advice agencies. The only difference is the number of organisational standards CABx are required to self-assess against.

Following peer review of your casework, your bureau is expected to demonstrate compliance with the 10 organisational standards relating to casework and referral in your self-assessment and application form.

The most recent audit report from CAS must also be submitted as part of your application to demonstrate compliance with all the organisational standards in the SNSIAP framework.

Following agreement with CAS, all CABx are now peer reviewed via direct access to their case files on CASTLE.

CABx are audited via a desktop review.

Guidance and forms

When self-assessing and applying for accreditation, CABx must use the CABx self-assessment and application form,[13] the CABx self-assessment summary form[14] and the self-assessment guidance for CABx.[15]

Cases to be reviewed must be accompanied by a consent form from the client. CAS has produced guidance on client consent and data protection for CABx.[16]

More information can be found at slab.org.uk/advice-agencies/scottish-national-standards-for-information-and-advice-partners/cab-accreditation.

Tackling Problem Debt Group

On 1 January 2019, the Scottish government took control of the Financial Conduct Authority (FCA) levy funding for Scotland.

It created a forum for discussing the future direction of debt advice in Scotland. The Tackling Problem Debt Group was formed from representatives of the government and other interested bodies such as Money Advice Scotland, CAS, COSLA, StepChange and the Scottish Legal Aid Board.

Its vision is for a free debt advice system that is:
- **user-centred.** Free debt advice must focus on responding to the needs of those who seek it. While the quality of service and availability should, as far as practicable, be comparable across Scotland, it should reflect the differing circumstances of communities and user groups and allow them to make choices that are right for them on how and where to seek help;
- **collaborative.** The free debt advice sector consists of many advice providers and funders. The expertise of each must be recognised, as is the value of overlapping services where these reach different communities or groups. However, we must also recognise that user needs can be well served by more joined-up services, where users can easily be referred from one provider to another. Sharing expertise can also reduce costs and workloads for advisers, leading to better morale and service provision;

Chapter 1: Debt advice: an outline
1. Professional debt advice

- **sustainable.** A free debt advice service must have a range and breadth of providers supported by adequate funding to allow them to survive. In turn, these advisers must have the requisite staff and expertise to provide a high-quality service to support users. Both goals require investment that finds the balance between supporting immediate service needs and developing services for the future.

It has since come up with a 'route map', with nine recommendations.

Scottish government's debt route map [17]
1. Ensure that levy funding reflects the needs and experiences of users and potential users of debt advice.
2. Develop a debt helpline that is Scottish-focused and better integrated with Scotland's advice landscape.
3. Develop a three-year funding model for levy-funded debt advice.
4. Operationalise the Funders Framework to bring more consistency and clarity to advice funding.
5. Develop a model of Scottish government levy funding that is transparent, independent and rigorously reviewed and evaluated for impact.
6. Develop a more integrated funding landscape for free debt advice.
7. Harness the potential of technology in a way that practically improves the experience of both providing and receiving debt advice.
8. Develop a workforce strategy for the free debt advice sector.
9. Ensure sustainable funding is available to achieve the outcomes identified above.

More detailed information on the route map can be found on the Scottish government website.[18]

Second-tier support from MATRICS consultancy

The MATRICS project (Money Advice Training, Resource, Information and Consultancy Service) provides the free-to-client money advice sector with training, consultancy support, information and resources to help ensure quality services for people with unmanageable debt throughout Scotland.

As money advisers are faced with increasingly complex cases, the MATRICS team provides second-tier support to ensure that the people working on the front line of money advice have somewhere to turn for guidance and support.

MATRICS is a partnership between Money Advice Scotland and CAS and has operated across the sector for almost 20 years.

For more information, email consultancy@matrics.org.uk or call 0845 123 2326.

MATRICS learn

MATRICS learn is a blended-learning platform developed to update learning approaches and allow advisers to progress their learning in a controlled, step-by-step way.

It is also used to accredit debt advisers who are not automatically accredited through their agency to deliver the Debt Arrangement Scheme and sign certificates for sequestration.

It is based on a 'flipped-learning' approach, putting the emphasis on the learner, not the tutor, and moving away from traditional behaviourist learning to social constructivist learning, where learners are encouraged to learn from each other.

The innovative programme is fully learner-centred and promotes knowledge input via bite-sized e-learning modules, followed by discussion groups and workshops considering practical examples to deepen understanding.

It is designed to help advisers progress their learning and deepen their understanding as they go through the learning pathway. Due to the current and expected demand for more debt advisers in Scotland, the MATRICS partnership has prioritised and expanded the provision of training for new debt advisers. Advisers can work through the elearning with self-assessment at their own pace and join the live peer and tutor groups for that crucial link to practical application and confidence building. To register, visit matricslearn.org.uk. You will be guided through the set-up process after you click 'create new account'. You must use a valid work email address to sign up. There is an opportunity to request that your Wiseradviser training record be transferred to MATRICS learn as part of the registration form. When you register, you are encouraged to start at level 1 and work your way through the stages.

The Financial Conduct Authority

The provision of debt advice is a regulated activity, which generally requires the adviser (or their employer) to be authorised by the FCA. Guidance on good practice is in the FCA's *Consumer Credit Sourcebook* (abbreviated to CONC), which is part of the *FCA Handbook* (available at handbook.fca.org.uk). Debt advice (debt counselling) for all agencies is defined by the FCA in the *Perimeter Guidance Manual* (PERG) which is part of the *FCA Handbook*.

For definitions of debt advice, see PERG17.5 and 17.7.[19]

The client's best interests

In any situation where money is owed, there are two parties whose interests may conflict. As a professional debt adviser, you should know that you cannot advise both parties in such a situation, and so you must be clear that you are working only for the interests of the client. This is true even if your employment is funded by the finance industry or another creditor, such as a local authority, or if you work for an organisation that seeks to be impartial.

The FCA's *Consumer Credit Sourcebook* makes it clear that all advice given, and action taken, must consider the best interests of the client and must take into account:
- their financial circumstances; *and*
- their personal circumstances, including the reasons for their financial difficulty and whether they are temporary or long term; *and*
- any other relevant factors, including any known or reasonably foreseeable changes in the client's circumstances.

You should also take into account whether the client is a vulnerable person, the options open to the client and the powers of the creditor to enforce the debt.

A professional attitude

As a professional debt adviser, you should be aware of your past experiences from which you may have developed a judgemental attitude towards some clients and/or creditors. Consciously avoid any personal bias and adopt a professional approach to the work you do.

You should also offer a high-quality, accessible service to all groups in society and should work towards understanding that debt can affect clients from different backgrounds in different ways.

A commitment to social policy

As a professional debt adviser, you should not allow the same recurring problems you encounter with clients to adversely affect the lives of others but should make known the lessons that can be learnt from your work to as wide an audience of policymakers as possible.

A sound knowledge of law and procedures

As a professional debt adviser, you should be knowledgeable and imaginative about the ways in which the law can be applied to mitigate the effects of debt. You should be able to offer and explain these to your clients. Advisers need to become acquainted with many areas of law and practice.

A commitment to developing the service

As a professional debt adviser, you should take regular opportunities to enhance your skills through training, research and education, and should participate in offering this to others, so that the practice of debt advice continues to be refined and developed.

You should register for regular updates from organisations such as:

- the FCA;
- the Accountant in Bankruptcy;
- the Scottish Courts and Tribunals Services;
- the Money Advice Trust;
- Money Advice Scotland's Basecamp;
- Debt Camel and others.

A systematic approach

As a professional debt adviser, you should apply a single systematic approach to each individual client. Also ensure that the advice you give is:
- in the best interests of that particular client; *and*
- appropriate to their individual circumstances; *and*
- realistic; *and*
- where an offer of payment is made, it is sustainable and based on a true and accurate assessment of the client's individual circumstances.

An ability to involve the client in informed choices

As a professional debt adviser, you should always try to involve the client, ensuring that they understand the implications of their situation and the steps you advise be taken. You can assist the client to make an informed choice by giving them all their available options and explaining the consequences before anything is done. Do not assume that a client is seeking a particular outcome, but establish what they want, and recognise that it may not necessarily be realistic or achievable.

Many advisers tend to put pressure on themselves to solve their clients' problems, and clients' expectations can add to this. Although advisers should always do the best they can for their clients, there may be times when the options are limited because matters have simply gone too far, and you cannot make the problem go away.

You should not feel that you have somehow 'failed' the client if you cannot make a problem go away, as they are still likely to need support in other ways.

Many debt cases involve distressing facts that can affect you and how you feel. Make sure you can share and discuss these sorts of issues with colleagues and your supervisor/manager.

Clients with mental health problems

There is a clear link between debt and mental health issues. According to the Royal College of Psychiatrists, one in four adults living in the UK experiences a mental health problem every year.[20] When combined with financial difficulties, mental health problems can affect not only the individuals concerned, but also the organisations with which they have relationships.

Chapter 1: Debt advice: an outline
2. The debt advice system

Many mental health conditions have no physical signs, and fluctuations in the severity and effects of an illness are common. In many cases, creditors are not aware that there is a mental health issue until payments have been missed and the collections process has reached an advanced stage. Even then, it may not be apparent whether the client is capable of conducting a financial transaction. Money advisers and creditors are not trained to diagnose mental health problems and often do not understand the implications. However, once a creditor is aware of the issue, it should have processes and systems in place to take account of the situation and should respond fairly and appropriately. More information can be found in Chapter 15.

2. The debt advice system

The debt advice system is a structured set of procedures and actions that should be worked through if you are to provide the best possible service to someone with debt issues.

It is designed to:
- maintain the client's home, liberty and essential goods and services;
- advise the client about their rights and responsibilities, and also the rights of their creditors;
- give the client the information they need to make informed choices to deal with their debt situation;
- treat all creditors equally;
- empower the client, where possible.

A systematic approach is essential because of:
- the large amount of information and paperwork generated by most debt enquiries and the need to avoid overlooking a particular strategy;
- the need to keep detailed records of the agency's work – both to ensure effective advice and follow-up, but also to enable case material to be used for evaluating the service, quality of advice assessments, peer reviews and for social policy development;
- the need to train new workers in a clearly defined set of skills and knowledge;
- the need to guarantee consistency despite the diversity of clients using the service;
- the need to protect the adviser from the strain of having continually to 're-invent the wheel'.

However, the system should not be seen as a straitjacket, and it does not prevent you working creatively and flexibly in the best interests of your client. Different agencies need to develop their own systems based on demand and resources, as well as any funders' requirements.

You must undertake a wide range of tasks to provide effective help to clients. In practice, the tasks may not necessarily be carried out in the order in which they are presented, and some tasks can be carried out simultaneously – eg, maximising income while waiting for information needed to check the client's liability for their debts. It is also common for tasks to be carried out more than once over the life cycle of a case.

Client authorisation

The client must provide a signed authority before you can contact third parties on their behalf. Most agencies have a standard authorisation form. You must also comply with data protection legislation and get your clients' consent to hold sensitive personal information about them and, if relevant, to share information about their cases with third parties – eg, for referral, monitoring or quality-checking purposes.

Stages of the debt advice process

There are six steps in the debt advice process which are covered in more detail in Chapter 3.
- Step 1: find out the whole situation.
- Step 2: identify and deal with emergencies.
- Step 3: check liability.
- Step 4: list creditors and priority and non-priority debts.
- Step 5: create the common financial statement.
- Step 6: maximise income and minimise expenditure.

Initial interview

At the first interview, it is good practice to point out:
- the agency's commitment to confidentiality; *and*
- the steps the agency will take and the steps the client has agreed to or is expected to take; *and*
- that the client should not incur any further credit commitments without discussing it first with you; *and*
- that the client should inform you of any change in their financial circumstances; *and*
- that a successful outcome cannot be guaranteed; *and*
- details of the agency's complaints policy and of the client's right to escalate complaints to the Financial Ombudsman Service.

Monitoring creditor practices

Debt advisers should keep a record of the collection techniques and tactics used by individual creditors. This is useful in any future choice of strategy. In addition, note practices or situations that continually cause hardship to clients and monitor which creditors are responsible.

The effectiveness of any pressure for change often depends on the ability of an agency to produce evidence in support of its recommendations. For this reason, case recording must be accurate and detailed, stored in a form that allows details of particular practices, and the hardship they cause, to be retrieved and patterns detected.

There are frequent changes in the law and procedures that affect debt, and agencies are often in a very good position to look closely at how these are working in practice. Agencies often carry out such exercises as part of a network of local and national debt services.

3. **Administration**

Good administrative systems and time management are essential to manage the debt advice process in an efficient way and to meet the client's needs appropriately.

The triage interview

Many agencies use preliminary or diagnostic interviews that do not involve providing advice, but are time-limited, fact-finding interviews designed to identify:
- what service the client needs; *and*
- any action that needs to be taken straight away; *and*
- the next steps, which might be:
  - providing information; *or*
  - signposting or referring the client to another agency; *or*
  - arranging for the client to receive further advice, either immediately or by appointment.

Making appropriate referrals

It is important to establish whether a case should be referred to a specialist or more experienced adviser, and whether there is a mechanism in place for referring cases, if appropriate, to other outside organisations.

Record key dates (eg, court hearings) and time limits so they are not missed, and adequate preparation can be made. It may be appropriate to keep a record of referrals to track the outcome.

Once a case is opened, keep a record of the case and the client's name and address to ensure the file can be accessed in the future should the client return after the case is closed.

In some situations, you may not do any work for the client, but instead signpost them to a more appropriate organisation.

Case recording

It is common for agencies to use an electronic case management system to support effective case recording – eg, CABx use the CASTLE system. A significant amount of information is gathered from a client at initial interview, but also through follow-up contact with the client and other relevant third parties. Effective case recording and written communication skills are vital attributes for a debt adviser.

If electronic case recording and storage of documents is not available, all documents relating to a case must be kept in an adequate file. Keep all the papers in date order. Incoming letters could be stored on one side of the file and outgoing on the other. You could also use dividers to separate each different creditor, so it is easy to access each debt and monitor its progress. Alternatively, papers relating to each creditor could be kept together with a separate sheet on file to indicate the action on each debt.

You must comply with data protection legislation and obtain your clients' consent to hold sensitive personal information about them and, where relevant, to share information about their cases with third parties – eg, for monitoring or quality-checking purposes.

Correspondence

Keep the client informed of each stage of the case and give them copies of correspondence from the creditor. Telephone conversations should be recorded in the file, including names of those spoken to and on what date. It is good practice to follow up the call with an email or letter from either you or the creditor, as appropriate, to confirm the information discussed if it is relevant to the case.

Reviews

Each case should be regularly reviewed to check that replies have been received, that preparation for any court hearings has been carried out, and what the next step in the case should be. A brought-forward diary system may be useful to ensure that important dates are noted and there are regular follow-ups to ensure they are not missed. There is no point keeping a file open if there is no further work to be carried out, or if the client has ceased to engage and is not responding to your attempts to make contact.

By managing the caseload, you also have a clearer idea of how many additional cases, if any, you can cope with.

Agencies should have processes in place to ensure that a percentage of individual advisers cases are reviewed by a suitably qualified person within the agency to monitor service quality, identify adviser training needs and provide ongoing feedback to advisers.

Chapter 1: Debt advice: an outline
Notes

Closing cases

At the outset, you should give the client an indication of how long the case will remain open. This gives you an idea of how many cases you are dealing with and when you can take on any more. As you are trying to empower the client, your aim should be that, once the work is done on the case, clients can continue with the work themselves. They should have the option of possibly returning in the future should they feel unable to deal with matters themselves or if there is a change of circumstance.

A case can be closed if:
- the strategy for the client is up and running successfully; *or*
- you have lost contact with the client and they have not responded to your attempts to contact them; *or*
- the client no longer wants help from the agency or is changing advisers; *or*
- the agency is no longer able to provide a service to the client.

Once a case is closed, you should inform all relevant parties in writing and keep your case management system up to date.

If the client returns, you can either reopen the case, or start a new one.

Notes

1. Professional debt advice
1. gov.scot/publications/scottish-national-standards-information-advice-providers-quality-assurance-framework-2009
2. gov.scot/policies/access-to-justice/improving-information-and-advice
3. gov.scot/publications/snsiap-competences-for-advisers-november-2016-update
4. slab.org.uk/app/uploads/2019/06/SNSIAPguidance.pdf
5. slab.org.uk/advice-agencies/scottish-national-standards-for-information-and-advice-partners/peer-review
6. slab.org.uk/advice-agencies/scottish-national-standards-for-information-and-advice-partners/cab-accreditation; slab.org.uk/advice-agencies/scottish-national-standards-for-information-and-advice-partners/type-2-3-accreditation
7. slab.org.uk/app/uploads/2019/06/SNSIAPguidance.pdf
8. slab.org.uk/app/uploads/2019/06/SNSIAPselfassessment_-_Fillable_Fields.pdf
9. slab.org.uk/app/uploads/2019/06/SNSIAPselfassessmentsummary_-_Fillable_Fields.pdf
10. slab.org.uk/app/uploads/2019/06/SNSIAPguidance.pdf
11. Email: adviceaudit@slab.org.uk
12. Email: SNSIAPAPPLICATIONS@gov.scot
13. slab.org.uk/app/uploads/2019/06/SNSIAPselfassessmentCABx_-_Fillable_Fields.pdf
14. slab.org.uk/app/uploads/2019/06/brandedSNSIAPselfassessmentsummaryCABx_-_Fillable_Fields-1.pdf
15. slab.org.uk/app/uploads/2019/06/brandedSNSIAPguidanceCABx.pdf

16 slab.org.uk/app/uploads/2019/06/
CAS_Guidance_on_DPA_and_consent_
for_CABx.docx
17 gov.scot/publications/debt-advice-
routemap-scotland
18 gov.scot/publications/tackling-
problem-debt-group-recommendations
19 handbook.fca.org.uk/handbook/PERG/
17/?view=chapter
20 rcpsych.ac.uk/mental-health/mental-
illnesses-and-mental-health-problems/
debt-and-mental-health

Chapter 2

Key skills

This chapter covers:
1. Interviewing (below)
2. Negotiating (p17)
3. Letter writing (p18)
4. Representing clients in court (p21)
5. Changing policy (p25)
6. Challenging poor debt collection (p28)
7. Budgeting advice (p33)

1. Interviewing

During the interview with a debt client, there are some features that are important to note.
- Make it clear to the client that the service is free, confidential and impartial and explain what this means in practice.
- Actively listening will help you build trust and rapport with your client and help you understand your client's situation and feelings. Be aware of how your own preconceptions or attitudes affect the interview process. Recognise any negative ideas you may have about borrowing and debt and address them.
- Reassure the client that they have done the right thing in seeking advice. Being in debt can be stressful and clients may feel embarrassed to talk about their financial problems. It is important to build the client's trust and to emphasise that they will not be judged for being in debt.
- Encourage the client to express their emotions to get these out of the way, so they can then concentrate on remembering, thinking and decision making as the interview progresses. For example, many people in debt fear imprisonment. This is not the case for the majority of debts, but this fear must be voiced if progress is to be made.
- Asking clients the question 'Is there anything you are particularly worried about?' can allow them to express their fears/other emotions. Clients may also have problems that initially do not appear to be debt-related – eg, relationship

issues. Clients need to be able to express whatever is important to them and their concerns so that they can then concentrate on sorting out their debts.
- Due to the numerous threats from individual creditors, many clients feel hopeless about their situation. Do not raise false expectations by dismissing these threats, but be positive and explain that it is possible to do something about it.
- Anticipate problems that the client may face. It is important that the client does not depart from decisions made as part of a strategy, but you are unlikely to be there when these decisions are tested. For example, you may agree with a client that, because they have been paying creditors who call at their home and not paying their priority creditors, the best course of action is to withhold all payments to unsecured creditors until the arrears on the client's priority debts have been cleared.
- This decision will not be tested until an unsecured creditor calls, perhaps late at night, making threats. The client may find it difficult to stick to their earlier decision unless you have already explored this possibility with them. Try to prepare them for any such occurrences.
- Partners, or other people who the client lives with may need to be consulted if a good decision (ie, one which is likely to be adhered to) is to be made. Many of the decisions taken involve third parties who may not be at the interview. Even if you consider that urgent action is required, it can generally be delayed long enough for the client to consult others. Occasionally, there may be compelling reasons for not doing so – eg, if there is a fear of violence.
- Tell the client about the service they can expect from you and the agency. Explain what is expected of the client and what you will do. This must be written down and a copy given to the client and one kept by the agency.
- Performing realistic tasks can empower the client – eg, switching fuel supplier or opening a new bank account. Modest tasks, such as asking a particular creditor about arrears, can help the client feel involved in the processes being carried out on their behalf. Although it is important to offer expertise and services, do not take over the client's life – and avoid creating dependency.
- Be impartial and do not assume you know what is best for the client. All options suitable to the client must be considered before any course of action is agreed.

2. Negotiating

Negotiation is a process of communication between the debt adviser or client and the creditor. It takes place over a period of time, with the aim of reaching an agreement that both sides find acceptable.

A decision must be made about whether it is appropriate for you to carry out the negotiation or whether it should be done by the client. Sometimes, it is more

Chapter 2: Key skills
3. Letter writing

empowering for an adviser to support a client by providing, for example, a financial statement and some standard letters, rather than negotiating themselves. In the past, creditors routinely rejected offers made by clients unless they were made by an advice agency, even though it was the same offer and based on identical information.

If the client has authorised you to negotiate with a creditor on their behalf, the Financial Conduct Authority (FCA) forbids creditors to refuse to do so or to contact clients directly and bypass their appointed representatives.

Similarly, creditors should not refuse to deal with clients who are attempting to negotiate their own repayment arrangements. A creditor who refuses to negotiate with an adviser or a client without a justifiable reason should be challenged.

You should conduct all negotiations with the aim of resolving the financial difficulties or debt problem, bearing in mind that the client's best interests are paramount. If the client is going to make payments, ensure that they do not offer more than they can afford.

Advisers are often in a powerful position in relation to creditors because no one in the credit industry wants to be accused (particularly publicly) of acting illegally or oppressively. If a debt adviser from a well-respected local or national agency contacts a creditor to negotiate on a client's behalf, the creditor will likely want to reach a settlement.

Debt advisers may want the creditor to accept payments or write the debt off.

This does not mean that creditors should routinely be expected to agree to every proposal that you put forward. On the other hand, if you think the creditor is being unreasonable and/or unrealistic, consider referring the matter to a more senior person in the creditor organisation with a view to using the creditor's complaints procedure and ultimately referring the matter to the Ombudsman, if necessary.

When confirming the client's financial situation to creditors, you should use the Common Financial Statement (see p57). Creditors should accept figures if they are within the spending guidelines and any figures above the guidelines can be explained.[1]

You should support your arguments by referring to any relevant code of practice or section of the *FCA Handbook* (generally, the *Consumer Credit Sourcebook*[2]).

3. Letter writing

Much negotiation begins with a letter or email. However, where clients present with an emergency situation, although communication with the creditor may have to be initiated by telephone and confirmed in writing later, it is more effective to send a letter or email in the first instance so that full details can be enclosed. Important changes to agreements reached through negotiation should always be confirmed in writing.

It is essential to send letters to the right place. In many cases, local branch offices are unable to deal with their customers' financial difficulties and most creditors have dedicated departments instead. Wherever possible, use the address and account numbers provided by the creditor when dealing with communications.

Letters should follow a basic format, as explained below.

Use simple language

Letters should be written in simple, clear language. 'Thank you for your letter of 11 June' is just as meaningful as 'Your communication of 11 June is gratefully acknowledged'.

Assume nothing

Correspondence, particularly initial letters or emails are generally read by someone who knows little or nothing about the client's situation. A letter should therefore contain all the background information needed to make a decision.

Holding letters

It is often necessary to write an initial letter or email requesting information that you require to advise the client and identify the available options. Such information includes:

- copies of any agreements, default notices and/or termination letters, where relevant;
- a statement of account, showing full details of the outstanding balance and how this is calculated;
- details of any court orders or other enforcement action.

The letter should also ask the creditor to put a hold on any further collection activity and to freeze any further interest and/or charges being added to the account until the information requested has been supplied and the client has had an opportunity to put forward their proposals for resolving the matter.

Any breaches of the Financial Conduct Authority's (FCA's) *Consumer Credit Sourcebook* by the creditor or debt collector should also be addressed in this letter. If there is an issue in relation to restarting the prescription clock, a standard holding letter or email should not be used and any letter sent to the creditor should not be an acknowledgment of the debt.

Chapter 2: Key skills
3. Letter writing

Use a framework

Many agencies have templates for standard letters. New or unusual situations may require individual letters. These are easier to write with a framework to follow.

- **Address.** The letter should begin with the address to which it will be sent, which must appear on your copy as well as the copy for the creditor.
- **Client and references.** Next comes the full name and address, including postcode, of the client and all references or other identifying numbers. Major creditors may have borrowers of the same name, so detailed identification is essential to avoid confusion.
- **Standard opening phrase.** This can usefully explain the agency's status. For example: 'The above has contacted us for advice about their financial affairs and we are now helping them to look at these as a whole.'
- **Outline the background.** Next, tell the story so far (although not necessarily in the holding letter, as you may not have all the details at this stage). It is essential to give all the necessary background and details. Go through the story in chronological order. Keep sentences short and factual. Avoid long explanations. Do not include demands or excuses. The statement of facts must include those on which you are basing the strategy, in particular any unusual expenditure or special circumstances of the client or the members of their household. So, if you are asking for a temporary suspension of payments and interest charges, make sure you explain that there is currently no available income or capital and set out the client's future prospects.
- **Make the request.** The next stage of the letter should be the request. This needs to be clearly and simply phrased. Do not be apologetic or circumspect – link the request to the facts outlined and make it appear to be an inevitable consequence of them. Where relevant, ask the creditor to (continue to) freeze interest and/or other charges to prevent the debt from increasing further. The letter should continue by stating when you propose the strategy should be reviewed. You can express this either as a fixed period *or*, with reference to other factors – eg, 'We will be happy to review this when Mr Parker gets a job.'
- **Add any special reasons.** After outlining the request, add the special reasons why this should be accepted. These may be obvious from the facts you have listed, but it is worth repeating them. If arrangements have broken down in the past or you believe a creditor will be resistant to the suggestion, however, it is useful to list whatever special reasons you can.
- **Provide details of any offer.** If you are putting forward an offer of payment, this should be clearly described – eg, 'The first payment of £... will be made on 27 August and following payments will be made on the 27th of each month.' You should also specify the method of payment. Advise your client to begin making the payments in accordance with the offer without waiting for confirmation from the creditor, as some creditors are prepared to accept offers

but do not notify their acceptance and then complain that the client has not kept to the payment arrangement.
- **Suggest an expected response.** Your letter could then suggest the kind of reply you expect – eg, 'We would be grateful if you could confirm, in writing, that this will be acceptable.'
- **Who the creditor should reply to.** Consider whether or not creditors should reply to the agency or to clients directly. If there is a heavy debt advice workload, it may be advisable to ask creditors to reply directly to their customers. It may be worth explaining why this is necessary. You should also include your contact details and availability (or alternative contacts where appropriate), so that creditors can contact you if necessary. Some creditors and collectors contact the client directly even when asked to reply to the agency, usually in an attempt to persuade the client to increase their repayment offer. This is a breach of the FCA's *Consumer Credit Sourcebook*.
- **Ending.** End the letter with conventional politeness, such as 'We are very grateful for your help in this matter', followed by 'Yours sincerely/faithfully'.

4. **Representing clients in court**

Most sheriff court cases take place in open court (ie, in public), so it is useful to know who is who, and what their roles are.

While procedures vary according to what procedure is being used, the general process in each case is roughly the same, as are the officers of the court.

Debt advisers need good verbal communication and presentation skills to represent clients in court action. It is good practice to attend court as an observer before carrying out any representation to see how the court process is carried out.

What happens in court

Court personnel

Sheriffs/summary sheriffs

The sheriff is the judge who hears the case and decides the claim. Sheriffs sit at the front of the court facing the public. They usually wear a wig and gown, although when hearing simple procedure claims they may dispense with this formality.

The Courts Reform (Scotland) Act 2014 created a new judicial office in the sheriff court known as the 'summary sheriff'. Summary sheriffs can deal with a range of the civil proceedings heard in the sheriff court, including family cases such as adoption, domestic abuse, appeals from the children's hearings, arrest warrants, extension of time to pay debts and simple procedure.

Sheriff clerks

Sheriff clerks are responsible for the organisation of the work of the sheriff court. In the courtroom, they call out the case name and record the decision of the

Chapter 2: Key skills
4. Representing clients in court

sheriff. In the sheriff clerks' office, they advise on court procedures and help with filling out court forms (although they do not give legal advice).

Bar officers
Bar officers are responsible for keeping order in the court and for various practical matters such as finding out if someone is in the right court. It is useful to know who they are and how to find them.

Who to speak to
If you are attending court on behalf of a client, try to contact both the sheriff clerk and the opposing side (solicitor) to let them know you will be there and are attending on behalf of the client.

Turn up early and try to negotiate with the opposing side before the case is called – eg, getting them to agree to a time to pay application.

Lay representation
A person involved in civil court proceedings without representation from a solicitor is referred to as a 'party litigant'. A party litigant can ask the court for permission for someone to help at the hearing. The court rules allow for two types of non-solicitor assistance during the court hearing.
- You can ask the court for permission for someone who is not a solicitor to speak on your behalf. They are referred to as a **'lay representative'**.
- If you intend to speak for yourself at the hearing, the rules allow someone to accompany you for moral support and advice, but they cannot speak for you. They are referred to as a **'courtroom supporter'** (or sometimes a lay supporter or **'McKenzie friend'**).

There are rules that provide for lay representation in the sheriff court. Different court rules apply, depending on the type of civil action that has been raised.
- Simple Procedure Rules – Part 2.
- Summary Cause Rules – Chapter 2 and Chapter 2A.
- Ordinary Cause Rules – Chapter 1A.
- Summary Application Rules – Chapter 1A.

Asking for the court's permission for a lay representative to speak on your behalf
You must complete a form to request permission for a lay representative to appear on your client's behalf. The lay representative must sign a declaration that the court will consider when deciding whether they are suitable. The forms are available from the Scottish Courts and Tribunals Service website.
Simple procedure – Form 2A (lay representation form).
Summary cause – Form A1 (statement by prospective lay representative for pursuer/defender).

Ordinary cause – From 1A.2 (statement by prospective lay representative for pursuer/defender).

Summary application – Form A1 (statement by prospective lay representative for pursuer/defender).

More information can be found at scotcourts.gov.uk/taking-action/lay-representation-in-civil-cases.

Do not try to act out with your competence. It may backfire on other amateur representatives and organisations.

The procedure

Normally, the case is called by the sheriff clerk and the creditor is asked to put their case forward, including what they want to happen.

Next, you or the client have the opportunity to do the same. Make sure you are prepared and have the necessary information and links to the legislation beforehand.

It is good practice to have a copy of all documents for the opposing side and the sheriff.

Next, there is a short discussion and, depending on which cause the hearing is in, the sheriff may decide there and then or arrange for a further hearing to hear evidence.

Be prepared to argue on a point of law and be clear what you are asking for.

Useful techniques

Plan well

Plan everything to be said in advance. Make sure it is logical and clear. Use notes where necessary. Rehearse presentations, if possible, particularly if you are a new representative. You should inform the court if you have not had time to obtain full instructions – eg, in the case of emergency hearings. It may then be in the client's best interests to request a continuation to allow them to engage with an advice agency, even if this means that the client may have an increased liability for the creditor's costs.

Be brief

Sheriff courts operate to very tight timescales and sheriffs may expect representations to be short and to the point. Avoid any repetition or wandering off the point.

Summarise

The court wants to know what order it is being asked to make and the reasons why it is appropriate to make it. A written summary of the case, briefly setting out the issues, the facts and any relevant legislation and caselaw is often helpful and can be handed out at the beginning if it has not been possible to circulate it in advance. Take copies for the sheriff and creditor's representative. This can then be expanded on in the presentation.

Prepare clear documents

Financial statements or other documents used to support a case should be clearly presented and photocopied for the sheriff and creditor's representative.

Tell the story

Explain the background to the case clearly and concisely in chronological order. Do not assume that the sheriff has read the papers.

Quote precedents and powers

Give clear references and explanations of any past cases cited in support of your case if it is unusual, and the legal powers on which it depends. Reference the court rules, any other legal enactments and any caselaw on which you intend to rely. Take copies for the sheriff and creditor's representative.

Admit ignorance

If stuck, it is better to admit this and ask for help rather than pretend otherwise. Provided your case appears reasonable, many sheriffs are helpful if they are asked. However, this should never be used as an alternative to thorough preparation of the case. Do not pretend to be a solicitor or allow others to assume wrongly that you are one.

Use court staff

Before the hearing, tell the sheriff clerk that you wish to speak on the client's behalf.

How to address the sheriff

The sheriff should be addressed as 'My Lord' or 'Your Ladyship'.

Look smart, be polite, speak clearly

Wear smart clothes (or apologise for your inability to do so – eg, if it is an emergency application). It is usually acceptable for lay representatives to dress less formally. Use standard English where possible; slang may not be understood and will almost certainly not further your case. Appear as confident as possible without being 'cocky'. Be respectful and pleasant. Use eye contact and smiles to retain the attention of the sheriff.

Know your own limits

Do not attempt to represent a client in court without being aware of all the possible outcomes.

5. Changing policy

If a particular law, practice, structure or policy adversely affects many clients or affects vulnerable groups of clients, debt advisers should work to change the policy.

When contacting individual creditors, stress that this is a general social policy approach and not an attempt to reopen a case that has already been discussed.

Other organisations can be helpful. The ways in which creditors deal with debt may be controlled or overseen by one of a number of organisations.

You should also pass on details to umbrella organisations, such as Citizens Advice Scotland, AdviceUK or Money Advice Scotland.

The Financial Conduct Authority

The Financial Conduct Authority (FCA) is responsible for regulating consumer credit.

Running a consumer credit business and other credit-related activities requires authorisation by the FCA. Debt counselling, debt adjusting and providing credit information services (ie, assistance to obtain details of credit reference files or information about how to change credit reference files) are also all credit-related activities requiring authorisation.

You can check whether a firm is authorised at register.fca.org.uk. Firms that are not authorised can be reported to the FCA helpline (tel: 0800 111 6768). It is a criminal offence to carry out a debt-related activity without the appropriate authorisation.

Local trading standards departments may be able to help resolve individual cases. As the regulator, the FCA cannot provide redress in individual cases.

Ofgem, Ofcom and Ofwat

The suppliers of fuel, telecommunications and water all have regulatory bodies which have varying powers to investigate and comment on their activities. The fuel regulatory bodies are responsible for preventing unlawful price increases or disconnections. They can also be useful in exercising pressure in other areas.

Trade associations

Many industries have trade associations. These are bodies that are regulated by their members but impose certain agreed standards as a membership condition.

Many trade associations have a code of practice or conduct, and all have a complaints procedure, which can be used to resolve individual cases.

Trade associations exist primarily to protect their members. However, they can be useful in changing the behaviour of an individual company, as trade associations do not want the good name of their members to be affected by the poor behaviour of one company. The peer group pressure they can exert, either through a complaints procedure or less formally, is probably much greater than the pressure an advice agency acting on its own could create.

Local councillors and MPs

Much debt is payable to local or national government. This includes council tax, income tax, VAT and rent. The statutory powers which the state has given itself to enforce these debts are considerable, so they are all priority debts. However, depending on the client's circumstances, some of these debts may not always need to be treated as a priority debt, so the client's situation may mean that diligence available to the creditor will have little or no impact on them. In addition, as government debts, they are subject to scrutiny by elected members – ie, councillors, MSPs and MPs. This can provide a powerful method of ensuring that the state's powers are not used in too draconian a fashion.

Elected members are often not aware of the measures being used by their officers to collect debts. For instance, many local councillors are unaware of the extent to which their authority uses enforcement agents (sheriff officers) and, once briefed by an advice agency, can raise this as an issue and change the way these debts are collected.

Ombudsmen

If the administration of debt collection by the state is poor and results in individuals experiencing hardship, a complaint can be made to the relevant ombudsman. Ombudsmen are not regulators and their primary role is to help resolve individual cases. They expect the client to give the creditor the opportunity to investigate their complaint and resolve the matter before referring the case to them.

The parliamentary, local authority and health service ombudsman

The Scottish Public Services Ombudsman (SPSO) is the final stage for complaints about councils, the NHS, housing associations, colleges and universities, prisons, most water providers, the Scottish government and its agencies and departments and most Scottish authorities.

Information on how to complain can be found on the SPSO website.[3]

The Adjudicator's Office

The Adjudicator's Office deals with complaints about the way things have been handled by HMRC (but not about the amount of tax or VAT the client has been asked to pay).

The Financial Ombudsman Service

The Financial Ombudsman Service handles complaints between clients and finance firms (including banks and building societies), complaints about firms with a consumer credit licence (including debt collectors and sub-prime lenders) and with complaints about debt advice providers (including not-for-profit providers and those that charge a fee).

Energy Ombudsman

For energy services, first make a complaint to the supplier and ask it to put the account on hold while it deals with the complaint. If, after 10 days, there has been either no response or an unsatisfactory response, the complaint should be escalated through the supplier's complaints procedure. Refer to its code of practice for details of how to do this. The case can be referred to the Energy Ombudsman either eight weeks after the complaint was made or after the supplier has issued a 'deadlock letter' – ie, negotiations have broken down and neither party will reconsider its position. The complaint must be referred to the Energy Ombudsman within 12 months of the deadlock letter being issued. Sometimes, the ombudsman can investigate an older complaint if the client has not received a deadlock letter.

Complaints about a solicitor

In Scotland, any complaints about a solicitor can be made to the firm in the first instance, then, if the client is still not satisfied, to the Scottish Legal Complaints Commission (SLCC).[4]

Monitoring local courts

Court procedures should be monitored on a local basis by debt advisers. Having collected information about how a particular court operates, it is important to decide whether pressure for change needs to be exerted on the court staff, the judiciary, or both.

Individual sheriffs are not open to being lobbied by groups about individual decisions or the types of decisions they are required to take. However, particularly if you work for a charitable organisation with a good reputation locally, it may be possible to arrange meetings with the sheriff principle to discuss how the advice centre can assist the courts in their work or other issues of mutual concern. In practice, this means it is generally possible to discuss procedures and engage the decision makers in an analysis of the effects of their judgments.

Local liaison groups

Some public services have liaison groups (eg, a local sheriff court users' group) and you should investigate whether any such groups exist (and perhaps advocate for them if they do not). Consider becoming a member to gain credibility through networking, and to change policies and procedures that are unhelpful or oppressive. Some groups may have existed for a long time with a fixed membership – eg, solicitors, members of the probation service and the police. You may have to spend time securing membership, but this may be rewarded with a direct line of communication to powerful local decision makers.

Using the media

Discussion with the various bodies outlined above can often result in useful changes that prevent continued injustice. However, it is often only when something becomes a live, public, political issue that real change can occur. It is important, therefore, to cultivate links with local and national media so that publicity can be gained for particular issues.

When considering whether to use the media, you must bear in mind general advice work issues, such as confidentiality. However, even if an individual client does not wish to have their case publicised, it may be acceptable for an anonymous description of the issues involved to be part of a media campaign. There is an almost endless demand from media organisations for examples of individuals who have suffered by being in debt. Many people do not wish to have their private affairs made public, but for others this can be an important way of regaining a sense of power after the experiences they have faced at the hands of creditors. It is certainly the way to bring an issue to public debate.

6. Challenging poor debt collection

Dealing with harassment

Many creditors harass clients. Much of this goes unreported and unchallenged and the client may even feel they deserve this treatment. Section 40 of the Administration of Justice Act 1970 defines harassment as trying to coerce a person to pay a contract debt by making demands for payment that are calculated to subject a person to 'alarm, distress or humiliation, because of their frequency or publicity or manner'.

Harassment can occur in writing or orally. It can include using obviously marked vehicles, calling repeatedly at antisocial hours, or visiting neighbours or places of work. Harassment occurs if a debt collector purports to be enquiring about a person but explains to neighbours why the enquiries are necessary. Harassment might also include posting lists of debtors in public. It includes abusive or threatening behaviour and all acts of violence. Any false representation that non-payment of a debt is a criminal offence, or that a person is a court official or other publicly sanctioned debt collector is also regarded as harassment.

Harassment is not a criminal offence but could give rise to civil action.

Because much debt collection activity takes place verbally over the phone, at the client's home and sometimes at their place of work, you should always ask how demands were made, exactly what was said, and check all written communication for evidence of inappropriate behaviour.

It is important to take urgent action to protect the client from further contact. Send a letter of complaint immediately, outlining the facts as understood and warning the collector and creditor that, if not resolved to the client's satisfaction, the complaint will be taken to the next level. In cases of violence or extreme harassment, inform the police and the local trading standards department as soon as possible.

Note: feedback from creditors suggests that some advisers do not act professionally when making complaints on behalf of clients – eg, by using rude, abrupt and sarcastic language. In addition, hearsay evidence is often reported as fact instead of, for instance, 'our client informs us that…'. The complaint letter should be objective and factual, and not personalised (unless the complaint is about the actions of an identified individual).

Next, advise the client to have no further contact with the collector or creditor until the matter has been resolved. This may involve politely, but firmly, refusing entry to the property or not answering the telephone. You should advise clients that, if they have expressed a wish to the collector or creditor not to be telephoned and that contact should be by letter only, this wish should be respected.

Advise the client to keep a diary recording details of any further attempted collection action. If possible, take practical steps to ensure that the client's friends, neighbours or relatives know about serious harassment and enquire whether they can provide a safe haven or support to them. Some agencies give clients a sheet of their letterheaded paper and advise them to show this to any collectors or creditors who visit and tell them to contact your agency.

The *Consumer Credit Sourcebook*

The Financial Conduct Authority produces the *Consumer Credit Sourcebook* (CONC), the specialist sourcebook for credit-related regulated activities. Chapter 7 applies to creditors or external debt collectors and the steps they can take to obtain payment of a debt due under a credit agreement.

It covers:
- clear, effective and appropriate arrears policies and procedures for dealing with clients who fall into arrears, including for the fair and appropriate treatment of clients who are particularly vulnerable (CONC 7.2);
- the treatment of clients in default or arrears, particularly the requirement to treat clients fairly (CONC 7.3);
- the requirement to provide clients with information about the amount of any arrears and the outstanding balance (CONC 7.4);
- pursuing and recovering repayments (CONC 7.5);
- exercising a continuous payment authority – ie, a mandate given by the client to, for instance, a lender, allowing it to take a series of payments from a debit or credit card without seeking express authorisation for every payment (CONC 7.6);

Chapter 2: Key skills
6. Challenging poor debt collection

- applying interest or charges (CONC 7.7);
- jurisdictional requirements (CONC 7.8);
- contact with clients (CONC 7.9);
- the treatment of clients with mental capacity limitations (CONC 7.10);
- misrepresenting the authority or the legal position with regards to the debt or the debt recovery process (CONC 7.11);
- creditors' responsibilities in relation to debt (CONC 7.12);
- data accuracy (CONC 7.13);
- settlements and disputed debts (CONC 7.14);
- statute-barred debts – ie, those that are too old to be recovered (CONC 7.15).

Specifically, the guidance states the following.
- If a creditor informs a client that it has decided not to pursue the debt, it must make them aware that the debt may still be sold by the creditor and the debt purchaser might decide to pursue the debt. **Note:** if the creditor has accepted a payment in full and final settlement of a debt, the creditor must formally and clearly confirm this (CONC 7.4.2R and 7.14.14R).
- A creditor must investigate if a debt is disputed on valid grounds or what may be valid grounds (eg, if the client is not the debtor, the debt does not exist or the amount being pursued is incorrect) and must provide information on the result of such investigations (CONC 7.14.3R and 7.14.5R).
- Creditors must not require someone to supply information to prove they are not the debtor in question (CONC 7.14.4R).
- Creditors must suspend debt collection activity if a client disputes the debt on valid grounds, or what may be valid grounds (CONC 7.14.1R).
- A creditor should not make undue, excessive or otherwise inappropriate use of statutory demands when seeking to recover a debt from a client (CONC 7.3.15G).
- Creditors must treat clients in default or in arrears difficulties with forbearance and due consideration (CONC 7.3.4R).
- If a client is in default or in arrears difficulties, a creditor must inform them that free and impartial debt advice is available from the free-to-client debt advice sector and refer the client to an agency. It appears that it is sufficient for a creditor to signpost a client to a debt advice agency or to the Money Advice Service by providing its name and contact details to the client (CONC 7.3.7AG).
- Creditors must not pressurise clients to pay a debt in a single lump sum or more than they can reasonably afford and must allow alternative, affordable repayment amounts if a reasonable offer is made (CONC 7.3.8G and 7.310R). For example, putting clients under pressure to draw a lump sum from a pension in order to pay a debt is likely to breach these requirements (CONC 7.3.10AG).
- Creditors must suspend recovery of a debt from a client for a reasonable period (ie, 30 days) if a debt adviser is assisting them to agree a repayment plan and

should consider extending this for a further 30 days if there is evidence of reasonable progress (CONC 7.3.11R and 7.3.12G).
- Creditors must suspend recovery of a debt from a client if notification has been given and it is reasonably believed that they lack the mental capacity to make decisions about their debt problems, unless or until a reasonable period has been allowed for relevant evidence to be provided (CONC 7.10.1R and 7.10.2G).
- Creditors must take reasonable steps to ensure that customer data is accurate and that accurate and adequate data is passed on to third parties, such as debt collectors, debt purchasers and credit reference agencies, to avoid cases of 'mistaken identity' (where the wrong person is pursued for payment of a debt) and to ensure that clients are pursued for the correct amount of any debt (CONC 7.13).

In relation to statute-barred debts, see the Prescription and Limitation (Scotland) Act 1973. CONC 7.15 states that a statute-barred debt ceases to exist and is no longer recoverable if:
- a relevant claim on behalf of the lender or owner has not been made during the relevant limitation period; *and*
- the debt has not been acknowledged by, or on behalf of, the customer during the relevant limitation period.

The detailed rules and guidance set out above are underpinned by a set of principles known as the *Principles for Businesses* (PRIN), which are set out in the *FCA Handbook*. Principle 6, which requires creditors to 'pay due regard to its customers' interests and ensure they are treated fairly', and Principle 7, which requires creditors to 'pay due regard to the information needs of its clients and communicate information to them in a way which is clear, fair and not misleading', are of particular significance when creditors are dealing with clients in financial difficulties and arrears.

Principle 6 requires a proper investigation of the client's personal circumstances, including what they can truly afford to repay and whether the client is a vulnerable person so that any payment arrangements agreed are appropriate. In January 2021, the FCA reminded debt purchasers and debt collectors that the requirement to treat customers fairly applied equally to them as to the original creditor.

The FCA has introduced a new Principle 12, known as the 'Consumer Duty' (a firm must act to deliver good outcomes for retail customers). Firms are required to apply the duty to new and existing products and services (including debt advice) from 31 July 2023.

Where the Consumer Duty applies, Principle 12 replaces Principles 6 and 7 as it sets a higher and more exacting standard of conduct than that which the existing principles would otherwise have required. The rules can be viewed at

Chapter 2: Key skills
6. Challenging poor debt collection

fca.org.uk/publication/policy/ps22-9.pdf and the guidance at fca.org.uk/publication/finalised-guidance/fg22-5.pdf. The new duty is underpinned by three rules setting out the key behaviours required by the duty (described by the FCA as the 'cross-cutting rules') which require creditors to:
- act in good faith towards retail customers; *and*
- avoid causing foreseeable harm to retail customers; *and*
- enable and support retail customers to pursue their financial objectives.

The duty does not have a retrospective effect and so actions or omissions occurring before the duty cames into effect are assessed in line with the rules in force at the relevant time. While no right of action through the courts for any breach of the consumer duty has been incorporated in the final rules, creditors will still be accountable through the Financial Ombudsman Service.

In February 2021, the FCA published its finalised guidance on the fair treatment of vulnerable customers with the stated aim of ensuring that vulnerable customers are treated fairly and that they experience the same outcomes as those of other customers. The FCA defines '**vulnerable customers**' as: 'customers who, due to their personal circumstances, are especially susceptible to harm, particularly when a firm is not acting with appropriate levels of care'.

The guidance sets out six areas the FCA believes creditors should focus on.
- Understanding the nature and scale of their customers' potential vulnerabilities and the impact of vulnerability on their needs.
- Training staff to identify phrases and behaviours that suggest customer vulnerability and then direct them to appropriate sources of assistance.
- Considering vulnerable customers at all stages of product and service design.
- Providing customer service processes that enable vulnerable customers to disclose their needs and responding flexibly.
- Ensuring communications are understandable by all consumers, taking into account the needs of vulnerable customers – eg, choice of communication channels.
- Monitoring and evaluating whether the needs of vulnerable customers have been met.

The guidance also points out the relevance of the Equality Act 2010 and that a breach of the Act is likely to be a breach of FCA rules and principles – eg, the requirement to make reasonable adjustments for a client with a disability.

The FCA said it intended to review the impact of this guidance within two to three years. The guidance can be found at fca.org.uk/publication/finalised-guidance/fg21-1.pdf. To help creditors understand their role in treating vulnerable customers fairly, the FCA published a set of frequently asked questions, which can be found at fca.org.uk/publication/documents/guidance-fair-treatment-vulnerable-customers-faqs.pdf.

Breaches of the *FCA Handbook* should first be raised with the creditor and/or debt collector concerned. If the matter is not resolved, the client should use the complaints procedure to escalate the matter to the Financial Ombudsman Service. Also raise the issue with the appropriate trade body – eg, the Finance and Leasing Association or the regulator (eg, the FCA).

Codes of practice

Many creditors have their own codes of practice. For example, all gas and electricity suppliers must have a code of practice on dealing with customers in financial difficulty. Other creditors subscribe to trade associations, which have codes of practice with which members should comply – eg, the *Finance and Leasing Association Lending Code*, the *Credit Services Association Code of Practice* and the Lending Standards Board's *The Standards of Lending Practice*.

Some regulators (eg, the FCA, Ofwat and Ofgem) issue guidelines on how to deal with customers in debt.

All of these codes set high standards, which creditors and collectors are expected to meet in their dealings with clients. *The Standards of Lending Practice* also requires subscribers to ensure that when they sell a debt, the purchaser agrees to comply with its guidance on handling financial difficulties. The *Finance and Leasing Association Lending Code* contains equivalent provisions. Although creditors and collectors often fall short of the standards set in the relevant code of practice, they are voluntary and cannot be directly enforced in the event of non-compliance. The only remedy is a complaint, which in some cases can be referred to an independent ombudsman.

This *Handbook* refers to codes of practice where relevant. It is often in a client's best interests to point out to a creditor or collector where there is non-compliance with a code of practice and request that it be complied with. In the case of collectors (and private enforcement agents), it is also worth copying in the creditor where the collector is collecting a debt on behalf of a creditor. This does not mean that a complaint should be made in every case. The aim of a complaint should be to achieve a better outcome for the client than currently appears likely and so, if a complaint is likely to impede rather than promote negotiation, you should discuss this with the client and consider deferring it.

7. Budgeting advice

Although advice on budgeting is not debt advice, you should use the procedures and skills described in other parts of this *Handbook* to assist clients to deal with their debts. Budgeting advice is now a separate area of advice work in its own right, but it can play a useful part in the debt advice process. Discussing a person's finances can be a sensitive subject so skilful interview techniques are required. Be careful not to impose your own values on a client.

Some agencies offer clients a session with a budget or financial capability adviser, prior to their debt advice appointment. In this session the adviser goes through the client's budget in detail and looks at ways in which they could maximise income and minimise expenditure. The budget can then be brought to the debt appointment.

There are particular problems when budgeting on a low income. Often, people on a low income only have access to the more expensive forms of credit. In the absence of credit, goods available are generally more expensive because it is impossible to buy enough to benefit from the lower unit prices charged for larger quantities. Similarly, a client may not have access to the cheapest sources of goods if transport is not available to the large out-of-town stores. Budgeting on a low income often requires purchasing inferior goods because money is not available to buy more expensive goods that would last longer and be much cheaper in the long run.

If poverty exists alongside other factors, such as disability, parenthood or the breakdown of a relationship, it is likely that budgeting is constrained by the time available, which in turn is constrained by the practical and emotional demands of these other situations.

The financial statement

Very often, the process of producing a financial statement enables a client to see the sources of their financial problems. When all items of expenditure have been listed, it is often clear that these cannot be met from available income. Ideally, if there is a need to cut expenditure, it will occur to the client themself. If this does not happen, you could suggest ways of budgeting and the likely results of such strategies to the client.

Be aware of vocabulary, body language and tone of voice, to avoid giving the impression that you are judging the client. Issues such as drinking, gambling and smoking must be addressed, and you should explain to the client that these are matters which creditors are likely to raise and so have to be discussed. Any suggested cuts in expenditure should be for the client's benefit.

On the other hand, this exercise may establish that the client is able to meet all their contractual liabilities together with any accruing charges as well as maintaining their essential expenditure, and consequently does not need debt advice or any of the strategies discussed in this *Handbook*.

Luxury or non-essential items

There are some items of expenditure that may, in comparison to the possible loss of other goods or services, be less essential.

- Cars are generally more expensive than is realised to buy, run, maintain, tax and insure. If a car is not necessary for personal and family mobility or work requirements, the client may need to consider either getting a cheaper car, selling it and/or doing without.
- In the past, telephones, particularly mobiles, have been considered a luxury. This is not always the case – eg, if someone's health might require them to call for assistance in an emergency or if someone has experienced racial abuse or domestic abuse and that could happen again. The phone may also be an important social lifeline or a means of making emergency help available to another person outside the client's home. However, if no such factors exist, particularly if phone bills are large, the possibility of doing without or changing to incoming calls only could be considered. If a mobile phone is used, the cost (which may be less than that for a landline on some tariffs and usage patterns) and the appropriateness of this should be explained. Clients who get universal credit (UC) (and have no earnings), income support, income-based jobseeker's allowance, income-related employment and support allowance or the guarantee credit of pension credit may be able to benefit from a low-cost phone package available from BT known as BT Essentials. BT and some other broadband providers, including Virgin Media, are now offering low-cost tariffs to clients on benefits. More details are available from Ofcom at ofcom.org.uk/phones-and-broadband/vulnerable-customers. The National Databank provides free mobile data, texts and calls to clients in need via the Good Things Foundation's network of community partners in partnership with Virgin Media, O2, Vodafone and Three. To find out how your agency can apply to join this network and the criteria for eligibility for assistance to clients, see goodthingsfoundation.org/our-services/national-databank.
- Cable or satellite television is expensive. If a client has an agreement that has already run for its minimum period, the adviser could discuss whether satellite TV is more important than other items on which the money could be spent. On the other hand, it may be part of a package, including the phone, in which case the overall cost may be justified.

The client's non-dependants

If the client is a parent and their adult son or daughter lives in their household, they may wish to charge them only a nominal amount for board. The client may want to keep the family together and this arrangement could save money – eg, by reducing childminding costs. In some cases, challenging the amount being paid by a non-dependant could lead to family disruption.

Faced with this difficult situation, a client may need information and support to make decisions. For example, if housing benefit or UC housing costs is being claimed, they need to know by how much this is reduced due to the non-dependant living with them. From the financial statement, a client can judge what might be a fair share of the total household expenditure to be attributed to the non-dependant.

Financial inclusion: MoneyHelper

Overindebtedness and poverty often go hand in hand, particularly in deprived communities where many people are on a low income and financially excluded – ie, they lack access to basic financial products, such as bank accounts, ways of saving and affordable credit. In addition, financially excluded people can find themselves paying more for essential services, such as fuel, insurance and essential goods, because they only have access to high-cost credit provided by sub-prime lenders or loan sharks.

An important factor in financial inclusion is 'financial capability'. The Money and Pensions Service's defines 'financial capability' as 'the ability to manage money well – both day-to-day and through significant life events'.[5]

Without financial capability, clients risk not getting value for money and the products they obtain not meeting their needs.

Advice on buying a specific financial product from a particular provider is a regulated activity that requires the adviser to be approved by the Financial Conduct Authority (FCA). However, free generic financial advice is available from MoneyHelper (which replaces and brings together the Money Advice Service, Pensions Advisory Service and Pension Wise). Provided by the Money and Pensions Service (MaPS), MoneyHelper is independent of both government and the financial services sector and aims to help people manage their money better by giving clear, unbiased money advice to help people make informed choices.

The service can be accessed at moneyhelper.org.uk. It publishes printed guides, tools and calculators, and provides support both online and over the telephone. The service is free and impartial, providing advice on budgeting, saving and borrowing, pensions, retirement planning, tax and benefits, but does not recommend specific courses of action, products or providers. It is available for everyone but is particularly targeted at people who are financially vulnerable and those at key life stages – eg, during pregnancy.

Credit unions

A credit union is one way of extending low-cost financial services to local communities. Credit unions are financial co-operatives owned and controlled by their members. Each credit union has a 'common bond' which determines who can become a member – eg, people living or working in a particular area. They offer savings facilities and affordable loans sourced from their members' savings.

By law, a credit union cannot charge interest of more than 3 per cent a month (42.6 per cent APR), although the average is 1 per cent a month (12.7 per cent APR). Many now provide current accounts, bill-paying services through budgeting accounts, a facility to allow payment of benefits directly into a credit union account, and savings accounts.

Credit unions, together with advice agencies, offer a range of potentially complementary services that can assist in tackling financial exclusion and overindebtedness. For example, a credit union can help clients gain access to financial services and manage their finances effectively, help and encourage them to save and budget, and may even be able to provide a loan to pay off debts. However, a loan – even at a much lower rate – is not always in the client's best interest and more effective solutions can identified through accessing debt advice within the debt advice sector.

There are issues to consider when signposting clients to a particular credit union. To preserve independence, you should stress that you are not an agent of the credit union and must not give clients unrealistic expectations of the assistance they can expect from it. Also, make it clear that signposting does not guarantee immediate access to financial services, such as a loan. Credit unions are not charities and should only lend to people who can repay. Provided the signposting is in the best interests of the client, the fact that they may be borrowing to pay off other debts should not be ruled out in all circumstances. Bear in mind that affordable credit is not the only financial service offered by a credit union, and that access to current and savings accounts also promotes financial inclusion.

It is important to remember that credit union loans are *generally* not regulated by the Consumer Credit Act 1974. A credit union loan is not regulated if the APR is at or below the statutory limit (currently 42.6 per cent). The provisions of the FCA's Consumer Credit Sourcebook (CONC), therefore, do not apply to them.

Credit union regulation
Credit unions need to apply to the Bank of England (bankofengland.co.uk/prudential-regulation/supervision/credit-unions) for authorisation and approvals and they must also register with the FCA (fca.org.uk/firms/credit-unions/consumer-credit) before they can offer financial services.

However, the FCA's *Principles for Businesses* (PRIN) apply, in particular PRIN 6, and so a complaint could be made to the Financial Ombudsman Service based on this – eg, unaffordable lending.

If the client defaults on a loan, the credit union becomes one of the client's non-priority creditors. Most credit unions negotiate debt repayment terms if a client has fallen into financial difficulties, but some tend to refuse low loan repayments (such as token offers) and may decide to impose membership restrictions on other products and services. If not treated as a priority, the client is likely to lose the benefits of membership.

Debt collection is a regulated activity and the CONC rules apply.

Notes

2. Negotiating
1 See aib.gov.uk/debt-solutions/
   common-financial-tool/common-
   financial-statement-cfs
2 handbook.fca.org.uk/handbook/CONC

5. Changing policy
3 spso.org.uk
4 lawscot.org.uk/for-the-public/client-
   protection/complaints-against-solicitors

7. Budgeting advice
5 See fincap.org.uk/en/articles/what-is-
   financial-capability

Chapter 3

The six stages of the debt advice process

This chapter covers:
1. Stage 1: find out the whole situation (below)
2. Stage 2: deal with emergencies (p45)
3. Stage 3: check liabilities (p49)
4. Stage 4: listing creditors and priority and non-priority debts (p51)
5. Stage 5: create the initial Common Financial Statement (p57)
6. Stage 6: maximise income and reduce expenditure (p62)

When clients are about to have their first interview with a debt adviser, they can feel embarrassed, ashamed, uncertain, judged and many other negative emotions. The stigma of debt can create barriers which may prevent a client from being open and honest about their situation. A debt adviser needs to reassure the client, build trust and ensure they feel safe about sharing their information.

This chapter looks at how to build that rapport with a client, to understand their whole situation and to work through the six stages of the debt advice process.

It is always possible that the stages may be in a different order than stated, or that you will deal with some of them together, but it is a useful tool to keep you on track.

1. Stage 1: find out the whole situation

During an initial interview, the debt adviser needs to uncover a variety of information from the client. To help gather this information, it is important to gain the client's confidence and reassure them about any misunderstandings they may have about the actions their creditors can take – eg, they may believe they can be sent to prison for non-payment or sheriff officers can enter their home at will.

The adviser must also explain the process of how they will deal with the client's case. Throughout the initial interview, the adviser must work with the client, demonstrating empathy and understanding to build trust and reassurance. This will allow the client to feel more comfortable sharing information about their situation, which will lead to a better outcome.

To fully understand the client's situation, the adviser needs to:
- explain the principles of debt advice;
- explain your remit;
- understand what has happened;
- reassure and start building rapport.

Explain the principles of debt advice

Debt advice follows five underlying principles – that the service offered is:
- free;
- confidential;
- impartial;
- non-discriminatory;
- non-judgemental.

These principles ensure that all people can access advice and that the advice they receive is unbiased and in the client's best interest.

Explaining these principles and what they mean to a client can reinforce the key message that their choices are respected and that they can be open and honest about their situation.

Explain your remit

A debt adviser should explain the role and boundaries of the agency, and what they can and cannot do. They should also explain what is expected of the client and what the debt adviser will do. A copy of this information should be provided in writing to the client as an action plan. This also helps to involve the client in solving their own problem.

Understand what has happened

It is important to understand what situation led the client into debt. This assists in developing strategies to help them and uncover other risks that could affect which solutions might be appropriate. Ask the client what led to the debt problem and what measures they may have taken to deal with it.

Reassure the client and start building rapport

Encourage the client to express their emotions, and then they can concentrate on remembering, thinking and decision making. Allow the client to voice their fears, even if they do not initially appear to be debt-related. Clients need to be able to express their concerns so that they can concentrate on solutions to their debt problems. Expressing their fears allows them to build trust with the adviser and enables the adviser to focus on dealing with misconceptions and unwarranted concerns.

Understand that all information obtained from the client is vital

For a debt adviser to help a client, they must gather information about the client's situation. The regulations that govern debt advisers and the Scottish National Standards for Information and Advice Providers (SNSIAP) both state that a client's circumstances must be verified as much as possible. All information that a client provides is important to identify an appropriate solution.

Information and evidence gathering

An adviser needs to collect the following information from a client. It is important that the client provides supporting information to show evidence that the information provided is accurate.

Personal information
- Name, address and telephone number, if possible.
- Details of members of the client's household.
- Client's housing situation.

Creditors/debts
- Names, addresses, account numbers of all creditors, including family and friends.
- Details of each debt and whether the debt is in joint names.
- Details of actions creditors have taken, including any legal action.

Statements and letters from creditors can be used as evidence.

Income
- Client's employment situation.
- Client's earned income (ideally by payslips – three if paid monthly, five if paid weekly).
- Details of any benefits the client receives – copies of award letters should be provided.
- Details of other income such as private pension, board from a lodger, savings and or insurance policies.

Assets
- Value of any property owned by the client and any equity.
- Details of other assets – eg, vehicles.

A recent property valuation or a mortgage statement could be used as evidence.

Expenditure
- The household expenditure.

Evidence for this can be copies of recent bank statements and bills.

Clients may be unable to provide all of this information during the initial interview and will have to provide this evidence during subsequent interviews.

Information for the client

The debt adviser needs to ensure the client is provided with relevant information that will help them to decide which action they should take and what will be required of them.

This information should include:
- written information about the service being offered;
- which debts will be included in any debt solution, and which will not be;
- impartial information on the debt solutions available to the client;
- the advantages and disadvantages of each debt solution;
- the suitability of each option.

They must also be warned of the risks and problems which may occur. This information could include that:
- creditors may still try to collect debts – this action could incur additional costs which increase the debt;
- the client's credit rating may be negatively affected;
- the client must meet priority commitments;
- correspondence from creditors should not be ignored, although advisers should be mindful of debts which may be, or near being statute-barred;
- entering into a repayment arrangement does not guarantee that current recovery or legal action will be suspended or withdrawn.

The adviser should talk through each item to ensure the client fully understands each point and provide a written copy of this information.

All information a client provides about their circumstances can affect the solutions which may be effective in their situation. This information needs to be verified and recorded to ensure accuracy and to meet the standards expected of debt advice agencies. It is also important to provide the client with information on what will happen and how the process works to ensure that all their decisions are well informed.

Client consent, privacy statements and UK GDPR

The UK General Data Protection Regulation (UK GDPR) and Data Protection Act 2018 together form a legal framework that sets out the requirements for how a person's data can be processed. There are six lawful bases for processing data under the UK GDPR – consent is one of them.

You require explicit consent to process sensitive personal data, known as 'special category data'.

Consent includes ensuring the client understands what you will be doing with their data, who it will be shared with and how it will be used. This information should be covered in a privacy statement and given to the client.

Without obtaining explicit consent from a client over how their personal data will be processed, an organisation/agency and an adviser may be at risk of substantial fines under UK GDPR.

Data protection principles

There are seven data protection principles:
- lawfulness, fairness and transparency; *and*
- purpose limitation; *and*
- data minimisation; *and*
- accuracy; *and*
- storage limitation; *and*
- integrity and confidentiality (security); *and*
- accountability.

Any data you process should comply with data protection principles.

Further details are available on the Information Commissioner's Office (ICO) website.[1]

Lawful basis

There are six lawful bases for processing data and each organisation should identify the correct lawful basis for how the personal data will be processed. The most common of these for debt advice processing are legitimate interest, consent and public task (for a public body).

Further details on are available on the ICO website.[2]

Consent mandate and privacy statements

A consent mandate is a form stating the client is giving the debt adviser consent to use the information they have provided. It must be easy to understand, concise and separate from any other information the client needs to review. It should avoid technical or legal jargon, unexplained abbreviations and confusing terminology. It must be written in a manner which the client understands.

It must include the following:
- the name of the debt advice agency and the names of any other controllers who will rely on the consent; *and*
- why the debt adviser needs the data; *and*
- how the debt adviser will use the client's data; *and*
- confirmation that the client can withdraw their consent at any time and, how to withdraw consent.

A privacy statement supports a consent mandate to ensure the client is aware of what will happen to the personal information they provide to the adviser.

It should include the following:
- who is responsible for the client's information; *and*
- how long the information will be kept; *and*
- who it will be shared with; *and*
- what information will be collected and shared; *and*
- who the client can contact if they have concerns over how their information is being used.

Consent includes ensuring the client understands what you will be doing with their data, who it will be shared with and how it will be used.

Explicit consent

Many debt advice organisations use consent as their lawful basis and use explicit consent to process special category data. When you are processing data that is special category data, you must have an additional legal basis.

The most common special category data legal basis for debt advice processing are explicit consent and a public interest condition. Explicit consent requires a clear and specific statement of consent which will be understood and signed by the client.

Special category data is data about someone's:
- health; *or*
- racial or ethnic origin; *or*
- sex life; *or*
- sexual orientation; *or*
- religious or philosophical beliefs; *or*
- political opinions; *or*
- genetic or biometric data; *or*
- trade union membership.

This data is considered more sensitive and therefore requires additional considerations before processing it.

Each organisation will have different approaches and applicable legal bases. You should refer to your organisation's data protection policies and procedures for further details.

Explicit consent can only be given if the client understands:
- why the adviser wants the data; *and*
- what they will do with it; *and*
- which organisation and any third parties are asking for consent; *and*
- they can withdraw consent at any time and how they can do that.

You should speak to your data protection officer or refer to internal policies and procedures about sharing data externally for advice. You should only ever share the minimum amount of data necessary to support the client.

Further guidance on data sharing is available on the ICO website.[3]

The client must actively opt in to give consent and a record must be kept of who consented when, how and what they were told.

2. Stage 2: deal with emergencies

There is usually something that triggers a client in financial difficulties to seek debt advice. It can be when they realise they can no longer manage their debt or when they receive a threatening letter or court paperwork.

These presenting issues are often the first matter the client raises with an adviser. They can be threats to the client's home, essential services, wellbeing or liberty. When these threats are immediate, they become emergencies and an adviser must treat them as such.

Emergencies need to be identified early in the interview process as they may require immediate action to avoid serious consequences to a client. An emergency threatens the client's wellbeing in the short term and must be treated as a priority.

This section looks at how to manage emergencies that you are sharing with a third party.

What is an emergency

An emergency is a situation that threatens the client's home, essential goods and services, or liberty if it is not dealt with promptly. It needs immediate action to resolve and takes priority over exploring the client's situation in detail.

Emergencies also involve the time you have to deal with the situation, rather than just the sanctions available to the creditor.

Common examples of emergencies

Sheriff officers are threatening to visit the client's home and/or remove goods today.

The client is facing the imminent loss of essential goods – eg, hire purchase goods that are about to be repossessed.

The client is about to be evicted for rent arrears.

The client is facing imminent disconnection of essential utilities.

A warrant has been issued for the client's arrest for an unpaid fine.

The client is due in court the next day.

The client has no money for food or electricity/gas.

A deadline for a response to enforcement action is approaching.

The client attends with an expired charge for payment.

Each of these is time sensitive and requires immediate action to avoid a detrimental effect on the client.

Chapter 3: The six stages of the debt advice process
2. Stage 2: deal with emergencies

The general strategy
- Check what stage the emergency is at and try to get some paperwork.
- Contact the creditor and ask for time to deal with the emergency.
- Ask the creditor what outcome they are looking for.
- Go over the client's options for dealing with the emergency.
- Look at the whole situation.
- Choose a strategy or strategies to deal with the emergency situation.

The following are some common solutions to some of the emergency situations listed above.

Sheriff officers are threatening to visit the client's home and/or remove goods
- Let the sheriff officers know you are dealing with the situation and ask them to hold action.
- Apply for a statutory moratorium for the client and advise the sheriff officers. This should prevent them from carrying out the exceptional attachment.
- You can then look at a solution to cover all the debts.
- See Chapter 9 for further information on attachments and exceptional attachments.

The client is facing the imminent loss of essential goods – eg, if hire purchase goods are about to be repossessed
- Check the paperwork to see what stage debt recovery is at. Speak to the creditor and ask what they want and if they will accept a time to pay offer (see Chapter 11).
- Check the agreement and see what the terms are. It may include a clause on insolvency, which you need to be aware of.
- Look at the options available and decide which route to take – ie, time to pay, a time order or a statutory debt solution. A statutory moratorium may prevent the recovery of money owed, but not the repossession of the goods.

The client is facing imminent disconnection of essential utilities
- Advise the supplier that you are dealing with the situation and ask for time to prepare a financial statement. Advise the client that they are in a multiple debt situation and that once you have all the necessary information you will be back in touch.
- Disconnection may be prevented if the supplier is contacted, and a debt repayment plan is arranged. As a last resort, this could also be rearranged by installing a prepayment meter. If the client is in a vulnerable group, fuel cannot be disconnected during winter months (from October to March).

The client is about to be evicted for rent arrears

Some options that may be available include:
- recalling the decree;
- applying for a Debt Payment Programme under the Debt Arrangement Scheme;
- looking at an insolvency solution to deal with the arrears of rent arrears.

Remember:
- Actions for repossession are generally in two parts: one for the money owed and one for repossession of the tenancy.
- The sheriff must be convinced to disallow the repossession action while the debt is being repaid.

A warrant has been issued for the client's arrest for an unpaid fine

Contact the fines enforcement officer at the appropriate court and advise them of how you are dealing with the situation. Advise them that you will get back to them with an offer once you have completed a financial statement. Suggesting that the client gets legal advice as soon as possible may also be appropriate.

The client is due in court the next day

Imminent court action may not be an emergency. Remember, you may still have the opportunity to recall the decree (or equivalent) if the client does not attend and is not represented. You can also apply for a 'time to pay order' (see Chapter 11) after the decree. It may also not be an emergency if the client cannot pay the debt and is considering bankruptcy as a debt solution.

Always find out the client's whole situation before making an offer under time to pay at court.

If your agency has a referral agreement with specialist housing advisers (eg, at the Civil Legal Assistance Office or Shelter), see if they will accept the client. They may be able to request a continuation in court.

The client has no money for food

Food banks provide short-term emergency support. Advisers should have local knowledge of what is available in their area. See also p65.

Advisers could also look at the Scottish Welfare Fund crisis grants for help or any other more immediate crisis assistance locally.

A deadline for a response to enforcement action is approaching

Apply for a statutory moratorium to stop any diligence that has not been actioned or started by the creditor and give you time to assess the client's situation in full. Remember to let the creditor/sheriff officers know that you have applied for a statutory moratorium, as they are not obliged to check the register. See Chapter 6 for more information.

Chapter 3: The six stages of the debt advice process
2. Stage 2: deal with emergencies

The client attends with an expired charge for payment

A charge for payment of money is a final notice from a creditor and gives the client 14 days to pay before the creditor can take further diligence against the client (eg, a wages arrestment). Options could include applying for a statutory moratorium (remembering that if diligence has already been actioned, then a statutory moratorium will not help). You can still contact the creditor and make an offer of payment for the client that is affordable, if that is what the client wants to do.

An overview of basic tactics to deal with emergency situations

An emergency requires actions to be taken with limited information and time available. Offers must not be made to creditors until the client's full situation is understood. Therefore, asking for more time is preferable to arranging a repayment scheme a client cannot maintain.

In emergencies, the action by the creditor needs to be halted or delayed. This often involves contacting the creditor to make them aware the client has contacted an agency to request assistance or is seeking assistance from an experienced debt adviser.

An experienced debt adviser has several options available depending on the type of emergency – eg:
- negotiate with the creditor;
- recall a decree;
- apply for an emergency payment;
- arrange a fuel prepayment meter to prevent disconnection;
- apply for time to pay through the court, if appropriate.

Signposting or referral

Emergency situations can occur when an adviser has little information about the client's full situation. They can give the adviser a limited timeframe to make a decision. Sometimes, simple actions such as signposting the client to another source of assistance may be appropriate. In cases where the emergency is more complex, seeking assistance from an experienced money adviser is advisable.

'**Signposting**' is making a client aware of other organisations that may be able to provide them with the advice, information or support they need. The client must be informed of the organisation's contact information and what they offer. The client must make contact with the organisation directly.

Referral involves actively transferring the case to another agency more suited to help the client.

The decision to refer the client is based on whether the case is beyond the scope of the agency or if the adviser does not have sufficient knowledge and experience to advise in this specific situation.

In these cases, the client should be given all the relevant information about the possible referral to help them decide if it is appropriate.

The client must be informed of likely costs, or eligibility for help with costs, if the agency charges for services.

The adviser should liaise with the other agency to ensure a smooth transfer. This involves ensuring the case records are accurate, up to date and stored in compliance with UK GDPR provisions.

Debt advisers should always know their remit and what they can and cannot manage. More experienced debt advisers can provide specific support for the adviser and the client.

3. Stage 3: check liabilities

When a client comes to an advice agency with a debt problem, one of the first things an adviser should do is check whether the client is liable for the debt they are presenting.

A liability only exist if the client:
- has entered into a valid contract – eg, bank loan, credit card, HP agreement, mortgage, secured loan;
- must pay it under legislation – eg, council tax, national insurance, income tax;
- has a court order – eg, fines, decision, decree, summary warrant.

The client is not responsible for other people's debt unless they entered into an agreement (eg, as a guarantor).

As in all areas of advice, sometimes the issues are quite complex, and advisers should always seek help before any action is taken if they are unsure.

Joint and several liability

Joint and several liability refers to two or more people being liable for it. Joint and several liability means they are both liable for 100 per cent of the debt.

Couples are only liable for each other's debts when:
- specific legislation makes them jointly liable – eg, council tax;
- both parties have signed the agreement – eg, a joint bank account;
- they have signed a guarantor agreement.

If the couple are jointly and severally liable, the creditor can pursue either party for the full amount of the debt.

If one partner has forged the signature of the other to obtain credit, the client could challenge the debt. However, the adviser should explain that this means they will be accusing their partner of fraud, which is a criminal offence.

Checking liability

There are many reasons why a client may not be liable for a debt. If the client is not liable, they should be able to challenge the creditor.

Some specific areas where an adviser should check for liability are as follows.

Debts after death

A client is not generally responsible for the debts of someone who died, whatever their relationship. They may be liable if the client had joint and several liability with the person who died and they both signed the agreement. This could include a mortgage, council tax or rent arrears.

Someone dealing with the estate of a person who has died has no personal liability for any debts that cannot be paid from the estate.

Creditors can make a claim against the estate of the person who died. This includes their money, personal possessions and property. See Chapter 18 for more information about what to do after a death.

Debt lapsed because of time

If there has been no acknowledgement or payment between the client and creditor for five years or more, and no court action has been taken by the creditor, the client may no longer be liable for the debt. If court action has taken place and resulted in a decree, this timeframe is extended to 20 years. For council tax debt, the period is also 20 years. This is a complex area of the law and advisers should read Chapter 12 for more detail.

Faulty goods

If goods or services provided to the client are faulty, the debt may be challenged. This especially applies to goods bought on credit through a third-party finance company or credit card. For goods or services to be faulty they would need to be:
- broken or damaged;
- unusable or not fit for purpose;
- not what was advertised.

Minors

If the client is under 16, they can only be responsible for a debt if it was for 'necessaries'. This is defined as 'goods suitable to the condition in life of a minor and their requirements at the time of sale and delivery' – eg, a mobile phone contract, clothes or food.

Incapacity

For an agreement to be valid, the client must have been aware of what they were doing when they made the agreement. The client must also understand what they were doing and remember making the agreement. If the client has a mental health condition which leads to limited mental capacity or has drug or alcohol problems, the debt may be challenged.

Undue influence/duress

If the client signed an agreement under coercion or without understanding the implications of an agreement, then the debt may be challenged due to undue influence or duress.

Examples of this include actual undue influence, such as if the client was subject to domestic or financial abuse, or presumed undue influence, such as if someone the client relies on for advice influenced them into signing the agreement through misrepresentation.

Fuel/beneficial user

Fuel companies can only seek to recover charges for energy consumed in the previous 12 months, unless the bill was sent before May 2018. If the client was not named on the fuel bill but lives in the property, they can challenge debt the fuel company claims the client owes, as beneficial users may not be liable for a fuel debt.

Could the debt be reduced?

Even if the client is liable for a debt, they may not be liable for the full amount. The adviser should consider whether the claim is incorrect – eg, due to a faulty gas meter, overestimated fuel bill, unreasonable charges or charges for goods which were not ordered.

4. Stage 4: listing creditors and priority and non-priority debts

It is important to identify all the people the client owes money to, including family members and friends. All creditors must be listed even if they are not in arrears with payments. This involves dividing all of the client's debts into priority and non-priority debts and taking copies of the most recent statements and letters from creditors.

Priority debts carry the most serious consequences if the client does not pay them. These may not be the largest debts or the debts with the highest interest rates. These are debts which can lead to serious problems for the client if they are not paid.

This section looks at how to identify priority debts and options for dealing with both priority and non-priority debts.

Chapter 3: The six stages of the debt advice process
4. Stage 4: listing creditors and priority and non-priority debts

Identify and list all debts

When collecting information from a client, it is important to obtain details of all the debts and creditors.

A client may not have all the information available during the initial interview. It is therefore important to agree how and when the information will be collected.

The client's credit reference file can help with gathering debt information if the client does not have all the paperwork. Remember that not all debt information is contained in a credit reference file – eg, local authorities rarely register council tax or rent arrears. There are three main credit reference agencies in the UK: Experian, Equifax and TransUnion.

Information about all creditors and the debts must be recorded in the client's case file.

The creditors

The following creditor information is required.
- The name, address and telephone number of each creditor – the exact name of the company is important, as many creditors may have similar names.
- Account/reference numbers – creditors may have a reference number to access information about a client, which should also be recorded.
- Letter references and contact details – any correspondence from a company with a letter reference should be recorded, along with any contact details.
- Agent's details – if a creditor is using a solicitor or a commercial debt collector, their details should be recorded separately. Details of the person who made the most recent contact should also be recorded. If the collector has purchased the debt, they are now the creditor. If they have not and are acting on behalf of the creditor, they are accountable to the original creditor. Creditors should notify clients when debts are passed on or sold to third parties.

The debts

The following debt information is required.
- Age of debt – when any credit was first granted, how long the agreement has run for and how long it has been unpaid for all factor into negotiation with creditors. Debts agreed upon a long time ago may be unenforceable through the courts, or their legal position may have changed.
- Reason for debt – it is important to ask the client what the reasons for the debt are. This can help you understand the background as to why the client is in debt.
- Priority of the debt – the debt should be recorded as priority or non-priority.
- The written agreement – if a debt is based on a written agreement, check that the client has seen it and has a copy. Agreements should be checked for any defects which may affect their enforceability. A copy may need to be obtained from the creditor. A debt that is not based on a written agreement may be unenforceable.

Chapter 3: The six stages of the debt advice process
4. Stage 4: listing creditors and priority and non-priority debts

- Liability – check if the client is responsible for the debt. This includes checking who is named on the agreement or what names are on the bills. These may include the client and a partner, friend or a relative who acted as a guarantor.
- Payments – the amount currently owing for each debt needs to be recorded and also whether the figure is approximate or exact. Contractual payments under any original agreement, any amendments, any arrears in payments and the payment method must also be noted.

The client should not be advised to stop or reduce payments to creditors before a repayment arrangement is agreed, unless it is clearly in their best interests to do so.

The client may need advice at this stage about:
- dealing with doorstep collectors;
- changing or cancelling standing orders;
- direct debit arrangements;
- continuous payment authorities;
- opening a new bank account or building society account if the current bank or building society is a creditor.

Online credit reference services can be helpful. The services below are online and free to use and could assist an adviser to gather information the client may no longer have paperwork for:
- creditkarma.co.uk;
- clearscore.com;
- moneysavingexpert.com/creditclub.

Other credit reference agencies can provide a statutory credit report posted to an address. Some agencies allow a third party to request a report with the client's consent. Agencies which provide this service are:
- transunionstatreport.co.uk/content/files/creditfile-app.pdf;
- experian.co.uk/downloads/consumer/Stat-Application-Form.pdf;
- equifax.co.uk/efx_pdf/CreditReportApplicationForm.pdf.

It is important that information is collected about all the client's debts, including those which are not in arrears. Details of each creditor and their agents must be recorded. Information on the age and reason for each debt, as well as the liability and payments, needs to be recorded. If the client does not have details on their debt or creditors, a credit reference service can help to provide more information. After identifying all the debts belonging to a client, an adviser can then identify which are a priority.

Priority debts

It is important for an adviser to understand and explain to a client the difference between priority and non-priority debts. Priority debts are dealt with differently

Chapter 3: The six stages of the debt advice process
4. Stage 4: listing creditors and priority and non-priority debts

from non-priority debts because of the actions (sanctions) a priority creditor can take.

Types of debt

Priority debts carry the most serious consequences if a client does not pay them, and this can lead to severe penalties for the client. Non-priority debts are still important and must be addressed but have less serious consequences for no payment.

Priority debts include mortgage, rent, court fines, council tax, TV licence, child maintenance, any loans secured against a client's home, fuel bills and hire purchase agreements for essential goods and services.

Sanctions and client needs

Non-payment of a priority debt may result in the client losing access to an essential service, their home, or imprisonment.

An adviser decides on the priority of debt through two rules:
- sanction of the creditor; *and*
- client need.

The sanction of the creditor is the action they can take against the client. The following are sanctions for different types of debt:
- mortgage or secured loan – repossession of client's home;
- rent – eviction;
- council tax – money taken from wages or bank account, bankruptcy or debt secured against the client's home, client's assets taken from their home;
- child maintenance – client's assets are taken from their home, money taken from wages, bank account or benefits received, imprisonment;
- criminal fine – client's vehicle impounded, money taken from wages, bank account or benefits received, imprisonment;
- tax, VAT or national insurance – client's assets taken from their home, money taken from client's bank account, client's PAYE tax code adjusted to recover debt, bankruptcy;
- decree – client's assets taken from their home, money taken from wages or bank account, or debts secured against client's home;
- TV licence – client receives a criminal fine;
- gas or electricity – client faces services being disconnected, decree, money taken from benefits received;
- hire purchase – client faces repossession of goods;
- telephone – client's phone line is disconnected.

Advisers must take into account the needs of the client and whether the creditor sanctions will have an adverse effect on those needs. This could be because of the creditor's importance to them (such as a debt to a family member) or because they believe the goods or services are essential (such as a telephone for a housebound client).

Dealing with priority debts

Priority creditors are paid first from the client's available disposable income. All other creditors take a share of the pro rata calculation from the remainder of the client's disposable income when the amount to be paid to priority debts has been agreed.

Immediate contact should be made with the creditor. If an immediate definite offer of payment is not possible, the adviser should ask the creditor for more time and for no further action, or for existing action to be suspended during this period. The client should be advised to continue paying towards their current liability, if possible – eg, pay ongoing rent charge while negotiating payments for arrears.

The client may be unable to make payments towards all their priority debts and will need to decide which priority debts are of most importance.

When considering how to deal with priority debts, an adviser should work through the following tasks:
- for secured loans, hire purchase/conditional sale agreements, the adviser should check whether the client has payment protection insurance which may cover repayments;
- for secured loans, hire purchase/conditional sale agreements, the adviser should also investigate whether the creditor followed the appropriate regulator's guidance to assess the client's ability to repay – if not, the debt may be challenged;
- for tax or VAT, the adviser should consider what enforcement is likely to be used and the effect on the client.

Calculation

The calculation is done by negotiation with the priority creditors, not on a pro rata basis (although you can ask them to accept a pro-rata payment).

Example

Jack's disposable income is £100 a month.

His adviser has negotiated a payment of £30 a month for the priority creditor, leaving £70 for the non-priority creditors.

Creditor	Balance	Payment offer
Creditor 1 (priority)	£500	£30
Creditor 2	£500	Pro rata
Creditor 3	£2,000	Pro rata
Creditor 4	£500	Pro rata

Creditors 2, 3 and 4 are offered a pro rata amount based on the remaining disposable income of £70.

Non-priority debts

Types of non-priority debt
The most common non-priority debts an adviser may deal with include:
- overdrafts;
- personal loans;
- bank or building society loans;
- money borrowed from friends or family;
- credit cards, store card debts or payday loans;
- catalogues, home credit or in-store credit debts.

Non-priority debts have less serious immediate consequences for non-payment than priority debts.

They are still important and need addressing, as they are often the majority of a client's debts. Note that non-priority creditors can eventually decide to take sheriff court proceedings against the client to deal with non-payment and enforce the judgment through the courts.

Dealing with non-priority debt
All non-priority creditors should be treated fairly. The client should not make full payments to one creditor while reducing payments to another.

There are several options available to deal with non-priority debt.

Token payment
When the client has little available income, no assets or capital and their situation is temporary, it may be necessary to offer payment by instalments of a token nature. This can satisfy the administrative system of a creditor and prevent them from taking further action. A token payment is usually £1 a month; larger amounts such £5 or £20 may be regarded as token payments by some creditors as the debt will never be repaid at that rate. This tactic can be used as a delaying tactic until the client's situation improves or another debt solution is chosen.

Freeze interest
When a repayment schedule of less than the original contractual payment is planned, or if the client cannot afford any payment at the moment, a request should be made to freeze all interest and other charges associated with the debt. This strategy should be used in combination with another strategy in the long term.

Informal moratorium
If the client has no money available for non-priority debts, the creditor should be asked to accept no payments for a three- or six-month period, after which the situation can be reviewed. If a request is made to a creditor to withhold action and

accept no payments, they must be asked to stop interest/charges at the same time to prevent the debt from increasing.

Pro rata payments
If the client cannot afford the minimum payment to any of their non-priority debts, they should make a reduced payment to all of them using a pro rata calculation. This option is available if a client has disposable income, a number of debts and no assets. The client's income should be distributed among all the non-priority creditors in a fair way. The amount of each instalment is directly proportionate to the total amount owed to that particular creditor.

> **Example: individual debt, divided by total debt, multiplied by the disposable income**
> Jack's disposable income is £70 a month. (See the priority debt example on p55.)
>
> | Creditor | Balance | Payment |
> |---|---|---|
> | Creditor 2 | £500 | £500 divided by £3,000 x £70 = £11.67 |
> | Creditor 3 | £2,000 | £2,000 divided by £3,000 x £70 = £46.67 |
> | Creditor 4 | £500 | £500 divided by £3,000 x £70 = £11.67 |
> | Total debt | £3,000 | |

5. Stage 5: create the initial Common Financial Statement

A financial statement is a document which gives creditors accurate details of the client's financial circumstances. It lists the client's income and expenditure and debts. It is essential for negotiating with creditors and helping the client to budget.

The process of completing the financial statement may start at the initial interview, or the client may have already started it before meeting the debt adviser.

What is a financial statement

A financial statement is a debt adviser's most important tool. It shows the details of a client's overall financial situation, including what they spend their income on, and helps identify where the client can increase their income or reduce their expenditure. It must show a true and accurate assessment of the client's circumstances.

It also acts as a plan for the future development of the case by helping to inform what debt options may be available to the client.

Chapter 3: The six stages of the debt advice process
5. Stage 5: create the initial Common Financial Statement

It is a Financial Conduct Authority (FCA) requirement that clients confirm the accuracy of the financial statement before it is sent to creditors. It is good practice to ask the client to check and sign that the financial statement is accurate to the best of their knowledge.

The Common Financial Statement

The **'Common Financial Statement'** (CFS) is a tool that provides a detailed budgeting format that enables an accurate overview of a client's income, expenditure, assets and liabilities. This tool assists with the preparation of realistic and sustainable repayment offers. The CFS improves communication and transparency between creditors and advisers negotiating on behalf of clients.

Supporting creditors will accept offers made by the CFS, providing those offers are made by independent money advisers based on expenditure trigger figures that follow the latest guidelines. It is recognised by a range of formal schemes and codes of practice.

The 'common financial tool' (CFT – see p61) is used to assess a client's situation against different statutory debt solutions. It uses trigger figures to determine if a client's expenditure is reasonable.

How to access the Common Financial Statement

The CFS is available to recognised debt advice agencies but not to the general public.

To use the CFS and access the associated trigger figures, you must apply for authorisation. Authorisation can be given to:
- a third-party organisation negotiating debt repayment offers for a client or providing financial advice on statutory debt solutions;
- an organisation involved in making decisions about debt repayment.

The CFS authorisation covers users at an organisational level. Therefore only one authorisation is required per organisation. To apply for authorisation, email the CFS mailbox: aib_cfs_enquiries_mailbox@aib.gov.uk.

It can be accessed through case management software such as CASTLE Debt, Microsoft Excel, PETRA, PGdebt 9, IIZUKA Case Manager, AdvicePro, Liquid Advice, MACS and Topaz.

How to complete the Common Financial Statement

It is important that information entered into a CFS from the client has been verified and evidence recorded in the client's case file.

When completing the CFS the first information entered is the client's:
- name;
- address;
- date of birth (optional);
- national insurance number (optional);

Chapter 3: The six stages of the debt advice process
5. Stage 5: create the initial Common Financial Statement

- number of dependants;
- number of vehicles.

Information relating to the agency (such as the case reference number and CFS licence number) is also entered.

The next stage is to record the client's income. This includes:
- income from employment or self-employment;
- certain benefits and tax credits;
- pension payments;
- rent or board received;
- any other source of income.

It is important to include all forms of the client's income and the frequency with which they receive it (weekly, fortnightly, annually). The form automatically converts all income to a monthly equivalent.

If the client has any assets or equity (such as property), these must be recorded and the box marked to show that this has been discussed with the client.

Next, the client's expenditure is recorded. This is listed under five categories: essential expenditure, phone, travel, housekeeping and other expenditure. **Note:**
- Priority bills and other essential expenditure should be listed first.
- Non-priority expenditure is then recorded. This includes travel, phone and housekeeping costs.
- For living and household costs, the client can average their spending based on information from recent shopping receipts or bank statements.
- A client must then think about other things they spend money on – eg, repairs, self-care and entertainment.

Once this information has been recorded, a list of priority and non-priority debts is entered. Priority debts should have been identified by this stage. Amounts owed need to be recorded, as well as any repayment offers made to priority debts. The information entered into the CFS must:
- be accurate and realistic; *and*
- note any fees or charges being made by the debt agency; *and*
- be provided to creditors as soon as the client has confirmed its accuracy; *and*
- be sent to the creditor only after obtaining the client's consent; *and*
- be sent to the client along with any accompanying correspondence.

When completing the CFS, the debt adviser must:
- take reasonable steps to verify the client's identity, income and expenditure; *and*
- notify the client as soon as possible if a creditor will not work with the adviser's agency; *and*

- seek explanations for any unusually high or low expenditure listed on the financial statement.

The trigger figures

'Trigger figures' represent pre-agreed levels for certain areas of household expenditure. They cover expenditure for telephone, travel, housekeeping and other costs. They identify reasonable levels of monthly expenditure when completing the CFA.

They are calculated from research by the government's Living Costs and Food Survey, which takes information from a random sample of lower-income UK households provided by the Office for National Statistics.[4] It collects information about spending patterns and living costs to reflect household budgets across the UK. Trigger figures are updated annually and published in April.

Trigger figures change depending on household sizes – for each additional adult or child in a household, the trigger figure will increase.

Trigger figures provide a guideline maximum figure for expenditure but not a minimum. The basic principle is that spending should be accepted as reasonable if it is within the relevant trigger figure amount. Spending above the trigger figure may be reasonable depending on the client's circumstances. An explanation of these circumstances should be included with the financial statement if expenditure is above a trigger figure.

The CFS collects information on a client's income, expenditure and debts, which can be presented to creditors to show that repayments are sustainable.

Information entered in the CFS must be verified to ensure it is accurate. For some expenses, trigger figures are used to measure whether expenditure is at a reasonable level. If expenditure levels are higher than trigger figures, an explanation must be provided, along with the CFS when it is sent to creditors.

How creditors use the Common Financial Statement

The FCA's *Consumer Credit Sourcebook* (CONC) is the specialist sourcebook for credit-regulated activities. It states that a creditor should pay regard to provisions in the CFS and use them when considering the client's repayment offer.

What will consumer creditors accept?

Creditors are advised by the Lending Standards Board (LSB) to accept the CFS if received from a debt adviser with the authority to act on behalf of their client. If repayment offers based upon expenditure fall within the trigger figures, they should not challenge them unless they believe the information in the CFS is incomplete or inaccurate.

Issues with local and UK government creditors

The CFS is currently not required to be used across central and local government organisations. They often use a non-standardised income and expenditure form.

These are not publicly accessible, therefore little information is available about spending and how disposable income is defined.

This can result in repayment rates being set by local and UK government creditors, which are unaffordable for the client. Often these types of creditors will look at a client's income and not their realistic expenditure.

Due to this, government organisations will not take into account that clients may have multiple governmental creditors that compete for payments from a client who cannot cover even one of the government creditors. HRMC expects 50 per cent of an individual's disposable income to be put towards their 'time to pay' arrangement, which may be unreasonable if the client has other priority debts.

For example, if a client owes both council tax and rent to the local council, the different departments will both be looking for 50 per cent of a client's disposable income, leaving the client at risk of being unable to pay other creditors.

Creditors are advised by the FCA's *Consumer Credit Sourcebook* and the LSB to accept a CFS and use it as evidence when considering a client's repayment offer.

Common Financial Tool

The Common Financial Tool (CFT) is used to assess household income and expenditure in order to set a contribution across all statutory debt solutions. It ensures consistency and transparency when assisting a client to assess one solution against another and allows for a comparison of the repayment under each solution.

It uses benchmark expenditure levels known as 'trigger figures' to assess reasonable levels of expenditure. These figures are set using the CFS. To use the CFS and access the trigger figures, you must apply for authorisation.

Notes for Guidance – Common Financial Tool provides detailed information and evidence requirements to support debt solution applications.[5]

The CFT uses common financial statement trigger figures to assess whether a client's expenditure is reasonable. If the client exceeds the trigger figures, they will have to provide a reasonable explanation, supported with evidence, with any application for a statutory solution.

Who can access the Common Financial Tool

The CFT can be accessed by someone:
- qualified to act as an insolvency practitioner and fully or partially authorised to act for a client in accordance with the Bankruptcy (Scotland) Act 2016 (the '2016 Act');
- working for an insolvency practitioner and who has been given authority by the insolvency practitioner to act on their behalf in providing money advice under the 2016 Act;
- working as a money adviser for an organisation that has been awarded accreditation at the type II level or above, against the Scottish National Standards for Information and Advice Providers (SNSIAP);

- approved for the purposes of the Debt Arrangement Scheme;
- working as a money adviser for a Citizens Advice Bureau which is a full member of the Scottish Association of Citizens Advice Bureaux – Citizens Advice Scotland;
- working as a money adviser for a local authority.

The standard financial statement

The standard financial statement is similar to the common financial statement but used in England and Wales only. It is not currently used in Scotland.

6. Stage 6: maximise income and reduce expenditure

Maximising the client's income is a key element of the debt advice process. Part of this is checking the client's entitlement to benefits and other ways to increase income, as well as finding ways for the client to reduce their expenditure.

Maximising income increases the amount of money the client is in receipt of and may increase their disposable income. This is achieved by identifying new income sources, such as benefits, grants or rebates and reducing the client's expenditure through budgeting, identifying non-essential expenditure and reducing the costs of bills.

This section looks at ways to maximise client income and reduce their expenditure.

Overview of maximising income

When an adviser is looking at the potential to increase a client's income or raise a lump sum there are some key questions they should ask.
- Is the client entitled to state benefits?
- Does the client have the correct tax code?
- Can the client claim maintenance from a former partner?
- Is it possible for non-dependants to pay more?
- Is the client eligible for a lump-sum payment from a charity or other source?
- Is the client able to rent out a room tax-free?
- Is the client eligible for home efficiency or home improvement grants?
- Can the client receive assistance from social work departments?
- Are there any insurance payments the client can claim?

Benefit check

A good starting point when investigating income maximisation is to check whether a client is receiving all the benefits they are entitled to. There are many

ways to categorise benefits, which can make the system appear very complex. Benefits fall into three main types.
- Earnings-replacement benefits – these benefits are based on national insurance contributions and are not means tested. If the client has worked or been self-employed in the past, they may qualify for a contribution-based earnings-replacement benefit. Examples of this type of benefit are contribution-based jobseeker's allowance, contributory employment and support allowance and retirement pension.
- Benefits that depend on a personal circumstance – these types of benefits are paid because the client has specific needs or falls into a certain category, such as having a child or a disability. Examples of this type of benefit are adult disability payment and child benefit.
- Means-tested benefits or tax credits – these top up a client's benefit and/or other income to a certain level, sometimes referred to as the 'safety net'. Which means-tested benefits a client can claim depends on their circumstances. Examples include universal credit, pension credit, Scottish child payment and housing benefit.

An adviser should perform a benefit check to find out what benefits a client may be entitled to. An online benefits calculator can highlight which benefits a client will receive and how much. Alternatively, the client should be referred onto another service that can advise them, such as a welfare rights organisation.

Tax allowances, rebates and tax codes

A client may be eligible to reduce the amount of tax they pay or to receive a tax rebate. When looking at a client's tax situation, the adviser should check the following.

Tax allowances

The personal allowance is a basic allowance available to most people. Clients who are married or in a civil partnership may be entitled to a transferable tax allowance which allows a set limit of underused personal allowance to be transferred from one partner to the other. If the client or their partner was born before 6 April 1935, they may be entitled to a married couple's allowance.

A client who is registered blind can claim a blind person's allowance for the whole tax year. This is in addition to the personal allowance.[6]

A backdated claim can be made for up to four years for any allowances, so check whether the client has not received an allowance to which they are entitled.

Tax rebate

A client who is unemployed or is laid off may be entitled to a tax rebate at the end of the tax year. This can be reduced or cancelled if they receive a taxable benefit. If HMRC has delayed paying the tax rebate, they must pay interest on it.

Tax code

If a client has an incorrect tax code, they may be paying more tax than they should or may be owed money for overpayment of tax. See gov.uk/tax-codes for help identifing when a client may have an incorrect tax code.

Child maintenance

If the client has children and is not living with the other parent, they may be entitled to child maintenance. Child maintenance may be paid voluntarily, by a court order or by an application to the Child Maintenance Service. Child maintenance does not count as income for means-tested benefits.

Charity payments

Many charities can provide payments to clients in need. Larger charities receive many applications for these payments every year and may place limits on who they are prepared to accept applications from. Less well-known charities, such as locally based charities or those with specific criteria, are worth researching as they may receive fewer applications.

Turn2us has a website which lists many charities that may be able to provide financial aid.[7]

Insurance payments

An adviser should check whether a loan is covered by insurance. If the reason for the client's debt is sickness or unemployment and they have payment protection insurance, then the insurance may make repayments towards contractual instalments. If the client has defaulted on payments, the adviser should check the insurance policy to see if it still provides coverage even after lapsed payments.

Other sources of financial help

Trade unions

An adviser should check whether the client is or has been a member of a union. Many trade unions have hardship funds to assist members and ex-members. Unions may also be connected to benevolent funds or charities linked with specific industries.

Civil compensation for damages

If the client has suffered an injury due to negligence, they may be able to submit a personal injury claim against the individual or organisation that was responsible for the injury.

Council tax discount or reduction

If clients have difficulty paying their council tax, they may qualify for council tax discount or reduction. Local authorities administer council tax discount and reduction schemes which are often means tested. Details can be found on local authority websites.

Food banks

Clients unable to afford food may be referred to a food bank. The client may be limited in the number of times they can use them in a set period. Some food banks also provide fuel vouchers to assist with gas and electric prepayment meters. Local foodbanks can be found through trusselltrust.org/get-help/find-a-foodbank. Local authority websites also have details on other sources of food help in the client's area.

Private and occupational pensions

Clients may be able to take pension benefits before the normal retirement age from an employer's (occupational) or a private pension scheme if they are a member. This is possible under specific situations such as the client being permanently incapable of work. Independent financial advice should always be sought before a decision is made to take pension benefits early.

To find areas where a client can maximise their income, an adviser should perform a benefit check to find out if the client is entitled to any benefits, check their tax code is correct and if they can receive additional allowances or a rebate, check for any child maintenance they are owed, check if any loans are covered by insurance, and check whether there is any available charitable assistance available.

Reduce expenditure

Carrying out a comprehensive exploration of the client's situation can identify opportunities to reduce expenditure. It is important to avoid being judgemental when looking at a client's expenditure.

Here are some areas you can look at with your client.

Utilities

Check whether the client can change to a cheaper utility provider. Check meter readings are accurate and up to date. Check they are on the most suitable tariff.

Satellite TV

Discuss with the client ways to reduce their subscription to a cheaper package or to Freeview.

Telephone, mobile and internet

The client may be able to combine all three of these into one cheaper package or find a package which offers benefits such as free evening calls.

Vehicles

If the client does not need a vehicle on a day-to-day basis, then selling it not only provides a lump sum of money but reduces their expenditure. They could also look at trading it in for a cheaper model (although this may increase running costs).

Meals at work

Preparing a packed lunch is cheaper than paying for pre-made food.

Non-essential items

The client could cut back on items such as dry cleaning, newspapers and meals out. Remember that what may seem non-essential to you may be essential to the client. Do not judge or assume cutting back on such things will be easy for them.

Council tax

Depending on the client's situation, they may be eligible to receive a reduction in council tax costs. Examples include:
- single person discount. If the client is over 18 and the property's sole occupier, they may receive a 25 per cent discount;
- severely mentally impaired exemption or discount. If the client and every adult living with them is severely mentally impaired, an exemption may apply. If all but one adult in the property is severely mentally impaired, a 25 per cent discount can apply.

Luxuries and non-dependants

Luxuries are items of expenditure which, in comparison to the possible loss of other goods or services, are considered less essential. These could be online video streaming services, a family car which is not used or an overly expensive mobile phone package. These items may be cancelled or the cost reduced.

If the client lives with non-dependants (eg, their adult children), they could ask for a nominal payment for board and to assist with household expenditure. In some cases, this can lead to family disagreements and should be handled carefully.

Challenging low spending

Clients can sometimes be unrealistic about their expenditure, which can affect their ability to keep to a repayment arrangement. They often underestimate or ignore some expenditure. Common examples include:
- food;
- smoking products;
- replacement of clothes and furniture;
- house maintenance and repair;
- work – eg, travel and lunches;
- running a car;
- birthdays and Christmas gifts.

Try not to suggest unreasonable ways to cut expenditure. It can have an adverse effect on the client.

Non-judgemental approach

Each client's situation is unique. Some expenditure may be considered as optional or a luxury. In these cases, the adviser may want to talk to the client about reducing or stopping the expense. It is important to listen to the client's reasons for the expenditure on a case-by-case basis without being judgemental.

Do not blame the client

Advisers must be careful not to focus too much on financial capability as a way of solving a client's debt problems. Trying to encourage a client to cut back on expenditure without offering them any long-term solutions can drive a client away. An adviser must be aware of this and approach the situation appropriately. It may be that the client simply does not have enough money to live on.

When looking at a client's expenditure, it is vital to avoid judging the client. The adviser should listen to the client's explanation of their expenditure and work with them to identify ways in which to reduce spending in the long term without overly affecting the client's wellbeing. This can sometimes be achieved by finding cheaper alternatives or other ways to reduce current costs rather than eliminating a service completely.

Notes

1. **Stage 1: find out the whole situation**
   1. ico.org.uk/for-organisations/uk-gdpr-guidance-and-resources/data-protection-principles/a-guide-to-the-data-protection-principles
   2. ico.org.uk/for-organisations/uk-gdpr-guidance-and-resources/lawful-basis/a-guide-to-lawful-basis
   3. ico.org.uk/for-organisations/uk-gdpr-guidance-and-resources/data-sharing

5. **Stage 5: create the initial Common Financial Statement**
   4. ons.gov.uk/surveys/informationforhouseholdsandindividuals/householdandindividualsurveys/livingcostsandfoodsurvey
   5. AiB, *Notes for Guidance – Common Financial Tool*, available at aib.gov.uk/publications/notes-for-guidance-common-financial-tool

6. **Stage 6: maximise income and reduce expenditure**
   6. gov.uk/blind-persons-allowance
   7. grants-search.turn2us.org.uk

Chapter 4

Household debt

This chapter covers:
1. Child support payments (below)
2. Spousal maintenance payments (p72)
3. Gas and electricity charges (p73)
4. Council tax (p79)
5. Water charges (p87)

1. Child support payments

Child maintenance is a general term used to describe all types of financial support paid for children, including voluntary arrangements and payments under a court order. In this *Handbook*, the term 'child support' is used to describe child maintenance paid by parents under the statutory scheme run by the Child Maintenance Service (CMS), which is part of the DWP.

Some clients may have historic arrears from a previous scheme run by the Child Support Agency (CSA). All CSA cases have now been closed and ongoing arrangements have ended.

Parents needing ongoing child support have been encouraged to make a 'family-based arrangement'. If a family-based arrangement is not possible, they can make an application to the CMS.

The legal position

Both parents have a duty to contribute to the costs of each 'qualifying child'.[1] A child who does not live with both of their parents is a qualifying child if they are under 16, or aged between 16 and 19 and:[2]
- child benefit is payable; *or*
- they are in full-time, non-advanced education; *and*
- they are not married or in a civil partnership.

Where one parent lives in a different household (the 'non-resident parent'), they are required to make payments to the parent who has day-to-day care of the child (the 'parent with care').

Chapter 4: Household debt
1. Child support payments

Special features

The CMS refers to non-resident parents as 'paying parents' and the parent with care as 'receiving parents'. The CMS calculates child support payments based on a percentage of the paying parent's gross weekly income. The percentage depends on the number of children the paying parent is paying for. This includes each qualifying child plus any other child that the parent has a family-based arrangement for. The gross income figure used is reduced to account for any 'relevant other children' – ie, a child for whom the paying parent or their partner gets child benefit.

The CMS charges the paying parent a 20 per cent fee in addition to each assessed amount of child support payment and the receiving parent pays 4 per cent of the assessed amount. There are no collection fees if the parties agree arrangements for the paying parent to make payments directly to the receiving parent (Direct Pay). To encourage Direct Pay, the CMS can advise about setting up a non-geographical bank account which has a central sort code and so does not give any information about the area in which the parent lives.

There are no set rules on how quickly child support arrears should be paid, although the CMS aims to clear arrears within a maximum of two years, at a rate of up to 40 per cent of the paying parent's income. However, enforcement officers have the discretion to extend this period in appropriate cases. All decisions relating to the collection and enforcement of child support are discretionary and the welfare of any child affected must be taken into account. This includes if the paying parent has a child in a new relationship. A client experiencing hardship should contact the CMS with full details of their circumstances, including how the collection rate impacts their ability to keep contact with their children. There is no right of appeal against a discretionary decision. However, a complaint can be made if the parent feels that they have been treated unfairly or there have been unacceptable delays or other maladministration. It can be helpful to get the client's MP involved. Complaints can be escalated to the Independent Case Examiner or the Parliamentary and Health Service Ombudsman.

If child support is being paid through the CMS's collection service, it can consider taking enforcement action as soon as a payment is missed. If child support is being paid directly to the receiving parent by the paying parent, the receiving parent should notify the CMS if a payment is missed. Otherwise, the CMS will not be aware of this. If the CMS decides to take enforcement action, it will also start managing ongoing payments through its collection service (and charge collection fees).

To avoid enforcement action, the paying parent should contact the CMS as soon as a payment is missed to explain why and make arrangements to pay.

Before escalating to tougher enforcement action, the CMS has other options including collecting earnings direct from parents' employers or different bank accounts. The first step in enforcement is usually to make a deduction from earnings order (see p308).[3]

The CMS has the power to accept lump-sum payments in full and final settlement of the arrears.[4] If an offer in full and final settlement is accepted, the paying parent has no further legal obligation to pay the rest of the arrears. The receiving parent has to agree. However, the CMS will investigate the offer before putting it to the receiving parent. If it thinks the paying parent can pay and there is a reasonable chance of getting back all the arrears, the CMS will insist on their paying the full amount.

When fully in force, the Child Support (Enforcement) Act 2023 will see families paid faster as it gives the CMS the power to issue its own liability orders to reclaim unpaid child maintenance.[5]

Appeal a decision about payment amounts

An appeal to an independent tribunal can be made if anything relating to the child support calculation is disputed. Get specialist advice if the client wants to appeal the assessment. Before you can appeal, you must contact the CMS to ask for the decision to be looked at again. This is called mandatory reconsideration.[6]

If you are unhappy with the outcome of the mandatory reconsideration, you can appeal to the First-tier Tribunal (Social Security and Child Support) within one month of getting the decision. If you submit your appeal after a month, you must explain why you did not do it earlier.

Enforcement

Other enforcement action (but not recovery of arrears from the estate of a deceased paying parent or deductions from benefits) requires a liability order from the sheriff court. Your client will then have 21 days to object to the liability order being made. The court must accept that the payments specified are due from the paying parent and have not been made, but it cannot question the child support calculation itself.

Liability orders made in any other part of the UK can be enforced in Scotland. If a liability order is made in Scotland, it can be enforced by:[7]
- charge for payment; *or*
- attachment and exceptional attachment, which may involve sheriff officers going to your home to value your belongings that could then be sold to pay off your arrears; *or*
- inhibition order.

If these methods are not successful, the CMS can take further enforcement action. If the court deems that the client has the means to pay but has 'wilfully refused or culpably neglected' to do so, the CMS can apply to court for an order to:
- send your client to prison for up to six weeks;[8] *or*
- disqualify your client from holding a driving licence for two years or (but not both) disqualify your client from holding a passport for two years;[9] *or*

- impose a curfew order for up to six months and an order for the client to be searched and any money found on them confiscated.[10]

Your client may also be subject to penalty payments of up to 25 per cent and this will not affect their liability to pay ongoing payment or to arrears.

The CMS can also apply to the court for an order preventing the disposal of assets if the paying parent has disposed of, or is about to dispose of, assets with the intention of avoiding the payment of child support.

The CMS has said it is only likely to use these powers in exceptional circumstances and only where arrears of over £1,000 remain outstanding. The CMS cannot seek both disqualification from holding a passport/driving licence and imprisonment.

The CMS can write off arrears if it considers that it would be unfair or inappropriate to enforce the liability and:
- the receiving parent has requested that it cease taking action on the arrears; or
- the receiving parent has died; or
- the paying parent died before 25 January 2010 and there is no further action that can be taken to recover the arrears from their estate; or
- the arrears accrued in respect of an 'interim maintenance assessment' made between 5 April 1993 and 18 April 1995; or
- it has advised the paying parent that the arrears have been permanently suspended and that no further action will be taken to recover them.

Appeals to the sheriff court are possible.

Debt Arrangement Scheme

Child maintenance arrears can be included in an application for a Debt Payment Programme under the Debt Arrangement Scheme. However, ongoing liability payment cannot be included.[11]

Insolvency

Any obligation to pay child maintenance will not be discharged in insolvency proceedings.

Checklist for action

Advisers should take the following action.
- Consider whether emergency action is necessary.
- Check liability.
- See whether an offer of full and final settlement can be made or request to have the arrears written off.
- Assist the client to choose an appropriate or suitable debt solution because this is a priority debt.

2. Spousal maintenance payments

When couples separate in Scotland, one partner can take action in the sheriff court or Court of Session to ask for financial assistance.

In Scotland, this is called 'aliment', not maintenance as in England and Wales.

Special features

Spousal aliment

'Aliment' is the Scots law term for regular payments of financial support for certain categories of relations, including spouses and civil partners. It can be by agreement between the parties or by court order.

The obligation of aliment can be owed by:
- spouses to each other;
- civil partners to each other;
- a parent to their child;
- a person who is legally obliged to support a child.

When considering whether to make a final award of aliment and how much to award, the court must consider:[12]
- the needs and resources of the parties; *and*
- the earning capacities of the parties; *and*
- all the circumstances of the case.

When awarding aliment, the court can order:
- periodical payments, for a definite or indefinite period or until a certain event occurs;
- payments of a special or occasional nature;
- the backdating of an award to either:
  - the date the action was brought; *or*
  - such later date as the court thinks fit; *or*
  - a date before the action was raised, if special cause is shown.

The court must take into account a mixture of the needs and resources of both parties both at the time of application and in the foreseeable future. Thus, variations and recall can be applied for if situations change.[13]

It can include money for essentials and other things like holidays and entertainment and may reflect the standard of living during the period when both partners were together.

The court will also look at resources including such things as income from a trust or investment, a company car or rent-free accommodation. Payments to a mortgage by the absent parent can also be taken into account. Where the paying partner has a new relationship, their partner's income may also be taken into account.

If advice on court procedures is required, debt advisers should not attempt to get involved and the client should be advised to consult a solicitor.

Enforcement
If a paying partner does not meet their obligations and the aliment has been awarded by decree, the receiving partner can take the usual enforcement action such as arrestment, attachment and inhibition.

Debt Arrangement Scheme
Aliment arrears can be included in an application for a Debt Payment Programme under the Debt Arrangement Scheme. However, ongoing liability payment cannot.[14]

Insolvency
Any obligation to pay aliment will not be discharged in insolvency proceedings.[15]

Checklist for action
- Consider whether emergency action is necessary.
- Check liability.
- Assist the client to choose an appropriate or suitable debt solution, as this is a priority debt.

3. Gas and electricity charges

Gas and electricity suppliers charge in a number of ways. Common payment methods include prepayment meters, quarterly accounts, direct debit and online schemes. Clients have a choice of supplier, although a supplier to whom arrears are owed can object to a transfer in certain circumstances. Ofgem regulates the industry. Suppliers must have codes of practice on the payment of bills and disconnection, including guidance for customers who have difficulty paying. You should obtain copies of the codes of practice of your clients' suppliers.

Suppliers are required to consider clients' ability to pay when recovering debts. Measures to support clients with prepayment meters and people with fuel debt mean that suppliers are expected to:[16]
- offer emergency credit to clients struggling to top up prepayment meters;
- offer clients 'friendly-hours credit' provided overnight, at weekends and on public holidays when their meters have run out or are running low;
- offer extra prepayment credit to clients in vulnerable circumstances to give them time to make alternative arrangements to pay;

- ensure they put clients in debt on realistic and sustainable repayment plans, including making proactive contact with clients and setting repayment rates based on ability to pay.

See CPAG's *Fuel Rights Handbook* for more information. It is available free at cpag.org.uk/handbooks.

The legal position

Electricity

A person is liable to pay an electricity bill if:
- they have signed a contract for the supply of electricity; *or*
- no one else is liable for the bill or their liability has ended (see below) and they are the owner/occupier of premises which have been supplied with electricity (known as a 'deemed contract').

A person is not liable to pay an electricity bill if:
- they have not a made a contract with a supplier; *and*
- someone else is liable to pay the bill, but their liability has not ended.

A person is no longer liable to pay an electricity bill under an actual or deemed contract if:
- they have terminated any contract in accordance with its terms (but they are still liable if they continue to be supplied with electricity); *or*
- they cease to be the owner/occupier of the property, starting from the day they leave the property, provided they have given at least two days' notice of leaving; *or*
- they did not give notice before leaving the property, on the earliest of:
  - two working days after they gave notice of ceasing to be an owner/occupier; *or*
  - when someone else becomes owner/occupier of the property and takes a supply of electricity to those premises.

This means that if the fuel supply is in the sole name of the client's partner who has subsequently left the home, the client is not liable for any arrears up to that date. However, they could be liable for the cost of any fuel supplied after this date, regardless of whether their partner has terminated the contract.

Advise clients to arrange for a final meter reading before leaving the property. If this is not possible, they should, at least, read/photograph the meter themselves to be able to check their final bill.

Gas

A person is liable to pay a gas bill if:
- they have signed a contract for the supply of gas; *or*

- no one else is liable for the bill or their liability has ended, but they have continued to be supplied with gas (known as a 'deemed contract').

A person currently liable under an actual or deemed contract remains liable until:
- they terminate the contract in accordance with its terms (but if they still occupy the premises and continue to be supplied with gas, they remain liable to pay for the gas supplied); or
- they cease to occupy the premises, provided they have given at least two working days' notice that they intended to leave; or
- if notice was not given before they left the premises, the earliest of:
  – 28 days after they informed the supplier that they have left the premises; or
  – the date when another person requires a supply of gas.

Advise clients to arrange for a final reading of the meter before leaving the property. If not possible, they should, at least, read/photograph the meter themselves to be able to check their final bill.

Special features of electricity and gas arrears

If there are arrears, fuel supplies may be disconnected. Therefore, this is potentially a priority debt. The prioritisation of the debt depends on the client's continued need for that fuel at their present address.

A supply can only be disconnected at the address to which the bill relates.

Note: a supplier cannot transfer a debt from a previous property to a new account and then disconnect that fuel supply for the previous debt.

It may be possible to reduce charges by switching supplier. Clients on a standard variable rate tariff could save money by moving on to a fixed rate deal with another supplier. If they have owed money for less than 28 days (eg, they have not yet paid a recent bill), they can usually change supplier in the usual way, and the debt is transferred to the new supplier.

Switching supplier while in debt after 28 days is subject to a protocol agreed between Ofgem and energy suppliers. If you have a credit account and a debt, your supplier can stop you from moving to a new supplier until you pay off your debt – this is referred to as 'debt-blocking'. If your current supplier blocks your request to switch, it must advise you on the best tariff for you, managing your debt and energy efficiency.[17]

Clients with a prepayment meter should be able to switch supplier and transfer a debt of up to £500 per fuel.[18] This happens under a debt assignment protocol.

A prepayment meter can only be fitted at the address to which the bill relates (unless the client requests otherwise).

Estimated bills

Estimated bills are a common way to accrue arrears. Many bills are based on estimated meter readings. Under their licence conditions, suppliers are only

Chapter 4: Household debt
3. Gas and electricity charges

required to obtain actual meter readings once every two years. If the estimated reading is different to the actual reading, the client should read the meter themself and ask for this reading to be used to avoid either an overpayment or an underpayment which could lead to arrears.

If the bill is estimated and the estimated reading is higher than the actual reading, it is possible to reduce the amount owing. The bill will explain (often by means of an 'E' next to a reading) whether an estimated reading has been given. Clients can read their own meters and provide the supplier with their reading, and so should never be disconnected on the basis of an estimated bill. You should ask the client to read the meter and request an amended bill. The roll-out of smart meters should, in theory, see the end of estimated billing as the meter sends consumption information to the supplier and allows accurate bills to be produced regularly.

When a client pays by direct debit, suppliers estimate future usage (eg, over the winter) when setting the amount of a direct debit. Suppliers should estimate based on the best and most current information available. You should, therefore, advise clients who pay by direct debit to regularly check their usage and provide accurate and up-to-date readings to suppliers where it appears a direct debit may have been set at an unreasonably high level.

Backbilling

When a supplier issues a bill, it can only seek to recover charges for energy consumed in the previous 12 months unless:[19]
- it has previously issued a compliant bill and is chasing previously billed charges; *or*
- the client behaves in an 'obstructive or manifestly unreasonable way' – eg, by physically preventing access to the meter or stealing fuel.

Ofgem has confirmed that it does not consider a client to be 'obstructive or manifestly unreasonable' when they do not supply a meter reading.[20] If clients do not respond to requests for a meter reading, suppliers should take a meter reading themselves to avoid billing based on estimates. This means suppliers will have to put more effort into obtaining meter readings from their customers.

Warm Home Discount

Clients on a low income (eg, getting pension credit) might also qualify for a £150 Warm Home Discount. See the section on Scotland at gov.uk/the-warm-home-discount-scheme for more details.

Extra support

As energy prices are volatile and bills are high, Ofgem recognises many people need extra support. It has published guidance to help advisers. You can see the latest version at ofgem.gov.uk/publications/energy-domestic-consumer-advice.

Chapter 4: Household debt
3. Gas and electricity charges

In 2022, Ofgem issued guidance to suppliers[21] and also sent them an open letter setting out the key regulatory expectations on suppliers when supporting customers in payment difficulty.[22] Ofgem expects suppliers to take the following actions in line with their licence obligations.
- Ensure customers can easily contact their supplier and are treated fairly when they do.
- Identify customers in vulnerable situations and provide additional support where appropriate, including ensuring that Priority Services Register data is up to date.
- Make proactive contact with customers in payment difficulty through a range of communication methods.
- Always take into account a customer's ability to pay, including before escalating the debt recovery process, giving due consideration to information provided by third parties representing them, including use of the Standard Financial Statement.
- Ensure prepayment meters are safe and reasonably practicable in every case and act quickly to change the meter to non-prepayment if necessary. Additional credit support should be offered to customers who have self-disconnected or self-rationed where it is in their best interest and/or where they are in a vulnerable situation. Involuntary fitting a prepayment meter under warrant is always a last resort and all other routes of debt recovery should be fully exhausted before applying for a warrant.
- Debt recovery action should always be fair and proportionate, and not escalated too quickly. Ensure third-party debt collection agencies treat customers fairly.

Force-fitting prepayment meters
From 18 April 2023, a new code of practice sets out how suppliers should deal with clients when considering whether to install an involuntary prepayment meter.[23] This means that a prepayment meter can be installed with a warrant, or a smart meter switched to prepayment meter mode, to recover debt owed without the client's consent. All suppliers have signed up to this code. The code requires suppliers (and their contractors) to:
- make at least 10 attempts to contact a customer before forced installation of a prepayment meter;
- carry out a site welfare visit before a prepayment meter is installed;
- refrain from all forced installations for the highest risk customers including:
  – households which require a continuous supply for health reasons;
  – people over 85 (where there is no other support in the property);
  – households with residents with severe health issues, including terminal illnesses or those with a medical dependency on a warm home;
  – where there is no one within the household who has the ability to top up the meter due to physical or mental incapacity;

Chapter 4: Household debt
3. Gas and electricity charges

- wear audio or body cameras on all warrant installation or site welfare visits to check for vulnerabilities (footage to be available for audit);
- give a £30 credit per meter (or equivalent non-disconnection period) on all warrant installations or remote switches as a short-term measure to remove the risk of customers going off supply;
- reassess the case once a customer has repaid debts owed and contact the customer to offer assessment of whether prepayment remains the most suitable and preferred payment method of choice for the customer.

From 8 November 2023, Ofgem guidance for vulnerable customers with prepayment meters provides for:[24]
- suppliers to refrain from involuntary installations for people aged over 75 with no support in their house and in households with children aged under two (this previously only applied to the people or households listed above);
- the voluntary code of practice which came into force in April 2023 (see above) to be made mandatory by becoming part of the suppliers' licence conditions, which, if broken, could result in enforcement action and fines.

Other assistance

Clients may be able to get a grant to pay off fuel debts. Some energy suppliers have trust funds to help customers who are in debt or may fund projects for the fuel poor. Grants are available for electricity and gas bills and may also be available to pay other essential household bills.

In response to increasing fuel prices, the British Gas Energy Trust (BGET) launched the British Gas Energy Support Fund and the Individuals and Families Fund to help British Gas customers with debts.[25] These new funds aim to help those who are most financially vulnerable with their fuel bills.

Auriga Services (which works with utility companies to assist customers who are vulnerable or in financial hardship) publishes a booklet summarising the schemes, called *Help with Water and Energy Bills*, available at aurigaservices.co.uk.

Clients can also take steps to help save energy and reduce fuel bills. The Energy Saving Trust offers free advice on ways to reduce fuel consumption and should be aware of grants that are available locally to help cover the cost of energy efficiency measures. See energysavingtrust.org.uk or telephone Home Energy Scotland on 0808 808 2282.

All suppliers must provide a range of free services (including quarterly meter readings) to clients who are on their Priority Services Register. This is available to clients who:
- have a disability or long-term health condition; *or*
- are over pension age; *or*
- have a hearing or sight condition; *or*
- are pregnant or have children under five; *or*

- have a mental health condition; *or*
- have experienced domestic abuse; *or*
- have extra communication needs – eg, they do not speak or read English well.

See CPAG's *Fuel Rights Handbook* for more details.

Checklist
- Contact the supplier and ask for forbearance and time to complete a financial statement.
- Explain that your customer may be vulnerable.
- Where possible, show a deficit budget making them vulnerable under the guidance.
- Look at a the Debt Arrangement Scheme or an insolvency solution for the arrears. (This would also show their financial vulnerability.)
- Consider whether emergency action is necessary.
- Check liability and whether the client is eligible for any assistance with the charges.
- Assist the client to choose an appropriate strategy as this is a priority debt.

4. Council tax

Council tax in Scotland was introduced in 1993 by the Local Government Finance Act 1992. It is a system of local taxation levied on domestic properties. It has two equal elements – a 'property' element and a 'people' element. It is administered by local authorities who are responsible for calculating liability, billing, collection and enforcement. In Scotland, this includes an amount for water and sewerage charges.

For more detailed information, see CPAG's *Council Tax Handbook*.

The legal position

The obligation to pay council tax is created by section 4(1) of the Local Government Finance Act 1992.

Special features

Property element
All domestic properties in Scotland have been valued and placed in one of eight valuation bands A to H. Any type of house or flat counts as a dwelling. Caravans count if they are the client's main home. Properties with multiple occupation with shared facilities may count as one or more dwellings, dependent on arrangements.

Chapter 4: Household debt
4. Council tax

The valuation of a property is based on what it would have sold for on the open market on 1 April 1991.

The Assessor does not normally adjust the valuation based on sale prices over time. They apply the comparative principle of valuation, which relies on comparing the physical and geographic features of the property to be valued with those of houses that sold around 1 April 1991.

The current bands are:

Range of values	Band
Up to £27,000	A
Over £27,000 and up to £35,000	B
Over £35,000 and up to £45,000	C
Over £45,000 and up to £58,000	D
Over £58,000 and up to £80,000	E
Over £80,000 and up to £106,000	F
Over £106,000 and up to £212,000	G
Over £212,000	H

The Council Tax Valuation List is a public document which contains the addresses and council tax bands for all domestic properties in the valuation area. It is available at the local Assessor's office or on the Scottish Assessors Association's website.

Certain properties are exempt, and advisers should check to ensure an exemption has been applied for, if appropriate.

People element

The tax assumes that two adults aged 18 or over live in each household. Nothing extra is payable if there are more than two adults. One adult living on their own receives a 25 per cent discount.[26] If there are no adults, there is a 50 per cent discount. If the latter applies, it may be that the property is exempt, and you should check whether this is the case.

When counting the number of adults in the household, certain people can be disregarded, and this should be checked. In addition, in certain cases, there are reductions for people with disabilities whose homes have been modified or if a disabled resident uses a wheelchair in the home. The disabled person does not have to be the person liable for the council tax.

Liability

A resident for council tax purposes is a person who is 18 years or over and occupies the property as their sole or main residence.[27]

If there are more than one resident with the same interest in the property (ie, joint owners or joint tenants), they are 'jointly and severally' liable. This means that all the people concerned can be asked to pay the full charge, together or as individuals. Members of a couple are jointly liable. A single bill is sent, either in the name of one of the persons concerned, or in both names.

Some people are disregarded and may be exempted from being counted as being residents living in the property. These include full-time students, people who are 'severely mentally impaired', unpaid carers, people held in detention and children under 18. They cannot be jointly and severally liable if there is someone else with the same status and legal interest in the property who is not exempt.

Annual council tax bills should be issued less any award of council tax reduction (CTR), exemption or discounts, and must arrive at least 14 days before the first instalment falls due. The local authority usually asks for payment by 10 monthly instalments, but this can be spread over 12 monthly instalments in certain circumstances.

A council tax bill is sent to each domestic property. There is a 'hierarchy' of liability, as follows:[28]
- resident owner of the whole or any part of the dwelling;
- resident tenant of the whole or any part of the dwelling;
- resident statutory tenant, resident statutory assured tenant, or resident secure tenant of the whole or any part of the dwelling;
- resident subtenant of the whole or any part of the dwelling;
- resident of the dwelling or any of the following:
  - the subtenant of the whole or any part of the dwelling under a sublease granted for a term of six months or more;
  - the tenant, under a lease granted for a term of six months or more, of any part of the dwelling which is not subject to a sublease granted for a term of six months or more;
  - the owner of any part of the dwelling which is not subject to a lease granted for a term of six months or more.

A resident of the property is usually responsible for paying the council tax unless:
- they rent and the owner has agreed to be responsible for paying it; *or*
- they live in a house in multiple occupancy (HMO); *or*
- they live in a hostel, nursing home or other accommodation where several individuals or households pay rent separately but share cooking or washing facilities; *or*
- they live in a convent, monastery or other religious community.

There is a right to appeal to the First-tier Tribunal (Local Taxation Chamber) against certain decisions, including liability, valuations, discounts, exemptions and CTR.

Exempt properties

Some properties are exempt for six months (or longer) – eg:[29]
- unoccupied and unfurnished new dwellings;

Chapter 4: Household debt
4. Council tax

- dwellings under repair;
- dwellings last occupied by charitable bodies;
- empty dwellings;
- dwellings last occupied by persons living or detained elsewhere;
- deceased owners;
- dwellings empty under statute;
- dwellings awaiting demolition;
- dwellings occupied by a minister;
- unoccupied dwellings for students;
- repossessed dwellings;
- agricultural dwellings;
- dwellings difficult to let separately – eg, granny flats.

Others are exempt indefinitely. These include properties:
- only occupied by one or more people who are in the UK under the Homes for Ukraine Sponsorship Scheme, where an approved sponsor provides the accommodation – this exemption only applies where it is their sole or main residence;[30]
- where the accommodation is provided with no payment in return, and only occupied by one or more people who are in the UK under one of the following schemes – this exemption only applies where it is their sole or main residence:[31]
    - the Afghan Citizens Resettlement Scheme;
    - the Afghan Relocations and Assistance Policy;
    - the Community Sponsorship Scheme;
    - the UK Resettlement Scheme;
    - the Vulnerable Children's Resettlement Scheme;
    - the Vulnerable Persons Resettlement Scheme.

Discounts, exemptions and reductions

Single person discount
A client may get a 25 per cent discount on their council tax bill if they are the only adult living in the property. This is not automatic and must be applied for.

Students, apprentices and trainees
Council tax does not need to be paid by anyone under 18, full-time students, student nurses and some apprentices or trainees.

Carers
Carers who live in the same property as the person they care for may get a discount on council tax. The carer must provide care for more than 35 hours per week.

The person receiving care must receive one of the following benefits:

- child disability payment (CDP) or disability living allowance (DLA) – care component at the middle or high rate;
- adult disability payment (ADP) or personal independence payment (PIP) – daily living component at any rate;
- attendance allowance (AA) or pension age disability payment (PADP) – at any rate;
- armed forces independence payment (AFIP).

The carer cannot look after their spouse, civil partner or a child under 18. It does not matter if the client is getting carer support payment or carer's allowance. Their income and savings will not affect whether they can get a discount.

Disabled clients

Clients may be eligible for the disabled band reduction scheme if they live in a larger property than would be needed if they or another occupant were not disabled.[32]

The client must show that they have either:
- an extra bathroom, kitchen or another room that is needed for the disabled person; *or*
- extra space inside the property for using a wheelchair.

The property must be the main home for at least one disabled person, either an adult or a child. It does not have to be the person responsible for paying the council tax.

Severely mentally impaired

People with certain severe mental impairments (SMI) are disregarded for council tax purposes. For council tax purposes, you are considered to have SMI if you have a severe impairment of intelligence and social functioning (however caused) that appears to be permanent. This includes where you are severely mentally impaired as a result of a degenerative brain disorder such as a stroke, Alzheimer's disease or other forms of dementia. The household is billed as if this person was not living there. If the person with SMI lives alone, they do not need to pay council tax.

A client qualifies for this if they have a permanent and severe learning disability or mental health impairment and are in receipt of, or entitled to one of the following benefits:[33]
- universal credit (UC) (the limited capability for work/limited capability for work and work-related activity element must be included);
- employment and support allowance (ESA);
- incapacity benefit or severe disability allowance;
- AA/PADP;
- CDP/DLA (middle or highest rate care component);
- ADP/PIP (standard or enhanced rate of daily living component);
- AFIP;

Chapter 4: Household debt
4. Council tax

- the disability element in working tax credit;
- income support (IS) including a disability premium because of incapacity for work;
- disablement pension for constant attendance at the increased rate;
- disability working allowance;
- unemployability supplement;
- constant attendance allowance or unemployability allowance payable under the industrial injuries or war pension schemes.

The client may qualify if they are entitled to any of these benefits but do not receive them due to their age – eg, for being too old. The disregard can still be awarded if they meet the criteria. The SMI exemption can be backdated – check with the local authority as significant backdates can sometimes be obtained which can extinguish council tax arrears.

Empty and unfurnished property
If the client's property is unoccupied, the local council may offer a discount for a limited amount of time if the client can prove:
- they are in the process of renovating the property;
- the property is for sale or rent.

The previous owner's or occupier's use of the property can affect the amount of the discount the client gets and the length of the discount.
If the property is unoccupied for more than 12 months, the council can charge a surcharge equal to double the normal rate of council tax.[34] The council has the discretion to:
- grant no discount for empty homes;
- increase the council tax by 100 per cent for certain properties which have been empty for one year or more.

Council tax reduction scheme
The CTR scheme can reduce a client's council tax bill if they have a low income. It is available to both homeowners and tenants in all council tax bands. The amount of CTR depends on:
- the amount of council tax the client is liable to pay;
- whether the working-age or pension-age rules apply;
- how much income and capital the client and their partner have;
- how many people are in the household, their circumstances and income.

CTR can reduce a bill to zero, but the client must still pay their water and sewerage charges. If the client has savings over £16,000, they will not be entitled to CTR unless they receive the guarantee credit of pension credit (PC).

Council tax valuation band

The owner of a property, or a person liable to pay council tax for it, can lodge a proposal to alter the council tax band in certain circumstances. The criteria can be found on the Scottish Assessors Association website.

You may want to use a rating agent to help you deal with issues such as appealing your rateable value or checking what the likely effect of any changes will be.

Before appointing a rating agent, make sure that you have a clear agreement on what they will do for you and what they will charge. Typically, tasks include valuing your premises to determine what the rateable value should be.

If there are grounds for a reduction, your agent can lodge an appeal and act as the point of contact with your local assessor. Remember that a reduction in your rateable value does not guarantee a reduction in your non-domestic rates bill.

Your agreement should clearly state what fees are payable to the agent and if these are affected if your rates bill is not reduced.

Members of the Royal Institution of Chartered Surveyors (RICS) or the Institute of Revenues, Rating and Valuation (IRRV) must follow a rating consultancy code of practice. You can contact RICS or one of their members for advice from a local chartered surveyor.

Appeals

The Local Taxation Chamber deals with appeals about council tax, water charges and non-domestic rates. It is part of the First-tier Tribunal for Scotland. It is a free service dealing with 'first instance decisions'. However, you have to pay your own costs, such as travel and professional fees, should you ask a rating agent, or other person, to represent you. For council tax, there is a right to appeal to the tribunal against certain decisions, including liability, valuations, discounts, exemptions and council tax reduction.

Arrears procedures

Council tax is normally paid in monthly instalments. If a payment is missed, the local authority sends a reminder notice giving the client seven days to pay the outstanding amount.

This reminder notice lists:
- the outstanding amount to be paid; *and*
- if this amount is not paid within seven days, the right to pay in instalments is lost and the outstanding amount for the financial year must be paid.

If the outstanding amount is paid but a payment is missed later in the year, the next reminder notice will state that if a third payment is missed in the same financial year, they will lose the right to pay in instalments without a reminder notice being sent out.[35]

Chapter 4: Household debt
4. Council tax

When a client loses the right to pay by instalments and fails to make payment of the outstanding amount for the financial year and the time limit for payment has lapsed, the local authority can apply to the sheriff court for a summary warrant.

The client cannot negotiate with the court before it is granted.

The amount due will have increased as there is an automatic penalty of 10 per cent if a summary warrant has been granted against the client.

The local authority must obtain a charge for payment before money can be recovered.

Enforcement

There is no court hearing as such for enforcing council tax and water debts in Scotland. It is done by summary warrant procedure.[36] More detailed information on summary warrants is in Chapter 7.

Once a summary warrant has been granted, a charge for payment must be served and expired before certain diligence can be carried out. Charge for payments expire after 14 days if the debt remains unpaid.

Diligence available to sheriff officers for the recovery of unpaid council tax is:
- arresting the client's earnings;
- freezing and taking money from the client's bank accounts;
- removing belongings from the client's home and selling them;
- sequestration.

Once a charge for payment has been issued, the client can apply for a time to pay order, which will allow them to make a repayment plan. It also stops sheriff officers from taking action against the client.

A statutory moratorium may also be used to stop enforcement after the summary warrant has been issued.

Third-party deductions

A third-party deduction scheme is used when a client has arrears and other methods to recover the debt have been tried. A threat of enforcement action must have been used before a third-party deduction can be applied for (unlike Water Direct (see p87) which can be applied for without the threat of enforcement action). A fixed amount is deducted from the client's benefits to clear the arrears.[37]

Third-party deductions can be made from UC, PC, IS, JSA or ESA. The amount is deducted from the client's benefit and paid directly to the creditor until the debt is cleared. Where there is more than one debt, a maximum of three deductions can be taken at any one time inclusive of council tax arrears.

Checklist for action

Advisers should take the following action.
- Consider whether emergency action is necessary.

- Check whether the property is exempt and the client is in receipt of all relevant discounts and reductions.
- Check liability for the debt, including any associated sheriff officer's charges. Consider whether there are any grounds for a complaint.
- Check whether an application for a statutory moratorium would be an appropriate course of action.
- Consider applying for the Debt Arrangement Scheme or an insolvency option. In the case of joint and several debts, where only one party opts for a formal debt solution, the other party can be pursued for the whole debt.
- Assist the client to choose a relevant strategy because this may be a priority debt.

5. Water charges

Water and sewerage in Scotland is publicly owned and run by Scottish Water on behalf of the Scottish government. All money collected goes towards improving the service and infrastructure.

The legal position

The Water (Scotland) Act 1980 lists most of the powers and duties associated with supplying water in Scotland.

The prices Scottish Water can set are determined by the Water Industry Commission for Scotland.

Domestic customers

Most domestic customers receive and pay for four services:
- supply of drinking water; *and*
- removal and treatment of sewage; *and*
- removal and treatment of surface drainage from private areas such as roofs and car parks; *and*
- removal and treatment of surface drainage from public areas such as roads.

Household water and sewerage charges are billed by local authorities for Scottish Water, and collected with council tax. Bills are issued annually and the amounts are listed separately. This joint billing and collection system enables water and sewerage bills to be linked to the council tax banding system and some council tax discounts also apply to water and sewerage charges.

The amounts payable by council tax band are available on Scottish Water's website.[38]

Most domestic water supplies in Scotland are non-metered. However, clients can have a water meter installed if they wish to pay for how much water they use.

Chapter 4: Household debt
5. Water charges

Domestic customers with water meters are directly billed by Scottish Water rather than by their local authority.

Some domestic properties have a private supply from Scottish Water that can be metered – eg, where the client permanently lives in a mobile home, charges are usually paid to the site.

If properties are exempt from council tax, there may still be a charge for water and sewerage.

Households that receive council tax reduction (CTR) automatically receive a reduction from their water and sewerage bill through the water charges reduction scheme. This is up to a maximum of 35 per cent from 1 April 2021. So, even if your client receives 100 per cent CTR, they still need to pay 65 per cent of the water and sewerage charges.[39]

Households with no occupants liable to pay council tax (eg, properties fully occupied by full-time students) are exempt from paying water and sewerage charges.

Many clients might believe that if they have a discount or CTR they do not have to pay for water. This is not the case.

Properties with a private septic tank are not liable for sewerage charges, just water.

Scottish Water has a Priority Services Register for people with additional requirements – eg, those with a disability or long-term illness, looking after very young children or who require water for medication.

Non-payment of water charges

If a client has not paid the water and sewerage part of their council tax bill, local authorities can begin recovery procedures.

Clients receiving certain benefits can have deductions made from their benefit to pay off their water debt. This is sometimes called 'Water Direct' or the DWP's 'third-party deduction' system. If a local authority uses the scheme, it can deduct two payments from your client's benefit – one to recover water and sewerage arrears, and one to cover current charges so they do not build up further arrears.

A fixed amount is deducted from benefit until the arrears are cleared. Deductions can be made from:[40]
- universal credit;
- income support;
- income-based and contribution-based jobseeker's allowance;
- income-related and contributory employment and support allowance;
- pension credit.

Local authorities do not need permission to take deductions of up to 25 per cent (15 per cent from April 2025) of a client's benefits. For amounts over this, the client must approve the deduction.

Summary warrant
The local authority can also use the summary warrant procedure to collect water debts. See Chapter 7 for more information about summary warrants.

Disconnection
Disconnection from the public water supply is not generally allowed for domestic customers in Scotland, only for non-domestic customers.

Complaints and redress
In the first instance, complaints should be addressed to Scottish Water.

If your client is still not satisfied, they can take it further by contacting Citizens Advice Scotland (tel: 0800 028 1456).

Ombudsman
If your client has completed the stages of Scottish Water's complaints process and the complaint remains unresolved, it can be escalated to the Scottish Public Services Ombudsman (SPSO).[41] The SPSO independently and impartially investigates complaints. A complaint can be started at spso.org.uk.

Non-domestic customers
All non-domestic customers in Scotland are charged on a metered basis, unless it is not practical to do so. Property and road drainage charges are based on the property's rateable value.

Water and sewerage charges for non-domestic customers are made up of six elements:
- a fixed charge for water;
- a volumetric charge for water;
- a fixed charge for wastewater;
- a volumetric charge for wastewater;
- property drainage;
- roads drainage.

Their supply may not come from Scottish Water, but a private retailer licensed by Scottish Water, such as Clear, SES Business Water or Veolia Water.[42]

Non-domestic customers can move between suppliers for the best deal.

Complaints
Complaints should be made to the company first, then Scottish Water, then the Ombudsman, as above.

Disconnection
Non-domestic customers can be disconnected. The guidance for this can be found on the Scottish Water website.[43]

Chapter 4: Household debt
Notes

Checklist for action
- Consider whether the client is eligible for any help or assistance.
- Check liability.
- Assist the client to choose a relevant strategy, as this could be a priority debt.

Notes

1. **Child support payments**
   1. s1 CSA 1991
   2. ss3(1) and 55 CSA 1991
   3. s31 CSA 1991
   4. s32 CMOPA 2008
   5. s2 Child Support (Enforcement) Act 2023
   6. gov.uk/child-maintenance-service/complaints-and-appeals
   7. s38 CSA 1991
   8. s40A CSA 1991
   9. s40B CSA 1991
   10. s28 CMOPA 2008
   11. Reg 2 DAS(S) Regs

2. **Spousal maintenance payments**
   12. s4 Family Law (Scotland) Act 1985
   13. s5 Family Law (Scotland) Act 1985
   14. Reg 2(1)(f) DAS(S) Regs
   15. s145(3)(f) B(S)A 2016

3. **Gas and electricity charges**
   16. Condition 27A SLC
   17. Condition 14.9 SLC
   18. Ofgem debt assignment protocol for prepayment meter customers letter, 12 May 2015, ofgem.gov.uk/publications-and-updates/decision-make-modifications-gas-and-electricity-supply-licences-reform-switching-process-indebted-prepayment-meter-customers-debt-assignment-protocol
   19. ofgem.gov.uk/what-do-if-you-get-back-bill
   20. Ofgem, *Decision: Modification of the electricity and gas supply licences to introduce rules on backbilling to improve customer outcomes*, ofgem.gov.uk/system/files/docs/2018/03/backbilling_final_decision_policy_document_-_march_5_-_website.pdf
   21. Ofgem, *Good Practice for Supporting Customers in Payment Difficulty*, September 2022, available at ofgem.gov.uk/publications/good-practice-supporting-customers-payment-difficulty
   22. Ofgem, *Regulatory Expectations on Supporting Customers in Payment Difficulty*, available at ofgem.gov.uk/publications/regulatory-expectations-supporting-customers-payment-difficulty
   23. Ofgem, *Involuntary PPM - supplier code of practice*, April 2023, available at ofgem.gov.uk/publications/involuntary-prepayment-meter-energy-supplier-code-practice
   24. ofgem.gov.uk/news/new-rules-installing-involuntary-prepayment-meters
   25. See bget.org.uk

4. **Council tax**
   26. s79 LGFA 1992
   27. s75 LGFA 1992
   28. s75(2) LGFA 1992
   29. Sch 1 CT(ED)(S)O
   30. s2 The Council Tax (Exempt Dwellings) (Scotland) Amendment Order 2022 No.124
   31. s2 The Council Tax (Exempt Dwellings) (Scotland) Amendment Order 2023 No.36
   32. s80(1)-(4) and (6)-(7) LGFA 1992; The Council Tax (Reductions for Disabilities) (Scotland) Regulations 1992 No.1335
   33. Art 4(2) The Council Tax (Discounts) (Scotland) Consolidation and Amendment Order 2003 No.176; The Council Tax (Discounts) (Scotland) Amendment Order 2023 No.25

34 The Council Tax (Variation for Unoccupied Dwellings) (Scotland) Regulations 2013 No.45
35 s22(4) The Council Tax (Administration and Enforcement) (Scotland) Regulations 1992 No.1332
36 The Council Tax (Administration and Enforcement) (Scotland) Regulations 1992 No.1332
37 Sch 9 SS(C&P) Regs

5. Water charges
38 scottishwater.co.uk
39 scottishwater.co.uk/your-home/your-charges/your-charges-2024-2025
40 gov.uk/bills-benefits
41 s16A Scottish Public Services Ombudsman Act 2002
42 A full list can be found at scotlandontap.gov.uk/suppliers/suppliers.
43 scottishwater.co.uk/business-and-developers/licensed-providers/connections-and-disconnections

Chapter 5

Consumer credit

This chapter covers:
1. Introduction (below)
2. The Consumer Credit Act (p93)
3. Pre-contractual information (p97)
4. Key elements of consumer credit agreements (p98)
5. Withdrawal, cancellation and cooling-off periods (p100)
6. Unfair relationships (p101)
7. Arrears notices (p103)
8. Default notices (p104)
9. Voluntary termination of hire purchase and personal contract purchase agreements (p104)
10. Time orders (p105)
11. Section 75 credit card protection (p107)
12. Early repayment rules under the Consumer Credit Act (p108)
13. Credit reference agencies (p108)
14. The Financial Conduct Authority's role (p112)
15. Financial Ombudsman Service and Financial Services Compensation Scheme (p112)

1. Introduction

The Consumer Credit Act 1974 (CCA 1974) was introduced to protect consumers and some small businesses using credit to buy goods and services in the UK.

The CCA 1974 was reviewed and amended by the Consumer Credit Act 2006 (CCA 2006) and further provisions were brought into force in the UK in 2010 (The Consumer Credit (Agreements) Regulations 2010) as a result of the European Consumer Credit Directive (which had been adopted in Europe in 2008).

Until 1 April 2014, the Office of Fair Trading (OFT) was responsible for overseeing the Consumer Credit Act. From 1 April 2014, the OFT closed and its functions were largely divided between the Competition and Markets Authority and the Financial Conduct Authority (FCA), which has assumed responsibility for regulating consumer credit.

Some parts of the Consumer Credit Act have been abolished, but most of its provisions remain in force and have been carried over into new rules made by the FCA in its *Sourcebook*. The specific rules for firms carrying out consumer credit activities are set out in the FCA's *Consumer Credit Sourcebook* (referred to as 'CONC').

In June 2022, the UK government began a process to change the CCA 1974 radically. The government will move much of the Act from statute to sit under the FCA – enabling the regulator to quickly respond to emerging developments in the consumer credit market, rather than having to amend existing legislation. It will also simplify ambiguous technical terms to make clear to consumers what protections they have. This is currently in the consultation phase and is expected to take many years to be completed because of the complexity of legislation.

Consumer credit legislation is complex. It is suggested that debt advisers get specialist advice when dealing with challenges to the CCA 1974.

European Consumer Credit Directive

Since 1 February 2011, lenders providing unsecured loans regulated by the CCA 1974 have to comply with guidelines imposed by the Consumer Credit (EU Directive) Regulations 2010. The directive made many changes, including rules on creditworthiness, the right of withdrawal, early repayment, adequate explanations of credit, credit reference agencies and credit intermediaries. Many of these amendments have since been omitted from the CCA 1974 and can now be found in the FCA's CONC.

2. The Consumer Credit Act 1974

What is the Consumer Credit Act 1974

The Consumer Credit Act 1974 (CCA 1974) protects the rights of consumers. It sets out how most retail lending and credit is handled in the UK. It determines how businesses that lend money or offer goods and services on credit conduct their business and advertise those products, as well as requiring them to be licensed by the Financial Conduct Authority (FCA).

The CCA 1974 regulates the relationship between consumers (ie, private individuals) and lending institutions (ie, creditors) where a credit or hire agreement is provided (ie, the relationship between lender and client).

The CCA 1974 only applies to 'regulated agreements', where the client is an individual (ie, a consumer) and where a statutory exemption does not apply.

The Act gives clients a variety of rights against lenders, such as the right to a 'cooling-off period' or to pay off their credit early, and lays down certain procedural requirements to control the lending process.

Chapter 5: Consumer credit
2. The Consumer Credit Act 1974

Regulated credit agreements

All credit agreements are regulated unless they are exempt. Most credit agreements that debt advisers come across are regulated credit agreements. The following are all common types of credit regulated by the CCA 1974:
- credit cards;
- hire purchase agreements;
- payday loans;
- personal loans;
- store cards;
- secured loans, but not if they are secured on a client's main residence, as these are classed as FCA-regulated mortgages.

Key terms for regulated credit agreements
Fixed-sum credit agreement
These are where a client borrows a fixed sum of money to be repaid over a fixed time, with fixed instalments and a fixed interest rate. Interest is added at the beginning of the agreement and repaid alongside the capital element of the credit over the period of the agreement. This means the monthly payments are the same every month during the payment period.

Running account credit agreements
A personal credit agreement that enables a client to receive loans from time to time from a bank or other lender provided that a specified credit limit is not exceeded. Interest is charged on the amount loaned during any period. Interest is added on at the end of every month and can vary depending on the amount outstanding. Credit cards are an example of running account credit.

Consumer hire agreements
An agreement (either running-account or fixed-sum) which is made by a client with an individual (the hirer) for the hiring of goods which:
– is not a hire-purchase agreement; *and*
– is capable of lasting for more than three months (that is, even if it is originally made for a shorter period, it is capable of being extended).

An example of this is hiring tools or hiring a car for a short period. The important aspect of this is that the goods are returned to the hirer.

Credit-token agreement
A regulated agreement for the provision of credit in connection with the use of a credit token. This can be for the supply of cash, goods or services on credit up to a set credit limit. In return, the client pays the creditor the full amount outstanding within a set time or by regular minimum instalments, with interest being charged on the full outstanding balance. An example of this is a credit or store card.

Restricted-use credit agreements
Credit (either running-account or fixed-sum) provided in such a way that the creditor controls its application or use. Restricted-use credit is also where there is an agreement to

Chapter 5: Consumer credit
2. The Consumer Credit Act 1974

finance a specific transaction (usually the sale of goods) between a client and a creditor.
An example of this is a store card (credit-token agreement) that can only be used in certain stores, or a loan taken out specifically for, say, the consolidation of debt.

Unrestricted-use credit agreements
An agreement under which the client is free to use the credit as they choose or where the client controls the application or use of the credit.

Hire purchase and conditional sale
In these contracts, the goods do not become the property of the client (hirer) until the final payment is made. If the client (hirer) cannot meet the normal payments, the goods will eventually be repossessed. However, if they have paid one-third or more of the purchase price, the goods are protected, and a court order is necessary for a creditor to repossess the goods. If the goods are on private property (eg, a driveway), a court order is always required.

Secured loan
The consumer puts up something of value as security for the loan. This is usually a house or car. If they cannot meet payments, the loan company will eventually force the sale of the property in order to recover their unpaid debt. Any surplus money raised from the sale is returned to the consumer.

Linked transactions
It covers transactions entered into in compliance with a term in the original agreement such as a life insurance policy entered into under a loan agreement. It does not cover a transaction for the provision of security for the original agreement. Certain transactions are said to be related to a regulated agreement. This is important in withdrawal from, cancellation of, and unfair relationships between creditors' and clients' provisions.

Exempt credit agreements

Certain forms of credit are not covered under the CCA 1974. They are often referred to as 'exempt agreements' and include:
- buy now pay later finance;
- charge cards (these are not credit cards – see p96);
- debts to individuals (including family and friends);
- debts to local government – eg, council tax and benefit overpayments;
- debts to unlicensed lenders – eg, loan sharks;
- mortgages;
- some credit union loans;
- agreements which include limited companies;
- certain types of business debts;
- agreements where the creditor is a local authority;
- an agreement that is for a fixed-sum credit that the client is required to repay in four payments or less within the year.

Chapter 5: Consumer credit
2. The Consumer Credit Act 1974

Key terms for exempt agreements
Charge cards
This is a running-account credit agreement which provides for the making of payments in relation to specified periods and requires that the entire credit be repaid in one instalment.
Mortgage
Certain agreements secured by land mortgages made by a local authority, authorised bank or building society. It can also apply to certain secured loans on the property. Regulation for this is found in the FCA's *Mortgages and Home Finance: conduct of business sourcebook* (MCOB).
Low-cost agreement
A client-creditor agreement where the creditor is a credit union and the rate of the total credit charged (ie, the APR) does not exceed 26.9 per cent. A client-creditor agreement which is of a type offered to a particular class of individuals and not offered to the public generally – eg, a loan by an employer to an employee.
High-net-worth exemption
The Consumer Credit Act 2006 (CCA 2006) allows 'high-net-worth' clients to opt out of CCA 1974 regulation. This applies where the client's net income is £150,000 a year or more, or where their assets are £500,000 or more (excluding their home and pension). (The client must sign a 'high-net-worth' declaration which must be certified by an accountant – banks can certify in-house.)
Agreements for business purposes
CCA 2006 introduced a business-related exemption: it does not regulate a consumer credit agreement by which the creditor provides credit exceeding £25,000, or a consumer hire agreement requiring the hirer to make payments exceeding £25,000, provided in each case that the agreement is entered into by the client or hirer wholly or predominantly for a business carried on, or intended to be carried on, by them.
Buy-to-let agreements
The CCA 1974 does not regulate certain consumer credit agreements relating to investment properties – typically 'buy-to-let' agreements.

Agreements with partial exemption

Certain agreements, while regulated by the CCA 1974, are exempt from some of its important provisions.
These include:
- small agreements where the total amount of credit involved does not exceed £50;
- hire purchase and conditional sale, which are excluded from the definition of small agreements.

This is just a selection of common types of debt, but there are many more which can be regulated or exempt. In some cases, a debt could be either, depending on the date it was taken out and the amount borrowed. For example, before 2008, debts over £25,000 were not regulated.

When a regulated agreement complies with all the formal requirements, it is 'properly executed'. This means it is legally binding and can be enforced by the creditor through the courts.

Agreements which do not comply with the formal requirements are 'improperly executed'. Whether or not they can be enforced through the courts depends on certain factors.

A court may allow an agreement to be enforced, depending on what is 'wrong with it'. For example, if the only thing wrong with it is the misspelling of the client's name or a typing error, it is likely the courts would grant permission to the creditor to enforce this agreement.

Debt advisers who are unsure whether their client's debt is regulated or exempt are encouraged to seek specialist advice.

3. Pre-contractual information

Creditors supplying goods, services or digital content must give certain key information (pre-contractual) to a potential client before providing any form of credit covered by the Consumer Credit Act 1974. This includes:[1]
- how long the agreement is for;
- how much repayments will be and when they are to be made;
- the amount of credit or the credit limit;
- the APR, interest rate charges and anything else applicable to the interest rates to be charged;
- the identity and address of the credit provider;
- the name and address of the credit intermediary (if applicable);
- the nature of the agreement;
- the total payable amount;
- the type of credit being agreed to.

Pre-contract information for on-premises contracts

Creditors supplying goods, services or digital content to a client using an on-premises contract must provide all of the following information in a clear, comprehensible way:[2]
- the main characteristics of the goods, services or digital content; *and*
- the creditor's trading name, address and telephone number; *and*
- the total price including all applicable taxes; *and*
- all additional delivery charges; *and*
- arrangements for payment, delivery and time for delivery; *and*
- the complaints-handling policy; *and*

- a reminder that they are under a duty to supply goods conforming to the contract; *and*
- whether there is any after-sales service or guarantee, and their conditions; *and*
- the duration of the contract and how it can be ended if it is indefinite; *and*
- the functionality of digital content; *and*
- the compatibility of digital content with hardware or software.

However, creditors do not have to supply this information if it is a 'day-to-day transaction' that is performed immediately – eg, selling goods in a shop.

There is no prescribed format for the information, except that it must be headed **'pre-contract information'**, handed to the client before the agreement is made and must be capable of being taken away to be studied. As there is also no prescribed period for providing the information, the creditor can give the pre-contract information document to the client and then immediately invite them to sign the actual agreement.

If the creditor does not comply with the pre-contract information requirements, the agreement is improperly executed, and the creditor needs the permission of the court to enforce it.[3]

Pre-contract information for distance contracts

Creditors selling to a client without face-to-face contact (ie, distance selling) must give clients all of the information listed below in good time before the client enters into the contract. They must provide this information in a clear, comprehensible manner that is appropriate to the type of distance communication used to make the contract – eg, mail order or digital television services.

The main characteristics of the goods, services or digital content are:[4]
- the creditor's trading name;
- the ttotal price of the goods or services, including all taxes;
- delivery and any other costs, where appropriate;
- in an indefinite or subscription contract, the total costs per billing period;
- if the client has a right to cancel, the time limit, conditions and procedures for cancelling;
- the duration of the contract, or if the contract is indefinite, the conditions for ending it.

4. Key elements of consumer credit agreements

A creditor should advise a potential client to consider all information before signing the credit agreement.[5] This ensures they are fully aware of the costs, legal responsibilities and the consequences of failing to make payments, such as late payment charges and possible legal action.

Prescribed and non-prescribed terms on consumer credit agreements

A credit agreement is not properly executed unless it contains all the prescribed terms and conforms to regulations made under section 60(1) of the Consumer Credit Act 1974 (CCA 1974) and is signed in the prescribed manner.[6] The consequence of a failure or omission to state fully and correctly any of the prescribed terms is to render the agreement improperly executed and, therefore, unenforceable except by order of the court.

'Prescribed terms' and 'non-prescribed terms' must be included in a regulated agreement for it to be properly executed.

Prescribed terms

Generally, prescribed terms should be set out first, followed by non-prescribed terms. A clear explanation of the client's obligations must be included above the signature box or space.

The prescribed terms are:[7]
- the amount of credit or credit limit (or how the credit limit is determined);
- the interest rate;
- details of the repayments expressed by reference to a combination of:
  - the number;
  - the amount;
  - the frequency;
  - the dates;
  - how they are determined;
  - any way in which the creditor can vary what is payable.

Non-prescribed terms

Certain other information, known as 'non-prescribed terms', must be included in an agreement for it to be properly executed:
- the consumer credit heading;
- the agreement is regulated under the CCA 1974;
- names and addresses of all parties to the agreement. Although this should be spelt correctly, it is very unlikely a court would decide an agreement was improperly executed if a name was incorrectly spelt;
- financial information expressed as a combination of:
  - the amount of credit or credit limit (or the manner it is to be determined);
  - that the total amount payable if fixed, or an estimate if the rate is variable;
  - the duration of agreements;
  - the timings of repayments;
  - the APR and whether it is variable;

- other financial information, including:
  - the description of any goods or services;
  - the cash price;
  - any advance payment – eg, a deposit;
  - the total charge for credit;
  - the rate of interest;
  - details of any security;
  - key information;
  - a statement of consumer rights, including cancellation rights (or, where applicable, a statement that the agreement is not cancellable);
  - default charges;
  - a signature box or space for both parties to sign;
  - a cancellation box (where appropriate);
  - a separate signature box for the client to confirm the purchase of any insurance product.

5. Withdrawal, cancellation and cooling-off periods

Withdrawal from agreements

There is a difference between the withdrawal and cancellation of an agreement. Clients cannot cancel an agreement before it has been made but can withdraw at any time until then. The effects are the same, restoring both parties to the position they were in before the making of the proposed agreement.

Cancelling a consumer credit contract

In most circumstances, when both parties have signed a consumer credit agreement, it becomes legally binding on both parties.

The right to cancel is also known as the 'right to withdraw'. This should not be confused with 'withdrawal from agreements' (see above).

Cancellation can be done verbally (if time is short) or (preferably) in writing, by post or email. It is good practice to follow a call to a creditor to cancel a credit agreement with a request to cancel the agreement in writing, by post or by email using the contact details provided in the agreement.

Cancellation of consumer credit contracts is governed by sections 67 to 73 of the Consumer Credit Act 1974 (CCA 1974).

There is an extended cooling-off period for credit cards and loans. For agreements made on or after 1 February 2011, the client can withdraw from an agreement within 14 days without giving any reason.[8] This applies to all regulated agreements except those:

- for credit of more than £60,260;
- secured on land.

The 14-day cooling-off period starts from the day the agreement is executed or, if later, from the day the client receives a copy of the agreement. Withdrawal can be made verbally or in writing.

In addition:
- the client must repay the credit and any accrued interest within 30 days;
- withdrawal from the agreement also includes withdrawal from any supplementary agreement – eg, PPI;
- the effect of withdrawal is as if the credit agreement had never been entered into.

Credit agreements at a distance and cooling-off periods

The CCA 1974 covers both credit agreements made at a lender's premises and those entered 'at a distance'. These are credit agreements made online, over the phone, in a client's home with a representative or elsewhere, such as a pop-up business stand.

The CCA 1974 acknowledges that for distance credit agreements, clients might be making a decision that is hasty or on reflection not suitable. For this reason, it provides a 'cooling-off period' during which clients have the right to cancel a credit agreement.[9]

Creditors must provide clients with a copy of their cancellation rights with the credit agreement. This must be sent by post or email within seven days. Clients then have five days (not including the day they received the documents) to cancel.

If a client decides to cancel, the credit agreement is treated as if it never existed. Clients must repay any monies or return any goods that have been received.

An example of a cancellable agreement is when a double-glazing salesperson calls on a client at home and persuades the client to sign a credit agreement for replacement windows.

6. Unfair relationships

The Consumer Credit Act (CCA 2006) amended the Consumer Credit Act 1974 (CCA 1974) to introduce the concept of an 'unfair relationship'. It relates to credit agreements entered into after 6 April 2007 or agreements which had not been repaid by a client before that date.[10] It provides greater protection to clients to redress unfairness in consumer credit agreements between a lender and a client (borrower). These provisions are in addition to the Financial Ombudsman Service's jurisdiction. They apply to regulated and non-regulated agreements, including exempt agreements, regardless of the amount of credit involved (except if the agreement is exempt because it is a regulated mortgage contract).

The CCA 2006 does not define an unfair relationship. It sets out, in general terms, factors that may give rise to an unfair relationship. These include:
- where the terms of the agreement or related agreement are deemed to be unfair to the borrower of the loan;
- how the creditor has exercised or enforced their rights under an agreement – eg, seeking to issue legal proceedings and recover the debt due;
- anything done (or not done) by, or on a lender's behalf, in respect to the loan agreement or a related agreement – eg, to the loan agreement itself, or an insurance policy running alongside it.

The provisions also relate to all second charge lending as long as the relevant agreement was entered into before 21 March 2016. Any second charge lending after 21 March 2016 is governed by the Financial Conduct Authority's *Mortgages and Home Finance: conduct of business sourcebook* (MCOB) regime and the provisions do not apply. 'Second charge lending' is when a client takes out a loan secured against their property when they already have a mortgage (the first charge).

In some cases, unfair contract terms may be sufficient in themselves to give rise to an unfair relationship, but the court can also look at:
- how agreements are introduced and negotiated; *and*
- how agreements are administered; *and*
- any other aspect of the relationship it considers relevant.

Both actions and omissions can be unfair. This includes actions or omissions on behalf of the creditor or suppliers (who are deemed agents of the creditor) and debt collectors. These include:
- pre-contract business practices such as misleading advertisements, mis-selling products, high-pressure selling techniques, and irresponsible lending;
- post-contract actions, such as demanding money the borrower has not agreed to pay and aggressive debt collection practices;
- failing to provide key information in a clear and timely manner or to disclose material facts.

The court must take into account all matters it thinks relevant, including those relating to the individual client and creditor. This means that a term or practice may not be unfair in a particular case because of the client's knowledge or experience, but may be unfair in another client's case if they are more vulnerable or susceptible to exploitation. There is also an expectation that clients will act honestly in providing accurate and full information to enable the creditor to assess risk.

Powers available to the courts include:

- making the lender/creditor repay the client some or all of the value of the loan;
- ordering the lender/creditor to release the client from all or a portion of the remaining balance of the loan;
- ordering the lender/creditor to release their claim on the property offered by the client as collateral;
- releasing the client from having to pay any penalties that may have resulted from the unfair relationship;
- changing the terms of the agreement or any related agreement, such as an insurance policy to protect payment required under the loan to make the terms fair to the client.

The unfair relationships provisions may be especially useful for clients facing court proceedings for enforcement of a debt or repossession, or where the restrictions on the ombudsman's jurisdiction mean that a client has no option but to resort to the unfair relationship provisions to challenge the creditor or defend the court action. However, they should be viewed as a remedy of last resort. Debt advisers should get specialist advice if considering using these provisions.

7. Arrears notices

Creditors must inform clients when their arrears reach a certain level, and that interest or charges may be accruing. This applies to most new and existing credit agreements. There are different provisions for fixed-sum and running-account agreements.
- **Fixed-sum agreements** – within 14 days of a client missing two scheduled payments under a fixed-notice credit agreement, the creditor must issue an arrears notice.[11] This 'notice of arrears' should be a specified form.
- **Running-account agreements** – if the client has missed two scheduled payments or is in arrears by the equivalent of two scheduled payments, before the next payment is due, the creditor must issue an arrears notice.[12] This 'notice of arrears' should be a specified form.

All arrears notices must be sent with a Financial Conduct Authority information sheet.[13]

When a client has received an arrears notice, they can apply for a time order through the courts. There is no requirement to wait for a default notice. See p105 for more information on time orders.

8. Default notices

If a client's credit agreement is regulated by the Consumer Credit Act 1974 (CCA 1974), the creditor must issue a default notice before any legal action can be taken. This notice is in the form of a formal letter explaining how the terms of the agreement have been broken and should include:[14]
- the client's and the creditor's name and address;
- details of the credit agreement and how it was broken;
- what action must be taken to repay the arrears;
- what action will be taken if the default notice is not complied with.

It must state that it is served under section 87(1) of the CCA 1974.

The default notice can be issued on most types of credit agreement for any amount of money owed. It instructs the client that they have 14 days to repay the amount they owe before a default is added to their credit file and that the creditor will take further action, including court action, to recover monies.

If the client pays the money owed under the default notice before the 14 days have passed, the default notice is not added to their credit reference file.

The default notice is only issued by a creditor when the client has missed between three and six months' worth of payments towards the debt. Default notices must be sent with a Financial Conduct Authority information sheet about defaults.[15]

9. Voluntary termination of hire purchase and personal contract purchase agreements

Hire purchase (HP) is a form of borrowing where the client does not own the goods. They are considered to be *hired* to the consumer until the final payment is made. Personal contract purchase (PCP) agreements are another common option for car finance. They are similar to HP but generally have lower monthly payments for the client. To take the title of the car, the client must make a 'balloon payment' at the end of the contract.

HP and PCP allow the client to voluntarily terminate the agreement early without any further payments being made when they have paid 50 per cent of the total cost of the credit (including any interest and charges).[16] They can only do this if they are not in default.

For HP agreements, this is generally halfway through the contract time – eg, on a 36-month contract 50 per cent is generally paid when month 18 has been cleared.

For PCP, it is slightly different because the total cost includes the balloon payment, so it may take longer to get to the 50 per cent mark.

In both instances, the client can terminate the agreement and hand the car back without having to pay any more to the contract. The amount to be paid to voluntarily terminate will be outlined clearly in the consumer credit contract the client signed when they took on the credit. Debt advisers are encouraged to check the client's contract to ensure it is correct.

10. **Time orders**

A time order is a request to the court for more time to pay a credit agreement.[17] A court can decide if a time order will go ahead, based on the client's and creditors' interests. Clients can only apply for a time order whether their credit agreement is regulated by the Consumer Credit Act 1974 (CCA 1974).

A time order can change the amount to be paid each month, the length of the loan and, occasionally, the interest rate.

It is especially useful if the client has a secured loan and creditors are threatening to repossess their home or if the client has a hire purchase (HP), personal contract purchase (PCP) or conditional sale contract as a successful time order application can stop a home or car from being repossessed.

Note that if the client already has had a time to pay direction (TTPD) or time to pay order (TTPO) granted by the court and has defaulted on this agreement, they cannot then apply for a time order.

Information on time orders is in section 129 of the CCA 1974. If a client also wants to stop their car from being repossessed, they must also make an application using section 135 of the CCA 1974 at the same time, asking the court to keep the car while they continue to make repayments under the time order. Section 136 can also amend the interest being paid.

See a recent case from Govan Law Centre.[18]

Time orders are applied for by a client under two different procedures.

- **Stand-alone application.** This is made before the creditor has raised court action and can be applied for when the client receives a notice of arrears from the creditor. Clients must submit Form 1[19] to the court and the creditor. The client incurs the cost of having it served on the other party.

  If the client has received a default notice which has expired, they can also apply for a time order using the same form. They do not have to serve notice of doing so to the creditor at this point. They must still submit it to court and are responsible for any cost associated with applying for a time order.

- **Time order when action has been raised in court.** When a creditor raises an action in court to recover money or take possession of goods, the client is sent a summons. This is a bundle of court papers, including a form which allows them to apply for a time order/TTPD. It is called 'Application in writing for a time to pay direction or a time order' (Form O3 – available from the sheriff court or online). It should be submitted before the expiry of the response date on the summons to the court. There is no cost for doing this.

Whichever procedure is used, the creditor informs the client and the court whether or not it is prepared to accept the time order application. If accepted, the court notifies the client and they must begin making payments.

If the creditor does not accept the time order application, the court sets a hearing date. The client and their representative must attend and make representations as to why the application should be accepted.

If it goes to court, the sheriff listens to both sides and decides whether the application is 'just'. Their decision is final. Clients should be made aware that if a time order application is not successful, the sheriff can grant a court order against them. Where this relates to an HP, conditional sale or PCP agreement, the sheriff usually also makes a possession order for the item to be returned to the creditor.

Ancillary order

At the same time as applying for a time order, clients can apply for an ancillary order to reduce the level of interest being charged by the creditor.[20] If granted, it means the loan is paid off sooner.

Sheriffs are often reluctant to grant ancillary orders, even when the level of interest being paid is high. Creditors argue that they are justified in setting the interest rate high because the client is a high-risk customer. If the client can show that the interest is exorbitant or unfair, the courts may be more inclined to award an ancillary order.

Advantages of a time order
- No decree is granted.
- The client's creditworthiness may not be affected.
- The client is in control of the situation and displays a sense of responsibility with consequential motivating effects. It is a proactive step for the client.

Disadvantages of a time order
- It only deals with one debt.
- Interest will continue to accrue at the original rate or the rate decided by the court.
- A time order is similar to a TTPD/TTPO, where the sheriff decides whether the repayment proposals are reasonable.

Time orders are rarely used and complex. Debt advisers should always seek specialist advice before helping clients with a time order.

11. Section 75 credit card protection

Transactions made by credit card are 'linked agreements' under the Consumer Credit Act 1974 (CCA 1974). This means credit card companies can be held responsible for misrepresentation and for defective goods or services costing between £100 and £30,000 if the seller is unwilling to remedy the situation. This could include a claim for damages due as a consequence of the misrepresentation or other breach.[21]

The credit card company has equal responsibility (or 'liability') with the seller if there is a problem with the things bought or if the company clients have bought from fails.

What section 75 covers

Clients can use section 75 when:
- the company has failed to supply the goods or services, or has supplied goods not up to standard;
- the company has misrepresented what it is supplying – eg, a software supplier says a software package will work with a particular computer when it does not.

To qualify for protection under section 75, clients must have spent between £100 and £30,000 on their credit card. This protection does not apply to anything bought using a debit card. **Note:**
- The £100 minimum amount applies to each item or set of items bought, rather than the total bill. For example, when buying tickets for an event, a 'family ticket' counts as one item but individual tickets for family members would not. If the individual tickets were less than £100 each, they would not be covered under section 75.
- Clients should first contact the company/creditor they purchased from, providing them with an opportunity to resolve the issue. The client should explain that they want them to help resolve an issue with something they have paid for using their credit card and would like them to consider the chargeback and section 75 process. They should include any supporting information they have – eg, receipts, invoices or other proof of payment, any correspondence about the goods/services purchased, contracts and terms and conditions, if available. If the company fails to respond or refuses a refund, a claim can be initiated against their credit card company.

Section 75 of the CCA 1974 outlines this protection in detail and should be referred to by a debt adviser who may be helping a client with an application.

If an application under section 75 is unsuccessful, the client can raise a complaint with the Financial Ombudsman Service (see p112). Their decision is usually final, although the client can ultimately raise an action in court, but should be made aware that this is costly and often not successful.

12. Early repayment rules under the Consumer Credit Act

A client can decide to pay off a regulated credit agreement early, in full or partially, after it is in place.[22] There is a formula to ensure that creditors can recoup costs associated with setting up an agreement; therefore, a lower percentage rebate is given for settlement during the earliest parts of a credit agreement.[23]

If a client requests a settlement figure from the creditor for a regulated credit agreement, the creditor must provide a statement of the amount required to settle the agreement, together with details of how the amount is calculated. They should reply to the client within seven days. The creditor must set the settlement repayment date 28 days after the request was made, to give the client time to consider and pay the early settlement figure.[24] The figure is the sum the client owes plus the interest owed less the statutory interest rebate they must apply.

13. Credit reference agencies

There is no right to credit, and most lenders decide credit applications based on 'credit scoring' – ie, a system used to assess the probability of applicants meeting their financial commitments, using information supplied on the credit application form, the lender's records (where available) and data from credit reference agencies. Different lenders use different systems, which should not only establish the likelihood of the applicant repaying but also whether they can afford to do so.

There are three main credit reference agencies in the UK: Experian, Equifax and TransUnion. They provide information about clients and their credit records. They do not:
- make the decision or express any opinion about whether clients should be given credit and are unable to tell clients why they have been refused credit; *or*
- keep 'blacklists' or details of clients' credit scores.

When a creditor informs a client that it is rejecting their credit application, based on information from a credit reference agency, the creditor must provide details of the credit reference agency, including the name, address and telephone number.[25] Failure to do so is an offence. This requirement does not apply to agreements secured on land.

Credit reference agencies usually keep details of:
- electoral roll entries;

- sheriff court decrees. These are held for six years from the date of judgment unless paid within one month when any record is removed;
- bankruptcies and protected trust deeds. These are held for six years from the date of sequestration or signing the trust deed;
- credit accounts. A record is held until the account is paid off and then for a further six years;
- whether the client has defaulted on a credit agreement. A record is held for six years from the date the default was registered, normally when the account is three to six months in arrears;
- mortgage repossessions, including voluntary repossessions. These are held for six years;
- aliases, associations and linked addresses – ie, any other names the client has been known by, previous addresses or correspondence addresses, and whether they share financial responsibility for an account with another person;
- a warning from Credit Industry Fraud Avoidance System (CIFAS) – a fraud avoidance system developed to protect people whose names, addresses or other details have been used fraudulently by other people to apply for or obtain credit. It does not mean that the client is being accused of fraud, but any credit applications may be checked out to ensure they are, in fact, the applicant;
- information from the Gone Away Information Network (known as GAIN) – ie, on clients who have 'gone away' without informing their lenders of a forwarding address. This information is held for six years;
- previous credit searches by lenders in the past two years. Several searches within a short period may indicate attempted fraud or over-commitment.

A client's credit file should only hold information about them and any other person they have a 'financial association' with – ie, joint account holders or applicants, or anyone who informs the agency that they have financial ties. This allows lenders to take account of information about anyone 'linked' to the client.

Although the client can ask a lender only to take account of information about them, this does not prevent the lender from carrying out checks to make sure that this is not intended to hide a partner's poor credit rating. If there is no financial association, the client should inform the agency so the link can be removed.

Useful publications

Experian has published a helpful guide called *Understanding Your Credit Information and How Lenders Use It*.[26]

The Information Commissioner's Office publishes a leaflet, *Credit Explained*.[27] The Information Commissioner has collaborated with the credit industry to produce a guidance document, *Principles for the Reporting of Arrears, Arrangements and Defaults at Credit Reference Agencies*.[28]

Recording defaults

Guidelines from the Information Commissioner state that a client's account should not be recorded as in default unless the relationship between the creditor and the client has broken down.[29] This means the client has been in arrears for at least three consecutive months on the contractual instalments or under an agreement to reschedule repayments. It should be recorded as 'in default' if such payments have not been made in full for six months. Accounts which are subject to repayment arrangements or debt management plans should only be recorded as in default if the client:

- is only making token payments. However, in this situation, they can ask the agency to record this (known as filing a 'notice of correction') if the creditor has not done so; or
- defaults on the arrangement and the arrears are equivalent to three months' payments under the original contract; or
- is making reduced payments, but no agreed arrangement is in place.

If the lender does not agree to accept reduced payments (including token payments), although any payments the client makes are reflected in the outstanding balance recorded, arrears continue to accrue, and a default may be recorded once the equivalent of three months' arrears is reached.

If a creditor fails to record a default within the three- to six-month period but, for example, delays registering the default until the client misses an agreed repayment, the Financial Ombudsman Service may order the creditor to backdate the registration. A default cannot be registered in respect of an irredeemably unenforceable agreement.

A zero balance on a credit reference report marked 'balance satisfied' (with or without the flag 'partially satisfied') indicates there has been a default, but that:

- the account has been paid in full; or
- the account was included in a trust deed that has been satisfactorily completed, or in a bankruptcy from which the client has been discharged; or
- the creditor has agreed to accept less than the full amount due in full and final settlement of the account.

If the information held is incorrect

A client can obtain a copy of their file at any time, free of charge.[30] As the different credit reference agencies hold different data from different credit providers, it is useful to get reports from the main three agencies. Request for reports can be made:

- **online** from:
  - Equifax (equifax.co.uk);
  - Experian (experian.co.uk);
  - TransUnion (transunion.co.uk); or

- **in writing.** The client must provide their full name and address (including previous names or addresses used in the past six years). See ico.org.uk/your-data-matters/credit for more information about making a written request.

Correcting information held on a credit reference file

If the client considers that any of the information in the file is wrong and is likely to cause prejudice as a result, they can write to the lender or the credit reference agency. However, as the credit reference agency would have to contact the lender to ask it to investigate the complaint, it might be quicker to write to the lender and send a copy to the credit reference agency. The client should state why the information is wrong and submit any supporting evidence – eg, that a debt has been paid. The agency must respond in writing within 28 days, stating either that it has corrected or removed the information, or done nothing.[31]

While the agency checks its accuracy, the information is marked 'account query'. If the agency fails to remove the information or the client disagrees with the proposed amendment, they can ask the agency to add their own 'notice of correction' to the file – eg, an explanation of how the debt arose. This must be up to 200 words and sent to the agency within a further 28 days. The agency must inform the client within 28 days if it accepts the notice. If it does not, the agency must refer the case to the Information Commissioner for a ruling.

If the client receives no response after writing to the lender and/or the credit reference agency, they can complain to the Information Commissioner. A client can also complain to the Information Commissioner if they believe inaccurate information is being held but a 'notice of correction' is not appropriate – eg, it should be completely removed. If the information about the client's credit history is factually correct, it is not removed just because they do not want it made public.

Subject access request

Under the General Data Protection Regulation, clients have the right to access the information that their creditors hold about them by making a 'subject access request'. No particular form of words is required so long as the client makes clear that they are asking for details of their personal data held by the creditor.

The creditor must respond within one month of receiving the request. In most circumstances, the creditor cannot charge a fee for complying with the request. A reasonable fee can be charged to cover administration costs where requests are excessive or unfounded or if the client requests further copies of the data.

Credit repair companies

Credit repair companies that claim to be able to 'clean up' credit reference files (for a fee) should be avoided. The information they give may be misleading or worse.

14. The Financial Conduct Authority's role

All UK financial services firms, investment firms and consumer credit companies must be registered and authorised by the Financial Conduct Authority (FCA).[32]

To be authorised, a company must meet the standards set by the FCA. An authorised firm can be investigated by the FCA if they do not meet these standards. The FCA can order authorised firms to stop trading, prosecute them and get compensation for consumers.

The FCA register lists all companies regulated by the FCA, including those regulated in the past. It contains information on the firm's contact details, what they are authorised to do and if they are covered by the Financial Ombudsman Service and the Financial Services Compensation Scheme. The register also contains information on firms offering financial products or services without the necessary authorisation. This includes firms operating financial scams listed with red text and a warning symbol. You can check whether a firm is authorised at register.fca.org.uk.

If a company is listed on the register as regulated, it must adhere to the FCA's strict rules. The FCA's *Consumer Credit Sourcebook* (CONC) details the rules businesses must follow. It is closely aligned with the Consumer Credit Act 1974 and all subsequent legislation and regulations.

15. Financial Ombudsman Service and Financial Services Compensation Scheme

Financial Ombudsman Service

The Financial Ombudsman Service (FOS) helps settle disputes between consumers and UK-based businesses providing financial services, such as banks, building societies, insurance companies, investment firms, financial advisers and finance companies.

The FOS can deal with complaints from clients about most financial matters, including:
- banking;
- insurance;
- mortgages;
- pensions;
- savings and investments;
- credit cards and store cards;
- loans and credit;
- hire purchase and pawnbroking;
- financial advice;

- stocks, shares, unit trusts and bonds;
- money-transfer operators.

Before the FOS can step in, the client must first give the business they are unhappy with the opportunity to deal with the complaint itself. The business has a maximum of eight weeks to resolve the complaint. If they do not resolve it within eight weeks or the client is not happy with the response, the client can refer it to the FOS. The complaints form is available at financial-ombudsman.org.uk/consumers/how-to-complain or you can phone 0800 023 4567.

The FOS has the authority to request or require a company to offer financial compensation, correct a client's credit file or offer an apology, as a means of dispute resolution.

More information can be found on the FOS website.[33]

Financial Services Compensation Scheme

The Financial Services Compensation Scheme (FSCS) is the UK's statutory deposit insurance and investors compensation scheme for customers of authorised financial services firms. It is an independent body, set up under the Financial Services and Markets Act 2000, and funded by a levy on authorised financial services firms. The scheme's rules are made by the Financial Conduct Authority (FCA) and are in the FCA *Handbook*.[34]

Information on how it operates can be found at fscs.org.uk.

Notes

3. **Pre-contractual information**
   1. *FCA Handbook*, CONC 4.7 and 6.3.4R
   2. The Consumer Contracts (Information, Cancellation and Additional Charges) Regulations 2013 No.3134
   3. CONC 4.2.3
   4. Reg 12 The Consumer Contracts (Information, Cancellation and Additional Charges) Regulations 2013

4. **Key elements of consumer credit agreements**
   5. CONC 4.2.3
   6. s61 CCA 1974

   7. Sch 6 The Consumer Credit (Agreements) Regulations 1983 No.1553

5. **Withdrawal, cancellation and cooling-off periods**
   8. Reg 25 The Consumer Credit (Agreements) Regulations 2010 No.1014
   9. s68 CCA 1974

6. **Unfair relationships**
   10. ss19-22 and Sch 3 paras 14-17 CCA 2006

Chapter 5: Consumer credit
Notes

7. Arrears notices
11 s86B CCA 1974
12 s86C CCA 1974
13 s86A CCA 1974; fca.org.uk/publication/information-sheets/arrears-may-2021-cmyk-a4.pdf

8. Default notices
14 s87 CCA 1974
15 s88(4A) CCA 1974; fca.org.uk/publication/information-sheets/information-sheet-default.pdf

9. Voluntary termination of hire purchase and personal contract purchase agreements
16 s99 CCA 1974

10. Time orders
17 s129 CCA 1974
18 citadvscot-my.sharepoint.com/:w:/g/personal/danna_higgins_cas_org_uk/EdTvv7LTTARHmhl5pCUxBEoB3s-8E0RlwIVFMD0VRgWw7A?e=zsBd1a
19 advicescotland.com/wp-content/uploads/2019/05/Time-Order-application.pdf
20 s136 CCA 1974

11. Section 75 credit card protection
21 s75 CCA 1974

12. Early repayment rules under the Consumer Credit Act
22 s94 CCA 1974
23 The Consumer Credit (Early Settlement) Regulations 2004 No.1483
24 s94 CCA 1974

13. Credit reference agencies
25 s157 CCA 1974
26 experian.co.uk/consumer/product-factsheets/understanding-credit-information.pdf
27 ico.org.uk/media/your-data-matters/documents/1282/credit-explained-dp-guidance.pdf
28 scoronline.co.uk/key-documents
29 *FCA Handbook,* CONC 4.7 and 6.3.4R
30 s158 CCA 1974
31 s159 CCA 1974

14. The Financial Conduct Authority's role
32 register.fca.org.uk

15. Financial Ombudsman Service and Financial Services Compensation Scheme
33 financial-ombudsman.org.uk
34 handbook.fca.org.uk/handbook/COMP/1/?view=chapter

Chapter 6

Statutory debt solutions in Scotland

This chapter covers:
1. Introduction (below)
2. The Common Financial Tool (p116)
3. The Debt Arrangement Scheme (p129)
4. The Minimal Asset Process (p150)
5. Full Administration Bankruptcy (p156)
6. Creditor petitions for bankruptcy (p165)
7. Protected trust deeds (p169)
8. Common rules in bankruptcy (p186)
9. Statutory moratorium on diligence (p199)

> **Future changes**
> At the time of writing, a Scottish government review of Scotland's statutory debt solutions was in its final stage. This may lead to changes to the solutions described in this chapter in the future.

1. Introduction

There are three types of personal insolvency in Scotland which a client can access. There are two bankruptcy options (Full Administration Bankruptcy (FAB) and the Minimal Asset Process (MAP)) and one voluntary arrangement (protected trust deed (PTD)). There are specific rules for each, and general rules that cover all three. The general rules are in section 8 of this chapter.

There are also creditors' petitions where the creditor can petition the sheriff court for a client's bankruptcy.

The Debt Arrangement Scheme (DAS) is not an insolvency option but allows the client to pay their debt off over a reasonable period and will freeze any additional interest or charges.

Chapter 6: Statutory debt solutions in Scotland
2. The Common Financial Tool

When making an application for MAP, FAB, DAS and PTD, debt advisers and insolvency practitioners are obliged to use the common financial tool (CFT) to assess a client's financial situation and their ability to contribute.

Note that bankruptcy is often referred to as 'sequestration' in Scotland and both terms are interchangeable.

Notes for advisers

The legislation and regulations around bankruptcy can be difficult to go through.

The Bankruptcy (Scotland) Act 2016 and the Bankruptcy (Scotland) Regulations 2016 cover most of the laws of bankruptcy in Scotland.

Although essential in the debt adviser's day-to-day work, we recommend that an adviser starts with the Accountant in Bankruptcy (AiB) guidance for trustees. This is an accessible document and covers most of the issues that arise on a case-by-case basis.

MATRICS learn has several e-learning modules on all forms of insolvency and an online class that Scottish advisers can access.

The AiB is an excellent source of information and guidance. Do not be afraid to give them a call or send them an email if you are unsure about any aspect of the insolvency process, MAP, FAB or PTD.

MATRICS is also on hand if you need to discuss a case.

2. The Common Financial Tool

The Common Financial Tool (CFT) must be used when making an application for the Debt Arrangement Scheme (DAS – see p129), Minimal Asset Process (MAP – see p150), Full Administration Bankruptcy (FAB – see p156) and protected trust deeds (PTD – see p169).

What is the Common Financial Tool

Debt advisers advising clients on Scottish statutory debt relief and management options are obliged to use the CFT when assessing a client's financial situation and ability to pay a contribution. A trustee must use the CFT to determine the amount of contribution payable in a PTD and bankruptcy and a debt adviser must use the CFT to determine the expected contribution payable under the DAS and on submission of a client's application for bankruptcy. The CFT is a mirror image of the Common Financial Statement (CFS). See p57 for more about the CFS.

The contribution payable by a client in a Scottish statutory debt solution is their surplus income over the lower of the client's expenditure or the 'trigger figures' (see p125).[1]

The client may be allowed an amount of expenditure that exceeds the trigger figures. The debt adviser/trustee must demonstrate the rationale for the increased expenditure by providing an explanation for each individual occurrence. Evidence should be retained and made available on request by the Account in Bankruptcy (AiB).

There is a requirement to obtain primary evidence associated with the categories included with 'essential expenditure' during the pre-application stage.[2]

The AiB's *Notes for Guidance: Common Financial Tool* are available on its website.[3] This section is based on that guidance.

Any person applying the CFT must have regard to the AiB guidance on:[4]
- the treatment of types of income and expenditure to be taken into account;
- how income and expenditure are verified by the debt adviser and the trustee;
- the conduct of debt advisers in carrying out their functions in relation to the CFT.

Common Financial Tool for sequestration applications

As it is not always possible to evidence fully a client's income and expenditure, the AiB recommends using the 'Additional information' section to explain why any income or expenditure cannot be evidenced. This should help prevent any unnecessary delays in processing a client's application for bankruptcy. Note that in MAP (benefits only) cases, there is no requirement to evidence expenditure.

Where no explanation has been provided and in the absence of evidence, the AiB may telephone the debt adviser to speed up the process. A debt adviser can contact the AiB at any stage of the application process to discuss and resolve any application matter. The AiB contact number is 0300 200 2850.

Where sufficient evidence/explanation has been provided, but additional work is necessary to confirm income and expenditure, to establish the amount of the debtor contribution order (DCO), the award of sequestration may still proceed. In these circumstances, the DCO amount is set based on the information available at the point of the award and a post-award check will be undertaken to get additional evidence/explanation.

Household composition

A comprehensive understanding of the household's income and expenditure gives the most accurate determination of the available income for any contribution. It is in the interest of both creditors and clients that an accurate calculation is completed.

The CFT captures the full household income and expenditure, including that of a client's partner or other non-dependant household members. Debt advisers/trustees should explore the entire household financial position wherever possible. Circumstances vary from case to case and it is not always possible or practicable to obtain the full household income and expenditure details – eg, a client's partner might be disinclined to volunteer information about their income or expenditure as they feel that they have no part in the client's financial position.

Chapter 6: Statutory debt solutions in Scotland
2. The Common Financial Tool

In these circumstances, the reasons that the full household circumstances have not been used in calculations should be recorded as part of the CFT assessment.

A decision not to use the entire household financial position must result from individual circumstances rather than the standard practice adopted by any debt adviser, trustee or organisation. It is feasible that two similar household circumstances may be encountered, with partner income information not available in only one case. The approach adopted may result in quite different levels of disposable income. In the interest of fairness for all parties, reasonable efforts must be taken to achieve an assessment that is transparent and based on a clear methodology.

A clear rationale must set out the basis of the income and expenditure calculation. Where the partner's income is not available, a calculation must be completed and set against the 'trigger figure' to establish whether trigger figures have been breached. However, the amount allowed for essential expenditure must reflect a reasonable contribution for the client which takes account of the household composition. For example, it may be reasonable to assume a 50 per cent contribution to housing and utility costs if the client has a partner but details of their partner's income are not known. This approach also applies in cases where all that is known is that the client makes a lump-sum payment towards the general running costs of the household.

Where the entire household income is known, the CFT assessment reflects the household position. However, the excess income figure calculated relates to the household and does not indicate the contribution that would be expected from the client. A fair and reasonable approach in these circumstances is to compare the client's income to that of the total household, producing a percentage figure. That same percentage is then be applied to the total household income surplus to calculate the client's surplus income. This results in a proportionate allocation of surplus income and ensures the client is not prejudiced in circumstances where a partner with a higher income creates an inflated household excess income figure.

Example
You have completed a CFT for your client based on the full household income and expenditure. Your client works part time and earns 30 per cent of the household income and their partner works full time and earns 70 per cent of the household income. There is £100 of disposable income. The client's disposable income is £30.

Adult non-dependants

An adult who normally lives in your home who is not your partner may be a non-dependant. Examples of non-dependants include grown-up children, relatives or family friends staying with you without a formal tenancy agreement. Where a non-dependant with earnings does not contribute towards household income, it may impact the client's current position. For example, having a non-dependant in a household disqualifies the client from a single person's council tax discount, resulting in a greater liability. It could be appropriate for an adult non-dependant with earnings to assume responsibility for these costs. If the adult non-dependant has no earnings, they may have the characteristics of a dependant on the client. If this impacts on the allowances used for calculating a contribution, an explanation of the circumstances should be provided.

Example
Betty's non-dependent son pays her £100 a month. Betty's trigger figures increase by the second adult amount which may allow additional spending within the trigger figures.

Dependent children

When assessing household income, the following count as a 'dependent child':[5]
- a child under 16 (or older if they are in approved education or training) for whom a client is entitled to claim child benefit;
- a child under 16 for whom a client has shared caring responsibilities but who does not reside in their home on a full-time basis.

A dependent child does not include young adults in the household who have their own means of support. This includes, for example, a non-dependant who has been denied access to certain state benefits through a sanction or any other restriction resulting from their own actions.

Income

Debt advisers/trustees should obtain documentary evidence to support the client's household income. Verification of income from third-party sources is sufficient – eg, proof of housing benefit (HB) confirmed by the local authority or universal credit (UC) entitlement confirmed by the DWP.

Income sources from which a contribution can be taken

Contributions can be taken from:[6]
- earnings;
- a private pension;
- annuities;
- grants;
- trusts;
- rents;
- maintenance or child support paid to the client;
- boarders or lodgers;
- non-dependant contributions;
- bursaries;
- foster care professional fees (excludes foster care allowance).

Chapter 6: Statutory debt solutions in Scotland
2. The Common Financial Tool

This is not an exhaustive list.

Note: for some annuities, grants, trust and bursaries, the individual terms and conditions of an agreement/award may indicate that a contribution cannot be taken.

Wages/salary from employment

Where the client's current income is derived from employment, pay slips for three months should be obtained. Where the client's income varies (eg, due to seasonal work, overtime or bonuses), it may be in the client's interest to obtain an average over a longer period of time up to a maximum of 12 months.

Any change in income after the DCO is fixed should be reviewed and, if the overall impact on the client's income and expenditure is that the DCO amount is no longer appropriate, reported to the trustee and a payment variation sought.

Any non-mandatory deductions should be questioned – eg, an employer voluntary savings scheme or additional private pension contributions.

Debt advisers/trustees should take account of any deductions taken through an earnings arrestment that would be defeated through entry into a statutory debt solution. It is not appropriate to verify wages from bank statements alone as these do not provide a comprehensive picture of the gross salary and any statutory or voluntary deductions that have been applied.

Example
Dean's net income after all deductions is £1,000, but included in the deductions is an earnings arrestment of £100. The amount noted on the CFT should be £1,100.

Self-employed income

The CFT does not include budgeting categories for business-related expenditures. As business and trading cases are generally complex, clients should be signposted to an adviser with relevant knowledge and experience. In self-employed cases, a business budget sheet must be compiled to account for the costs of running their business. The client can then work out how much money they can 'draw' from their business, and this amount can be included as income in the CFT.

If the client does not have an accountant to prepare a business budget sheet, they can contact Business Debtline on 0800 197 6026 or visit its website at businessdebtline.org for support.

Benefits and tax credits

Where income is from UC, other benefits or tax credits, evidence should be obtained from recent award letters or other written confirmation from the relevant department. It is also possible to verify income from bank statements to clarify the amount and frequency of payment.

Entitlement to disability benefits (eg, adult disability payment (ADP) or disability living allowance (DLA)) is not based on a client's other household income and is assessed against specific mobility or care needs. These payments must be taken into account in any assessment of income and expenditure. However, debt advisers/trustees should take into account any related increase in expenditure that may arise to meet these transport or care needs. If the client wishes, this income can be offset against any additional expenditure in these categories, such as adult care costs or travel.

Carer's allowance/carer support payment should be taken into account for income purposes, although it is expected that the actual expenditure for the person's caring responsibilities match or exceed this payment.

Household income may include HB or the UC housing cost element for help with rent. Discretionary housing payments (see p441) should be shown separately. In assessing the household position, the most transparent way to record information is to show the HB/UC in full as an income, with associated housing costs shown in full as expenditure.

Where a client's income is solely from benefits, no contribution is taken during a bankruptcy or protected trust deed. However, a voluntary contribution can be made from benefits if the client is repaying debts through the DAS.

Pensions

All pension income needs to be listed in the CFT income category.

Pension contributions that have been increased recently, which could be considered excessive, should be questioned and it should be established if the client received regulated pension advice before increasing the contributions. If the pension contributions are considered to be excessive, the client may be required to pay a higher contribution amount.

Note that advice on any decision to reduce or increase pension contributions falls within the boundary of regulated pension advice and is therefore outside the remit of advice from debt advisers/trustees. If the client has any queries about their pension contribution, they should be referred to an appropriate regulated financial adviser.

Bursaries

Where income is from a bursary, it may be possible to take a contribution from it if there is a calculated surplus income. This depends on the circumstances of each case.

Debt advisers/trustees should consider the bursary's rules and conditions. It is acceptable to exclude the bursary as a source of a contribution payment, where the bursary is for a specific purpose (such as funding specific expenditure) or where a condition of the bursary states that the bursary will be reduced as a direct result of taking a contribution from it. The debt adviser/trustee must explain how they have treated a bursary and why they have adopted that approach.

Chapter 6: Statutory debt solutions in Scotland
2. The Common Financial Tool

Redundancy payments

If a client has received a redundancy severance payment before or after bankruptcy/granting a trust deed, or proposing a DAS Debt Payment Programme, it is important that the debt adviser/trustee identifies if any aspect of the payment is income in lieu of wages.

Pay in lieu of notice (PILON) should be considered as the client's income over the period it has been paid for.

When a client is made redundant and receives a severance payment from their employer, the question arises as to whether this payment or part of it vests in the trustee – ie, it becomes the property of the trustee and no longer belongs to the client.[7]

This question was considered in an application by Patrick McGrail under section 78(11) of the Bankruptcy (Scotland) Act 1985.[8] The sheriff did not issue a written judgment, but the AiB understands the facts of the case to be as follows. During the relevant period,[9] Mr McGrail was made redundant and received a severance payment of £5,050. This was made up of four elements:

- statutory redundancy payment: £810;
- payment in lieu of notice: £810;
- company ex gratia payment: £1,000;
- additional payment based on years of service and wages: £2,430.

The trustee conceded the PILON was income but claimed the remaining £4,240 as 'acquirenda'. This approach was later approved by the sheriff. The client disputed this approach and applied to the sheriff for this amount be excluded from vesting in the trustee under section 78(11) of the Act. The sheriff held that: the statutory redundancy payment of £810 fell to be regarded as alimentary in nature and therefore as income which did not vest in the trustee; the other payments made by the company which were voluntary did vest in the trustee. When dealing with payments made on redundancy, it is necessary for trustees to identify the part which represents the client's statutory entitlement and care will be required in those cases, such as the McGrail case, when it is company policy to pay an enhanced sum. In some cases, such an enhanced sum might be loosely termed the 'redundancy payment'. It is important to advise a client that they need to inform their trustee if they are made redundant and to provide a breakdown of payments.

> **Income or acquirenda?**
> Statutory PILON: income
> Enhanced or voluntary PILON: acquirenda
> Statutory redundancy pay: income
> Enhanced or voluntary redundancy pay: acquirenda
> Other ex-gratia payments: acquirenda

Child maintenance

Child maintenance payments paid to the client should be included as an income from which a contribution may be deducted. This payment is paid to the adult for the maintenance of the child, with any outgoings being deducted for the child as per the appropriate trigger figures.

Evidence of maintenance contributions can be provided in the form of a court award, notice from the Child Maintenance Service, bank statements or a note provided by the paying parent, confirming the amount and frequency of the payments received. This evidence should be retained.

If the money is paid directly to the child, no contribution should be taken.

Income from which a contribution cannot be taken

Contributions cannot be taken from:[10]
- bereavement allowance;
- bereavement support payment;
- Best Start grants;
- category A, B, C and D retirement pensions (including additional pension);
- carer's allowance and carer support payment;
- carer's allowance supplement;
- child benefit;
- child disability payment;
- child tax credit;
- DLA, ADP or PIP;
- early years assistance;
- employment and support allowance;
- foster care allowance;
- guardian's allowance;
- HB;
- income support;
- industrial injuries disablement pension;
- jobseeker's allowance;
- pension credit;
- kinship allowance;
- maternity allowance;
- Scottish child payment;
- short-term assistance;
- social fund payments;
- UC;
- widowed parent's allowance;
- winter heating assistance;
- working tax credit.

Chapter 6: Statutory debt solutions in Scotland
2. The Common Financial Tool

This is not an exhaustive list. Increase of benefit for an adult or child dependant are included.

Assessed contribution
The contribution assessed from the client's surplus income must not exceed the total earned income as this would result in a contribution being deducted from the client's benefits. No contribution can be taken from a benefit payment.

General assets
Consideration of the valuation of assets is important if clients are considering statutory insolvency solutions as these may vest or be conveyed to the trustee.

Heritable property (the client's home)
Before establishing whether a debt solution is the appropriate action, the equity position of the client's property should be ascertained. This allows the client to obtain a realistic valuation and potentially safeguard their home.

If a client enters into the DAS, the property is excluded from the arrangement and a valuation is not required.

Vehicles
A valuation of the client's vehicle(s) should be obtained from an independent recognised source such as The Parkers guide (parkers.co.uk), mycarcheck, AutoTrader or on headed paper from a car dealership/garage. The AiB may also obtain a vehicle valuation.

The AiB does not accept valuations from webuyanycar, Arnold Clark, Motorway or any company that provides quick access to cash from a vehicle sale.

If the valuation is lower than could be expected for the make, model and year of the vehicle (eg, due to damage or or high mileage), an explanation for the low valuation and the source of the valuation must be provided. Additionally, debt advisers/trustees should confirm why the use of the vehicle is required. This could include the need to travel to work or that a vehicle is required for a specific reason such as ill health impacting on mobility. Other factors can also be taken into account – eg, rural locations and access to amenities and shops.

The valuation of a vehicle is important as bankruptcy legislation only provides for clients to retain ownership of a vehicle of up to £3,000 in value and where it is reasonably required. Incorrect advice at the outset may result in the vehicle being sold by the trustee in bankruptcy.

Insurance policies
Debt advisers/trustees must obtain documentary evidence of all insurance policies held and establish whether there is any immediate realisation value. The onus is on the client to clarify the position. The surrender value of any life insurance

policy must be established before a bankruptcy application. If the surrender value exceeds £1,000, the client is not eligible for bankruptcy through the MAP route.

Maintenance of insurance policies is acceptable if each policy is relevant and the cost is not excessive. Clients should be advised that if insurance policy premium costs are excessive, they may be asked to pay a higher contribution.

Note that advice on changing life insurance cover provision or disposing of an insurance policy falls within the boundary of regulated financial advice and so outside the remit of advice from debt advisers/trustees. If the client has queries about their life insurance policies, they should be referred to an appropriate adviser.

Expenditure

The CFT expenditure categories are:
- essential expenditure;
- phone costs;
- travel costs;
- housekeeping;
- other expenses.

Debt advisers and trustees should always investigate whether a client's declared expenditure could be considered too high or too low. Except for essential expenditure, there are 'trigger figures' for each category.

Trigger figures

Trigger figures assist debt advisers/trustees to determine whether the amounts included in the financial assessment are acceptable or whether they should be subject to further investigation or the provision of additional evidence of expenditure.

It is important that the CFT trigger figures do not form the starting point for an assessment of expenditure. The CFT assessment should include details of the client's actual circumstances.

Only when the full expenditure has been established and relevant evidence, or explanation, obtained, should the client's financial circumstances be compared to the trigger figures.

The AiB, the trustee or trustee acting under a protected trust deed can allow expenditure over the trigger figures.[11] An explanation of why this expenditure is required must be provided, along with supporting evidence. Consideration will be given to whether this allowance is reasonable in the circumstances. For example, the client may be locked into a phone contract or paying for a phone for a child they do not live with in order to remain in contact.

Chapter 6: Statutory debt solutions in Scotland
2. The Common Financial Tool

Essential expenditure

Bankruptcy applications submitted to the AiB in which the client's sole income is derived from state benefits do not require evidence supporting the expenditure in the CFT. Only proof of benefits is required. In every case, the supporting evidence should, however, be obtained and retained by the debt adviser/trustee as per regulatory requirements.

The essential expenditure category does not include a set trigger figure. Debt advisers/trustees must verify all the expenditure within this category (except for evidence of a TV licence) as relevant documentation should be available. Advisers should use their judgement in determining accurate essential expenditure figures. Further checks should only be made in exceptional circumstances – eg, where energy costs are deemed excessive in relation to the property type.

The following categories should be evidenced by original documentation or by examination of payments made from the client's bank account:
- rent;
- ground rent, service charges, factor fees;
- mortgage;
- other secured loans;
- mortgage endowment/mortgage PPI;
- council tax;
- building and contents insurance.

Essential expenditure also includes other costs not directly related to housing costs. Evidence should be available for the following expenditure items from correspondence/bills from the organisations involved or from bank statements:
- pension and life insurance;
- magistrate or sheriff court fines;
- child maintenance;
- hire purchase/conditional sale;
- childcare costs;
- adult care costs.

Evidence should be kept for two years from when the bankruptcy was awarded.

Energy costs

Evidence, or a written explanation to support declared expenditure on gas, electricity and other fuels (eg, coal, oil, Calor gas and solid fuel) can include:
- future consumption estimates determined by a qualified fuel adviser;
- annual consumption projection statements from the fuel companies;
- historic utility bills;
- direct payments recorded in bank statements.

The AiB only requires sight of supporting evidence/estimates if it has been determined that the spend will exceed a specific amount. This could vary based on the energy price cap, so check the CFT guidance for updates.[12]

Council tax

It is beneficial for the client's council tax payments to be calculated over a 12-month period rather than 10 months. This ensures a more accurate monthly expenditure throughout the term of a possible DCO.

A request can be made to a local authority for the client's council tax payments to be made in 12 instalments. However, such a change is at the local authority's discretion and may depend on the payment method.

A council may suspend a client's right to pay their council tax in instalments if they are made bankrupt or grant a trust deed. If this happens, their DCO amount may have to be varied if council tax was originally included in the client's expenditure calculation.

Hire purchase

Careful consideration must be given to any hire purchase (HP) or conditional sale agreements that are in force. Checks should be made to establish if there is a clause whereby an agreement becomes null and void if the holder is made bankrupt or subject to insolvency proceedings. Debt advisers/trustees must ensure that they obtain proof of the type of agreement the client has entered into, as some clients are not aware of the distinctions between different types of credit agreements.

This expenditure may be allowed if the items included are essential and the payments are reasonable in the circumstances. An explanation of the expenditure allowed should be included in the CFT to highlight the items and the reason for the expenditure. Whether items bought on this type of credit agreement are essential depends on the client's situation – eg, a car providing the only way of travelling to work would be deemed as essential.

If an item is not considered essential, debt advisers/trustees should refer the client to a specialist organisation, such as Advice Direct Scotland or Trading Standards Scotland for advice about cancellation rights and any costs involved.

If the client has declared they are making a payment towards a third party's HP agreement or paying a reasonable amount directly to a third party for the use of a vehicle that they will not own, these payments may be treated as a legitimate expenditure, provided the client can evidence the payments made and the reason for the payments. However, consideration must also be given to the need for the client to make the payments, and they may be disallowed if the payment amounts are in excess of the client's needs.

Trigger figure categories

Telephone costs

Debt advisers/trustees should get evidence of expenditure relating to home and mobile phone contracts. This should be available from sources including original correspondence/billing, online account information or through other evidence such as the purchase of pay-as-you-go top-up credits. It may be more difficult to verify pay-as-you-go credit than contract information, but information should be available from bank statements or the mobile phone company records.

If mobile phone costs are high, the reason for this should be explored and consideration must be given as to whether the existing expenditure is allowable or sustainable in the future. Where trigger figures are breached, evidence must be obtained and options to reduce future expenditure explored with the client.

Travel costs

Verifying travel costs can be difficult as fares are often paid in cash with little or no evidence retained. Therefore, advisers should take a flexible approach and assess travel costs based on the client's circumstances (eg, location, health, mode of transport and proximity to work/amenities) and agree on what is reasonable.

It may be possible to verify expenditure in specific circumstances – eg, where a client has a season ticket or where petrol purchases can be verified on bank statements.

If the trigger figures are breached, the debt adviser/trustee must provide supporting evidence and/or an explanation to support the reason for the required travel and the amount of expenditure declared. If proof of expenditure cannot be provided, the reason for this must be given.

The debt adviser/trustee should also ensure that they discuss with the client any ongoing maintenance and servicing costs for any vehicle and include such in the CFT expenditure figures.

Housekeeping

Housekeeping covers most of the day-to-day living expenses, including household food, provisions and consumables. The evidence for this expenditure is normally obtained through scrutiny of bank statements. However, this does not cover all expenditure items, as some transactions within this category involve smaller cash purchases or transactions in a range of different shops.

Where the final assessed housekeeping expenditure is within the trigger figure limits, trustees and creditors are unlikely to query the allowance or seek further evidence. Therefore, the debt adviser/trustee does not need to obtain evidence of smaller amounts of expenditure included in the figures, if this is not easily forthcoming. However, any excessive spending or breaches of trigger figures should be documented, and evidence provided.

Expenditure on tobacco and alcohol is allowed, although the debt adviser/trustee should negotiate with clients to try to minimise the costs. It is possible that an allowance may result in a client having to make some concessions in other areas of expenditure.

Where additional spending is required on medical grounds that is not funded from a declared disability benefit, either a breakdown of spending, with details of any purchases related specifically to the medical requirement, or a summary explanation from the debt adviser, should be provided. The guidance highlights that an award of DLA (or ADP/PIP) acts as an indicator to increased expenditure in other categories.

Where there are pet costs, an explanation, and evidence where possible, should be produced. If pet insurance is being paid for, this must be evidenced.

Other expenditure

Other expenditure includes a range of expenditure that is not categorised alongside general housekeeping – eg, haircuts, meals at work or school, socialising, Christmas and birthdays. Verification of such expenditure may be difficult to obtain through documentation or examination of bank account activity.

Evidence should be available to support certain items within the other category – eg, amounts paid towards cable, satellite and internet access. These items should be supported by original documentation from the providers.

A more flexible approach should be adopted in assessing the expenditure associated with the other items within this category. Similar to other expenditure categories with associated trigger figures, any expenditure where the trigger figure is breached requires suitable evidence and/or explanation of the expenditure.

Contingency provision

Clients can have an expenditure of up to 10 per cent of the surplus income calculated, allocated as a contingency allowance or saving provision.[13] A maximum contingency allowance of £20 a month is permissible for each assessment.

Debt advisers/trustees should consider including the contingency allowance in every case, as it is in all parties' interest that the client has funds available to meet the cost of unexpected future liabilities.

Example
Harry's CFT assessment results in surplus income of £100, with no contingency provision. It can be recalculated with up to £10 included in the other expenditure category, resulting in a revised surplus of £90.

3. The Debt Arrangement Scheme

The Debt Arrangement Scheme (DAS) allows someone in debt to repay their debts in full through a Debt Payment Programme (DPP). Payments are made over an extended period based on what they can afford. Creditors can take court action against the client during DAS but cannot enforce it through diligence. It is the only statutory debt management plan in the UK. It is *not* insolvency.

The parties involved

There are five main parties involved in DAS: the client, the creditor, the debt adviser or continuing debt adviser, the payments distributor and the DAS administrator (the Accountant in Bankruptcy – AiB).

The client

The client (an individual) is someone who owes or is due to pay money to an individual or a company. There is no maximum or minimum amount of debt the client must owe to access the scheme. The client must have disposable income to repay these debts over a reasonable time. A client can apply for a DPP if their income is only from benefits, but they must be able to show they have surplus funds available. The client must have one or more debts.

The creditor

The creditor is an individual or a company owed money by a client under the terms and conditions agreed when the credit was provided. A collection agency working on behalf of a creditor is not the 'owner' of the debt.

In some cases, creditors sell debts to collection agencies. This makes the collection agency the owner of the debt and a party to the DPP. The creditor must make clear to whom the DAS payments are to be made if not directly to themselves.

Payments distributors

Approved payments distributors collect the client's payment to the DPP and distribute it pro rata to creditors. The payments distributor is often the same organisation as the debt adviser. The AiB can be nominated as the payments distributor.

The DAS administrator

The DAS administrator is the AiB, appointed by Scottish Ministers to administer and supervise the entire DAS process in line with statutory requirements. The AiB can also be nominated by clients to act as a payments distributor.

The DAS administrator:
- approves, suspends or revokes the approval of debt advisers;
- approves or rejects applications for a DPP;
- approves or rejects applications to vary a DPP;
- approves or rejects applications to revoke a DPP;
- sends notices to the parties in a DPP of the decision to approve or reject an application for approval, variation or revocation of a DPP;

- sends notice of recall of any arrestment of the client's property or income, where the client's DPP is approved (in some instances, all of the above notices are sent by the continuing debt adviser rather than the DAS administrator);
- maintains the DAS Register;
- approves and revokes the approval of payments distributors;
- when requested, reviews a decision to approve or reject an application for a DPP, to vary a DPP or to revoke a DPP;
- corrects accidental errors in any determination, including incorrect information provided by a third party.

The debt adviser

Debt advisers in the free sector (eg, in Citizens Advice Bureaux (CABx) and local authorities) can become DAS-approved debt advisers (see p132). DAS-approved debt advisers give advice to clients and, if appropriate, prepare and submit applications for approval of a DPP. They also assist clients in nominating a payments distributor (see p130) to deal with the transmission of the DAS payments from the client to their creditors. A client can only apply for a DPP if they have obtained advice from a DAS-approved debt adviser about their financial circumstances and the effect of the proposed programme.

After the debt adviser submits the application, and it has been checked and issued to creditors, the DAS administrator takes on the responsibility for carrying out the administration of the DPP. If the client requires further money advice during the period of the approved DPP, the DAS administrator will recommend that the client contact a debt adviser.

The functions and duties of a debt adviser include:[14]
- considering and discussing with the client the options for dealing with their debts and the best course of action;
- assisting the client in maximising income;
- liaising with creditors on behalf of a client;
- advising the client about responsible budgeting;
- using the Common Financial Tool (CFT) to assess a client's available surplus income;
- submitting a moratorium application form to AiB;
- assisting the client with and advising on an application for approval, variation or revocation of a DPP or an application for the review of a determination;
- preparing and submitting an application for approval of a DPP to the DAS administrator for consideration;
- preparing and submitting an application to vary or revoke a DPP on behalf of a client, if required;
- providing lay representation in court, if suitably trained and instructed by the client.

Who can be an approved debt adviser

If you were approved by the DAS administrator as a DAS-approved debt adviser before 1 July 2011, you continue to be approved unless the DAS administrator revokes or suspends that status.

You can be an approved debt adviser if you:[15]
- are qualified to act as an insolvency practitioner in accordance with the Insolvency Act 1986; *or*
- work for such an insolvency practitioner and have been given authority by the practitioner to act on their behalf as a debt adviser for DAS; *or*
- are a debt adviser working for an organisation which has been awarded accreditation at type II level or above in accordance with the Scottish National Standards for Information and Advice Provision (see p3); *or*
- are a debt adviser working for a CAB which is a full member of Citizens Advice Scotland (see p5); *or*
- are a debt adviser working for a local authority.

A DAS-approved debt adviser must not advise a client with whom they have an association – eg, their partner or family member.

If you want to become a DAS-approved debt adviser but do not meet the criteria, you can apply to the DAS administrator.

You must:[16]
- apply in writing, either electronically incorporating an image of your relevant organisation or on headed note paper, stating your name and business address;
- include a statement of your suitability to act as a debt adviser for DAS;
- provide evidence of any relevant training undertaken;
- enclose a valid criminal record certificate (a disclosure Scotland certificate) dated less than 12 months before the date of your application.

The DAS administrator aims to respond to your application within 10 days and may approve your application if satisfied you are a fit and proper person and have undergone training the relevant training.[17]

Who cannot be an approved debt adviser

You cannot become an approved debt adviser if you are:[18]
- a sheriff officer or messenger-at-arms, or an employee of such a person;
- a person or body providing financial services, or financial advice other than money advice, in the course of a business or otherwise for profit, or an employee of such a person, unless the person is:
  – a solicitor;
  – a chartered or certified accountant;
  – a credit union;
- a person providing debt collection services, or an employee of such a person;
- a person convicted of an offence involving theft, fraud or other dishonesty;

- a person subject to a bankruptcy restrictions order (including an interim order) or bound by a bankruptcy restrictions undertaking, under legislation in Scotland, or England and Wales or Northern Ireland;
- a person in respect of whom a court has made a disqualification order, or who has had a disqualification undertaking accepted under the Company Directors Disqualification Act 1986;
- a person whose approval to be a DAS-approved debt adviser is revoked or suspended.

Period of approval as a debt adviser

There is no set period of approval in DAS. You must meet the criteria to become an approved debt adviser or have been approved by the DAS administrator. Unless your circumstances change and you no longer meet the criteria, or your approval is revoked or suspended for any reason, the approval continues for an indefinite period. If you intend to resign as a client's debt adviser, you must assist the client to find a replacement debt adviser before you resign.

Although debt advisers are approved as individuals, they are granted DAS-approved status by virtue of their employment/engagement with a money advice organisation. Hence, they are subject to the terms and conditions of any contract or code of conduct issued by their employer.

Advice organisations are responsible for ensuring the information retained on the DAS's eDEN case management system is correct and that it is only relevant staff who have permissions to use the system. When a member of staff leaves, or no longer requires access to the system, the organisation's manager/supervisor is responsible for deleting the user from the system. If they are unable to do so, or the individual is the manager/supervisor, they should contact the DAS administrator as soon as possible with a request for the user to be deleted.

All organisations should be encouraged in terms of GDPR and general good housekeeping to monitor their staff access to the system at least every quarter. All eDEN users are reminded of the data protection statement, which must be complied with every time they are logging in to use eDEN.

Revocation or suspension of a debt adviser

The DAS administrator can revoke or suspend an adviser's DAS-approved status.[19] The AiB provides written notice of any intention to do so.

Preparing the application

The debt adviser must apply for a DPP using eDEN, the DAS IT system. Neither the adviser nor the client needs to sign the application form. However, the debt adviser must tick the declaration box on the form that the client has been given advice and has consented to proceed with the application without signing it.

If the client prefers to sign the form, you can print the completed application from eDEN, ask the client to sign, and post to the DAS administrator.

Moratorium on diligence

Sections 195 to 198 of the Bankruptcy (Scotland) Act 2016 allow for a moratorium on diligence if the client intends to apply for a DPP, trust deed or sequestration. The client or the debt adviser can submit the application for a moratorium.

The AiB enters all moratoria granted on the Register of Insolvencies and the DAS Register, where they remain for six months.

During the moratorium period, creditors cannot enforce payment of any debt. They may not serve a charge for payment, commence or execute any diligence to enforce any debt owed by the client, or petition for sequestration.

Only one moratorium is permitted in any 12-month period, except in cases where a client has previously been in a joint DPP which has been revoked due to a relationship breakdown or the death of one of the clients. In these circumstances, the client may apply for another moratorium within 12 months.

The moratorium entry on the DAS Register and Register of Insolvencies is removed or amended on the earliest of:
- six months from the date entered on the register have elapsed and a DPP application has not been received; *or*
- the date a notice is entered on the DAS Register that an application for a DPP has been received and is yet to be approved – provided that the application is made before the six-month moratorium period has ended.

If you or the client have made a moratorium application, and you do not submit an application on behalf of the client before the six months have finished, the client loses any protection against creditor enforcement action.[20]

The client is therefore open to enforcement action by their creditors after the six months, unless and until a DPP application is received by the DAS administrator and issued to creditors. Protection starts again from the date the DPP proposal is sent to creditors, and remains in place until the DPP is approved or rejected.

Eligibility for a debt payment programme

To be eligible for a DPP, the client must:[21]
- be habitually resident in Scotland. This is difficult to define exactly. The person should have their main residence in Scotland, be registered to vote there, normally have their bank account there and pay their bills there. It excludes anyone temporarily residing in the country, who is working in Scotland but has their 'home' elsewhere, or is in Scotland on holiday. If you are not sure, contact the DAS administrator;

- have one or more debts;[22]
- not have a conjoined arrestment order. There is an exception to this. If a client has a conjoined arrestment order and a creditor (it does not matter whether this creditor is involved in the conjoined arrestment order or not) has tried lawfully to enforce another debt due, the client can apply for a DPP;
- not be a party to a protected trust deed (see p169). A client who has been granted a trust deed which has become protected is precluded from having a DPP if they have not been discharged from the trust deed;
- not currently be bankrupt – ie, they have been made bankrupt and they have not yet received their discharge in Scotland, England, Wales or Northern Ireland;
- not be subject to or bound by a Bankruptcy Restrictions Order (including an interim order) or bankruptcy undertaking in Scotland, England, Wales or Northern Ireland.

If the client only has one debt, they cannot apply for a DPP if the debt is being paid under:[23]
- a time to pay direction under the Debtors (Scotland) Act 1987;
- a time to pay order under the Debtors (Scotland) Act 1987;
- a time order under the Consumer Credit Act 1974.

Joint applications

Clients can apply for a joint DPP if each of them is liable for a debt which the programme covers.

To apply in joint names, the clients must be spouses or civil partners (or living together as spouses or civil partners). Both clients must be eligible to apply and meet the criteria to apply in their own names.

There is no requirement for married clients or clients in a relationship to apply jointly. Each client can apply for an individual DPP instead, if they prefer.[24]

There are times when only one client in a relationship has surplus income. For example, where only one partner is in paid employment, or where both partners are employed but one's income is too low to provide a viable basis for a sole DPP. Provided the clients meet the eligibility criteria and the criteria for a joint DPP, they can apply together. In these circumstances, the incomes, or income, can be regarded as joint.

Preparation for an application for a DPP

Before completing and submitting an application for a DPP on the client's behalf, the debt adviser must do the following.
- Ensure the client fully understands the implications of applying for a DPP, including that it will be recorded on the public DAS Register.
- Prepare a full statement of the client's income and expenditure, using the CFT.

Chapter 6: Statutory debt solutions in Scotland
3. The Debt Arrangement Scheme

- Agree with the client on how much of the surplus income will be offered as a contribution to the DPP.
- Confirm with the client if any rent or mortgage arrears are to be included in the DPP.
- Confirm the level of debt with each creditor.
- Check whether the client has any assets that could be sold or lump-sum payments that may be made as part of the DPP.
- Inform the client of the standard conditions which apply if the DPP is approved.
- Inform the client of any discretionary conditions that may be applied if the DPP is to be approved.
- Confirm whether the client wishes to offer the sale or remortgage of their home as a discretionary condition. This is entirely the client's choice.[25]
- Agree the method by which the client will make their regular instalment – eg, by standing order or payment from wages.
- Remind the client that, if the DPP is approved, they must pay their first instalment within 42 days of the approval.

You must check the details of all debts included in the DPP with each creditor prior to the submission of the DPP to the DAS administrator. The application needs to be completed as fully as possible. It is essential that you provide the following:
- correct creditor details (not a collection agency acting for the creditor, unless the creditor has a named authorised representative on eDEN or the debt has been sold on). For example, if the debt is for council tax arrears, the council should be added as the creditor not the sheriff officer collecting the debt; *and*
- creditor sort codes, account numbers and reference numbers relating to the debt; *and*
- the correct level of debt.

You should now be in a position to complete the application on eDEN. Remember to attach a copy of a scanned signed client mandate allowing you to act on the client's behalf. The information on the mandate should be exactly the same as the client information added to eDEN – ie, if the client has a middle name or initial on the mandate, this should also be on eDEN. If you do not have the facility to scan the mandate, you can fax or post it. However, the case will not be accepted until this document has been received by the DAS team.

Where you are nominating the AiB as payments distributor, you must upload to eDEN the documentary evidence used to complete your client identification checks. This is allows the AiB to expedite the payment set-up, allowing the DPP to start and finish earlier, minimising disruption to the client and creditors. You should also be aware that all cases are given a completeness check by the DAS administrator, and if the information is not consistent, the case will be returned to the adviser for clarification and rework.

The application

The debt adviser submits the DPP application via eDEN.

The application is received by the DAS administrator. If there is information missing, the application is returned to the debt adviser for rework. When all the information on the application is complete, the DAS administrator circulates the application to creditors. The application is then recorded in the DAS Register, showing the date the application was issued to creditors.

The request to creditors to consent to the DPP application

The DAS administrator issues, via eDEN (if the creditor is registered) or mail, a request to consent to the DPP application to each creditor. All letters will be sent on the same day that the DPP is proposed to creditors using eDEN.

Creditors have 21 days from this date to respond to the proposal. This becomes the relevant date on which the application is made.

All interest, fees, penalties or other charges are frozen from the date the application is recorded on the DAS Register, and the request to creditors to consent is issued. They remain frozen until the DPP application is rejected, or an approved DPP is completed or revoked.

The request to consent gives creditors all the information they need to make a decision to accept or reject the proposed DPP application. It extracts information from the application form to give as much information as possible so that creditors can correctly identify the debt and understand the payment proposal being offered.

The form states:
- the client's details (name, address, postcode and date of birth);
- the client's financial statement;
- how much of the client's surplus income will be offered as a contribution to the DPP (if the client does not wish to use the full surplus);
- any rent or mortgage arrears which have not been included in the DPP;
- details of the joint client, if applicable;
- the total amount the client owes the creditor;
- the percentage of the total debt owed that will be repaid by the client after the fees have been deducted (net amount of debt);
- sort codes, account numbers and reference numbers (if known);
- the amount the creditor will receive in each instalment;
- the frequency of the proposed payments to the creditor;
- the proposed length of the DPP, any lump-sum payments or realisation of assets.

Creditors must respond within 21 days from the date of the request. If they do not, they are deemed to have consented to the DPP terms (this does not apply if the DPP is only for a single debt).[26]

There are three possible responses from each creditor:
- consent – the creditor responds within 21 days and agrees to the proposal;
- deemed consent – the creditor does not respond within 21 days. In this case, the creditor is deemed to have agreed to the proposal, unless the DPP is only for a single debt, where it will be treated as if the creditor has not consented;
- non-consent – the creditor responds within 21 days and does not agree to the proposal.

After 21 days, if at least 90 per cent in value of creditors have consented (or are deemed to have consented) to the DPP, the DAS administrator must approve the DPP automatically regardless of the amount of the debt or the length of the proposed programme. The DAS Register is updated to show the DPP approval date ('original decision date' and 'DPP start date') and that no 'fair and reasonable test' was carried out. However, single-debt DPPs are subject to the 'fair and reasonable test', unless the sole creditor has actively consented to the DPP proposal.

Where at least 10 per cent in value of creditors object (or where the DPP is for a single debt and the creditor has not responded within 21 days), the DAS administrator must approve a DPP proposal that is fair and reasonable. The DAS administrator will consider all creditors' responses and whether it is appropriate to approve the DPP. In deciding whether a programme is fair and reasonable, the DAS administrator considers the criteria set out under regulation 25.[27]

Rejection of a DPP proposal

If the DAS administrator does not approve a DPP application, all parties are notified via eDEN or in writing.

The DAS Register is amended to show the date the decision was taken, but does not have a 'DPP start date'. Protection from diligence continues for 14 days from when the DAS administrator enters the notice of rejection on the register.

The client can request a review of the determination within 14 days of the day they are notified of the rejection. Advisers can also request a review on the client's behalf. The DAS Register is amended to show the date a review application has been received.[28]

The client can make a subsequent application to the DAS administrator for approval of a DPP. However, they cannot submit a further moratorium application if they have had a moratorium granted within the past 12 months.

The effect of approval of a DPP on the client

A client with an approved DPP is subject to the standard conditions and any discretionary conditions imposed by the DAS administrator.

When a DPP is approved, any existing arrestment against earnings or property is recalled. The DAS administrator (or continuing money adviser (see below)) sends a notice of recall to each employer or party with possession of or property arrested. Earnings or property in the hands of a third party (arrestee) is released for the client's use.

> **Continuing money advisers**
> A money adviser is classed as a continuing money adviser where they provide ongoing advice to a debtor and carry out administrative functions – eg, during a DPP and insolvency practitioners who do DAS work.

Where property is attached and the client has already been notified of the auction date (before the date of making a moratorium application, or the date of application for the DPP), the removal and sale of the client's property may still proceed.

A debt adviser must include details of an arrestment order on the DPP application form. If the client has a conjoined arrestment order, the DAS administrator notifies the clerk of court. In effect, this recalls the order. Therefore, if a creditor is receiving any monies as a result of an order, these payments stop as the debt should thereafter be paid through the DPP.

If a debt has been omitted from the DPP due to oversight, it may be possible to include it through a variation to the DPP (see p141).[29]

A creditor can apply to vary a DPP, to adjust any debt balance due to them which is incorrect. However, for cases approved from 4 November 2019, the creditor must apply to make the change no later than 120 days from the date of approval. Applications can be made after 120 days, but the creditor must show good cause as to why the application could not have been made earlier. Clients must not receive further credit while they have a DPP, except:[30]
- credit approved by a variation of a DPP;
- credit up to a maximum of £2,000, with certain restrictions;
- further credit given as part of a cyclical loan agreement which was already in operation when the DPP was approved, where the payment to the DPP made by the client does not vary because this credit has been given;
- trade credit incurred by the client in the ordinary course of business. If the client applies for this credit, they must give the creditor written notification of their DPP;
- credit for emergency repairs. If the client applies for this credit, they must give the creditor written notification of their DPP;
- credit for reasonable funeral expenses for an immediate family member. If the client applies for this credit, they must give the creditor written notification of their DPP.

If a creditor gives credit to a client with a DPP other than for reasons above, the creditor cannot take action to recover this debt. Neither can they serve a charge for payment or commence any diligence to enforce payment or petition for the sequestration of the client's estate, until after the DPP is completed or revoked.

Clients in a DPP are not permitted, under the standard conditions, to apply for or obtain credit other than in specific circumstances, as set out above. Therefore, if a client obtains credit in any other circumstances, or without informing the creditor (where required) that they are currently in a DPP, this may be grounds for the DPP to be revoked.

Creditors must not try to persuade a client to withdraw from a DPP or to make additional payments in respect of a debt included in the programme. If the client receives reminder letters or demands for payment which may have been electronically generated by the creditor's administration system, you should inform the DAS administrator. Debt advisers should advise clients to expect annual default statements from creditors, as this is a requirement under the Consumer Credit Act 1974.

The effect of approval of a DPP on creditors

The approval takes effect from midnight of the day before the day the notice appears in the register.

Once the DPP is approved, it is not competent for creditors to serve a charge for payment or to commence or execute any diligence to enforce any debt owed by the client.

Creditors cannot make an order granting warrant for sale of attached land or a satisfaction order.

Creditors cannot petition for the client's sequestration.

Creditors must, on request by a continuing debt adviser to the client, or by the DAS administrator, provide a statement of all the client's liabilities. Creditors must also notify any debt adviser or the DAS administrator of any liability where they have security against another person who is joint and severally liable.

Where a DPP is approved and the client has previously granted a trust deed which was not protected, the trust deed in effect ceases to exist. Therefore, it is unlikely that the creditor will receive a dividend from that trust deed agreement.

Administration process following approval of the DPP

Following the DPP approval, the payment distributor is notified via eDEN and they arrange the start of the client's payments. They also receive full details of the payment programme via eDEN. Only payments distributors approved by the DAS administrator can be used to distribute payments in a DPP.

Where the debt adviser has not established payment details for creditors, the payments distributor contacts the creditors to make the necessary payments.

The payments distributor contacts the client to set up their payments. The payments distributor is only responsible for managing payments in a DPP. If there are enquiries other than in relation to payments, the client is referred to their debt adviser.

Administering a DPP

General

If the client makes the agreed payments as they fall due, the payments distributor should not need to contact the debt adviser or the DAS administrator.

If the client fails to make an instalment or underpays, the payments distributor contacts the client and notifies the DAS administrator via eDEN with details of the missed payment. If the client contacts the DAS administrator or their payments distributor to advise they are having difficulty making payments, they are referred to their debt adviser urgently.

Depending on the reasons for the missed payment (eg, a change in circumstances), it may be appropriate to consider a variation.

If the client makes an overpayment, the payments distributor makes a pro rata overpayment payment to all the creditors.

If the client makes a payment under the agreed amount, the payments distributor pro ratas this payment to all creditors. If the client regularly makes lower payments than the agreed instalment amount, eDEN calculates how much has been underpaid. When the underpayments total the equivalent of an instalment amount or more, eDEN automatically logs a 'missed payment'.

The DAS administrator issues an annual review to the client to confirm there have been no changes in circumstances which may affect the DPP. If the client reports any changes, the DAS administrator directs them to their debt adviser.

Application for a variation

The average length of a DPP is around six years. Within the DPP period, there may be times when the client's personal circumstances change, meaning the DPP may need to be varied.

DAS legislation allows the client, debt adviser or a creditor to apply to the DAS administrator to vary the DPP.

Variations can result in:
- the amount the client pays in each instalment increasing or decreasing;
- the frequency of the payments changing;
- the length of the DPP increasing or decreasing;
- new conditions being attached to the DPP.

Remember, the client should continue to make their agreed payments even when an application for variation has been submitted, as any missed payments may result in the DPP being revoked.[31]

Short-term financial crisis payment break

When an immediate (and often temporary) crisis requires immediate action, debt advisers can approve a variation under the short-term financial crisis payment break (STFCPB) criteria. This acknowledges that sometimes people have an immediate crisis which means they cannot make their payment. The definition of 'crisis' is at the adviser's discretion. If unsure whether your client's circumstances constitute a crisis, seek guidance from the DAS administrator.

> **Example**
> Danny needs his car to get to work. It breaks down and needs to be fixed. Instead of incurring debt to pay the repair or making a full variation application, Danny's adviser believes he has experienced a crisis which justifies not making the DAS payment. The adviser processes a STFCPB immediately on eDEN.

Debt advisers can process a STFCPB via eDEN. Creditors are not required to give prior consent.

Notification of the approval is sent to all creditors, the debt adviser, the payments distributor and the DAS administrator.

A client can have up to two STFCPBs approved in a rolling year.

STFCPBs can be applied retrospectively to a missed payment, but only if the next payment is not yet due.

The reasons for the deferral are shared with the DAS administrator and creditors and adviser should be careful about sharing the client's personal information.

> **What if the client is paying by direct debit?**
> If a client is making payments to their DPP by direct debit, the payment is requested three days before the agreed payment date. This is not an AiB process, but is a direct debit instruction processes. Therefore, if the debt adviser processes a STFCPB on eDEN in the three days prior to a direct debit being due, they must notify the payments distributor separately via eDEN conversations so that the payment can be returned to the client. The adviser should make the client aware of this at the point of agreeing the STFCPB.[32]

Payment break variation

Where a client cannot make payments due to a change in circumstances which goes beyond a short-term crisis, the debt adviser can establish if the income shock requires a variation application for a longer payment break. A client can apply for up to a six-month payment break if their disposable income has reduced by 50 per cent or more and it is considered the reduction will last for the period of the break. **Note:** when applying for a payment break variation, the income and expenditure (CFT) fields on eDEN must be completed. Advisers must ensure they have seen evidence of the reduction in the client's disposable income has been reduced by 50 per cent or more.[33]

The payment break suspends payments and interrupts the DPP period. The DPP will be extended by the corresponding time period.

Creditors should not contact the client or issue demand letters during this period.

After the payment break has finished, the client should recommence payments as agreed in their DPP. During this time, the client may seek debt advice to reconsider their debt management options.

There is no limit to the number of times a client can apply for a payment break variation during the DPP, provided they meet the necessary criteria. Before approving the variation, the DAS administrator considers whether the client has had a previous payment break and takes note of creditor comments.

All other variation types

For variations where there has been a material change in the client's circumstances, the income and expenditure section of the variation application must be completed in full. eDEN automatically populates the income and expenditure fields using information from the original DPP application, if the case was created after 1 July 2011. For cases created and approved before that date, eDEN does not hold the original information. Ensure the income and expediture information is amended to reflect the client's current financial circumstances. This may mean looking at the income and expenditure in the most recent variation on the case. For pre-July 2011 cases with no previous variations on eDEN and the information and expenditure has not changed, you must input sufficient information to allow the system to use the existing surplus income.

The adviser must apply for a variation to a DPP to the DAS administrator through eDEN.

When an application for a variation is issued to creditors, or approved automatically, the DAS administrator records it in the DAS Register. It shows in the section for 'variations', with the date of application and date of decision (where relevant), and the status of the applications – eg, 'issued' or 'approved'.

Only 'debt change' variation applications from debt advisers must be sent to the DAS administrator in the first instance. When the application has been checked, the DAS administrator issues the variation proposal to creditors. All other types of variation application are issued straight to creditors, or approved automatically if the term of the DPP is reduced.

When filling in the 'reason for variation' and 'supporting information' boxes, ensure that any detailed or personal information is put in the 'reason for variation' box as this is only visible to the adviser and the DAS administrator. Information in the 'supporting information' box should be general and anonymised, as this is shared with creditors.

The variation notification gives all parties 21 days to submit comments. After 21 days, the DAS administrator makes a decision on the variation application. Creditors who fail to respond during the 21 days are deemed to have consented to the proposed variation. The DAS administrator must agree to a variation where:[34]
- a client agrees with all the creditors that the programme should be varied;
- a client and a creditor agree that the client no longer needs to pay the creditor all or part of what is owed;
- the DPP was approved before 1 July 2007 and the client wishes to apply for the freezing of interest, fees and penalties on their debts;
- the effect of the variation reduces the term of the DPP;
- a liability of the client has been discharged by a creditor applying composition;
- all creditors in the DPP have consented to the variation;
- the variation has the effect of reducing the length of the DPP.

The DAS administrator may approve a variation subject to the 'fair and reasonable' criteria where:[35]
- there has been a material change of circumstances which may include an increase or decrease in the client's income;
- a debt due at the approval of the programme was omitted from the DPP or wrongly assessed for the DPP because it was overlooked, or someone made an error or for some other reasonable cause;
- future debt, which was not quantifiable when the DPP was approved, becomes due for payment – eg, if the client has a debt which they do not have to start paying for some months;
- a contingent debt, which was not quantifiable when the DPP was approved, becomes due for payment – eg, if the client has been a guarantor for someone else's debt and the creditor has called up the guarantee;
- the client has an emergency and needs credit to meet an essential requirement;
- circumstances have reduced the client's disposable income by 50 per cent or more, and the client wishes to have a payment break of up to six months.

If a creditor is applying for a variation, they must first have attempted to agree to the variation with the client. A debt adviser should try, on the client's behalf, to agree a variation with the creditors first as the DAS administrator takes their views into account.

DAS administrator to apply for a variation

The DAS administrator may propose a variation in exceptional circumstances, with the client's consent. This happens, for example, where creditors write off debt or refuse to accept funds, but do not apply for variations to remove the debts. This is purely an administrative function, and can only be done if the effect of the variation is to reduce the DPP term. The DAS administrator writes to the client advising of the intention to propose a variation, inviting them to contact the AiB or their debt adviser if they have any questions.

Notification of a variation

The DAS administrator sends a notification through eDEN if the client or a creditor has applied to vary the DPP. The DAS administrator allows the debt adviser, the creditors and the client up to 21 days to submit comments.

When the DAS administrator is determining whether a variation is 'fair and reasonable', they consider:[36]
- the fair and reasonable criteria;
- the client's views;
- the views of the other client in the case of a joint DPP;
- the views of a creditor taking part in the programme and of any creditor making the application;
- the views of any debt adviser who has provided advice to the client;
- whether any expenditure of the client declared in assessing disposable income appears to be necessarily incurred by the client;
- any payment break variation previously approved;
- any other factor the DAS administrator considers appropriate;
- whether approval may be made subject to a discretionary condition under regulation 28.

The DAS administrator notifies the following of the variation decision:[37]
- the client;
- the debt adviser;
- the payments distributor;
- the creditors taking part in the DPP;
- the client's employer (where the DPP is being paid by means of a payment instruction to the employer).

The notification informs all parties of the approval or rejection of the variation, including the reasons for the decision, via their chosen communication method.

The DAS administrator updates the DAS Register. The variation shows in the section for variations, with the date of application, date of the decision and the 'approved' status.

The DAS administrator must send all creditors details of the amended DPP, which provides:
- the client's details (name, address, postcode and date of birth);
- the client's financial statement;
- how much of the client's surplus income will be offered as a contribution to the DPP (including where the grounds for the variation are that the client has had a change of circumstances, and the client does not wish to use the full surplus income);

Chapter 6: Statutory debt solutions in Scotland
3. The Debt Arrangement Scheme

- details of the joint client, if applicable;
- the total amount the client owes the creditor;
- the percentage of the total debt owed that will be repaid by the client after the fees have been deducted (net amount of debt);
- sort codes, account numbers and reference numbers (if known);
- the amount the creditor will receive in each instalment and the frequency of the proposed payments to the creditor;
- the proposed length of the DPP;
- any lump-sum payments or realisation of assets;
- the revised end date of the DPP.

Following the approval of the variation, the DAS administrator notifies the payments distributor who arranges to make the agreed changes to the DPP.

If the client is paying their instalment through their wages, the client must provide an updated payment mandate using Form 3 to their employer.

Unless a payment break variation has been approved or there has been a change to the frequency of the payments, the client should arrange to make the varied payment under a programme in time for the next scheduled payment to the programme, and within one month of the DPP variation being approved.

If the DAS administrator rejects the variation application, the creditors should continue to receive payments as agreed in the DPP.

The client, the debt adviser or a creditor can request a review of the variation decision. If unsatisfied with the outcome of the review, the client or the creditor can appeal to the sheriff, on a point of law, against this decision.

Revocation of a DPP

The DAS administrator can revoke a DPP.[38] They must revoke a DPP where a client has:
- submitted a debtor application for bankruptcy, which has been awarded; *or*
- a trust deed which has gained protected status; *or*
- died.

The DAS administrator records the revocation date on the DAS Register. This stays on the register for six weeks after the revocation.

The DAS administrator notifies all parties that the DPP is revoked. All payments agreed in the DPP stop. Where a DPP was revoked because the client applied for bankruptcy, which was awarded, or granted a trust deed which has become protected, creditors can reapply any interest, fees and charges to the debt 14 days after the date of revocation. However, this debt is now to be included in the bankruptcy or protected trust deed, where applicable. The client's details are recorded on the Register of Insolvencies, when they are bankrupt or in a protected trust deed.

Where a DPP was revoked upon the death of a client, creditors cannot take enforcement action or reapply interest, fees and charges until six weeks have elapsed from the revocation date.

Application for revocation

An application for revocation can be made by the client in writing, or the debt adviser on the client's behalf, or by a creditor taking part in the DPP.[39] The debt adviser should apply via eDEN. **Note**: there has to have been a breach of the regulations before a revocation application can go ahead.

The DPP can be revoked by the DAS administrator:[40]
- if a client fails without reasonable cause to satisfy a standard or discretionary condition;
- the client has knowingly made an untrue statement in an application for approval or variation of the DPP;
- if a payment to be paid under the DPP becomes due, and a sum totalling the equivalent of three months' worth of payments is outstanding;
- in the case of a joint DPP, where the parties no longer qualify to be part of a joint DPP.

If the DAS administrator proposes to revoke the DPP following the receipt of an application, they inform:
- the client;
- the client's debt adviser;
- each creditor in the programme;
- any creditor who has made an application for variation of the DPP.

The revocation proposal gives all parties to the DPP four weeks to provide information or reasons why the DPP should not be revoked.

Determination of a revocation

Only the DAS administrator can make a determination on an application for revocation. They consider:
- any statement made by, or on behalf of, the client;
- the nature of any failure or untrue statement;
- any factor that may indicate whether or not the programme will be successful;
- any representations made by the client or creditors;
- any other appropriate factor.

If an application for revocation is approved, the DAS administrator informs:
- the client;
- the client's debt adviser;
- the payments distributor;
- the client's employer, if the DPP instalments are being paid directly from the client's wages;
- creditors taking part in the programme.

The notice is issued by the DAS administrator and includes the reasons for the decision. All payments agreed in the DPP stop and the DAS administrator removes the client's details from the DAS Register.

Creditors can consider whether enforcement action is required, or appropriate, to recover the debts.

The client is required to pay the debts under the terms and conditions under which the debt was originally provided. However, creditors cannot take any enforcement action until 14 days after the revocation.

Creditors can also apply interest, fees and charges to the debt after 14 days. If the client, the debt adviser or a creditor requests a review of the revocation decision, creditors must wait a further 28 days before taking enforcement action or adding interest, fees and charges.

If dissatisfied with the outcome of the review, the client or a creditor can appeal to the sheriff on a point of law against this decision.

If the DAS administrator decides to reject an application to revoke the DPP, all parties are informed of the decision. The client should continue to make the payments agreed in the DPP.

Revocation of a joint DPP

In a joint DPP, the debt adviser or either client can apply for revocation where they split up or one of them dies.[41] See p135 for who can have a joint DPP.

Where the clients no longer meet these criteria for a joint DPP, the DPP can be revoked. The clients are protected from creditor enforcement for six weeks following the date of revocation. In effect, this means the AiB treats both clients as if they have made a moratorium application in their own names.

This allows both clients to seek money advice without fear of a creditor taking action against them. Only joint DPPs which are revoked as a result of the clients' relationship breakdown get this protection. It does not apply if a joint DPP has been revoked due to a breach of the regulations.

If the DPP has been revoked due to the death of one of the clients, the revocation has no effect for six weeks. Creditors cannot apply any interest, fees or charges to the debt during this six-week period. The debt adviser should bear this in mind if the surviving client wishes to apply for a DPP in their own name. In addition to the above protections, if a joint DPP has been revoked as a result of a relationship breakdown or a death, a client has the right to apply for a moratorium, even if they have already had a moratorium within the preceding 12 months.[42]

There is further protection where the client applies for a DPP in their own name within 21 days of the revocation of the joint DPP. In this case, the creditors cannot apply any interest, fees or charges to the debt.[43]

You should treat any joint and severally liable debt as if each client owes the full outstanding amount. This protects each client if their ex-partner does not pay. The creditor can apply to vary the client's DPP if the debt is paid in full before the end of the agreed DPP period. Therefore, the client should not overpay.

However, it is good practice for the client and debt adviser to monitor this situation, and apply for a variation if required and if the creditor fails to do so.

If the client applies for a new DPP more than six weeks after the previous joint DPP was revoked, interest, fees and charges may be applied to the client's debts, subject to the discretion of the creditor. Advisers should assist the client in these circumstances by submitting an application within six weeks. The client is still protected from creditor enforcement action up to the end of the six weeks.

Completion of a DPP

The DPP reaches completion when the client has made all payments as agreed or has made a lump-sum payment equal to the sum of all outstanding payments. Completion of the DPP is at the time specified when the DPP was first approved, or if it has been varied, at the most recent variation. If the client has missed any payments or has made underpayments, the length of the DPP is extended accordingly.

The debt in the DPP will have been paid in full, minus the fees paid to the DAS administrator or payments distributor.

If the creditors agree in writing to the completion before the scheduled end of the programme, the DPP can be treated as if it has been completed – eg, if all the creditors agree to write off the outstanding debt. In these circumstances, the debt adviser must apply for a variation to adjust the balances to allow the DPP to be completed. Where the debt adviser or the client wishes to negotiate payment of a reduced lump sum amount in exchange for early settlement, the adviser must apply for a 'partial settlement' variation on eDEN. The adviser should follow the guidance set out for partial settlement variations on the AiB website.[44]

The payments distributor notifies the completion to:
- the DAS administrator;
- any continuing debt adviser;
- the client;
- each creditor taking part in the programme.

The DAS administrator informs the client's employer that the DPP has completed, if payments were being made directly from the client's pay.[45]

If any party has any enquiries about the completion of the DPP, or if a creditor does not believe the debt has been fully paid, they should contact the DAS administrator.

Composition

The DAS administrator, with the client's consent, can make an offer of composition to each creditor after 12 years from the date of approval of the DPP and where 70 per cent of the total debt due in the DPP has been paid.[46] The 12 years must not include any periods where the client was on an approved payment break. If all creditors agree, the DPP will be completed. If not all agree, the DPP duration may be reduced.

A creditor who accepts the offer agrees that the client's liability to repay that debt is discharged. A creditor who does not respond to the offer within 21 days is deemed to have accepted the offer.

If all creditors accept (or are deemed to have accepted) the offer, the DAS administrator sends written notification of the completion of the DPP to:
- the client;
- any continuing debt adviser;
- the payments distributor;
- the employer, where DPP payments are being made directly from the client's pay;
- the creditors in the DPP.

The DAS administrator keeps a record of creditor acceptances. If the offer of composition is not accepted by all creditors, the DAS administrator must vary the DPP to remove the debts owed to the creditors who accepted the offer, or who are deemed to have accepted.

The DAS administrator sends written notification of the effect of the variation to:
- the client;
- any continuing debt adviser;
- the payments distributor;
- all creditors continuing to take part in the programme;
- the employer, where DPP payments are being made directly from the client's pay.

Note: the AiB has been advised by the creditor sector that debts included in a DPP which is completed using composition under the regulations will be recorded with the credit reference agencies as 'partially settled'. Any queries on this point should be directed to creditors or the credit reference agencies.

4. The Minimal Asset Process

What is the Minimal Asset Process

Minimal Asset Process (MAP) bankruptcy was introduced in 2015 by the Bankruptcy and Debt Advice (Scotland) Act 2014. It replaced the previous Low Income Low Assets bankruptcy process. It is designed to allow clients with few or no assets a faster and easier route through the bankruptcy process. A MAP bankruptcy is suitable for clients who cannot afford to pay back their debts within a reasonable time, or not at all, and have no disposable income and no assets.

Chapter 6: Statutory debt solutions in Scotland
4. The Minimal Asset Process

There are no fees for a MAP application as the debtor contribution order (DCO) must be zero.

When a client wishes to apply for bankruptcy, the debt adviser decides whether to apply for MAP or Full Administration Bankruptcy (FAB). The Accountant in Bankruptcy (AiB) checks when the application is submitted to ensure all information and evidence has been provided and that the application meets the specific criteria.

MAP is a form of bankruptcy where specific criteria apply, and it has some advantages for the client over the FAB process.

Some advantages of MAP bankruptcy

MAP allows a client to write off up to 100 per cent of their qualifying debt while a trustee deals with creditors.

Creditors cannot take legal action against the client to recover their debt. This includes interest, fees and charges which are frozen.

Creditors can only claim for the outstanding balance due as at the date of sequestration.

It stops or removes the effect of any existing diligence such as wage arrestment, bank arrestment and deduction of earnings orders.

The process is designed to be simpler, quicker and less onerous on the client.

Discharge of debts is six months, compared to 12 months for a FAB and 48 months for a protected trust deed.

Some disadvantages of MAP bankruptcy

Clients may find their employment prospects harmed.

Clients cannot act as a director of a limited company or be involved in the financial management of a limited company.

Clients cannot act as an MP or a justice of the peace.

The client's credit rating will be adversely affected for six years.

For six months after discharge, if they apply for credit of £2,000 or more (or any amount if they owe debts of £1,000 or more), they must inform the creditor that they were bankrupt in the previous six months which may limit their access to credit.

They may be in breach of contractual obligations by being made bankrupt such as tenancy, car lease agreements and employment contracts. These have to be checked before recommending bankruptcy to a client.

Service providers (eg, gas or electricity suppliers) may change how they want to receive payments from the client by using a prepayment card or meter.

Banks may freeze or close accounts after a client is declared bankrupt.

Bankruptcy is recorded on the Register of Insolvencies for at least one year after discharge. It is a public register which is available for everyone to search.

Qualifying criteria

There are several qualifying criteria an applicant must meet for MAP. These include the following.[47]
- The applicant has been assessed by the common financial tool (CFT) as requiring to make no debtor's contribution.
- The applicant has been in receipt of payments, of a kind prescribed, for at least six months ending with the day on which the debtor application is made.
- The total of the debts (including interest) on the application date is not more than £25,000. There is no minimum amount.
- The total value of the debtor's assets (leaving out of account any liabilities) on the application date does not exceed £2,000.
- The applicant has no single asset with a value over £1,000.
- The applicant does not own land.
- The debtor has been granted a certificate for sequestration of the debtor's estate.
- In the 10 years before the application is made (or such other prescribed period), no award of sequestration (MAP) has been made against the applicant.
- In the five years before the application is made, no award of sequestration has been made against the debtor in pursuance of:
  - an application made by the debtor other than by virtue of this subsection; or
  - a petition.

Route into a MAP

Entry into the MAP is by an authorised person (see p197) signing a Certificate for Sequestration (see below) which states that the client cannot pay their debts as they fall due. This must be dated no more than 30 days before the application is made.

An expired charge for payment or statutory demand or any other form of apparent insolvency cannot be used as a route into a MAP.

Certificate for Sequestration

A Certificate for Sequestration of the client's estate is a certificate granted by an authorised money or debt adviser (or other authorised persons) certifying that the client cannot pay debts as they become due.[48] See p197 for who is an authorised adviser and how to apply for a certificate.

No fee can be charged for completion of the certificate.[49]

Revocation or suspension of an approved debt adviser

The AiB can revoke or suspend an approved debt adviser if they fail to apply the CFT accordingly or do not maintain records of advice given.

A debt adviser must obtain evidence of a client's income and expenditure and retain all records for two years and provide this information to the AiB on request.[50]

Making an application

An application for a MAP is made by an authorised debt adviser (or insolvency practitioner) via BASYS, the AiB's electronic application system. The application must be accompanied by a completed Certificate for Sequestration (see p152).

Appointment of trustee

Unlike under the FAB or a protected trust deed, under the MAP, the client cannot appoint their own trustee. The AiB is always the trustee in a MAP bankruptcy. They may ask another insolvency practitioner to act as their agent in a case, but the AiB remains the trustee.

Included and excluded debts

In a bankruptcy, the general rule is that all debts must be included, but not all will be discharged. In a MAP application, the most notable exception to this rule is student loans. This ensures that the debt limit of £25,000 is not exceeded as student loans do not discharge. It must be included in the application, but a tick box allows you to exclude it from the total debt calculation.

Hire purchase debts do not need to be included where the client is making regular payments. They should be entered as ongoing expenditure.

An obligation to pay aliment or a periodical allowance payable on divorce is not discharged by:[51]
- any liability to pay a fine or other penalty due to the Crown;
- any liability to pay a fine imposed in a justice of the peace court;
- any liability under a compensation order (within the meaning of section 249 of the Criminal Procedure (Scotland) Act 1995;
- any liability to forfeiture of a sum of money deposited in court under section 24(6) of the Criminal Procedure (Scotland) Act 1995;
- any liability incurred because of fraud or breach of trust.

Debt advice

A client must take advice from an authorised debt or money adviser (or insolvency practitioner) who will assist them in making the application. A client cannot make an application on their own.

The client must also be issued with a Debt Advice and Information Package.[52]

Fees

There are no fees for a MAP application as there cannot be a contribution.[53]

If the client has £1 of disposable income, they are moved to the FAB process.

Chapter 6: Statutory debt solutions in Scotland
4. The Minimal Asset Process

BASYS

MAP applications are processed via BASYS, the AiB's online tool. Paper applications are still acceptable in specific circumstances, but are very rare. Paper forms and guidance from the AiB on completing the application on BASYS can be found on the AiB website.

Advisers can be registered by their organisation to use the system once they have been through the appropriate training.

The application is in two parts.

Part 1 contains, among other things, the client's personal details, income and expenditure, assets and liabilities.

Part 2 requires the client to sign several legal statements, including the statement of understanding and the statement of truth and contains a warning that:

'It is a criminal offence under section 8(4) or 218(1) and (2) of the Bankruptcy (Scotland) Act 2016 for you to make a false statement in this form in relation to your assets or business or financial affairs, to not disclose any material fact in this statement or make a material misstatement unless you can show that you did not know that statement was false and had no reason to believe it was false.

On summary conviction, you may be liable to a fine of up to £5,000 or to imprisonment for a maximum period of three months or to both. If you deliberately do not disclose all relevant information or if you deliberately make a false statement when completing this form, you may become subject to bankruptcy restrictions.'

If the client deliberately does not disclose all relevant information, or if they deliberately make a false statement when completing the form, they may become subject to bankruptcy restrictions, a fine or even imprisonment.

Therefore, by completing the forms, the client has stated that they have been given advice and that they will comply with the trustee over the 48-month period following the award of bankruptcy. Ensure you point this out to the client before you make the application.

Try to ensure that your client is aware what they are signing. Some advisers get the client to sign a copy of the warning for their records.

BASYS allows an adviser to enter all the details of income, expenditure, assets and liabilities as well as other necessary information for the application.

Once the application is made, it is assessed by the Insolvency Registration Team at the AiB who decides the application and whether it qualifies for the MAP or FAB process.

If the application is incomplete, the client will be sent a further information letter, with a copy sent to the adviser. The client has 21 days to provide the requested information. Failure to do so may result in the application being refused.

Chapter 6: Statutory debt solutions in Scotland
4. The Minimal Asset Process

BASYS allows the adviser to upload documents such as the Certificate for Sequestration, charge for payment, pay slips, bank statements and any other information required by the AiB.

Training on BASYS can be accessed by advisers via the MATRICS learning programme and from the AiB website (see p161).

Statement of undertakings and statement of truth

When making the application, the client must sign a Statement of Undertaking and a Statement of Truth to confirm they have understood the process and their legal obligations. See Appendix 3 for the text of the statements.

The client and adviser may complete the Statement of Truth, Statement of Undertaking and Certificate for Sequestration electronically as long as an 'averring statement' is provided by the client. This statement must include the client's full name, address and date of birth as well as a short statement giving the adviser authorisation to submit an application on their behalf.

Note: it is a criminal offence to make a false statement in these forms, to not disclose any material facts or make a material misstatement unless you can show that you did not know that statement was false and had no reason to believe it was false.[54] On summary conviction, you may be fined up to £5,000 or to imprisoned for a maximum of three months, or both.

If you deliberately do not disclose all relevant information or if you deliberately make a false statement when completing this form, you may become subject to bankruptcy restrictions. Therefore, the client will have stated that they have been given advice and that they will comply with the trustee over the 48-month period following the award of bankruptcy. Ensure you point this out to the client before you make the application.

Debtor contribution order

In MAP cases, there must be a zero contribution (or the client must have benefits-only income), so advisers should work with the client and the CFT to try and get the contribution to zero, or even show a negative budget.

This is important because if the CFT is not completed correctly, the AiB may change the contribution and move the client onto the FAB process, lengthening the discharge process.

If the AiB refuses to award a MAP bankruptcy, the client can request a review within 21 days if they disagree with the AiB's decision. The client can further appeal to the sheriff court within 14 days if they disagree with the review decision.[55]

Variation of the debt contribution order

If the client's situation changes during the first six months before the discharge of their debts, they must inform the AiB. The AiB may then vary the DCO and move the client to the FAB process.

The AiB quashes the DCO in MAP cases after six months. If the client's income then changes, the DCO cannot be varied.

Duration of the bankruptcy

There are different rules for discharge of debts and for complete discharge from the client's obligations under bankruptcy.

A client who applies for the MAP is obliged to comply with their trustee for 48 months after the date of sequestration, despite being discharged of their debts after six months.

This applies to aquirenda over the 48-month period after the date of sequestration and any change of income in the first six months of the bankruptcy. A client whose income changes within the first few months, and now has a disposable income, is moved to the FAB procedure. Try to ascertain whether this will be the case with your client and advise accordingly.

Date of sequestration

The date of sequestration is the date when it is awarded by the AiB.[56]

This date is important for a number of reasons, including calculating when creditors' claims are taken from, how much the debt claimed for will be, and when discharge happens.

Vesting of the estate

On the date of sequestration, the estate of the client 'vests' in the trustee. This means that the estate is legally transferred to the trustee whose duty it is to manage and realise that estate for the benefit of the creditors.[57] This includes moveable and non-moveable assets (ie, money in the bank and property), although in a MAP bankruptcy, the client must have no or little assets to qualify.

Note: where the client has more than £1,000 in a bank account, even if is for paying bills, it counts as an individual asset and the client will be moved to the FAB procedure.

The client has a legal duty to inform the trustee of all assets and signs a Statement of Truth to that effect (see Appendix 3).

Non-payment

As there is a zero DCO, non-payment does not apply in a MAP bankruptcy.

5. Full Administration Bankruptcy

What is Full Administration Bankruptcy

Full Administration Bankruptcy (FAB) is for clients who do not qualify for the Minimal Asset Process (MAP) bankrutpcy. FAB is a useful option for clients who cannot afford to repay their debts in a reasonable time, or not at all, and they have few or no assets or no chance of coming into any in the next four to five years.

When a client wishes to apply for bankruptcy, the debt adviser decides whether to apply for FAB or MAP. The Accountant in Bankruptcy (AiB) checks when the application is submitted to ensure all information and evidence has been provided and the application meets the specific criteria.

Creditor petitions (see p165) also fall within the FAB process.

Some advantages of FAB bankruptcy
Bankruptcy allows a client to write off up to 100 per cent of their qualifying debt while a trustee deals with creditors.
Creditors cannot take legal action against the client to recover their debt. This includes interest, fees and charges which are frozen.
Creditors can only claim for the outstanding balance due as at the date of sequestration.
It also stops or removes the effect of any existing diligence (such as wage arrestment, bank arrestment and deduction of earnings order) and prevents the instigation of new diligence by the client's creditors.
The debtor is discharged of their liability when their discharge is granted. The debtor's discharge will be considered at 12 months and may be granted, but it is dependent on their co-operation.

Some disadvantages of FAB bankruptcy
Clients may find their employment prospects harmed.
They cannot act as a director of a limited company or be involved in the financial management of a limited company.
They cannot act as an MP or a justice of the peace.
The client's credit rating will be adversely affected for six years.
They may be in breach of contractual obligations by being made bankrupt, such as tenancy, car lease agreements and employment contracts. These have to be checked before recommending bankruptcy to a client.
Service providers (eg, gas or electricity suppliers) may have concerns over how they provide a service to a client. They may change how they want to receive payments from the client by using a prepayment card or meter.
Banks may freeze or close accounts after a client is declared bankrupt.
Bankruptcy is recorded on the Register of Insolvencies for at least one year after discharge. It is a public register which is available for everyone to search. Data retention information can be found at aib.gov.uk/contact/privacy-and-data-protection.

Qualifying criteria

There are several qualifying criteria an applicant must meet for FAB. These include the following.[58]

Chapter 6: Statutory debt solutions in Scotland
5. Full Administration Bankruptcy

- The total of the debtor's debts (including interest) at the date of the application must be £3,000 or over (or other such sum as may be prescribed).
- An award of sequestration has not been made against the debtor in the five years ending on the day before the date the application is made.
- The debtor has obtained the advice of a money adviser.[59]
- The debtor has given a statement of undertakings (including an undertaking to pay to the trustee, after the award of sequestration of the debtor's estate, an amount determined using the common financial tool).

The debtor must:[60]
- be 'apparently insolvent' (see below); *and*
- have been granted, within the prescribed period, a certificate for sequestration of the debtor's estate; *or*
- have granted a trust deed which, by reason of creditors objecting, or not agreeing, to it is not a protected trust deed.

They must pay the fee of £150 (fee waivers are available).

Routes into FAB

Entry into FAB is by the 'apparent insolvency' route or by an authorised person signing a Certificate for Sequestration which states the client cannot pay their debts as they fall due (see p197).

Apparent insolvency

'Apparent insolvency' is constituted by any one of the following:[61]
- an expired charge for payment; *or*
- an expired statutory demand; *or*
- granting a trust deed; *or*
- a decree of adjudication is granted; *or*
- where a debt included in a Debt Payment Programme (DPP) under the Debt Arrangement Scheme (DAS) is revoked.

The usual way to prove apparent insolvency is to have an expired charge for payment or statutory demand.

A **'charge for payment'** can be issued to the client after a decree has been awarded in the sheriff court (or First-tier Tribunal) or a summary warrant has been issued. It gives the client 14 days to make payment, otherwise the creditor can begin diligence against them on the 15th day after service.

If your client has a charge for payment and it is near the expiry date, you could look at registering a statutory moratorium for the client. This stops the creditor from carrying out diligence for six months and prevents them from presenting a bankruptcy petition to the court against your client.

A **'statutory demand'** is a demand for payment from the client in a prescribed form. There is no need to have a decree or other document of debt (summary warrant) before serving a statutory demand and it is usually a sign that the creditor intends to serve a bankruptcy petition on your client.

When dealing with a statutory demand, and if the client wants to avoid bankruptcy, you should advise the client to deny the debt and return the form to the creditor within the timescale, which is 21 days from the date of service.

This makes the creditor take the normal court route for debt recovery where your client will have the opportunity to defend themselves.

On the other hand, if the client wants to go through the bankruptcy process, you could ignore the statutory demand as the creditor may follow it up with a creditor's petition and save your client the fee for applying.

See p165 for more information about creditor petitions.

Certificate for Sequestration

A 'Certificate for Sequestration' of the client's estate is a certificate granted by an authorised money or debt adviser (or other authorised persons) certifying that the client cannot pay debts as they become due.[62] See p197 for who is an authorised adviser and how to apply for a certificate.

No fee can be charged for completion of the certificate.[63]

Making an application

An application for FAB is made by an authorised debt adviser (or insolvency practitioner) via BASYS, the AiB's electronic application system. The application must be accompanied by a completed Certificate for Sequestration or proof of apparent insolvency.

Appointment of trustee

Under the FAB rules, there are two ways to have a trustee appointed.
- The first is to make an application and not to nominate a trustee. In this case, the AiB is the trustee. The AiB may then allocate the case to one of their contracted insolvency providers for administration, but they remain the trustee.
- The other way is to get the agreement of an insolvency practitioner and nominate them to be the trustee. This can be advantageous as the client can contact them before making the application and discuss how the bankruptcy will be run, how much the debtor contribution order (DCO) may be and how assets will be dealt with.

If the client has a reasonable contribution to make, it may be better if they appoint a trustee to look after their case.

Debt advisers should have a couple of insolvency practitioners to run cases by before making any applications. Remember to set up proper referral procedures

Chapter 6: Statutory debt solutions in Scotland
5. Full Administration Bankruptcy

and ensure you get feedback from both the insolvency practitioner and the client on the progress and administration of their case.

The insolvency practitioner must agree to be the trustee and complete Form 12. This form is included in Part 2 of the application. A copy can also be found at aib.gov.uk/publications/debtor-application-part-2.

Included and excluded debts

In a bankruptcy, the general rule is that all debts must be included, but not all will be discharged.

Hire purchase debts do not need to be included where the client is making regular payments. They should be entered as ongoing expenditure.

An obligation to pay aliment or a periodical allowance payable on divorce is not discharged by:[64]

- any liability to pay a fine or other penalty due to the Crown;
- any liability to pay a fine imposed in a justice of the peace court;
- any liability under a compensation order (within the meaning of section 249 of the Criminal Procedure (Scotland) Act 1995;
- any liability to forfeiture of a sum of money deposited in court under section 24(6) of the Criminal Procedure (Scotland) Act 1995;
- any liability incurred because of fraud or breach of trust.

Debt advice

A client must take advice from an authorised debt or money adviser (or insolvency practitioner) who will assist them in making the application. A client cannot make an application on their own.

The client must also be issued with a Debt Advice and Information Package (DAIP).[65]

Fees

The application fee for FAB is currently £150.

Fee waivers are available for clients with no disposable income[66] or if they have been in receipt of certain benefits for the past six months – eg, universal credit, pension credit, employment and support allowance, child tax credit or working tax credit (in certain circumstances).[67]

BASYS

FAB applications are processed via BASYS, the AiB's online tool.

Advisers can be registered by their organisation to use the system once they have received the appropriate training.

Chapter 6: Statutory debt solutions in Scotland
5. Full Administration Bankruptcy

BASYS training
Training on BASYS can be accessed by Scottish advisers via the MATRICS learning programme.[68]
The AiB also has a useful training tool which can be accessed on their website.[69] Advisers will have to register to gain access.

The application is in two parts.
- Part 1 contains, among other things, the client's personal details, their income and expenditure, assets and liabilities.
- Part 2 requires the client to sign several legal statements, including the statement of understanding and the statement of truth. It also contains a warning:

'It is a criminal offence under section 8(4) or 218(1) and (2) of the Bankruptcy (Scotland) Act 2016 for you to make a false statement in this form in relation to your assets or business or financial affairs, to not disclose any material fact in this statement or make a material misstatement unless you can show that you did not know that statement was false and had no reason to believe it was false.

On summary conviction, you may be liable to a fine of up to £5,000 or to imprisonment for a maximum period of three months or to both. If you deliberately do not disclose all relevant information or if you deliberately make a false statement when completing this form, you may become subject to bankruptcy restrictions.'

If the client deliberately does not disclose all relevant information, or if they deliberately make a false statement when completing the form, they may become subject to bankruptcy restrictions, a fine or even imprisonment.

Therefore, the client has stated that they have been given advice and that they will comply with the trustee following the award of bankruptcy. Ensure you point this out to the client before you make the application.

Try to ensure that your client is aware of what they are signing. Some advisers get the client to sign a copy of the warning as well as the statements of undertakings and truth for their records.

BASYS allows an adviser to enter all the details of income, expenditure, assets and liabilities as well as other necessary information for the application.

Once the application is made, it is assessed by the Insolvency Registration Team at the AiB which decides the application and if it qualifies for the MAP or FAB process.

If the application is incomplete, it can be returned to the adviser for more information. They have 21 days to update the information. It also allows the adviser to upload documents such as the Certificate for Sequestration, charge for payment, wage slips, bank statements and any other information required by the AiB.

Statement of undertakings and statement of truth

When making the application, the client must sign a Statement of Undertaking and a Statement of Truth to confirm they have understood the process and their legal obligations. See Appendix 3 for the text of the statements.

Debtor contribution order

In FAB cases, there can be a zero contribution (or the client must be in receipt of benefits only for the previous six months). The fee can be waived (see p160).

Completing a full, comprehensive and sustainable budget is important because if the common financial tool (CFT) is not completed correctly, the AiB may vary the contribution when it awards the DCO, making the client worse off and having to make an unaffordable and unrealistic contribution.

Variation of the debtor contribution order

The client has a duty to notify the trustee of any change in income and expenditure and if they acquire any assets during the 48-month period after bankruptcy is awarded.

If your client has a drop or increase in income and expenditure, they can have the DCO varied. This includes reducing the DCO to zero. If their income increases or their expenditure decreases, their DCO may be increased.

In a FAB, a payment of £0 counts as a contribution. This zero contribution counts as a payment and the bankruptcy still finishes at the end of the 48-month period. This is one benefit of bankruptcy over a trust deed where missed payments are added on at the end.

A variation can be applied for by contacting the trustee or by returning a completed debtor statement of affairs.[70]

Payment break

Where a client is struggling to make payments due under a DCO, they can apply to the trustee for a payment break of up to six months.[71]

Only one payment break is allowed during the the DCO.

A client can request a payment break if:
- there has been a reduction of at least 50 per cent in the client's disposable income (as determined using the CFT) as a result of:
  – unemployment or a change in employment;
  – a period of leave from employment because of:[72]
    – the birth or adoption of a child;
    – the need to care for a dependant;
    – a period of illness of the client;
    – divorce, the dissolution of civil partnership or separation from a person to whom the client is married or with whom the client is in civil partnership;
    – the death of a person who, along with the client, cared for a dependant.

- the client has not previously applied for a payment break in relation to a DCO applying after the sequestration of their estate.

An application for a payment break must specify the period during which the client wishes payments to be deferred.

The length of the payment break lengthens the period of the DCO accordingly – eg, if the client takes a break for three months, the DCO is extended from 48 months to 51 months.

If the trustee thinks the application to be fair and reasonable, they can grant the payment break and impose any conditions they think are reasonable.

The trustee will notify the client, creditors and any relevant third party of the decision. The client can ask for a review of the decision not to award a payment break within 14 days of the decision. The AiB Independent Review Team will review the decision and issue their guidance to the trustee within 28 days.

Any further appeal must go to the sheriff court within 14 days of the review decision. The sheriff's decision is final.

Payment break or variation?
The client has an option to apply to the trustee to vary to DCO to zero or to ask for a payment break. The client may be better off registering a zero contribution rather than taking a payment break, as the zero contribution does not lengthen the timescale.

Debtor's account of current state of affairs

Every six months the client is sent a 'Debtor's account of current state of affairs' on Form 27.[73]

On receipt of this, the trustee reviews the DCO.

If your client's situation has changed, make sure they complete and return the form properly as it will be used to reassess the DCO.

It is good practice for the client to come back to you for help with this on the first few occasions.

Duration of the bankruptcy

There are different rules for discharge of debts and for complete discharge from the client's obligations under bankruptcy.

A client who applies for FAB is obliged to comply with their trustee for 48 months (or until they are discharged) after the date of sequestration, despite being discharged of their debts after 12 months. This applies to aquirenda over the 48-month period.

The client also has an obligation to inform the trustee of any changes to income, so the DCO can be varied during the 48-month period. It can be increased if the client misses any payments or where the client and trustee agree, for example, to a payment break.

Wilful non-payment of any monies due can lead to the 48-month period being extended accordingly.

Date of sequestration

The date of sequestration is the date when sequestration is awarded by the AiB.[74]

This date is important for a number of reasons, including calculating when creditors' claims are taken from, how much the debt claimed for will be, and when discharge normally happens.

Vesting of the estate

On the date of sequestration, the estate of the client 'vests' in the trustee. This means that the estate is legally transferred to the trustee whose duty it is to manage and realise that estate for the benefit of the creditors.[75] This includes moveable and non-moveable assets – ie, money in the bank and property.

The client has a legal duty to inform the trustee of all assets and sign the Statement of Truth (see Appendix 3).

Non-payment

When the client misses two payments, the trustee can write to the client's employer and ask them to deduct the amount due. This is done on Form 19, available on the AiB website.[76] The employer must deduct the money and send it to the trustee. They can also charge for this, on a scale similar to an earnings arrestment.[77]

The trustee can also vary the amount if they see fit.

Evidence and information

A debt adviser must obtain evidence of a client's income and expenditure and retain all records for a two years and provide this information to the AiB on request.[78]

Checklist

- Ensure that you fully complete the CFT and that the DCO is complete, accurate and sustainable.
- Ensure that you have included all income and expenditure. This is in case the AiB disagrees with any of the expenditure and varies it downward, leaving a contribution.
- Complete a full budget with the client and do not ignore any expenditure that should be included just because the disposable income is at zero. If the budget is negative, it shows a clearer picture of the client's situation.
- Get someone to check the application before submitting it if you are new to debt advice.

- If you have any issues or are uncertain about anything, contact MATRICS or the AiB and run it past them.
- Make sure you advise the client about gratuitous alienations, unfair preferences and acquirenda and check to make sure FAB is the correct solution for the client over the long run.
- Ask whether the client may inherit or come into any assets within the next 48 months.
- The AiB guidance notes for trustees are an excellent place to look and simple to read.
- If in doubt, seek advice from a more experienced adviser.

6. Creditor petitions for bankruptcy

What is a creditor petition for sequestration

An individual creditor or a group of creditors owed £5,000 or more can petition the sheriff court for a client's bankruptcy.[79] The application must be through the court, not the Account in Bankruptcy (AiB).

All creditor petitions go down the Full Administration Bankruptcy (FAB) route.

Debt Advice and Information Package

At least 14 days (and not more than 12 weeks) before the creditor petitions the court, they must serve the client with a Debt Advice and Information Package.[80]

A copy of the document can be found at aib.gov.uk/publications/debt-advice-and-information-package.

Apparent insolvency

'Apparent insolvency' for a creditor's petition is generally constituted by an expired charge for payment or expired statutory demand.

A charge for payment expires 14 days after it is served and a statutory demand expires 21 days after service. The creditor must then use this evidence of apparent insolvency to lodge a petition in court within four months of the date of presentation of the petition.

A revoked Debt Payment Programme (DPP) under the Debt Arrangement Scheme (DAS) can also constitute apparent insolvency.[81]

Charge for payment

A charge for payment is issued to the client after a decree (or equivalent) has been issued. It gives the client 14 days to make payment. On the 15th day after service, the creditor can begin diligence against the client, including making an application to the court for the client's bankruptcy.

Full Administration Bankruptcy procedure

All creditor petitions are administered under the FAB procedure.

See the section on FAB starting on p156 for more information on individual issues and procedures.

Application to the court and intimation to the client

The client receives a copy of the creditor's application.

A sheriff officer may give notice on behalf of an intimating party by:
- delivering the intimation personally to the receiving party (the client); or
- leaving the intimation in the hands of:
  - a resident at the receiving party's dwelling place (home); or
  - an employee, agent, or representative at the receiving party's place of business.

Where a sheriff officer has been unsuccessful in intimation in accordance with the above, the sheriff officer may give intimation by:
- depositing it in the receiving party's dwelling place or place of business; or
- leaving it at the receiving party's dwelling place or place of business in such a way that it is likely to come to the attention of that party.

It may also be delivered to a solicitor acting on the client's behalf.

Notification is by Form 5.7.

A client is served with:
- a citation in Form 6.3–A; and
- a copy of the petition for sequestration in Form 6.1.A; and
- a copy of the form of certificate of citation in Form 6.3B.

They must also complete Form 6.2, which is a statement that the creditor has checked both the Register of Insolvencies (for a statutory moratorium) and the DAS Register (for a DPP).

All creditor bankruptcy forms can be found on the Scottish courts website.[82]

Warrant to cite

When the court receives the paperwork, it issues the client with a 'warrant to cite'.[83] This states the date when the client must appear in court to justify why sequestration should not be awarded.

If the client does not give good reasons, or fails to appear, the sequestration is automatically awarded.

When a creditor applies for a client's bankruptcy, the date of sequestration is the date on the warrant to cite.

Court hearing

All creditor petitions proceed through the sheriff court, not the AiB. Lay representation is available.[84]

At the hearing, the client has the chance to state why sequestration should not be awarded.

There are a couple of defences that may work for your client.

- If a statutory moratorium has been applied for before the petition was presented to court, they could argue that it should not be awarded as they are protected by the moratorium.[85]
- If the client already has a DPP approved and it is for the same debt, the petition is invalid.[86]

If the client has applied for a DPP, but it has not yet been awarded, or if the client intends to apply, they can ask that the petition be continued for up to 42 days or longer to allow you the time to make an application to the DAS and have a DPP awarded.[87] This is at the sheriff's discretion, but most sheriffs allow time to make an application for a DPP.

If the DPP is revoked or refused, the creditor can restart proceedings.

If sequestration is awarded, the sheriff appoints an interim trustee/trustee whose duty is to safeguard the estate for the creditors. This may be the AiB, or the creditor may appoint their own trustee who is appointed by the court and agrees to be the trustee.

The interim trustee may call a meeting of creditors and, in most cases, they are appointed as the permanent trustee. Where the AiB is interim trustee, there is not normally a statutory meeting of creditors.

Costs and fees

All costs associated with a creditor's petition (including AiB fees) are paid by the creditor and claimed for in the client's bankruptcy.

There are no costs involved with appearing in court to defend the granting of a petition (apart from solicitor's costs if the client decides to employ one).

Concurrent proceedings

Where a petition has been presented to the court, the client cannot apply for their own bankruptcy or a protected trust deed.[88]

Recall

Recall of a creditor's petition can be made to the AiB where the client is able to pay their debts in full, and to the sheriff court where the client was not apparently insolvent. You should seek further guidance on this.[89]

Dealing with a creditor petition

Dealing with a statutory demand

A statutory demand should be served personally on the client by a sheriff officer or messenger-at-arms together with an additional copy of the demand.

If your client receives a statutory demand,[90] they have the option of admitting the debt or denying the debt.

Unlike a charge for payment, a creditor does not need to have taken the client to court for the debt. They can simply serve a statutory demand and wait until the 21 days expire, constituting apparent insolvency, then petition for the client's sequestration.

The easiest way to deal with a statutory demand is to deny the debt and send the form back to the creditor. This sent be done by recorded delivery and arrive at the creditor no later than three weeks after the date of service. In this scenario, the creditor must proceed through the normal court process allowing the client to deal with it according to the court regulations.

If your client does not respond, the creditor begins sequestration proceedings through the sheriff court. So, ensure that your client responds accordingly within the set time.

Statutory moratorium on diligence

Where a statutory demand or charge for payment has been served and expired, and your client has not responded, but no proceedings have yet been started, you may consider applying for a statutory moratorium on diligence.

The moratorium stops any bankruptcy proceedings against your client and specifically the presentation of a petition for your client's sequestration.[91]

You then have six months to work out a suitable debt solution for your client without the fear of a petition for sequestration being awarded.

Application for a Debt Payment Programme

Once a DPP has been applied for, and it includes the debt craved for in the application, a creditor cannot serve a petition for sequestration for six weeks after the client's intimation to apply has been entered in the DAS register. Once approved, the petition is halted and if the client defaults on the DPP and it is revoked, the creditor can restart the proceedings.[92]

If the DPP application is rejected, there are a further 14 days for applying for a review and then another 28 days for the review to be considered.

When a DPP is awarded, it is not competent to petition for a client's sequestration.[93]

Apply for a continuation at court

If the client has already been presented with a petition and the case is being heard at court, it is too late to apply for a statutory moratorium. You could ask for a continuation of the case for a maximum of 42 days to allow you time to make an application for a DPP. This is at the sheriff's discretion.[94]

Checklist
- Consider returning a statutory demand and denying the debt within the relevant timescale.
- Apply for a statutory moratorium if you think a creditor may present a petition to court. A statutory moratorium will stop proceedings so long as it is in place before the petition is presented to the court.
- Consider applying for a DPP and ask for a continuation at court to allow this to go ahead.
- Check that the court had jurisdiction. It may be possible to recall the sequestration if the case has been dealt with in the wrong court, although this may only delay the process.

7. Protected trust deeds

What is a trust deed

A trust deed is a voluntary, legally binding agreement between a client and their creditors, operated by and through an insolvency practitioner.

It is insolvency in the wider sense, but not bankruptcy as such. It is governed in much the same way and there are more similarities than differences, as many of the same rules apply across all insolvency solutions.

A trust deed can be unprotected or obtain protected status and become a protected trust deed (PTD).

Under a PTD, creditors cannot pursue the debts owed to them, giving the client the same protection from creditors as bankruptcy. This is the main reason to have the trust deed protected. A PTD is suitable for a client who cannot pay their debts within a reasonable timescale and wishes to exclude the family home, although that is not always possible.

Voluntary trust deeds for creditors are covered in Part 14 of the Bankruptcy (Scotland) Act 2016 ('the Act').

All the forms used in a PTD can be found at legislation.gov.uk.[95]

Some advantages of a protected trust deed

It is not bankruptcy and might be more useful to a client whose job excludes them from being bankrupt.

Your client can discuss the terms of the trust deed and come to an agreement with the trustee before they sign. This can be useful in working out how disposable income is to be assessed, how assets are to be realised and specifically if the family home is to be excluded. The trustee deals with all creditor correspondence and queries.

Chapter 6: Statutory debt solutions in Scotland
7. Protected trust deeds

All interest and charges on the debts are frozen on the date the trust deed is signed.

Your client makes one affordable monthly payment, normally for 48 months.

Once the trust deed is given protected status, no further action can be taken against the client by their creditors.

After completion of the terms of the trust deed, the client is discharged from their debts and all included remaining debt will be written off.

Some disadvantages of a protected trust deed

Your client must pay contributions towards their debts for at least 48 months.

Having a trust deed will affect your client's credit rating for six years from the date the trust deed is signed.

Joint trust deeds are not possible.

If the client's situation changes, there is no zero contribution available (as there is in bankruptcy). Therefore, it may last longer than 48 months.

The creditors may not agree to the terms and the trust deed may not gain protected status, and the client may have to look at bankruptcy as a result.

Secured creditors may still take action to take possession of a debtor's home if they fall behind with mortgage payments.

If any new debts are taken on after a trust deed is signed, the debtor is not protected from legal action by these new creditors. Servicing new debts may affect the debtor's ability to maintain the agreed monthly contributions.

Role of the Accountant in Bankruptcy

While trust deeds are a voluntary agreement between the client and their creditors, the Accountant in Bankruptcy (AiB) acts as a regulator, supervising the performance of trustees, and trust deeds cannot gain protected status without the consent of the AiB.

Who can sign a trust deed

To be able to sign a trust deed and have it protected, the client must be:[96]
- a living individual; *or*
- a partnership; *or*
- a limited partnership; *or*
- a trust; *or*
- a corporate body; *or*
- an unincorporated body.

Joint trust deeds are not allowed.

The client must not:[97]
- be someone whose estate has been sequestrated if the trustee in the sequestration has not been discharged;
- be a limited company;

- have unsecured debts under £5,000 (including interest) at the date the trust deed is granted.

Partnerships

Partnership trust deeds are possible. In such cases, each partner, plus the partnership as a whole, needs to sign a trust deed. It cannot all be rolled into one.

Take advice from an insolvency practitioner if this situation arises.

Consequences

The main consequence of signing a trust deed is if it does not gain protected status because of creditor objections. In this case, the client will most likely need to look at sequestration as an option. This could be particularly difficult if the client wants to exclude their family home from the trust deed, as this will not be possible in sequestration.

Signing a trust deed also constitutes apparent insolvency and creditors can use this to bankrupt the client. They have a set period of five weeks in the process in which they can do this.[98]

The trust deed has an effect on the client's credit file and is registered for six years after the date of signing.

It may also have an effect on your client's employment, and you should check this is not the case before you make a recommendation.

Fees

There are no upfront fees to enter into a trust deed, although the client must be able to make a contribution or realise assets to pay fees and a return to the creditors.

The trustee has a fixed fee for a trust deed, plus costs and outlays. The trustee takes their fees from contributions and realisation of any assets. They also receive a percentage of all contributions or of asset realisation.[99]

Included and excluded debts

All debts must be included, but all may not discharge (ie, student loans).[100]

The same general rules apply as for bankruptcy (see p160).

Routes into a protected trust deed

There is no requirement to be 'apparently insolvent' (see p158) before signing a trust deed as with bankruptcy. The signing of the trust deed itself constitutes apparent insolvency.[101]

A client simply makes an appointment with an insolvency practitioner (or is referred by an adviser) and, after discussion as to its suitability and after taking time to consider it, agrees to sign the trust deed.

Advisers can refer on to an insolvency practitioner if they think the client would benefit from it. If they do, they should ensure that there is some follow up on the referral and check that the client is happy with the agreement. You should also receive confirmation that the trust deed has gained protected status.

Most advisers already have prepared a statement of income and expenditure, assets and liabilities with the client to make the insolvency practitioner's job easier. This could form the basis of the trust deed if the trustee agrees.

Operation of a trust deed

Trust deeds are administered by the trustee through ASTRA, the AiB's electronic case management system.

Registration of the trust deed

Once the trust deed has been signed, the trustee must send a notice (Form 1[102]) to the AiB who enters it in the Register of Insolvencies.[103] This begins the process.

Gaining protected status

No later than one week after registration in the Register of Insolvencies, the trustee must send all known creditors:[104]
- a copy of the signed trust deed; *and*
- a copy of the statement of claim (Form 2); *and*
- a copy of the notice (Form 1); *and*
- a statement of the client's affairs, prepared by the trustee, containing:
  - a list of the client's assets and liabilities;
  - a statement of the client's income and expenditure as at the date on which the trust deed was granted (Form 2A);
  - a statement as to the extent to which those assets and that income will not vest in the trustee;
  - a statement as to whether the creditors are likely to be paid a dividend and the amount of the dividend that is expected to be paid (Form 4);
  - a statement that on request the trustee must provide a copy of any valuation of the client's assests made by a third party, any statement showing the amount due by the client under a security and any document showing the client's income;
  - a copy of any agreement referred to in section 175(1) of the Act (heritable property);
  - a statement explaining the conditions which need to be fulfilled before the trust deed will become a protected trust deed and the consequences of it so becoming;
  - a statement, in such form as may be prescribed for the purposes of the above, of the trustee's anticipated realisations from the trust deed;
  - details of any protected trust deed within the six months preceding the notice, whereby they were discharged or refused discharge.

If a client has had a PTD within six months of the new notice, the trustee must also give creditors these details.

Trustee proposals for protection can be found in Form 3.

Where the client makes a contribution from income, there must be a statement and evidence that the contribution is in accordance with the Common Financial Tool (CFT).[105]

Creditor responses

Creditors reply to the trustee, agreeing or disagreeing that the trust deed should be protected. They must do so within five weeks from the date of registration of the trust deed. (Usually, four weeks after being informed.)

If more than half of the creditors, or a third in total value, do not agree to the trust deed becoming protected, it does not become a PTD.[106] Creditors who do not respond are deemed to have accepted.

Examples
There are seven creditors and four object to the trust deed gaining protected status. It does not become protected because more than half of the creditors object.

The total debt is £12,000. One creditor who is owed over £4,000 objects to the trust deed gaining protected status. It does not become protected because that creditor is owed a third of the value.

During the five weeks, creditors may also apply to the court for the sequestration of the client's estate (as signing the trust deed constitutes apparent insolvency), and the trust deed then cannot be used.

On application by a creditor, the sheriff grants the sequestration only if they are satisfied that to do so is in the creditors' best interests. In this case, the trustee may apply to the court for the client's bankruptcy and administer the case as a bankruptcy, where the Full Administration Bankruptcy rules apply. These terms should be included in the trust deed itself. This is at the sheriff's discretion, so there is no guarantee that the trust deed will gain protected status and be successful, and the client may end up bankrupt. This can affect the possible exclusion of the family home, and clients must be made aware of this.

Insolvency practitioners can give advice on whether they think the trust deed will gain protected status, as they will likely know which creditors will agree, and which will oppose it becoming protected.

Speak to the potential trustee about this before making a recommendation.

Sequestration petition by a qualified creditor to the sheriff court

A qualified creditor who is not a notified creditor or who has notified the trustee of their objection to the trust deed within the relevant period may present a petition to the sheriff for sequestration of the client's estate:[107]
- not later than five weeks after the date of registration under section 169 of the Act of the notice mentioned in that section; *or*
- at any time if the creditor avers that the provision for distribution of the estate is, or is likely to be, unduly prejudicial to a creditor or class of creditors.

The sheriff must be satisfied that it is in the best interests of the creditors before it is granted.[108]

If the petition is successful, the client is declared bankrupt, and the petitioning creditor may appoint another insolvency practitioner or the AiB to administer the bankruptcy.

Registration for protection

The trustee sends the AiB all the responses from creditors along with a statement by the trustee that those creditors, if any, who have objected in writing to the trust deed during the relevant period do not constitute a majority in number, or a third or more in value, of the creditors.

The AiB must register the trust deed in the Register of Insolvencies as a protected trust deed if, among other things:
- it has received all the documents required;
- the conditions set out in sections 164 to 170 of the Act have been met;
- it is satisfied, in accordance with the CFT, with the amount of the contribution determined.

Where the client makes a contribution from income:[109]
- a statement that the amount of the contribution is in accordance with the CFT as assessed by the trustee; *and*
- any evidence or explanation required in applying the CFT.

The AiB notifies the trustee that the trust deed has, or has not, gained protected status.

The trustee must, within seven days of being notified, notify the client and every creditor known to the trustee that the trust deed is registered as a PTD, or has been refused protected status.

Date of protection

When the AiB registers the trust deed in the Register of Insolvencies as a PTD, this is known as the 'date of protection'. From this date, creditors cannot pursue the client or attempt to use any diligence against them.[110]

Effect of protected status

Where a trust deed has protected status, all creditors are bound by the terms of the PTD. Section 172 of the Act covers the general effect of protected status over diligence.

The client cannot make an application for sequestration while the PTD subsists.

During a PTD, a secured creditor cannot:[111]
- make a claim under the PTD for any of the debt in respect of which the security is held. This means that the secured creditor, if they have agreed to be excluded from the trust deed, is also bound by the terms of the trust deed; *or*
- take diligence against the assets conveyed to the trustee under the PTD; *or*
- petition for the sequestration of the client during the subsistence of the PTD.

On the date of protection, any current earnings arrestment, maintenance arrestment or conjoined arrestment order cease to have effect.[112]

A deduction from earnings order is not 'competent' after the date of protection to secure the payment of any amount due by the client under a maintenance calculation in respect of which a claim could be made under the trust deed.

The execution of an earnings arrestment or the making of a conjoined arrestment order is not competent, after the date of protection, to enforce a debt in respect of which the creditor is entitled to make a claim under the trust deed.

Therefore, protection from diligence from creditors is achieved by the trust deed gaining protected status.

Unprotected trust deeds

In a trust deed which has not become protected, there is no statutory procedure to close the trust deed. It is normal practice for a receipt for the final dividend to incorporate a discharge of the trustee and a discharge of the client. Creditors who have not acceded to the trust deed have no requirement to grant a discharge to the client.

Basically, an unprotected trust deed brings no guarantee of an end to the debt for the client and creditors may still pursue them for the money owed.

A better alternative is for the trustee to sequestrate the client and bring the trust deed to an end with the agreement of the creditors. This clause should be inserted into and be part of the trust deed itself.

Duration of the trust deed

The normal duration of a protected trust deed is 48 months, although it can be extended if the client has any problems paying the contributions or if there are assets to be realised. Think of it as being 48 payments to be made over any period.

Whereas in bankruptcy the client can register a zero contribution and this counts as a payment in the 48-month period, when a client misses a payment in a trust deed, the trustee may add on another month (or more) to allow the client to catch up. This is a disadvantage of a trust deed over a bankruptcy.

Client's early discharge from a protected trust deed

The Protected Trust Deeds (Miscellaneous Amendment) (Scotland) Regulations 2024 introduced changes to how PTDs can be ended earlier than 48 months and came into effect on 1 July 2024.

Where a trustee believes the following circumstances exist, they can apply to have the trust deed ended early, and the client discharged of their debts before the 48 months are completed. The circumstances are:[113]
- the client can no longer meet their obligations under the trust deed; *and*
- there is no reasonable prospect of them being able to resume meeting their obligations under the trust deed in the foreseeable future.

The trustee must first seek the agreement of the creditors.

Creditors can object, and if a majority in number or a third in value object, the trust deed cannot be ended early.

If this is the case, the trustee can apply to the AiB for a review.

The AiB will consider the application and determine whether it is satisfied that, taking into account all the circumstances, it is fair and reasonable for the debtor to be discharged from the trust deed.[114]

If it refuses, an appeal under section 188 of the Act is possible.

Contribution

The client must sign an agreement, contained within the trust deed, to make regular contributions, or realise assets, or both, during the period of the trust deed.[115]

The trust deed must state that during the payment period, the client is to pay any contributions from income for the benefit of creditors (including, where the client is an individual, any contribution required by the CFT) at regular intervals.

The payment period is:
- 48 months starting on the date the trust deed is granted; *or*
- a period shorter than 48 months, as determined by the trustee; *or*
- longer than 48 months as:
  - determined by the trustee where there has been a period during which the client has not paid those contributions; *or*
  - agreed between the client and the trustee.

In calculating contributions, the whole of the client's surplus income over the amount allowed for expenditure in the statement of the client's income and expenditure supplied must be applied.

Note that contributions from a client cannot be taken from benefits only, but if there is a mixture of benefits and income, they can. However, the contribution amount cannot be any more than the earned income.

Non-payment

When non-payment occurs, a trustee can extend the period of the PTD and/or demand payment from the client's employer.[116]

When a client signs a trust deed, they sign a statement that, in the event of non-payment, their employer can be contacted, and the trustee can demand payment from the employer.

This can happen when the client misses two consecutive payments to the PTD.

The employer must make the deduction and pass the money on to the trustee or they will become liable for the payments. They can also charge a fee for this comparable to that where an earnings arrestment is in place.

Deductions from the client's earnings

Where a client is required to pay to the trustee a contribution from income for the benefit of creditors, and where the client fails to pay on two consecutive occasions, the trustee can insist that a deduction is made direct from the client's wages.[117]

Employee's payment instruction

Following a request by the trustee, the client must give their employer an instruction (using Form 4A) to make:[118]
- deductions of specified amounts from their earnings; *and*
- payments to the trustee of the deducted amounts.

Trustee's payment instruction

The trustee may directly give the client's employer an instruction (in Form 4B) if the client fails to comply.[119] The employer must comply with any instruction given.

If agreed between the client and the trustee, the client may also give the client's employer a variation to an instruction (Form 4C).

Employer's duty

The instruction having been delivered, the employer must:
- deduct the specified sum on every payday; *and*
- pay the sum deducted to the trustee as soon as it is reasonable to do so.

Where an employer fails without good cause to make a payment due under an instruction, the employer is:
- liable to pay on demand by a trustee the amount that should have been paid; *and*
- not entitled to recover from a client the amount paid to the client in breach of the instruction.

An employer may, on making a payment due under an instruction:
- charge a fee; *and*
- deduct that fee from the balance due to the client.

Chapter 6: Statutory debt solutions in Scotland
7. Protected trust deeds

This may cause the client serious problems either due to a reduction in earnings, increased costs or the CFT not being completed correctly, and a sustainable budget not being properly worked out for the client. It may also cause friction at work for some people.

If the client is suffering financial hardship, and it is not of a short-term nature, they should contact the trustee and revisit the CFT and agreed contributions, and perhaps look at sequestration as an alternative.

This involves the trustee resigning and the client may end up with all their debt back, despite having made several payments to the trust deed already. See p181 on non-performing trust deeds.

Third-party payments

If a client cannot make a contribution from their income for a trust deed, it is possible that a third party can contribute for them – eg, a friend or family member. The third party should not be subject to an insolvency or debt arrangement themself.

The trustee makes a payment agreement with the third party. This agreement may not be enforceable and, in the event of non-payment, the third party cannot be forced to pay. The trustee must inform the creditors if this is the case. The trustee should also advise the third party to take independent legal advice.

Where the agreement is unenforceable, it may lead to the creditors refusing protected status.

If the third party stops paying, and any third-party agreement is unenforceable, the PTD fails, and the client will be made bankrupt or be stuck in limbo in the PTD (see p181).

This could be useful where a trust deed would be a clear solution for the client but they cannot afford it. Take advice before considering this option.

Exclusion of the family home

In a trust deed, it is possible to exclude the family home and any equity in it. This is done with the agreement of the secured creditors. This is not possible under bankruptcy procedures and can be an advantage of a trust deed.

To be successful, the secured creditors must agree not to claim in the trust deed, and then the unsecured creditors have to agree to allow the trust deed to gain protected status.

If the unsecured creditors refuse to agree to the trust deed gaining protected status because of the exclusion of the family home (and any equity), the trustee can vary the trust deed to include it or look at sequestration as another option.

Before the client grants the trust deed:[120]
- the trustee must provide the client and the secured creditor with a valuation, made by a chartered surveyor or other suitably qualified person, of the dwellinghouse (or part) which is to be excluded from the estate;

- the client must obtain the secured creditors' agreement not to claim under the trust deed for any of the debt in respect of which the security is held, and any agreement so obtained must be set out in Form 1A.

This excludes the secured debt from the trust deed and the trustee can ignore any equity in the home.

More detailed guidance can be found in section 2.8 of the AiB's notes for guidance for trustees.[121]

Dealing with the family home where it is not excluded from the trust deed

Section 175 of the Act (agreement in respect of client's heritable property) applies where the client may have some equity that could be realised by the trustee but not enough for the trustee to sell the home. For example, if there is equity of £2,000 in the property at the time of signing the trust deed, the trustee would be looking to realise the £2,000 without having to sell the property and make the client homeless.

If the trustee does not realise the full amount of available equity in the family home, the trustee must give an equity statement to creditors and AiB.

The trustee has the following options:
- payment by the client (see below);
- paymeny by a third party (see below).

Explore these options when considering making a referral for a trust deed. For more information, see section 2.9 of the AiB's notes for guidance for trustees.[122]

Payment by the client

Where there is some equity in the property, the trustee may continue the trust deed for a longer period to allow the client to make up the amount of the equity.

This can involve the client making extra payments after the normal 48 months to make up the difference. In the example above, the client could offer the trustee £200 a month for 10 months or £100 a month for 20 months, extending the trust deed period to 58 or 68 months respectively. This increases the length of the trust deed but ensures the client does not lose their home.

Payment by a third party

The trustee can agree with a third party (eg, a close friend or family member) to make up the equity in the home so that the creditors do not lose out. The third party can make the contributions alongside the client's normal contributions over the 48-month period.

Using the example above, they could pay £2,000 over 48 months (£41.67 a month). This avoids the trustee having to sell the property.

Agreement where there is little or no equity

Where the trustee has obtained a valuation of the property and there is very little or no equity, they can agree to relinquish their interest for a nominal fee – currently around £550. This is done through an agreement in Form 1B.

The fee can be paid by the client at the end of the trust deed, or a third party can contribute during the term (see p178).

These options can be discussed with a trustee before the client signs the trust deed, which is one of the main advantages of a trust deed over bankruptcy (although this can also happen if you appoint your own trustee in bankruptcy – see below).

Failure to comply with the written agreement can lead to the trustee cancelling the agreement and proceeding with the sale of the property.

If the client contends the sale of the property, the trustee must apply to the sheriff to sell the property.

If your client has equity in their property, take advice first from an insolvency practitioner. It might not exclude them from an insolvency option.

Appointing your own trustee

In a trust deed, you must appoint your own trustee. You cannot appoint the AiB.

The trustee is usually an insolvency practitioner. They must agree to be the trustee.

An advantage of this is that your client can discuss the terms of the trust deed and agree the terms with the trustee before signing it.

However, your client should be made aware that the trustee has a dual role: firstly, to give advice to the client before signing the trust deed, and once the trust deed is signed, the trustee acts on behalf of the creditors.

You should keep a list of preferred insolvency practitioners you make referrals to, and monitor their performance and attitude to the client.

Trust deeds contents

The terms of the trust deed can be different and different insolvency practitioners may have different styles, but there are some details which all trust deeds must have.

The trust deed must state:[123]
- that all of the client's estate, unless excluded (eg, the family home), is conveyed to the trustee;
- that the client agrees to convey to the trustee, for the benefit of creditors generally, any estate (wherever situated) which:
  – is acquired by the client during the four years beginning with the date on which the trust deed is granted; *and*
  – would have been conveyed to the trustee had it been part of the client's estate on the date on which the trust deed was granted.

Where the client's home, or part of it, is excluded from the estate conveyed to the trustee, the trust deed must also include details of any secured creditor who has agreed not to claim under the trust deed for any of the debt in respect of which the security is held.

Before the trust deed is granted, the trustee must advise the client that granting the deed may result:[124]
- in the client's estate being sequestrated;
- in the client's being refused credit (before or after the client's discharge);
- subject to any exclusion mentioned in the trust deed definition, in the client not being able to remain in their current place of residence;
- subject to any such exclusion, in the client being required to relinquish property which they own;
- in the client's being required to make contributions from income for the benefit of creditors;
- in damage to the client's business interests and employment prospects; *and*
- in the trust deed becoming public information.

The trustee must provide the client with a Debt Advice and Information Package. The trustee and the client must both sign a statement to the effect that the trustee has fulfilled their duties.[125] In the future, clients will also be provided with a trust deed information document.[126]

Termination provisions

Trust deeds should contain provisions on termination. Such provisions, if complied with, will be effective in terminating the trust deed.

For example, trustees should ensure that the style of trust deed used contains provisions for ending the trust deed on sequestration and/or on final distribution of the estate.

Dealing with non-performing trust deeds

In some cases, which could be due to changes in a client's circumstances, a loss of income or an incomplete CFT having been done, the client may find that they cannot continue to make payments, as agreed, to their trust deed.

In this case, there are a few options open to the trustee.

Continue the trust deed for a longer period

The first option is usually to extend the trust deed for a longer period to see if the client's situation improves and they can restart their contributions. This can increase the length of the trust deed by months or years.

Discharge of the trustee

Another way to deal with a non-performing trust deed is for the trustee to discharge themselves from the case and to give the client back their debts, basically refusing to discharge the client from their liability.

The trustee must inform the AiB why this is the case and complete the appropriate refusal of discharge form.[127] (This only applies to trustees who are part of the protocol agreement.)

The trustee will use any monies collected to pay fees and, if possible, a dividend to the creditors.

The client is not discharged from their debts, but is freed from the constraints of the trust deed. In effect, the client gets their debt back, plus interest. They can then look at another debt solution such as a DPP under the Debt Arrangement Scheme, or sequestration.

The trustee must inform the AiB why they are not discharging the client.

If the AiB disagrees with the trustee's decision, the trustee will be contacted to discuss the refusal. Where the trustee and AiB do not agree, the AiB will seek to issue a direction to the trustee which can then be challenged.

Discharge of the trustee and the client

A third way to deal with a non-performing trust deed is for the trustee to discharge the client and themself if they believe that the client has tried their best to conform to the terms of the trust deed but has failed to complete the agreed 48 payments.

The trustee must inform the creditors and ask their permission to discharge the client. If all creditors and the AiB agree, the trustee can discharge the client, then themself and the period of the trust deed is over.

The AiB guidance for trustees states:[128] 'It would not be appropriate to refuse to discharge a client because of circumstances beyond their control, such as:
- a change of circumstances which prevents them from paying any contribution payable under section 168 of the 2016 Act...
- if an asset realises an amount less than originally estimated by the trustee on Form 3.'

A client in this situation should explain to the trustee that they cannot keep up the agreed payments, that they have tried their best to do so and the situation is unlikely to improve. They should ask the trustee to discharge them and bring the trust deed to an end.

Discharge of the client

Discharge is conditional on the client co-operating with the trustee and the terms of the trust deed. The client does not need to have paid all contributions and realised all assets to be discharged. The trustee must be satisfied that the debtor has co-operated with them and met the obligations of the trust deed. The trustee applies to AiB for the debtor discharge on Form 5.[129] The trustee can refuse to discharge the client (see p183).

The AiB then registers the discharge in the Register of Insolvencies. The date of discharge is the date on which it is registered.[130]

The trustee must notify the client with a copy of Form 5 and every known creditor of the date the client has been discharged. The trustee can charge a reasonable fee for a letter of discharge which is chargeable against the client's estate.

Form 5 can be used by the client as proof of discharge.

On discharge from the PTD, the client is discharged from any outstanding unsecured debts and obligations for which they were liable at the date that they granted the trust deed.

There are some important exceptions to this rule.

A PTD does not discharge a debtor from:[131]
- any liability arising after the date on which the PTD was granted;
- any liability or obligation mentioned in section 145(3) of the Act;
- any liability for a debt in respect of which a security is held if the secured creditor has agreed not to claim under the trust deed for any of the debt in respect of which the security is held.

Trust deed protocol

A 'trust deed protocol' has been developed by the AiB and other industry bodies. It sets out operational process changes introduced to promote good practice, improve transparency in the PTD administration process and provide greater clarity on the AiB's PTD supervision roles and responsibilities.

The protocol complements the AiB's PTD *Notes for Guidance* for clients, creditors and trustees about PTD administration.

As it is a voluntary code of conduct, there is currently no legal requirement for PTD trustees to consent to and comply with the protocol. In the future, it could be incorporated into legislation. In the meantime, Scottish Ministers and the AiB would like PTD trustees to consent to the terms of the protocol so there is consistency in the administration of all PTDs.

The insolvency practitioners agreeing to abide by the protocol have agreed to only accept referrals for trust deeds from the Financial Conduct Authority (FCA) authorised firms. So, if bad advice is given, the client should have some redress to the FCA on the behaviour of the firm. This could be appropriate where the client's situation has not been properly assessed by the CFT and/or no advice letter has been given out. See p186 for information about complaints.

The FCA is currently developing proposals that would ban the payment of fees to debt packagers.

Ban on debt packager referral fees

The FCA announced a ban on referral fees, and other forms of commission or remuneration paid by debt solution providers to debt packagers, from October 2023.[132]

The ban covers 'any commission, fee or any other financial consideration, received by a debt packager firm, directly or indirectly, from a debt solution provider in connection with the firm referring customers to a debt solution provider, or any other related services '.

The FCA stated its reasons for introducing the ban:

'a. The consumers affected by the consequences of mismanagement of the conflict of interest often show signs of vulnerability, which may affect their ability to assess already complex options.

b. We have seen widespread non-compliance with existing rules even after we set our expectations on how the conflict of interest should be managed.

c. We have taken action against individual firms previously, but the scale of the noncompliance has meant this is not an effective way to stop it occurring throughout the wider market while using our resources effectively.'

Exclusions

The ban will not apply to not-for-profit debt advice firms or to regulated providers of debt solutions (including debt management plans) who have a different business model to debt packagers. The FCA says: 'The conflict of interest from referral fees is less acute in the case of such firms who provide debt solutions themselves.'[133]

However, the FCA has also introduced new *Perimeter Guidance* (PERG) making it clear that referring a client to debt solution providers who only offer one option will now be looked at as being debt advice, and therefore, insolvency practitioners may no longer have the exemption from FCA compliance. The FCA says: 'IPs [insolvency practitioners] who act as lead generators should also consider if they need authorisation, since their exclusion from carrying out regulated activity may not apply in this situation.'[134]

This may cut the number of PTDs being awarded and may end up in more work for the not-for-profit sector as clients seek alternative advice.

Trustee's refusal to discharge the debtor

A trustee can refuse to discharge a client of their debts.[135]

If, on request of the debtor, or at the end of the 48-month payment period, the trustee considers that an application for the client's discharge is not appropriate, the trustee must inform the client in writing and state:
- the reasons why they do not consider discharge appropriate; *and*
- that the client is not discharged from their debts; *and*
- the client's right to appeal the trustee's decision.

A copy should be sent to the AiB within 21 days of the trustee issuing their notification. If the trustee refuses to discharge the client, they are not discharged from their debts.

The trustee may still seek their own discharge from the creditors, even if they refuse to discharge the client.

It is good practice for the trustee to notify the creditors if the client is to be discharged or not.

Where the PTD is administered in line with the PTD protocol, when wishing to refuse the client's discharge, the trustee must first submit to the AiB a 'Refusal of Debtor Discharge' document.[136]

Due to the significant implications for a client if they are not discharged from their PTD debts, the trustee is asked to explain the reasons for their decision in an agreed format, for AiB to consider, before the issue of the notice to the client.

If the AiB disagrees with the trustee's decision, it contacts the trustee to discuss matters.

Accountant in Bankruptcy direction to trustee

If the trustee and the AiB cannot agree and it remains the trustee's wish that the client is not discharged, the AiB may issue a 'Direction to the Trustee' directing the trustee to discharge the client.[137] This direction can be appealed by the trustee.[138]

Court direction

The client can further seek a direction from a sheriff, if they do not agree with the intention of their trustee to withhold their discharge.[139] A direction can be asked for at any time.

Appeals

A client may also appeal a decision to the sheriff court within 21 days.[140]

Discharge of the trustee

Once the final distribution of the trust deed has been made, and the client has been discharged or refused discharge, the trustee can apply to the creditors and the AiB for their own discharge. This ends the trust deed.

Details of the discharge process for client and trustee can be found in section 186 of the Act and section 10 of the PTD.

The trustee is required to seek their discharge from creditors within 28 days of the final distribution under the PTD.

The trustee applies to the creditors and the AiB using Form 6 in the Protected Trust Deeds (Forms) (Scotland) Regulations 2016. The final distribution date is considered to be the date the estate is no longer under the control of the trustee.

The trustee's discharge depends on the consent (actual and deemed) of a majority in value of creditors within 14 days of the issue of Form 6.

A creditor who does not respond to the form within 14 days from the date it is issued is deemed to consent to the trustee's discharge.

The discharge of the trustee releases them from any liability to the creditors in respect of any act or omission in exercising the functions conferred on them by the Bankruptcy (Scotland) Act 1985 and the Bankruptcy (Scotland) Act 2016, except for a liability arising from fraud.

If the creditors refuse to discharge the trustee, the trustee has a right of appeal to a sheriff.

Within 28 days of the discharge of the trustee, the trustee sends a statement to the AiB in Form 7 and the AiB will record this in the Register of Insolvencies. This brings the protected trust deed to an end.

Recall

There is no recall procedure for a trust deed.

Complaints

In the first instance, complaints about a trustee in a trust deed should be made to the trustee. If that is unsuccessful, the client can raise a complaint with their registered professional body through the Insolvency Service Complaints Gateway.[141] They can then apply to the AiB for a direction and, if that fails, go to the sheriff court for a direction from the sheriff.

Complaints about insolvency practitioners are made to the Insolvency Service. It issues the complaint to the relevant registered professional body and oversees the response.[142]

Checklist

- Have a list of insolvency practitioners you can contact to make a referral.
- Check that a PTD is the correct solution for a client.
- Fully explain the pros and cons of a PTD to the client.
- Check to see if the family home can be protected.
- Check what will happen with any vehicles.
- Fully complete a common financial statement.
- Tell the client to come back to you if there are any problems.

8. Common rules in bankruptcy

The Accountant in Bankruptcy (AiB) provides guidance to trustees and debt advisers in *Notes for Guidance – Bankruptcy (Scotland) Act 2016 (as amended)*.[143] It covers most of the small detail and is easier read and to understand than the legislation. It applies to Minimal Asset Process (MAP) bankruptcy, Full Administration Bankruptcy (FAB) and creditor petitions.

Separate guidance is issued for protected trust deeds (PTDs).

Income

At the date of sequestration, income vests with the trustee, but it does not during the bankruptcy period. However, the trustee is entitled to seek a contribution from such and will be 100 per cent of the disposable income – the debtor contribution order (DCO). In a MAP application, this must be zero.

What the income from which a contribution can be taken is listed in Appendix A of the Common Financial Tool guidance.[144] See also p119.

Pensions

If the client receives a pension and it falls into the 'approved' category, it may be classed as income and a contribution may be sought by the trustee. The pension itself does not vest in the trustee.

However, some 'unapproved' pensions can vest in the trustee. This is a complicated matter. It is covered by the Occupational and Personal Pension Schemes (Bankruptcy) Regulations 2002. Get advice from the AiB if this comes up.

Child support

At the date of sequestration, any arrears of child maintenance are included in the bankruptcy application and discharges.

If a deduction from earnings order (DEO) is in place, the bankruptcy stops it and there should be no further collection of the arrears after the date of sequestration.

The DEO should be noted on the BASYS online system so that the AiB can get it stopped.

The client must continue to pay ongoing liabilities.

Redundancy

When a client receives a redundancy payment, it can be difficult to determine what counts as income (and therefore subject to a contribution) and what vests in the trustee as 'acquirenda' (see p192). The AiB guidance helps clarify this for advisers:
- statutory pay in lieu of notice (PILON): income;
- enhanced or voluntary PILON: acquirenda vested in the trustee;
- statutory redundancy pay: income;
- enhanced or voluntary redundancy pay: acquirenda vested in the trustee;
- other ex-gratia payments: acquirenda vested in the trustee.

Once a client has received their statutory redundancy payment, the trustee should consider whether a contribution or increased contribution should be sought.

Where this occurs, or is likely to occur, seek guidance from the AiB before making an application.

Criminal injuries compensation

The compensation itself does not vest in the trustee, but they can seek a contribution from any payments made.

If this happens before the client's discharge from MAP, it could lead to them being moved onto the FAB process.

Seek clarification from the AiB before making the application.

Critical illness

Any lump-sum payments from a claim for critical illness vests in the trustee.

Any income received is also subject to a contribution. This could lead to an increase in the DCO.

This could lead to both acquirenda and an increase in disposable income.

In a MAP case, ensure you ask the client these questions, as it may lead to the case being transferred to the FAB process.

Assets

When making an application, clients are expected to detail all their income, assets and liabilities. Assets can include money held in a bank account, vehicles, property and life insurance policies.

Most, but not all, assets 'vest' in the trustee and it is their duty to try and realise the full value for the benefit of the creditors.

For MAP, there are limits on assets held, as follows.
- The total value of the client's assets (leaving out of account any liabilities) on the date the client application cannot exceed £2,000 or such other amount as may be prescribed.
- No single asset of the client can have a value which exceeds £1,000 or such other amount as may be prescribed.
- The client cannot own land.

Note: if the client acquires assets after discharge (six months), they may still need to inform the AiB, as per section 3 of the Statement of Undertakings, and the case will be moved to the FAB process.

Money in bank accounts

When a trustee is appointed, they may notify all banks of their appointment and ask if there are any assets, in the form of money, in the account. They are then entitled to this money which forms part of the client's estate.

In a MAP, if there is more than £1,000 held in a bank account(s), the client will be refused the MAP application and moved to the FAB process.

Chapter 6: Statutory debt solutions in Scotland
8. Common rules in bankruptcy

If the client has more than one bank account, these can be counted as one single asset.

If they have a joint account, they will be deemed to have half of the asset.

Make sure that the client has less than this when they make the application. Timing can be vital.

In some cases, the client's bank account may be frozen. This will be because the bank has received notification from the trustee that the client is bankrupt.

Although a bank will not allow a bankrupt to maintain a normal current account, it is possible to have a bank account, as long as it does not allow an overdraft or the provision of credit.

This can happen even when there is no money in the account and can cause problems for ongoing bill payments etc.

To deal with this, the client is issued with a letter, along with their award certificate, which states the trustee has no objections to the client operating an account/s if they hold less than £2,000 after the award of bankruptcy. This letter must be taken to the nearest branch of the bank that has frozen the account.

It may also be advisable that the client gets a new, clean bank account before they apply for their own bankruptcy. Many banks operate a basic bank account for bankruptcy clients.

If there is a joint account, this can also be frozen and it is advisable to get both parties to open a separate account each before making the application.

Life assurance policies

These also vest in the trustee as part of the client's estate, and how the trustee deals with them will depend on whether there is a surrender value or not.

Any policy which has a surrender value will vest in the trustee for the duration of the bankruptcy and the trustee should attempt to realise the asset by surrendering the policy or having a third party buy out the trustee's interest.

If the surrender value of the policy is more than £1,000, the client will not qualify for a MAP.

Any policy which does not have a surrender value should be treated as a non-vested contingent asset which will vest in the trustee for a period of four years from the date of sequestration.

Should the asset be realised, it will form part of the client's estate and vest in the trustee for the benefit of the creditors.

If the policy is put 'in trust', it does not vest in the trustee.

However, if the client is the beneficiary of the trust, and it becomes due during the four years from the date of sequestration, it does then vest in the trustee.

It may be worthwhile asking the client to make sure all policies are put in trust for a family member and not themselves. You can do this with the help of a regulated financial adviser. There is usually no fee for this.

Further reading on trusts can be found at legalandgeneral.com/insurance/life-insurance/guides/life-insurance-trusts.

Vehicles

Vehicles worth £3,000 and under, and are needed by the client, do not vest in the trustee and are not counted as an asset.[145]

Vehicles worth over £3,000 exclude the client from entry into a MAP. They must go down the FAB route.

The following can be used to obtain a valuation:
- a reputable car dealer that clearly highlights the condition of the vehicle and the reasons for the valuation (eg, damage, high mileage);
- an independent car dealer, preferably on headed paper, highlighting the condition of the car and the reason for the valuation;
- Parkers (and similar companies) who provide an online valuation.

Valuations from companies offering quick access to cash (eg, WeBuyAnyCar, Arnold Clark, Motorpoint or Motorway) cannot be used to obtain a valuation. These companies offer below book price valuations.

If a client is unable to provide a valuation on headed paper as the dealer may be in a rural area, a full explanation from the money adviser detailing the condition of the car and the reason for not being able to provide a formal valuation must be provided.

Be aware that while this may go some way to progressing a case, it may not be possible in every case.

Remember that the AiB might value the vehicle and come up with a different valuation, so be careful and maybe get two or three valuations before applying if it is close to the £3,000 limit.

See the AiB *Debtor Application – evidence requirements checklist*.[146]

The family home

Under MAP criteria, your client cannot own any property. Therefore, if your client does own it in part or in whole, they must look at the FAB procedure.

For FAB, the family home is an asset and will vest in the trustee as at the date of sequestration.

If your client lives with someone and the title deeds are in the other person's name, it does not become part of the client's estate or vest in the trustee.

To be sure about this and if there are any doubts, obtain a copy of the title deeds from the Registers of Scotland.

If the title deeds are in the client's sole name, 100 per cent of the equity vests in the trustee. If it is in joint names, 50 per cent vests in the trustee. How the trustee deals with the asset is determined by how much equity there is. Where there is extensive equity, the trustee will more than likely want to sell the property and realise it for the benefit of the creditors. Where there is little or no realisable equity, the trustee has further options.

Tenancy agreements

When the client is declared bankrupt, there may be clauses within the tenancy agreement that nullify the agreement and can terminate the tenancy.

Therefore, check your clients' tenancy agreement before recommending bankruptcy.

Gratuitous alienation

This applies to all personal insolvency solutions.

A 'gratuitous alienation' is when property owned by the client is transferred to another person for free or less than its worth[147] – eg, if a client passed ownership of a house or vehicle to a spouse or family member before bankruptcy in an attempt to hide it.

The trustee can challenge an alienation which took place up to five years before the date of sequestration if the person receiving the alienation is a close family member or associate. If the person receiving the alienation is not an associate of the client, the time limit is two years. Remember, if a client owns property, they do not qualify for MAP.

If a trustee discovers that assets have been transferred, they can pursue the asset through the court, gain a decree of reduction and return it to the client's estate.

They can pursue both assets and money derived from the sale of assets.

An alienation can also be challenged by the creditors if they have information to that effect.

The court will not grant a decree of reduction if:
- immediately, or at any other time, after the alienation, the client's assets were greater than their liabilities; *or*
- the alienation was made for adequate consideration; *or*
- the alienation was:
  - a birthday, Christmas or other conventional gift; *or*
  - a gift made, for a charitable purpose, to a person who is not an associate of the client; *or*
  - a gift which, having regard to all the circumstances, it was reasonable for the client to make.

Unfair preference

This applies to all personal insolvency options.

An unfair preference is a payment made by the client to a creditor which is prejudicial to the interests of the other creditors[148] – eg, paying off a family debt just before going bankrupt.

The trustee could raise a statutory action for the 'reduction' of an unfair preference if it took place less than six months before the date of sequestration. If successful, the creditor who benefited will have to refund some or all of the money to the trustee.

Make sure you ask your clients if they have paid any debts in the last six months which could be consideredan unfair preference.

Acquirenda

This applies to all insolvency options.

Acquirenda are assets that the client gains up to four years after the date of sequestration – eg, an inheritance or lottery winnings.

During the period of insolvency, the client must notify their trustee of any acquired assets within 48 months of the date of sequestration.

This is included in the Statement of Undertakings in a bankruptcy (see Appendix 3) and within the terms of a trust deed.

Acquirenda received during a MAP may result in a conversion to the FAB process.

Assets discovered after the trustee's discharge

Where a trustee discovers that the client had assets during the 48-month period after the date of sequestration, but they were unaware of it at the time and later is made aware of them, the trustee can be reappointed for the purpose of 'in-gathering' the asset.

This must be done within five years of the date of sequestration, the asset must be of a value more than £1,000 and there must be a dividend to the creditor, or the asset will be returned to the client.

The process for discharged cases where an asset is discovered is as follows.
- Step 1: assets are identified and their value established.
- Step 2: review case for claims:
  – if there are any claims, the case is automatically sent for reopening;
  – if there are no claims, the trustee writes out giving them 21 days to submit a claim.
- Step 3:
  – if a claim is received, the case is reopened;
  – if no claims are received, the case is not reopened.

To reopen, there has to be a return to the creditor. So, if no claims are in the case, there is no point in reopening it.

Financial education

All clients can be asked to complete a course of financial education by their trustee. This should be done within the first six months of the bankruptcy.[149]

Failure or refusal to complete the course could lead to the client being refused discharge.

A client can be excused from completing the course if they cannot participate bacause of ill health, disability or mental illness, or if they have already finished the course within five years from the date of sequestration.

The client can be asked to complete a series of modules including budgeting and financial planning, saving, borrowing, insurance, tax, financial life stages (eg, renting or buying a home, having a baby and loss of employment) and welfare benefits.[150]

Interest on debts

Statutory interest applies at 2 per cent above the Bank of England base rate at the date of sequestration, but only where the debts can be repaid in full. In all other cases, there is no interest applied as this is frozen on the date of sequestration.[151]

Recall

Recall of a sequestration can be done in two ways.
- Recall through the AiB can only be done where the client can afford to pay all the debt owed plus trustee fees and outlays.
- Recall can be asked for by a client or a trustee, including the AiB.

Where the client believes they should not have been sequestrated, or for a reason such as the client not having been apparently insolvent, they can apply to the sheriff court to have it recalled.

For creditor petitions, all recall applications go through the court.

Bankruptcy Restriction Order

A Bankruptcy Restrictions Order (BRO) can be made by the AiB or the sheriff where a client behaves inappropriately before or after the date of sequestration.[152]

BROs were introduced to deter clients from misbehaving or being dishonest and to provide businesses and creditors with a level of protection. A BRO can help ensure that those who abuse the bankruptcy process face the consequences of their actions. This can include an appearance in front of a sheriff if the AiB deems the client's behaviour has been exceptionally serious.

It is normally made after the date of sequestration and before the discharge of the client (six months), but can be made after this time on application to the court by the AiB.

There are two time limits for this.
- Where the AiB make the order, it can last for between two and five years for less serious cases.

- Where the sheriff makes the order, it can last for between five and 15 years for more serious cases.

Trustees (or agents) have a duty to report any misconduct to the AiB.

What can be deemed as misconduct?
– Not co-operating with your trustee during the period of your bankruptcy.
– Incurring debts that you knew you had no reasonable chance of repaying.
– Giving away assets or selling them at less than their value.
– Deliberately paying off some creditors in preference to others.
– Gambling or making rash speculations or being unreasonably extravagant.
– Failing to keep or produce records that would explain a loss of money or property.
– Fraud or a fraudulent breach of trust.
– Causing your debts to increase by neglecting your business affairs.
– Failing to supply goods or services that have been paid for.
– Carrying on a business when you knew or ought to have known that you could not pay your debts.
– Failing to supply accurate information for the granting of a certificate for sequestration.

Restrictions

During the BRO period, the following restrictions apply.
- The client must disclose to a credit provider that they are subject to a BRO if they (alone or jointly with another person) wish to get credit of more than £2,000.
- The client must disclose to a credit provider that they are subject to a BRO if they wish to get credit of any amount and already have debts of £1,000 or more.
- The client must disclose to those they wish to do business with the name (or trading style) under which they were made bankrupt.
- The client cannot act as the director of a company or take part in its promotion, formation or management unless they get the court's permission to do so.
- The client cannot act as an insolvency practitioner or as the receiver or manager of the property of a company on behalf of debenture holders.

There are other restrictions that restrict jobs or positions a client can be appointed to.

The restrictions apply after the client has been discharged from bankruptcy for a further period of between two and 15 years, depending upon the level of the client's misconduct or dishonesty before and during their bankruptcy.

Where a BRO is being considered by either the AiB or the sheriff, they must inform the client who has 14 days to reply why the BRO should not be awarded.

Once the BRO is made, the client can apply to the court to have the BRO cancelled or the terms varied.

Non-compliance
If a client fails to comply with a BRO, they can be brought to court and ultimately they can face imprisonment.

Examination of the client
Where a trustee is not satisfied with a client's behaviour or they need more information, they can request the client or any other 'relevant person' to come to a meeting to discuss the issue.

Where the client or other relevant person refuses or does not give the requested information, the trustee can apply to the courts for a hearing before a sheriff.

Failure to comply and attend can lead to a fine, a period of imprisonment of less than three months, or both.

Discharge of the client and the trustee
Part 11 of the Bankruptcy (Scotland) Act 2016 covers the discharge process for both the client and the trustee.

Client discharge
In a FAB case, the client is normally discharged from their debts in 12 months.[153] This does not mean they have no other responsibilities under the bankruptcy. The acquirenda rules still apply for 48 months after the date of sequestration. However, discharge is not automatic and needs to be requested by the trustee. The trustee must recommend the client's discharge to the AiB within 10 months of the date of sequestration. Alternatively, they can recommend that the client is not discharged. This could be due to non-co-operation with the trustee or non-compliance with the DCO.[154] If the situation is resolved, the trustee can submit a subsequent report to recommend the client's discharge. Where the AiB is the trustee, it follows the same process and decides, within 12 months of the date of sequestration, whether to discharge the client or not.

In a MAP case, the client is normally discharged from their debts in six months.[155] This does not mean they have no other responsibilities under the bankruptcy. The acquirenda rules still apply for 48 months after the date of sequestration. Where the trustee disagrees that the client has co-operated fully, they can delay their discharge. Where the client has co-operated fully with the trustee, the client is automatically discharged six months after the date of bankruptcy. A certificate of discharge is issued automatically and posted to the client.

When the client is discharged, they are discharged of any liabilities due at the date of sequestration.

However, not all debts discharge. For example, an obligation to pay aliment or a periodical allowance payable on divorce is not discharged by:[156]
- any liability to pay a fine or other penalty due to the Crown;
- any liability to pay a fine imposed in a justice of the peace court (or a district court);
- any liability under a compensation order (within the meaning of section 249 of the Criminal Procedure (Scotland) Act 1995);
- any liability to forfeiture of a sum of money deposited in court under section 24(6) of the Criminal Procedure (Scotland) Act 1995;
- any liability incurred because of fraud or breach of trust.

While being discharged of their debts, the client still has obligations under the bankruptcy and the acquirenda rules apply.

Trustee discharge

Where the trustee has completed their administration of the client's estate, and where the DCO has been completed satisfactorily, they can apply for their own discharge.[157] The trustee must also notify the client and the creditors of the application for discharge. After 14 days and if no objections have been lodged (and further time for appeal if required), the AiB discharges the trustee. The discharge is entered on the Register of Insolvencies. This effectively ends the period of sequestration for the client.

Complaints

Complaints about how the AiB, acting as trustee (in all MAP cases the AiB is the trustee), can be made direct to the AiB through its complaints procedure.

If there is an agent acting on the AiB's behalf, the complaint should be addressed first of all to them.

If the client is still not satisfied, then they can complain to the AiB.

If the client is still not satisfied with a decision of the trustee, they can either raise an action (appeal a decision of the trustee) in the sheriff court or, make a complaint to the Scottish Public Services Ombudsman (SPSO). See spso.org.uk for how to do this.

The SPSO can investigate several areas of complaints including:
- a complaint that has not gone through the AiB full complaints process;
- events that happened, or that your client became aware of, more than a year ago;
- a matter that has been, or is being, considered in court;
- a complaint regarding a data protection or freedom of information matter;
- a complaint for which there is another process by which you can complain – eg, a decision by a trustee which can be appealed to a sheriff.

Debtor contribution order

DCOs are regulated by Part 6 of the Bankruptcy (Scotland) Act 2016.

All bankruptcy cases have a DCO, even if it is zero.

The DCO is decided by the AiB, not the debt adviser.

When the client has taken advice from a debt adviser and they have used the CFT, all surplus income must be used as a contribution. (Unlike DAS where the client does not have to make a full contribution.)

In MAP cases, there must be a zero contribution (or the client must have benefit-only income), so advisers should work with the client and the CFT to try to get the contribution to zero, or even show a negative budget.

This is important because if the CFT is not completed correctly, the AiB may change the contribution and move the client onto the FAB process, lengthening the discharge process.

If the AiB refuses to award a MAP bankruptcy, the client can request a review within 21 days if they disagree with the AiB's decision. The client can further appeal to the sheriff court within 14 days if they disagree with the review decision.[158]

Certificate for Sequestration

A Certificate for Sequestration of the client's estate is a certificate granted by an authorised money or debt adviser (or other authorised persons) certifying that the client cannot pay debts as they become due.[159]

No fee can be charged for completion of the certificate.[160]

Who is an authorised person?

An authorised person includes anyone who:[161]
- is qualified to act as an insolvency practitioner under section 390 of the Insolvency Act 1986; *or*
- is an individual who works for such an insolvency practitioner and has been given authority by that practitioner to act on the practitioner's behalf as a money adviser for the purposes of the DAS; *or*
- works as a money adviser for organisations which have been awarded accreditation at type II level or above against the *Scottish National Standards for Information and Advice Providers* (see p2); *or*
- works as a money adviser for a Citizens Advice Bureau which is a full member of Citizens Advice Scotland (see p5); *or*
- works as a money adviser for a local authority; *or*
- is approved for the purposes of the DAS.

A debt adviser must grant a certificate only if the client can demonstrate that they are unable to pay their debts as they become due.

The certificate must be in Form 2, be signed by the debt adviser and the client, be on the organisation's headed paper and be less than 30 days old.

A copy of the certificate can be found in Schedule 1 of the Regulations or on the AiB website.[162]

Before granting a Certificate for Sequestration, an authorised person must give the client advice on:[163]
- their income and expenditure in accordance with the CFT;
- the evidence required to confirm their debts;
- the Debt Advice and Information Package;
- the options of a voluntary repayment plan, debt payment programme under the DAS or a trust deed;
- the consequences of sequestration and that an award of sequestration, if granted, is recorded in a public register and may result in:
  – their being refused credit or being offered credit at a higher rate (before or after the date of being discharged);
  – their not being able to remain in their current place of residence;
  – damage to their business interests and employment prospects;
  – their still being liable for some debts;
  – their past financial transactions being investigated;
  – other restrictions or requirements being imposed.

Who cannot be approved debt advisers

The following cannot be approved debt advisers.[164]
- A sheriff officer or messenger-at-arms, or an employee of such a person.
- A person or body providing financial services, or financial advice other than debt advice, in the course of a business or otherwise for profit, or an employee of such a person, unless the person is a solicitor or chartered or certified accountant.
- A credit union registered under the Co-operative and Community Benefit Societies Act 2014 or the Industrial and Provident Societies Act 1965 by virtue of section 1 of the Credit Unions Act 1979.
- A person providing debt collection services, or an employee of such a person.
- A person convicted of an offence involving theft, fraud or other dishonesty.
- A person subject to a BRO (including an interim order) under section 155 or 160 of the Bankruptcy (Scotland) Act 2016 or subject to a BRO, or bound by a bankruptcy restrictions undertaking, under schedule 4A of the Insolvency Act 1986.
- A person in respect of whom a court has made a disqualification order under section 1, or who has had a disqualification undertaking accepted under section 1A, of the Company Directors Disqualification Act 1986.
- Persons without a licence from the Money Advice Trust to use the Common Financial Statement.

Revocation or suspension of an approved debt adviser

The AiB can revoke or suspend an approved debt adviser if they fail to apply the CFT accordingly or do not maintain records of advice given.

A debt adviser must obtain evidence of a client's income and expenditure and retain all records for two years and provide this information to the AiB on request.[165]

Award by the Accountant in Bankruptcy

Bankruptcy, by whichever route is taken, is awarded by the AiB and advertised on the Register of Insolvencies.

There are exclusions from advertising if the client has a genuine reason for that information not to be made public. The AiB must agree that publication would likely jeopardise the client's safety or welfare – eg, where they are fleeing an abusive relationship and do not want to be found. Apply by completing the 'sensitivity obligation' section on the application. The client may have to provide evidence – eg, a police report.

The AiB can refuse to award bankruptcy if it thinks the application is inappropriate or return it to the adviser if it thinks it is incomplete. The adviser then has 21 days to update the application, or it will be refused.

9. Statutory moratorium on diligence

In April 2015, the Bankruptcy and Debt Advice (Scotland) Act 2014 introduced a statutory moratorium on diligence providing protection for those needing time to get advice, resolve their debt problems and consider the most appropriate solution. It is now covered under Part 15 of the Bankruptcy (Scotland) Act 2016.

What is a statutory moratorium

A **'statutory moratorium'** is a six-month period which prevents creditors taking any diligence action against a client.

If a client is thinking of applying for bankruptcy, a trust deed or the Debt Arrangement Scheme (DAS) and requires more time to think things over, but they (or you) are concerned about what their creditors could do in the meantime, an application for a statutory moratorium can be made.

What can a statutory moratorium do

A statutory moratorium can:[166]
- stop the service of a charge for payment;
- stop a creditor's application for bankruptcy;
- stop the service of a wage arrestment;

- stop the service of a bank arrestment and freeze the process of an ongoing bank arrestment;
- stop or freeze an application for an attachment;
- stop or freeze an application for an exceptional attachment.

Creditors can still follow the debt collection process, serving arrears and default notices, etc. as well as registering defaults on the client's credit file. They can also apply charges and interest and contact the client.

What can a statutory moratorium cannot do

A statutory moratorium cannot:[167]
- stop an application to the courts for a decree;
- stop a decree being issued;
- stop an earnings arrestment that is already in place;
- stop a creditor's petition for sequestration that has already been applied for;
- stop a direct earnings attachment (DEA), deductions from earnings order (DEO) or other non-diligence procedures;
- stop an inhibition from being applied;
- stop a charge for removal being served or an eviction;
- stop repossession in a hire purchase or similar agreement;
- stop an energy provider installing a prepayment meter.

Creditors can still follow the debt collection process, serving arrears and default notices, etc. as well as registering defaults on the client's credit file. They can also apply charges and interest and contact the client.

Making an application

An application can be accessed and submitted to the Accountant in Bankruptcy (AiB) through the Register of Insolvencies homepage.[168] Form 33 is used where the applicant is an individual person or the executor of a deceased person's estate. Form 34 is used for entities – eg, partnerships or trusts.

Alternatively, the forms can be completed, signed, scanned and emailed to the AiB's insolvency registrations team at moratorium@aib.gov.uk or posted to Moratorium Application, IRT, Accountant in Bankruptcy, 1 Pennyburn Road, Kilwinning KA13 6SA.

It is recommended that clients read the AiB's privacy statement before completing the form.[169]

If the moratorium is granted, the AiB registers this on the Register of Insolvencies and the DAS Register. From this date, the client thas six months to decide whether they want to proceed with an application for a statutory debt option. During the six months, the creditors cannot commence diligence, serve a charge for payment or apply to the court for the client's bankruptcy.

In most cases, the client can only apply for one statutory moratorium in a 12-month period.

Period of moratorium

A moratorium ends six months from the day it was registered in the Register of Insolvencies or earlier if:[170]
- an entry is made in the Register of Insolvencies recording the award of sequestration of the estate;
- an entry is made in the Register of Insolvencies recording that a trust deed granted by the person has been granted or refused protected status;
- an entry is made in the DAS Register recording the approval of a Debt Payment Programme (DPP);
- written notice is made from the client or on their behalf withdrawing the moratorium.

Adviser tips

Using a statutory moratorium is all about timing. As a client can only access it once in any 12-month period, do not waste the chance.

It only covers the diligences listed in the legislation and does not work with DEAs and DEOs. Other solutions can be found for these.

It gives you and your client time to work out a longer-lasting debt solution suitable to their needs.

When you or the client have lodged a statutory moratorium, remember to inform the creditors who could serve a charge for payment or commence diligence – eg, a sheriff officer recovering council tax arrears as they have no statutory duty to check the Register of Insolvencies.

The situation with bank account arrestments can be confusing. Most creditors do not need to serve a charge for payment before arresting a bank account. Only local authorities and HMRC need to complete this stage. Therefore, the earliest you should apply would be when the decree has been awarded and extracted if the debt is not for council tax.

When a bank arrestment has been served, a statutory moratorium stops the money being automatically released after 14 weeks, allowing you or the client time to challenge the arrestment in court or apply for a bankruptcy or protected trust deed (PTD).

Chapter 6: Statutory debt solutions in Scotland
9. Statutory moratorium on diligence

Ready reckoner

Where in the process	What a statutory moratorium does and does not do	Adviser tactics
Debt letters	A moratorium has no effect at this time.	Do not apply.
Default notice	A moratorium has no effect at this time.	Do not apply.
Writ, summons or claim	A moratorium has no effect at this time.	Do not apply.
At court	A moratorium has no effect at this time.	Do not apply.
Summary warrant granted	A moratorium does not stop a summary warrant from being granted. A summary warrant in pursuit of council tax arrears is followed by a charge for payment.	Do not apply at this stage; wait until the charge for payment has been served.
Decree granted	A moratorium does not stop the decree being granted, but does stop the charge for payment being served. It also prevents a bank arrestment being executed (non-summary warrant) as there is no need for a charge for payment to be served for this process.	Apply at this stage (or wait until the decree has been extracted) to prevent a bank arrestment. Remember, for a bank arrestment (not under summary warrant), there is no need to serve a charge for payment so this would be the earliest time to apply. Only summary warrant debts need to serve a charge for payment before arresting a bank account.

Chapter 6: Statutory debt solutions in Scotland
9. Statutory moratorium on diligence

Stage	Normal process	Moratorium action
Decree extracted	The normal process is that once a decree has been awarded, there is a 14-day time limit to allow for appeals to be made. The creditor then has to 'extract' the decree before executing diligence.	Apply at this stage to prevent a bank account arrestment. Remember only the local authority/HMRC needs to serve a charge for payment before executing a bank arrestment. If the debt is for council tax, wait until the charge for payment has been served and almost expired.
Charge for payment served	Apply at this stage and it prevents a wage arrestment, attachment or exceptional attachment being served. It also prevents a creditor from applying for the client's bankruptcy as an expired charge constitutes apparent insolvency.	Apply at this stage to prevent further diligence being carried out.
Statutory demand served	When a statutory demand is served, it is an indication that the creditor is considering bankruptcy, as once expired it constitutes apparent insolvency.	Send the statutory demand back and deny the debt. This makes the creditor follow normal court and diligence procedures and takes it back to the writ/summons/claim stage. Or apply for a moratorium once the 21-day limit is almost up, which stops a creditor's petition for bankruptcy.
Bank account arrested	A moratorium does not lift the bank arrestment but freezes the money in the account. The bank cannot send it to the creditor.	Apply at this stage to freeze the money and then look at a DPP, PTD or bankruptcy and the client may get the money returned once in place.

Chapter 6: Statutory debt solutions in Scotland
9. Statutory moratorium on diligence

Earnings arrestment schedule served	A moratorium does not stop a wages arrestment that came into force before the moratorium period commenced.	No use in applying here; the client is too late if the arrestment has been executed. Try looking at a time to pay order (TTPO), DAS or insolvency options.
Attachment	A moratorium stops the attachment unless the goods have been removed for auction or notice of auction has been given.	Apply to freeze the process. Use a TTPO or apply to have the attachment recalled. DAS and insolvency are also options.
Exceptional attachment	A moratorium stops the exceptional attachment unless the goods have been removed for auction or notice of auction has been given.	Apply before the goods have been removed or the notice of auction has been given. Use a TTPO or apply to have the attachment recalled. DAS and insolvency are also options.
Mortgage repossession proceedings	A decree for repossession is normally in two parts – one for payment of money (arrears) due and the other for repossession. A moratorium does not stop the repossession proceedings, but it can be used to stop the claim for money as with all other forms of diligence.	Apply for a moratorium to prevent diligence for the money part of the claim. In this case, a DAS may be the best option, include the arrears within the DPP. This is at the sheriff's discretion. Ask the sheriff to continue the case to set up a DPP for the arrears. Take advice.

Chapter 6: Statutory debt solutions in Scotland
Notes

Eviction proceedings	A decree for eviction is normally in two parts – one for payment of money (arrears) due and the other for eviction. A moratorium does not stop the eviction proceedings, but bankruptcy may be used to stop the claim for money as the debt will no longer be 'lawfully due'.	Apply for a moratorium to prevent diligence for the money part of the claim. In this case, a DAS or bankruptcy may be the best option as a bankruptcy including the arrears may stop the proceedings going ahead and a DAS can include the arrears. This is at the sheriff's discretion. **Note**: the proceedings may include a ground for eviction due to other reasons. Take advice.
Direct earnings attachment	No effect. It does not stop or freeze the DEA.	Do not apply for bankruptcy. A DAS or a PTD could work here.
Deduction from earnings order	No effect. It does not stop or freeze the DEO.	Do not apply for bankruptcy. A DAS or a PTD could work for arrears only.
Inhibition	No effect. It does not stop or freeze the inhibition.	Do not apply.

Notes

2. **The Common Financial Tool**
    1. Reg 15 B(S) Regs; reg 3 CFT(S) Regs
    2. CFT guidance, ss1 and 1.8
    3. aib.gov.uk/publications/notes-for-guidance-common-financial-tool
    4. Reg 15 B(S) Regs; reg 3 CFT(S) Regs
    5. CFT guidance, s2.18
    6. CFT guidance, Appendix A
    7. s86 B(S)A 2016
    8. Sheriff Murphy, Glasgow Sheriff Court, 10 August 1990
    9. Defined by s79(5) B(S)A 2016
    10. CFT guidance, Appendix A
    11. Reg 15(3) B(S)A Regs; reg 3(3) CFT(S) Regs

Chapter 6: Statutory debt solutions in Scotland
Notes

12 aib.gov.uk/publications/notes-for-guidance-common-financial-tool/6-essential-expenditure#publication-content
13 s16 B(S)A 2016

3. The Debt Arrangement Scheme
14 Reg 12 DAS(S) Regs
15 Reg 8 DAS(S) Regs
16 Reg 9 DAS(S) Regs
17 Reg 9 DAS(S) Regs
18 Reg 10 DAS(S) Regs
19 Reg 11 DAS(S) Regs
20 Part 15 B(S)A 2016
21 Reg 21 DAS(S) Regs
22 Reg 20 DAS(S) Regs
23 Reg 21 DAS(S) Regs
24 Reg 22 DAS(S) Regs
25 Reg 28(4) DAS(S) Regs
26 Reg 23 DAS(S) Regs
27 Reg 25 DAS(S) Regs
28 Reg 25 DAS(S) Regs
29 AiB Debt Arrangement Scheme Guidance for debt advisers, 7.6
30 Reg 33 DAS(S) Regs
31 Reg 36 DAS(S) Regs
32 Reg 11 DAS(S) Regs
33 Reg 37(h) DAS(S) Regs
34 Reg 38 DAS(S) Regs
35 Reg 38 DAS(S) Regs
36 Reg 38 DAS(S) Regs
37 Reg 39 DAS(S) Regs
38 Part 8 DAS(S) Regs
39 Reg 41 DAS(S) Regs
40 Reg 42 DAS(S) Regs
41 Reg 22 DAS(S) Regs
42 s195(1) B(S)A 2016
43 Reg 4(4) DAS(IFP)(S) Regs
44 Reg 46 DAS(S) Regs
45 Reg 46 DAS(S) Regs
46 Reg 15 DAS(S) Regs

4. The Minimal Asset Process
47 s2(2) B(S)A 2016
48 Reg 8 B(S) Regs
49 Reg 9 B(S) Regs
50 Reg 7 B(S) Regs
51 s145 B(S)A 2016
52 Reg 11 B(S) Regs
53 s2(2)(i) B(S)A 2016
54 ss8(4) and 218(1) and (2) B(S)A 2016
55 Part 6 B(S)A 2016
56 s22 B(S)A 2016
57 Part 5 B(S)A 2016

5. Full Administration Bankruptcy
58 s8 B(S)A 2016
59 s4(1) B(S)A 2016
60 s2(8) B(S)A 2016
61 s16 B(S)A 2016
62 Reg 8 B(S) Regs
63 Reg 9 B(S) Regs
64 s145 B(S)A 2016
65 Reg 11 B(S) Regs
66 Reg 7B BF(S) Regs
67 Reg 7A BF(S) Regs
68 matricslearn.org.uk
69 aib.gov.uk/systems/basys
70 s95 B(S)A 2016
71 s96 B(S)A 2016
72 s96 B(S)A 2016
73 legislation.gov.uk/ssi/2016/397/schedule/1
74 s22 B(S)A 2016
75 Part 5 B(S)A 2016
76 legislation.gov.uk/ssi/2016/397/schedule/1
77 s94 B(S)A 2016
78 Reg 7 B(S) Regs

6. Creditor petitions for bankruptcy
79 s7 B(S)A 2016
80 s3 B(S)A 2016
81 s16 B(S)A 2016
82 scotcourts.gov.uk/rules-and-practice/forms/sheriff-court-forms/bankruptcy-forms-2016-rules; Sch 1 AoS(SCB) Rules
83 s22 B(S)A 2016
84 Ch4 AoS(SCB) Rules
85 s197(3)(c) B(S)A 2016
86 s4(3) DAA(S) 2002
87 s23(3) B(S)A 2016
88 ss17 and 18 B(S)A 2016
89 s29 B(S)A 2016
90 legislation.gov.uk/ssi/2016/397/schedule/1
91 s197(3)(c) B(S)A 2016
92 Reg 30 DAS(S) Regs
93 s4(3) DAA(S)A 2002
94 s23 (3) B(S)A 2016

7. Protected trust deeds
95 legislation.gov.uk/sdsi/2016/9780111033173/schedule
96 s164(1) B(S)A 2016
97 s164(2) B(S)A 2016
98 s177(1)(a) B(S)A 2016
99 s183 B(S)A 2016
100 s184 B(S)A 2016
101 s16 B(S)A 2016
102 legislation.gov.uk/sdsi/2016/9780111033173/schedule
103 s169 B(S)A 2016
104 s170 B(S)A 2016
105 s170 B(S)A 2016
106 s171(1)(c) B(S)A 2016

107 s172 B(S)A 2016
108 s177(1) B(S)A 2016
109 s171 B(S)A 2016
110 s163 B(S)A 2016
111 s172(3) B(S)A 2016
112 s173 B(S)A 2016
113 s184B B(S)A 2016
114 s184C B(S)A 2016
115 s168 B(S)A 2016
116 s174 B(S)A 2016
117 s174 B(S)A 2016
118 s174(2) B(S)A 2016
119 s174(3) B(S)A 2016
120 s166(2) B(S)A 2016
121 aib.gov.uk/publications/notes-for-guidance-protected-trust-deeds-bankruptcy-scotland-act-2016
122 aib.gov.uk/publications/notes-for-guidance-protected-trust-deeds-bankruptcy-scotland-act-2016
123 s167 B(S)A) 2016
124 s167 B(S)A) 2016
125 s167 B(S)A) 2016
126 s10(2) BD(S)A 2024
127 aib.gov.uk/debt-solutions/protected-trust-deeds/ptd-protocol
128 PTD protocol, para 9.1, aib.gov.uk/publications/notes-for-guidance-protected-trust-deeds-bankruptcy-scotland-act-2016/8-debtors-discharge/84-effect-of-discharge#publication-content
129 legislation.gov.uk/sdsi/2016/9780111033173/schedule
130 s184(2) and (3) B(S)A 2016
131 s184 (6) B(S)A 2016
132 Policy Statement PS23/5, available at fca.org.uk/publication/policy/ps23-5.pdf
133 Policy Statement PS23/5
134 Policy Statement PS23/5, para 1.23
135 s184(4) B(S)A 2016
136 aib.gov.uk/debt-solutions/protected-trust-deeds/ptd-protocol
137 s179(1) B(S)A 1996
138 s188(1) B(S)A 1996
139 s189(1) B(S)A 1996
140 s188 B(S)A 1996
141 gov.uk/government/publications/insolvency-practitioners-guidance-for-those-who-want-to-complain/insolvency-practitioners-guidance-on-how-to-complain-about-an-insolvency-practitioner
142 gov.uk/government/publications/insolvency-practitioners-guidance-for-those-who-want-to-complain

8. Common rules in bankruptcy
143 aib.gov.uk/publications/notes-for-guidance-bankruptcy-scotland-act-2016-as-amended
144 aib.gov.uk/publications/notes-for-guidance-common-financial-tool/appendix-a-income-sources-from-which-a-contribution-can-be-taken#publication-content
145 s2(3)(b) B(S)A 2016
146 aib.gov.uk/publications/debtor-application-evidence-requirements-checklist
147 s98 B(S)A 2016
148 s99 B(S)A 2016
149 s117 B(S)A 2016
150 Reg 25 B(S) Regs
151 Reg 26 B(S) Regs
152 Part 13 B(S)A 2016
153 s137(2) B(S)A 2016
154 s137(4)(a) B(S)A 2016
155 s140 B(S)A 2016
156 s145 B(S)A 2016
157 s148 B(S) A 2016
158 Part 6 B(S)A 2016
159 Reg 8 B(S) Regs
160 Reg 9 B(S) Regs
161 Reg 3 B(CS)(S) Regs
162 aib.gov.uk/publications/form-2-certificate-for-sequestration
163 Reg 6 B(S) Regs
164 Reg 5 B(S) Regs
165 Reg 7 B(S) Regs

9. Statutory moratorium on diligence
166 s197 B(S)A 1996
167 s197 B(S)A 2016
168 roi.aib.gov.uk/roi/Moratoriums/Moratorium/Create
169 aib.gov.uk/contact/privacy-and-data-protection
170 s198 B(S)A 2016

Chapter 7

Money claims in the sheriff court

This chapter covers:
1. Introduction (below)
2. Simple procedure (below)
3. Ordinary cause (p220)
4. Summary warrant (p230)

1. Introduction

In Scotland, civil actions are handled by local sheriff courts, which are arranged into six sheriffdoms led by a sheriff principal. Sheriff courts have exclusive jurisdiction over all civil cases with a monetary value up to £100,000.

2. Simple procedure

This section covers simple procedure money claims in the sheriff court. The Act of Sederunt (Simple Procedure) 2016 ('the Simple Procedure Rules') provides the rules of court, forms and a set of standard orders.

Simple procedure replaced small claims actions in November 2016. It is used for money claims of £5,000 and less. It is designed to be quicker, cheaper and easier to follow for those raising an action or defending an action against them. There are rules for each step in the process and corresponding forms. It is raised in the sheriff court when a claim is made against a party known as a 'respondent'. Decisions are made by a sheriff or a summary sheriff. Solicitors are not required under simple procedure but can be used.

Sheriff and summary sheriff

The Courts Reform (Scotland) Act 2014 created a new judicial office in the sheriff court, known as the **'summary sheriff'**. A summary sheriff sits in the sheriff court, but with a restricted jurisdiction. They are able to conduct simple procedure and summary cause cases (under £5,000 in value). In this chapter, when we refer to '**sheriff**', this includes summary sheriffs, as under simple procedure they have the same powers.

How an action is raised

Before an action can be raised, the claimant must try to resolve the dispute by negotiation or by using alternative dispute resolution (ADR). For example, the claimant might write to the person or company that they have a dispute with. Going to court should always be a last resort.

How an action is raised is covered in Part 3 of the Simple Procedure Rules.

Simple procedure is initiated by the submission of a claim form (Form 3A), which provides the court with details on the following.
- **The parties.** In any simple procedure action, the claimant and the respondents are the only parties. The person who makes the claim is called the 'claimant'. The person the claim is made against is called the 'respondent'.
- **Circumstances of the dispute.** The claimant outlines in Parts D1–4 of the claim form all information they want to be considered in their dispute.
- **What the claimant is seeking.** The claimant outlines in Part D5 of the claim form what they are seeking from the respondent.
- **Why the claimant should succeed.** The claimant outlines in Part D7 of the claim form what they are seeking from the respondent.

Simple procedure claims should be submitted using Civil Online at scotcourts.gov.uk/taking-action/civil-online-gateway. If it cannot be submitted electronically, the claimant must contact the local sheriff court to seek the approval of the sheriff for the claim to proceed in paper format.

After the form has been registered, the court issues a timetable of actions to be taken. These actions include the deadlines to serve the claim form to the respondent and for the respondent to reply to the court.

Provisional orders

Provisional orders protect or secure the claimant's position before the sheriff makes a final decision in a case. Part 20 of the Simple Procedure Rules outlines how the claimant can apply for provisional orders.

There are three types of provisional orders a claimant can request.[1]
- **Arrestment on the dependence** under section 15A(1) of the Debtors (Scotland) Act 1987 – this is an order freezing the respondent's goods or money held by a third party.
- **Inhibition on the dependence** under section 15A(1) of the Debtors (Scotland) Act 1987 – this is an order preventing the respondent from selling their home or other land, or taking out a secured loan.

Chapter 7: Money claims in the sheriff court
2. Simple procedure

- **Interim attachment** under section 9A(1) of the Debt Arrangement and Attachment (Scotland) Act 2002 – this is an order preventing the respondent from selling or removing their goods.

Filing and serving documents

When completing Form 3A, the claimant decides whether they want to 'send' or 'formally serve' the claim form (C.10). If they choose to send the claim form, they must follow Part 6 in Schedule 1 of the Simple Procedure Rules.

Part 6.7 Simple Procedure Rules: How can a party send something to another party?

(1) A party may send something to another party in one of four ways:

(a) posting it to that party or that party's representative using a next-day postal service which records delivery;

(b) emailing it to that party or that party's representative, using an email address given on the claim form, 'response form' or 'time to pay application';

(c) making it available to that party or that party's representative using the portal on the Scottish Courts and Tribunals Service website;

(d) delivering it to a document exchange of which that party or that party's representative is a member.

(2) If none of those ways has worked, a party may send it to another party by sheriff officer using one of the methods of formal service mentioned in Part 18.

If the documents are to be 'served' formally, that may only be done by a solicitor, a sheriff officer or the sheriff clerk and must follow Part 18.

When these rules require a document to be formally served, the first attempt must be by a next-day postal service which records delivery. If service by post has not worked, a sheriff officer may formally serve a document in one of three ways:
- delivering it personally; *or*
- leaving it in the hands of a resident at the person's home; *or*
- leaving it in the hands of an employee at the person's place of business.

If the claimant is required to formally serve the documents (in the claim) on the respondent, they must also complete Form 6C and return it to the court.

Timetable

After a claim form has been accepted, the sheriff clerk issues a timetable for the case to the claimant. This includes:
- **the last date for service.**[2] This is the date by which the claim form must be formally served on the respondent. This must normally be three weeks before the last date for a response. **Note:** if the respondent does not live in a European

Union (EU) member state, the last date for service must normally be six weeks before the last date for a response, and if the respondent is a business with no place of business in an EU member state, the last date for service must normally be six weeks before the last date for a response; *and*
- the last date for a response.[3] This is the date by which the respondent must respond to the claim.[4]

Changing the timetable

The claimant, respondent and the sheriff can request the timetable be changed. This could be because of issues with serving the claim – eg, an address unknown or the form being served late. If the sheriff agrees to the timetable change, the sheriff clerk issues a new timetable to all parties.

Fees

In most cases, there is a fee for lodging a claim for simple procedure. Exemptions can be applied for if the claimant is eligible – eg, if they receive certain means-tested benefits. You can check the latest fees and exemption criteria at scotcourts.gov.uk/taking-action/court-fees.

There are also other costs if the claimant wishes to appeal. See scotcourts.gov.uk/rules-and-practice/fees/sheriff-appeal-court-fees for more information.

Understanding a simple procedure claim form

When a respondent is served a simple procedure claim form, it contains:
- a copy of the 'claim form' (Form 3A). This will have been completed by the claimant and should detail all the issues relating to the claim, including why the claim should succeed;
- a blank 'response form' (Form 4A). This form should be completed by the respondent and returned to the court before the expiry of the date for response if they want to respond to the claim;
- a copy of the timetable for the claim;
- a blank 'time to pay application' (Form 5A). If the respondent admits the claim but wants time to pay, they should complete this form and return it with the 'response form' (Form 4A) before the last date for response.

Responding to a simple procedure claim form

The respondent has three options when they receive a simple procedure claim form or they can opt to 'do nothing' and ignore the claim.

Admit the claim and settle it before the last date for a response

If the respondent wishes to avoid a court decision being made against them, they can settle the claim with the claimant before the deadline for a response. This avoids a court order being registered against the client and damaging their credit rating. Form 4A must be completed and returned to the court.

If the claim is settled this way, the claimant informs the court and the claim is dismissed.

Admit the claim and ask the court for time to pay

The respondent may admit the claim and ask to pay the sum by instalments or within a specified period. They can ask for time to pay by completing a 'time to pay application' (Form 5A) and return it using Civil Online,[5] by post or by handing it to the sheriff clerk's office.

After the application for time to pay has been received, the sheriff clerk sends a copy of the application with a 'time to pay notice' (Form 5B) to the claimant. The claimant then has two weeks to respond. The claimant either consents or does not consent to the time to pay application by competing and returning Form 5B to the sheriff court.

If the claimant has refused to consent to the time to pay application, a hearing will be set by the sheriff. If the claimant does not respond to Form 5B, the sheriff may call a hearing or may decide to grant or refuse the time to pay application.

Dispute the claim or part of the claim

If the respondent wishes to dispute the claim, a response must be sent to the court before the response deadline. This is done by completing sections C and D on Form 4A. The sheriff will then consider it and can take one of the following actions:
- refer both parties in the case for ADR;
- arrange a case management discussion;
- arrange a hearing;
- consider whether or not to make a 'decision' about the claim without a hearing;
- dismiss the claim or make a 'decision' because the claim is unlikely to be successful.

Do nothing

This is often used when waiting for proof of apparent insolvency or if the respondent has multiple debts and is looking to access a statutory option. The sheriff can in this instance make a 'decision in absence'. See p216 for more about decisions.

Alternative dispute resolution

ADR involves an informal meeting where parties express their views in private and attempt to reach a mutually agreeable solution. This process is also known as 'simple procedure mediation'. An independent mediator assists parties in identifying the issues and exploring possible resolutions. The mediator is not a decision maker; it is for the parties to decide on the terms of any agreement.

If mediation is successful, the court proceedings may be formally concluded without the need for any further input from the parties.

The majority of mediations are held face to face, but can be held by telephone or online. It should be noted that this can be expensive and, depending on the outcome, may increase court costs for all the parties involved.

Civil Online

Civil Online is an online service used for simple procedure cases. It is used to submit case documents and allows the parties involved to raise and respond to claims. It also contains up-to-date information about the case.

Civil Online can be accessed via Scottish Courts and Tribunals home page.[6]

What happens in a case

Part 7 of the Simple Procedure Rules outlines what happens after a response form has been received and what happens if no response form or time to pay application is received by the last date for a response.

When a response is received

After a response form has been received and looked at by the sheriff, certain actions will be taken.

If the response form indicates that the respondent admits the claim and will settle the claim before the date for response, the sheriff does not have to send orders to either party.

If the claimant then sends an 'application for a decision' to the court within two weeks of the last date for response, the sheriff can:[7]
- dismiss the claim; *or*
- make a decision awarding the claimant some or all of what was asked for in the claim form; *or*
- where a decision cannot be made awarding the claimant some or all of what was asked for in the claim form, order the claimant or the parties to come to court to discuss the terms of the decision.

When sending an 'application for a decision', the claimant must also send the court evidence that the claim form was formally served on the respondent.

If the claimant does not send an 'application for a decision' to the court within two weeks from the last date for a response, the sheriff must dismiss the claim.

When a time to pay application is received

If the respondent admits the claim and asks for time to pay, the sheriff does not have to send written orders to the parties.

Chapter 7: Money claims in the sheriff court
2. Simple procedure

Under Part 5 of the Simple Procedure Rules, if the respondent sends a time to pay application to the court, the sheriff clerk must send a copy of it to the claimant along with a time to pay notice.

If the claimant consents to a time to pay application, they must indicate consent on the time to pay notice and send it to the court within two weeks of receiving the notice. The sheriff may then grant the time to pay application and decide the case.

If the claimant objects to a time to pay application, they must indicate objection on the time to pay notice and send it to the court within two weeks of receiving the notice. The sheriff may give the parties an order arranging a time to pay hearing. The sheriff then decides the case and whether to grant or refuse the time to pay application.

If the claimant does not respond to a time to pay application within two weeks of the time to pay notice, the sheriff decides the case and whether to grant or refuse the time to pay application.

When no response/time to pay application has been received

If no response form or time to pay application has been received by the court from the respondent by the last date for a response, the sheriff does not have to send written orders to the parties.

If the claimant then sends an 'application for a decision' to the court within two weeks of the last date for response, the sheriff may:[8]
- dismiss the claim; or
- make a decision awarding the claimant some or all of what was asked for in the claim form; or
- where a decision cannot be made awarding the claimant some or all of what was asked for in the claim form, order the claimant or the parties to come to court to discuss the terms of the decision.

If the claimant does not send an 'application for a decision' to the court within two weeks from the last date for a response, the sheriff must dismiss the claim.

Orders (including standard and 'unless' orders)

Part 8 of the Simple Procedure Rules details the orders the sheriff uses to manage or decide a case. Orders may be given to the parties in writing, using the Order of the Sheriff Form (Form 8A). Orders may also be given to the parties in person at a hearing, case management discussion or discussion in court. Written orders must be signed or authenticated electronically by the sheriff or the sheriff clerk.

The sheriff may give 'standard orders' in typical situations. The sheriff may give parties a standard order, give parties an amended version of a standard order, or give parties an order customised to their case.

The full list of standard orders can be found in Schedule 3 of the Simple Procedure Rules.

The sheriff may give a party an order which states that 'unless' that party does something or takes a step, the sheriff will make a decision in the case, including:
- dismissing the claim;
- awarding the claimant some or all of what was asked for in the claim form.

If that party does not do the thing or take the step that they were ordered to, the sheriff may make a decision in the case including:
- dismissing the claim or part of the claim;
- awarding the claimant some or all of what was asked for in the claim form.

Pause and restart

Pausing and restarting claims is covered in Part 9 of the Simple Procedure Rules. Any party in the simple procedure action can request the claim be paused by completing an Application to Pause (Form 9A) and sending it to the other party. If the other party objects to the claim being paused, they must send the application to pause form to the sheriff court within 10 days of receipt, outlining why they object. The sheriff then reviews the application to pause and any objections, and issues one of the following three orders:
- grant the application, and pause the progress of the case; *or*
- refuse the application, and the progress of the case continues; *or*
- order both parties to appear at a discussion in court, where the sheriff will consider whether to pause the progress of the case.

The case is then paused until any party involved in the claim requests it is restarted by completing an Application to Restart (Form 9B) and sending it to the other party. The other party can object to the claim being restarted in the same manner as the application to pause. The sheriff reviews the application to restart and any objections, and then issues one of the following three orders:
- grant the application and restart the case; *or*
- refuse the application, and the case continues to be paused; *or*
- order both parties to appear at a discussion in court, where the sheriff will consider whether to restart the case.

The sheriff clerk must present to the sheriff a case which has been paused for six months or more. The sheriff then sends the party/parties involved written orders, stating that action must be taken otherwise the case will be dismissed.

Example

The respondent asked for the claim to be paused (which was granted), but the claimant did not ask for the claim to be restarted and six months have passed. The sheriff sends written orders to the claimant stating that they must apply for the claim to be restarted. If they ignore the written orders or do nothing, the sheriff dismisses the claim. Any time limits to this are set out in the written orders sent by the sheriff.

Chapter 7: Money claims in the sheriff court
2. Simple procedure

Going to court

If a respondent wishes to defend a claim or has applied for time to pay which has been objected to, they may need to go to court for a hearing in front of a sheriff. The respondent can attend court by themselves or can be represented by a solicitor. They can also be represented by a lay representative or/and be supported by a courtroom supporter. If the respondent represents themselves, they act as a 'party litigant'. The other party may represent themselves, be represented by a solicitor or be represented by a lay representative.

> *Points to remember*
> All parties should arrive in plenty of time and check with the court officers to find which court the case will be heard in.
> Parties should have all the evidence they intend to rely on with them. The court informs all parties what and what not to bring when it sets the date of the hearing.
> The case may be continued, so all parties should be prepared to discuss alternative dates.

Lay representation and courtroom supporters

A **'lay representative'** is someone who is not a solicitor or advocate who can represent a respondent in court in relation to civil matters (such as debt payment). The respondent should still attend court even if they have a lay representative.

Lay representatives are commonly Citizen Advice or local authority debt advisers. They cannot charge for their service and can do anything the respondent can do if they were defending themselves, such as speaking on their behalf. They can request that the court communicate with them when the response form (Form 4A) is returned.

Lay representatives must ask the court's permission to act on a client's behalf and submit a Form 2A to the court. Sheriffs can remove permission for a lay representative to act at any time within the process.[9]

A **'courtroom supporter'** is not a lay representative but usually a friend or relative who can attend a hearing with either party to lend quiet support. They may sit beside or behind the party they are supporting and can provide moral support, help manage their documents, quietly advise on points of law and procedure and take notes. Any party in a simple procedure action can ask for a courtroom supporter to be admitted to the hearing and must do so in writing before the hearing. The sheriff can deny their request.[10]

The decision

A decision (court order) is equivalent to a decree (court order) in other actions. Part 13 of the Simple Procedure Rules deals with decisions.

A decision may be made at almost any point after the Response Form (Form 4A) has been received. A decision may be made at a case management discussion, at a hearing or after the sheriff has considered the written evidence. At the end of a hearing, the sheriff may either make a decision there and then, or may take time to consider before making a decision. If the sheriff takes time to consider a decision, the decision must be made within four weeks from the hearing date. The parties will be sent a Decision Form (Form 13A) outlining what has been decided by the sheriff and also sets out the sheriff's decision about expenses.

The sheriff may make any decision which resolves the dispute between the parties, including a decision which:[11]
- orders the respondent to pay the claimant a sum of money;
- orders the respondent to deliver something to the claimant;
- orders the respondent to do something for the claimant;
- dismisses the claim (or part of the claim) made by the claimant;
- absolves the respondent of the claim (or part of the claim) made by the claimant. A decision which absolves the respondent in a claim means that the claimant cannot make a claim about the same subject against the respondent again.

After the decision

This section outlines what can be done by either party after a decision has been made by a sheriff.

Appeal

Once a decision has been made, the parties have four weeks to appeal the sheriff's decision. An appeal can only be on a point of law and the parties cannot appeal a decision if they can apply for the decision to be recalled. If any party wants to appeal a decision, they must send a completed appeal form (Form 16A) to the court and all parties involved in the claim within 28 days of receiving the decision form. The sheriff completes an appeal report (Form 16B), which outlines the legal questions which the Sheriff Appeal Court will answer in the appeal.

Recall

Any of the parties in a claim can apply to recall a decision made by a sheriff in five situations by completing an Application to Recall (Form 13B) and sending it to the court. These situations are:
- where the sheriff dismissed a claim because the claimant did not send the court an 'application for decision' within two weeks from the last date for a response;
- where the sheriff decided because the respondent did not send the court a 'response form' or 'time to pay application' by the last date for a response;
- where the sheriff dismissed a claim because the claimant did not attend a discussion or hearing;
- where the sheriff has decided because the respondent did not attend a discussion or hearing;
- where the sheriff dismissed a claim because neither party attended a discussion or hearing.

If the sheriff dismissed the claim, a party can only apply for recall within two weeks of the claim being dismissed.

If the sheriff made a decision (other than dismissal) in the case, a party may apply for recall at any time before the decision of the sheriff has been fully implemented. A party can only apply to have a decision of the sheriff recalled in a case once.

When a respondent completes an Application to Recall, they should outline the reasons for the recall – eg, why they do not appear at the hearing or 'what the defence to the action will be'. If the sheriff made a decision following an application for a decision and the respondent wants to dispute all or part of the claim, the respondent must include a completed Response Form (Form 4A) with the application to recall. The claimant has 10 days to object to the application.

If it is the first Application to Recall by that party, the sheriff sends the parties an order to attend a discussion in court. After this, the sheriff considers whether to recall the decision.

Decision in absence

If the respondent did not attend and was not represented at the hearing, the sheriff can grant a 'decision in absence'. If the respondent wants to admit the claim and ask for time to pay or deny the claim (or part of the claim) and has a defence, then before any diligence (eg, bank arrestment and wages arrestment) is fully implemented, they can apply to recall the decision (see p217). If the respondent has already had diligence fully implemented, they cannot recall the decision.

Case dismissed

If a sheriff dismisses a claim, any party can apply to recall the claim. They have two weeks from the date of the dismissal to lodge the claim. This is done by completing Form 13B. The claimant is more likely to utilise recall in this instance.

Extracted decision

Part 15 of the Simple Procedure Rules deals with how the successful party enforces a decision when it has been extracted. When a decision has been awarded by the sheriff court in favour of the claimant and no recall or appeal has been lodged, then generally the claimant will want to enforce the decision. They must wait 28 days from the date of the decision before they can enforce the decision. After the 28 days, they can serve the respondent with a charge for payment which gives the respondent 14 days to settle the debt before the claimant enforce diligence.

Changes to the Simple Procedure Rules and forms

From 31 May 2023, there are changes to how a simple procedure claim is treated.[12]

Rule changes
The rules have been amended to:
- clarify the circumstances in which the sheriff clerk may formally serve the claim form; *and*
- clarify the sheriff's powers designed to ensure the effective management of cases; *and*
- make new provisions which facilitate a claim form or response form being served electronically by email service; *and*
- clarify the procedures for the issue of a decision form/alternative decision form, the recall of a decision and for hearings on expenses; *and*
- improve procedures for lodging documents and other evidence with the court before a hearing.

In addition, the application forms have been streamlined by consolidating several forms into a flexible 'additional orders application' which the parties can use to ask the sheriff to make orders. Part 9 of the rules is therefore deleted and substituted by a new Part 9 regulating the procedure for these applications.

Forms and standard orders
Forms and standard orders have been revised, and the content streamlined to take account of and to align with the overall procedural rule changes made throughout the instrument. In particular:
- Form 3A (claim form) and Form 4A (response form) now include party details and orders sought in a summary front page, and all sections of the forms relating to contact preferences now incorporate options for online (ie, via Civil Online), by post and by email;
- a new standard form (Form 9A – Additional Orders Application) replaces 13 forms[13] which are now omitted;
- Form 13A (decision form) is revised and includes a section for noting the sheriff's reasons (where they have taken time to consider the decision);
- standard orders 1, 2 and 7–10 are revised to make reference to the new additional orders application and amended court procedures;
- a new standard order 3, simplifies the process of making a decision without a hearing;
- standard order 6 is revised to warn the recipient about the potential outcomes of non-compliance with an 'unless order';
- a new standard order 14 is provided for use in cases with additional respondents.

In addition, forms have been reformatted to improve accessibility.
Details are on the Scottish Courts and Tribunals Service website.[14]

3. **Ordinary cause**

Introduction

The ordinary cause procedure was introduced in Schedule 1 of the Sheriff Courts (Scotland) Act 1907. It was amended by the Act of Sederunt (Sheriff Court Ordinary Cause Rules) 1993 (the 'Ordinary Cause Rules').[15] It is used in the sheriff court for most money claims over £5,000 (and, from 2014, to a maximum of £100,000). It is a complex procedure which has been amended many times since its introduction, and it can be costly for all the parties involved.

Ordinary cause procedures cover more than money claims. They can be used in actions for:
- personal injuries claims;
- family actions, including divorce;
- dissolution of civil partnerships;
- applications for orders relating to children – eg, residence and contact.

Although an experienced debt adviser can represent in certain aspects of an ordinary cause action, it is recommended to get expert legal advice.

Most debt advisers see clients who are being pursued under ordinary cause for repayment of debt. Actions under ordinary cause can be raised for a variety of different debt types including:
- credit cards;
- personal loans;
- store cards;
- mortgage arrears;
- hire purchase agreements.

How an action is raised

Chapter 3 of the Ordinary Cause Rules deals with raising an action. An ordinary cause action is raised with an initial writ (Form G1). The pursuer must send or take the initial writ to the relevant sheriff court.

> **Which is the relevant sheriff court?**
> The relevant sheriff court is generally the court that has jurisdiction in the action. For example, where the pursuer lives in Glasgow, but the defender lives in Edinburgh, generally the action would be raised in the jurisdiction that covers the defender, so the action would be raised in Edinburgh. There are exceptions to this, and legal advice should be sought by the pursuer before raising the initial writ if they are unsure about the correct jurisdiction.

Chapter 7: Money claims in the sheriff court
3. Ordinary cause

A fee must be paid to start the action. Information about fees payable and whether an exemption can be claimed by the pursuer can be found on the Scottish Courts and Tribunals Service website.[16]

The pursuer is then asked about their case and the action they want the court to take. This is written down as part of the initial writ. The pursuer asks for the court to issue an order to allow them to 'serve the initial writ' on the defender.[17] The court then sends the paperwork back to the pursuer so that they can start the action by serving it on the defender. It is the pursuer's responsibility to serve the initial writ.

A Form of Citation (Form O4) is served on the defender. The defender has 21 days to respond after being served the writ.

Understanding an ordinary cause initial writ

The heading
This details which court will hear the case.

The instance
This details who the parties involved are. In an ordinary cause action, the person raising the action is called the 'pursuer' and the person the action is raised against is called the 'defender'.

The crave
This is the part in the initial writ that sets out what the pursuer is asking for – eg, if they are claiming the defender owes them money, they 'crave the court' for a court order for payment of that money.

They also often ask for interest on that amount at 8 per cent per annum, and for their expenses in raising the action.

The condescendence
This outlines the facts of the case that the pursuer is relying on. It is laid out in numbered paragraphs.

The condescendence should provide details of what the debt is for, the type of agreement it was, when it was signed and which payments have been made and missed. It should also state when a default notice was served and when the agreement was terminated. If the action being raised refers to a regulated agreement, the pursuer should include details and evidence of the same in the initial writ.[18]

The condescendence is an important part of the initial writ. If a defender intends to dispute the debt or part of the claim, it is important to check that the facts the pursuer has written are correct.

221

Chapter 7: Money claims in the sheriff court
3. Ordinary cause

Plea-in-law

This sets out the legal arguments for the order craved of the court based on the facts alleged in the condescendence.

Serving an initial writ

There are specific rules about service, which must be looked at carefully. Chapter 5 of the Ordinary Cause Rules outlines the steps that should be taken by the pursuer to serve an ordinary cause writ. Various forms must be completed and accompany the initial writ. In a money claim action under ordinary cause, a Form O7 (Notice of Intention to Defend) and a Form O5 (Time to Pay Application) should be included with the initial writ.[19]

The forms and initial writ can be served on the defender by recorded delivery post or using sheriff officers.

Alternatively, if the pursuer's and defender's solicitors have been in contact previously, the parties might agree that it can be served on the defender by sending it to their solicitors. This is called 'acceptance of service' by the defender's agent.

Postal service must be by first class recorded delivery. The envelope must contain a notice which states that it contains a citation from the relevant sheriff court, with a return address for the sheriff clerk's office in the event that service is unsuccessful. If service is unsuccessful, the court returns the papers to the solicitor for reserve; or sheriff officers can serve the writ by handing it to the defender personally or depositing it at their address. The original writ, warrant and productions should be sent to sheriff officers with the copies to be served. The sheriff officer returns the originals to the court, along with a Certificate of Citation (Form O6). This is the form used by the sheriff officer stating that they have served the citation documents on the defender and details the method used to do so.

Once it has been served, the client (defender) has 21 days to inform the court of their intention to defend the action. If they wish to defend the action, they must lodge a Notice of Intention to Defend (Form O7).

What happens after service of an initial writ

The client (defender) has several options on how to deal with the initial writ. They can:
- admit the claim and settle the debt;
- admit the claim and apply for time to pay;
- dispute the claim, or part of the claim;
- do nothing;
- counterclaim.

Admit the claim and settle the debt

If a writ for action has already been raised and served, the client (defender) would need to directly contact the creditor/pursuer or their solicitors to agree full payment of the debt, including any associated legal fees *before* the last date for response.

If they pay the full debt and expenses, the pursuer or their solicitor contacts the court to advise the claim is settled in full. This avoids a court order being registered against the client (defender) and damaging their credit rating.

Admit the claim and apply for time to pay

Time to pay allows the client (defender) to pay the money owed in instalments. If the creditor does not object to the application, it may be granted. However, if the creditor objects, a hearing is arranged where the sheriff decides if the time to pay should be awarded.

If the client misses more than two instalments, and the third becomes due, the time to pay fails and the creditor can go forward with normal diligence methods against the client.

Form O5 must be completed correctly and returned to the court before the expiry of the response date.

Dispute the claim

If the client wishes to dispute the claim, they must have a reason to do so. The client must dispute the claim before the expiry of the notice period in the initial writ. This is done by returning Form O7 to the sheriff clerk. There is a fee payable to the courts, but a client may be able to get a fee exemption.

Both parties must submit their defences within 14 days of the expiry of the notice period in the initial writ. The defence should have numbered paragraphs corresponding to the paragraphs in the pursuer's condescendence. The defence should include pleas in law for the defender supporting their defence.

When the form is returned, the sheriff clerk usually submits an options hearing date. This hearing allows the sheriff to hear the pleadings of the parties. The sheriff then decides what options are available. They may:
- decide the case;
- set a date for a proof hearing, which is similar to a civil trial, hearing evidence on the factual matters in the dispute;
- set a 'debate' if legal questions of law need to be dealt with.

Do nothing

This is a suitable option if the client (defender) admits the claim but is waiting for proof of apparent insolvency or if client has multiple debts and is looking to access a statutory option – either self-sequestration or waiting for a creditor petition for their sequestration. Note that 8 per cent judicial interest is added to a claim after a decree in absence is granted and the amount being claimed on the initial writ may increase by the time a statutory debt option has been accessed and completed.

Chapter 7: Money claims in the sheriff court
3. Ordinary cause

If the client (defender) opts to do nothing, the pursuer submits a 'minute' to the sheriff, after the expiry of the notice period contained in the writ, and asks for the court order (decree). This usually results in them obtaining a court order in their favour. If the sheriff decides the action is incompetent (eg, when the court does not have jurisdiction), they may refuse the decree.

Counterclaim

This is claim made by a defender against the pursuer in an existing action between the same parties.[20] Three conditions must be met in order to bring a counterclaim.
- The counterclaim could have formed a separate action.
- It would not have been necessary in that separate action to call another person as defender other than the pursuer.
- The subject matter of the counterclaim either:
  - forms part of the pursuer's action; *or*
  - arises out of the grounds of it; *or*
  - is necessary for the determination of issues between the parties; *or*
  - has arisen due to reconvention.

This is complex law and, if the client (defender) wants to counterclaim, they should be signposted or referred to a solicitor. Note that it can be expensive to counterclaim.

> *Reconvention*
> 'Reconvention' is where one party (A) can raise a counterclaim against another party (B) in circumstances which would normally be outside the territorial jurisdiction of the court. This is allowed because B has already brought an action against A in A's jurisdiction.

Lay representation

A lay representative is someone who is a not a solicitor or advocate who can represent a defendant in court about civil matters (such as debt payment). The defendant should still attend court if they have a lay representative.

Lay representatives are commonly Citizen Advice or local authority debt advisers. They cannot charge for their service and can do anything the defendant can do if they were defending themselves, such as speaking on their behalf.

Lay representatives must ask the court's permission to act on a client's behalf and submit a Form 1A to the court. Sheriffs can remove permission for a lay representative to act at any time during the process.[21]

Agencies have procedures in place to ensure an adviser meets all the standards required to be a lay representative. It is especially important to understand your boundaries when dealing with complex legal case work and to know when to refer cases to suitably qualified legal experts.

Chapter 7: Money claims in the sheriff court
3. Ordinary cause

Going to court

If a client (defender) wishes to dispute a claim or has applied for a time to pay direction (TTPD) which has been objected to by the pursuer, they must go to court for a hearing in front of a sheriff. The client can attend court by themselves or can be represented by a solicitor. They can also be represented by a lay representative for most aspects except appeals.[22]

If the client represents themself, they act as a 'party litigant'. A solicitor may represent the other party.

> *Points to remember*
>
> All parties should arrive in plenty of time and check with the court officers to find which court the case will be heard in.
>
> Ordinary cause actions are complex and the process in court can be very formal.
>
> Always wait to be addressed by the sheriff, and address them as 'My lord', 'My lady', 'Sir' or 'Madam'. Lay representatives must use 'My lord' or 'My lady'.
>
> Generally, a sheriff asks the pursuer why they have raised an action (the defender must not interrupt).
>
> The sheriff asks the defender 'what is it you want?' Where the defender is seeking a TTPD, they should state this clearly at the outset. Then explain clearly why the time to pay application is reasonable – eg, client is on benefits. Refer to the income and expenditure form orginally submitted.
>
> If the defender is disputing the claim, they should state this to the sheriff and say they are seeking the action to be dismissed. They should further explain why it should be dismissed – eg, the debt is extinguished.
>
> If the defender has any additional paperwork they want the sheriff to look at that has not already been submitted to the court, they must bring three copies with them to court (one for themselves, the sheriff and the pursuer).
>
> If the sheriff asks the defender a question, they should be prepared to answer it if able to. If they cannot answer it, tell the sheriff they cannot answer.
>
> If the sheriff asks the pursuer a question, wait for them to finish speaking.
>
> If the sheriff is taking notes while you are speaking, stop and wait for them to look up from the bench before continuing.

Options hearing

An options hearing is the first time the case is heard before a sheriff. They hear the pleadings of the parties and then decide what option is best suited to the case.

The sheriff may:
- decide the case for either party; *or*
- set a hearing on a preliminary point that requires both evidence and submissions on the law (this is known as a 'proof before answer'); *or*

- set a hearing on a preliminary point that requires only legal submissions: this is known as a 'debate'; *or*
- set a hearing on the merits of the case that requires evidence to be established before the court (this is known as a 'proof hearing'); *or*
- if they think the parties need to address further issues before fixing the substantive hearing, set a date for a procedural hearing and ask one or both parties to deal with certain matters before that date.

The options hearing can be rescheduled once, for no more than 28 days after the original options hearing.

Decisions made in court

When an ordinary cause action comes before the court, the sheriff has several options when deciding on a claim. This varies depending on the action that has been raised, but, in most money claims, the options available to the sheriff include:
- grant the court order (decree) in favour of the pursuer (see below);
- grant a disputed TTPD (often referred to as an 'instalment decree') (see below);
- dismiss the action/decree absolvitor (see p227);
- decree in absence (see p227).

Chapter 30 of the Ordinary Cause Rules covers decrees, extracts and executions.

Grant the decree in favour of the pursuer

If after listening to all the evidence, the sheriff grants the order in favour of the pursuer, it means the defender has lost the claim. The pursuer may also ask for expenses to be awarded to them. The pursuer must then wait 14 days before they can extract the decree. This is to give the defender time to appeal if they wish.[23]

After 14 days, they can take further steps to recover any monies claimed. This means the defendant is served with a charge for payment for money and given 14 days to repay the debt in full before the pursuer can proceed to further diligence – eg, wages arrestment or sequestrating the defendant.

If the defender did not appear in court and a decree was 'granted in absence' in favour of the pursuer, there may be an opportunity to recall ('repone') the decree (see p228). In these cases, the pursuer must wait 14 days to extract the decree.

Grant a disputed time to pay direction

If a defender has submitted a time to pay application which has been challenged by the pursuer, the sheriff hears arguments from the defendant and the pursuer. The sheriff can grant a decree to the pursuer and grant time to pay to the defender at the same time. This allows the defender to repay the debt at the amount offered in the application, and, although a decree has been awarded, the pursuer cannot take any further action against the defender while the TTPD is being paid. If the defender fails to make the agreed payments and the TTPD fails, the pursuer can extract the decree without waiting and begin to pursue further diligence.

Dismiss the claim

If the sheriff dismisses the claim, it means the court has ruled in favour of the defender. In this case, the pursuer's claims are rejected, and no court order or decree is granted. There are certain instances when the sheriff can dismiss a claim which can include:
- where the pursuer fails to appear at a hearing or submit paperwork to the court;
- when the sheriff finds in favour of the defendant;
- where the pursuer 'abandons' their claim.

If the case is dismissed, the pursuer can raise the same claim again against the defender, unless 'decree absolvitor' is awarded.

> ### *Decree absolvitor*
> This legal term is from the Latin meaning 'let him be acquitted'. The defender is absolved of any responsibility in the claim. It also prevents the pursuer from raising the same claim again. It is therefore important when the sheriff dismisses a claim that the defender requests 'decree absolvitor'. A sheriff may ask the defender or their solicitor if that is what they want before awarding and the answer should always be 'yes'.

Decree in absence

This is a decree granted in favour of the pursuer where the defender did not respond in any formal way to the court summons, or does not appear in court on the day. Approximately 80 per cent of cases passing through the sheriff court are undefended.

> ### Other common terms in ordinary cause actions
> '**Averment**' is a statement of fact which is set out in the written pleadings. Every averment is something that the party is offering to prove in the action before the court.
> '**Jurisdiction**' is the official power to interpret and apply the law. In Scotland, there are a number of different courts and tribunals. They are given powers to deal with different types of cases. These powers define the 'jurisdiction' of the particular body. A court cannot deal with matters which are beyond the scope of the powers it has. Where an applicant asks the court to do something beyond its powers, the application is said to be 'incompetent' or 'out with its jurisdiction'.
> '**Motion**' is the name given to any formal request by a party asking – or moving – the court to make an order. Use of the words 'motion' or 'moving' helps to distinguish such requests to the court from informal comments or suggestions made in correspondence to the clerks. The latter will not necessarily be drawn to the attention of the court.

'**Move**' is when a party makes a formal request to the court, they are said to move the court to do something, or move that it be done.

'**Sist**' is an application made where a party wishes to pause all procedure in proceedings. It brings about a temporary halt to the case and is at the discretion of the sheriff. Usually, a motion to sist must specify the length of time sought in respect of the sist. Either party in a claim can request a sist, either in person in court or by lodging a motion (incidental application).

Post-decree

When decree has been awarded, the options available to the client (defender) are limited by the time available and the action they have taken previously.

Appeals

Appeals are made on a point of law whereby one of the parties claims that the sheriff got the law wrong in a previous hearing of the case. Any party wishing to initially lodge an appeal has 14 days from the awarding of the decree to do so. Appeals are lodged with the Sheriff Appeal Court Civil in Edinburgh and then, if they go further, to the Court of Session Inner House. An appeal may even end up going to the Supreme Court of the UK. Lay representatives cannot lodge an appeal for their client (defender or pursuer), and any client wishing to appeal a judgment should be advised to seek legal advice. An accepted appeal stops the pursuer from extracting a decree for further diligence until the appeal is heard and decided.

Reponing

A '**reponing note**' is a request to reopen a case where decree in absence has already been granted. This is made on the basis that there was a good reason for the missed deadline. It is not the same as an appeal. A decision can only be reponed where it has not been implemented in full. If the decision has only been partially implemented, the judgment which has not been implemented can be reponed.

Reponing notes have to contain specific information, detailed in the Ordinary Cause Rules.[24] It is important that advisers are aware of reponing rules and have an understanding of what is required. Lay representatives cannot represent clients in a reponing and are unable to draft a reponing note. Advisers should contact a solicitor as soon as it becomes apparent the reponing note procedure is applicable.

Clients (defenders) often require representation from a solicitor. While a client can represent themselves, it is not advisable as the procedure is complex.

Reponing notes must be lodged with the sheriff clerk before full implementation of a decree in absence. Reponing notes cannot be used in all circumstances, and they are not guaranteed to be granted.

Reponing notes can be lodged if there is a full and substantial reason for a client failing to appear and there must be a stateable defence to the action.

Once a reponing note has been lodged, it is put before the sheriff by the sheriff clerk, to obtain a warrant to serve to the pursuer. There is a charge for lodging a reponing note.

A reponing note suspends any diligence based on the decree.

The sheriff can refuse a reponing note. If this happens, an appeal can be made to the sheriff principal or the Court of Session.

A reponing note must include an explanation of the failure to appear and details of the proposed defence. It will be subject to a hearing even if it is not opposed. Unlike minutes for recall in summary cause court procedure, there is no template form to be used for drafting reponing notes. The application is made to the court by 'minute' – the procedure for making an application by minute can be found in Chapter 14 of the Ordinary Cause Rules.

The form of a minute must contain:
- **a crave**: a formal statement on behalf of the defendant explaining what they are seeking. It explains the minute seeks to repone the decree in absence;
- **a condescendence**: statement of facts supporting the crave, it explains the reasons for the defender's absence and lack of response to the initial writ;
- **pleas-in-law**: the concise legal propositions setting out the merits of the case. It sets out the defender's proposed defence.

A reponing note should not be drafted without legal advice.

Time to pay order

A time to pay order (TTPO) is a request to the court after a decree has been awarded and the formal process of diligence has begun (once a 'charge for payment' or a bank arrestment has been served or an action for adjudication has commenced) to make payments to repay the debt in instalments. It is similar to a time to pay direction (TTPD) in that it stops any further diligence against the defendant.

A TTPO cannot be used when the debt is:[25]
- over £25,000; *or*
- for an award in connection with a divorce; *or*
- for maintenance; *or*
- for income tax, VAT or car tax.

The application form to apply for a TTPO is DSA 2. Unlike a TTPD, it is not included in the initial writ and it is not available via the Scottish Courts and Tribunals Service website under Ordinary Cause Rules. The sheriff clerk's office should have copies and most advice agencies have copies or know how to access a copy.

Unlike the TTPD, the DSA 2 has more room to include further details – eg, if the defender has other debts. The form must be returned to the correct sheriff court. There are time limits, but these can vary. Any delay in returning a TTPO could affect the defender's ability to stop or reverse other forms of diligence. It is therefore good practice to request a statutory moratorium at this stage.

If the pursuer does not object to the offer, the sheriff grants the TTPO after 14 days, effectively freezing any future diligence while it is in place.

If, however, the pursuer objects to the TTPO, a date for a hearing in court is fixed, which should be attended by both parties. The sheriff listens to both sides and decides whether to award the TTPO.

If a TTPO is awarded and the client has a change in circumstances which makes meeting the payment difficult, they can apply for a variation to reduce payments.

Generally, TTPOs are expected to clear debts within approximately two years. This time frame is not in any legislation, but has become custom and practice in court and should be taken into account when looking at TTPO as a viable option.

If two payments are missed and the third payment is due, the TTPO fails. It cannot be applied for again.

If a defender has had previous TTPDs which failed, they cannot apply for a TTPO. If, however, a defender applied for a TTPD before the decree which was refused, this does not preclude them from applying for a TTPO.

4. Summary warrant

Summary warrants are similar to court orders but are issued for certain types of debt such as council tax, income tax or non-domestic business rates. Summary warrants do not allow the client an opportunity to defend the action in front of a sheriff. It is awarded in their absence.

What is a summary warrant

When debts are for council tax arrears or HMRC or Revenue Scotland debts, they can be processed through a summary warrant. This allows local and central government creditors to achieve the equivalent of a court judgment much more quickly. Summary warrants bypass the court's normal processes and act faster than a typical court action.

A summary warrant is similar to a court order and allows further actions to be taken against a client should money not be recovered. The warrant details the amount due and who to contact for payment. Usually, this is the sheriff officers rather than the creditor. The debt is increased by a 10 per cent surcharge.

Court action is usually preceded by the creditor contacting the client requesting payment to be made.

Pre-court procedures

If a client fails to pay an instalment of council tax, they are issued with a first reminder notice stating the amount which must be paid within seven days. If the amount is not paid within seven days, the client may lose the right to pay the remainder of the account by instalments. The remaining balance for the financial year becomes due and must be paid within an additional 14 days. If the full balance is not paid, the creditor can apply to the sheriff court for a summary warrant.

There are similar procedures for HMRC or Revenue Scotland debts.

Court process

Summary warrant procedure generally minimises the expense of enforcement and collection. A summary warrant is obtained by application to a sheriff. The application needs to be accompanied by a certificate from the creditor stating that:
- the persons specified in the certificate have not paid the sums due;
- the creditor has demanded payment of the relevant payable sum from each such person;
- 14 days have expired without payment being made.

The certificate must also provide the amount due by each person specified in the application. A single application for a summary warrant can cover a number of clients. This makes the enforcement of debts covered by this process more efficient than processing individual applications. Assuming the above requirements are complied with, the sheriff must grant a summary warrant.

The summary warrant recovery process

When a summary warrant is issued, 10 per cent of the debt amount is added to the total amount of the debt. The summary warrant, once issued, can be used by the creditor to instruct sheriff officers to implement the court order. Sheriff officers serve the client with a formal charge for payment (even for a bank arrestment). The charge for payment does not need to be given to the client directly and may just be posted through the client's letterbox. At the same time, the creditor must also issue a Debt Advice and Information Package.

The charge for payment gives the client 14 days to pay the debt in full. If the debt is not paid within 14 days, the sheriff officers can commence the following diligence:
- attachment;
- money attachment;
- arrestment;
- earnings arrestment.

Dealing with a summary warrant

Before deciding how to deal with the summary warrant, a full assessment of the client's situation should be carried out, including whether they have other debts and if their assets at risk. There is no recall procedure for a summary warrant, so other solutions must be investigated.

Statutory moratorium

Applying for a statutory moratorium can prevent the creditor from issuing a charge for payment and give you time to work with the client to come up with a suitable strategy. As summary warrant debts must serve a charge for payment before executing diligence, the client could wait until the charge for payment has been served before applying.

Debt Arrangement Scheme

The debt can be entered into a Debt Payment Programme under the Debt Arrangement Scheme. The usual fair and reasonableness tests apply (see p129).

Insolvency

Debts due under a summary warrant can be discharged under any of the insolvency options (see Chapter 6).

Time to pay order

If the client only has one debt, they can apply to the court for a time to pay order. The court and the creditor have to accept the offer for it to be successful. See Chapter 11 on time to pay directions and orders.

Notes

2. **Simple procedure**
    1 Part 3.8 SPR
    2 Part 3.11 SPR
    3 Part 3.12 SPR
    4 r4.2 Simple Procedure Rules
    5 scotcourts.gov.uk/taking-action/civil-online-gateway
    6 scotcourts.gov.uk/taking-action/civil-online-gateway
    7 Part 7.2 SPR
    8 Part 7.4 SPR
    9 Parts 2.2 and 2.4 SPR
    10 Parts 2.5 and 2.6 SPR
    11 Part 13.4 SPR
    12 Act of Sederunt (Simple Procedure Amendment) (Miscellaneous) 2022 No.211

Chapter 7: Money claims in the sheriff court
Notes

13 Omitted forms: Form 3B (further claimant form); Form 3C (further respondent form); Form 3E (change of timetable application); Form 9A (application to pause); Form 9B (application to restart); Form 9C (additional respondent application); Form 9D (application to amend); Form 9E (abandonment notice); Form 9F (application to represent); Form 9G (incidental orders application); Form 10B (recovery of documents application); Form 10C (application to open confidential document); Form 10D (special recovery of documents application)
14 scotcourts.gov.uk/rules-and-practice/rules-of-court/sheriff-court---civil-procedure-rules/simple-procedure-court-rules/simple-procedure-rules

3. Ordinary cause
15 SI 1993 No.1956
16 scotcourts.gov.uk/taking-action/court-fees/sheriff-court-fees
17 Chapter 5 OCR
18 Part 3.2A OCR
19 Part 5.2(2) OCR
20 Sch 1 Ch 19 OCR
21 Sch 1 1.A.2(6) OCR
22 scotcourts.gov.uk/taking-action/lay-representation-in-civil-cases
23 Ch 30.4 OCR
24 Ch 8 OCR
25 s5 D(S)A 1987

Chapter 8

Housing debt

This chapter covers:
1. Social housing sector (below)
2. Private rented sector (p240)
3. Mortgage arrears (p250)

> **Future changes**
> At the time of writing, the Housing (Scotland) Bill proposed reforms to the private and social rented sectors. This includes the designation of rent control areas, duties to consider delaying evictions and provisions for homelessness prevention. Check the online version of this *Handbook* for updates.

1. Social housing sector

Clients may find themselves struggling to pay their social housing rent. Social landlords may do all they can to give their tenants advice and support, but this varies in practice. Evictions are traumatic for clients and their families and can be costly for landlords. Eviction should always only be used as a last resort.

Currently, all social housing eviction processes for arrears under £5,000 are by summary cause in the sheriff court.

Pre-court processes

Before a landlord can start court action to evict a tenant because they have rent arrears, they must complete a set of pre-action requirements. This ensures an 'action for possession' is used only as an option of last resort. An **'action for possession'** is where the landlord requests the court to grant a decree for eviction to take back control of the property and evict the tenant.

Pre-action requirements

The Housing (Scotland) Act 2010 introduced pre-action requirements that landlords must complete before a notice can be served on a tenant to recover possession of the property due to rent arrears.

These pre-action requirements protect tenants by:

- creating more consistency in practice between landlords;
- ensuring landlords and tenants explore different ways to resolve rent arrears;
- ensuring that eviction is only used when there is no other option.

Before a landlord can go to court to pursue a possession action, they must complete the following actions.[1]
- Tenants must be given clear information about the terms of the tenancy and any rent or other financial obligation owed to the landlord.
- Tenants must be given help and advice on their eligibility for help with housing costs or financial assistance.
- Tenants must be given information on where they can get help to manage debts.
- The landlord must make a reasonable effort to agree on a payment plan including future rent and arrears.
- The landlord must encourage tenants to contact their local authority.

The landlord must not pursue a possession action before they have considered:
- universal credit and housing benefit applications;
- actions the tenants are taking to pay off the arrears;
- whether the tenants are adhering to an agreed payment plan.

For further information on pre-action requirements, see Shelter's online information.[2]

Notice of proceedings for recovery of possession

Once the landlord has met the pre-action requirements, a notice can be served on the tenants explaining that proceedings for possession of the property can be raised, and the grounds for doing this. This is a 'notice of proceedings for recovery of possession' (commonly known as a 'notice of proceedings').[3] It must specify:[4]
- the grounds for recovery of arrears;
- the reason why possession is being sought;
- the date when recovery proceedings may be raised;
- steps taken by the landlord showing compliance with the pre-action requirements.

If the grounds for recovery include rent arrears, a section is included listing each pre-action requirement. Landlords mark each action as complete and provide brief details of their actions to comply with the legal requirements.[5]

When proceedings begin

Possession proceedings cannot begin until at least four weeks after the notice has been served.[6]

Proceedings must take place within six months from when the notice was served. If they do not, a new notice must be served.

You can read more about the grounds for eviction at mygov.scot/eviction-council-tenants/reasons-for-being-evicted.

Summary cause process

If the landlord is a council or housing association and they take the client to court, the case is dealt with:[7]
- under the summary cause procedure if the arrears are under £5,000;
- under the ordinary cause rule if the arrears are over £5,000. Get special advice.

The summons

The proceedings start with a summons being served on the tenant. This is only served once the notice period has passed. Usually, the case cannot be called into court until 21 days have passed from the summons being served.[8] This period may be shorter in specific cases.

The summons lists who the parties are, the address of the property the landlord is seeking to repossess and the grounds for seeking repossession. It includes a 'statement of claim', the part of the summons where the landlord outlines the case and gives the tenant fair notice of the case against them. This often contains details such as the period the rent has remained unpaid and how much is due. If basic information is not provided, the summons may be dismissed as incompetent.

The original summons is registered with the court by the landlord. A copy of the summons is formally delivered to the client. This summons explains what the pursuer (landlord) wants from the client. For example, if the landlord is attempting to evict the client, the summons explains it is an action for recovery of possession of heritable property.

The summons is sent to the client's home, workplace or other known address by recorded post or delivered personally by sheriff officers.

Responding to the summons

The summons contains a section called 'the claim'. This explains what the landlord is looking for and why – eg, recovery of the property due to rent arrears or antisocial behaviour. The client should respond to the summons before the return date if they dispute any of the facts of the claim. Applying for a time to pay direction is not an appropriate action as it only allows time to pay the debt, but a decree may still be awarded for eviction.

If the client fails to respond before the return date, they can go to court on the court date (the calling date) to explain why they should not be evicted.[9]

Lay representation

A lay representative is a person authorised by a client to help them prepare and conduct a civil legal action.

Chapter 8: Housing debt
1. Social housing sector

Lay representatives are allowed to do anything a client can do to prepare and conduct their case. Lay representatives cannot accept payment for this service.[10]

Points to remember

All parties should turn up in plenty of time and check with the court officers to find which court the case will be heard in.

Always wait to be addressed by the sheriff and address them as 'My lord', 'My lady', 'Sir' or 'Madam'. Lay representatives must use 'My lord' or 'My lady'.

Generally, a sheriff asks the pursuer why they have raised an action (the defender must not interrupt).

If the sheriff asks the defender a question, they must be prepared to answer it if they are able to. If they cannot answer, tell the sheriff.

If the sheriff asks the pursuer a question, wait for them to finish speaking.

If the sheriff is taking notes while you are speaking, stop and wait for them to look up from the bench before continuing.

Court terms and outcomes

Continuation

A continuation of an action allows for the case to be continued to another date. It is only a temporary postponement and allows the client time to make an arrangement with the landlord, seek money advice or make an application for benefit.

This order is made by a sheriff. The client, lay representative or landlord can make a request to the sheriff to have a case continued.

Heritable summary cause actions are either continued[11] in or adjourned[12] on one occasion only for a period of up 12 weeks. No further continuations or adjournments can be granted unless there are exceptional circumstances. This may vary from court to court. The sheriff's decision is final.

Sist

Sisting of an action allows a temporary halt of proceedings.

Unlike continuation, with sisting, the case comes off the court agenda. To reawaken the case, the landlord must make an incidental application to the court to recall the sist. This often happens when the client defaults on a payment arrangement.

Dismiss

If a case is dismissed by the sheriff, it means they feel there is no case to hear.

This may happen if the landlord has requested the case be dismissed, the landlord has not followed the proper procedures to bring the client to court, or the arrears have been cleared.

Chapter 8: Housing debt
1. Social housing sector

If the case was dismissed because the landlord did not follow procedures correctly but the grounds for the case remain, the landlord can start legal action against the client again from the beginning. If it was dismissed for any other reason, it is the end of the case.

Decree

A decree is a court order. When a creditor is seeking a decree against a client, they are asking the court to make a decision in their favour. A creditor usually seeks three craves (ie, demands). For housing cases, they are likely to be for:
- the clients to be evicted;
- eviction and repayment of rent arrears;
- for the expenses of the action.

Decree time limits

A decree specifies a period of time during which the landlord can start the eviction process. The decree prescribes a maximum period of six months starting from the date the decree was extracted.[13] The time limit may be less than this, but not more.

Note:
- If a landlord evicts the tenants within this time, the tenancy ends.
- If the landlord does not evict them within this time, the order ceases to have effect.
- If the client continues to fail to pay rent, the landlord must meet the pre-action requirements before further court action can be taken.

Post-court action

When the court grants a decree for possession of the property due to rent arrears, the tenancy is not ended on the date the court granted the decree. It ends when the landlord recovers possession of the property.

Minute for recall

A decree can be recalled through an application for a 'minute for recall'. This can only be applied for if a decree was granted and neither the client nor anyone representing the client appeared in court.[14]

For summary cause procedures, Forms 30 and 30a must be completed.

Recall can take place any time before the sheriff's decision has been fully implemented, even up to the date an eviction was planned.[15]

A client, qualifying occupier or landlord can recall a decree. A 'qualifying occupier' is someone who uses the property as their home and who is:[16]
- a member of the tenant's family aged over 16;
- assigned part of the property or subletting part of the property with the landlord's consent;
- lodging with the tenant with the landlord's consent.

When a decree can be recalled

If the decree includes a decree for eviction, a minute for recall can be applied for at any time up to the point of eviction.[17]

If the decree relates only to money, an application for a minute of recall can be applied for up to 14 days after the execution of a charge of payment or execution of an arrestment, depending on which took place first.

If the decree is for both eviction and money, each part can be recalled separately. The part of the decree relating to money should be recalled within 14 days of the execution of a charge or of an arrestment, whichever occurs first. The part relating to eviction can be recalled up to the point of eviction. Complicated recalls should be referred to a solicitor specialising in housing law.

Appeal

If the client wants to appeal, they should be signposted or referred to a legal professional.

An appeal can be made if the landlord or client disagrees with the sheriff's decision. The person making the appeal is called the 'appellant' and the other party is the 'respondent'.

The applicant must lodge a note of appeal with the sheriff clerk within 14 days of the final decision made by the sheriff.[18] The appeal sets out the points of law on which the appeal is made. A fee must be paid to make the appeal.

A 'draft' is issued within 28 days of the appeal being made. The draft details the facts the sheriff has found proved in the case, the legal findings and legal questions which will be considered at the appeal hearing.[19]

Charge for removing

The landlord notifies the tenant of their eviction date by sending a 'Form of Charge for Removing'. This is served by a sheriff officer. An example of a charge for removing is in the Schedule to the Removing from Heritable Property (Form of Charge) (Scotland) Regulations 2011.

The client is usually given 14 days to leave the property. If the tenant does not leave by the eviction date, sheriff officers write to the tenant to inform them when the eviction will be enforced. The tenant must have at least 48 hours' notice.[20]

See the Shelter website for further information.[21]

Dealing with rent arrears at court

- **Debt Arrangement Scheme (DAS):** it does not stop an eviction as it just gives time to pay the arrears. However, some landlords may agree to stop any recovery/eviction action if the arrears are included with a DAS Debt Payment Programme.
- **Insolvencies:** this may depend on each local authority or housing association and if a decree has already been granted. In the case of sequestration, many

registered social landlords may agree to allow the tenant to retain their tenancies and agree to write off any rent arrears up to the date of sequestration.
- **Recall:** you could ask the sheriff to recall the decree if the debt is subject to an insolvency or DAS.
- **Grants:** some organisation or charities may award a grant/hardship payments to pay off the arrears to stop an eviction.
- **Negotiate:** it is never too late to try to negotiate a payment option to pay off the arrears.

2. Private rented sector

Civil cases relating to the private rented sector are no longer dealt with as a summary cause action raised within the sheriff court. Since 1 December 2017, these cases have been transferred to the First-tier Tribunal for Scotland (Housing and Property Chamber). This section looks at possession for rent arrears cases.

The First-tier Tribunal for Scotland (Housing and Property Chamber)

Landlords can apply to the tribunal for eviction and repossession orders where they consider that they have ground(s) for eviction. This covers all tenancies in the private sector.

Members of the chamber comprise legal members and ordinary members. Ordinary members are surveyors or housing members. When they consider and decide a case they are referred to as a tribunal. A tribunal may comprise:[22]
- a legal member alone; *or*
- a legal member and one ordinary member; *or*
- a legal member with two ordinary members.

This chapter looks at how an application for rent arrears and/or repossession is carried out in the chamber. Different types of tenancies have slightly different procedures, but, for simplicity, we concentrate on where the same rules apply.

Tenancy types and procedures

The first step in giving housing advice is to determine the type of tenancy, the legislation it is covered by and the legal procedures that can be used to evict a client.
- Tenancies that began before 1 December 2017 are **assured and short-assured tenancies** and are regulated by the Housing (Scotland) Act 1988.
- Tenancies that began on or after 1 December 2017 are **private residential tenancies**) and are regulated by the Private Housing (Tenancies) (Scotland) Act 2016.

Short-assured tenancies and assured tenancies

A **short-assured tenancy** under the Housing (Scotland) Act 1988 is one where you rent from a private landlord or letting agent and:[23]
- the tenancy started after 2 January 1989 but before 1 December 2017; *and*
- the initial tenancy agreement was for at least six months; *and*
- before the tenancy started, the landlord issued an AT5 form.[24]

If no AT5 form was issued, the client has an assured tenancy.

A short-assured tenancy has an end date, but a landlord has to follow the right process if they want the client to leave. Otherwise, the tenancy is automatically renewed. This is called 'tacit relocation'.

A model short-assured tenancy agreement is at gov.scot/publications/private-residential-tenancy-model-agreement.

Assured tenancies are those which are not short-assured tenancies and were issued before 1 December 2017. They are regulated by the Housing (Scotland) Act 1988.

The procedures for eviction are very similar and the landlord must also take the client to the tribunal if they want to evict them.

The client should also have a lease agreement where the terms of the let are stated. It is essential to obtain a copy and check the agreement is valid.

Grounds for eviction

Under an assured and short-assured tenancy agreement, there are varying ways that a landlord can evict a tenant. The landlord must specify which ground for eviction they are using.

The full grounds for eviction are in Schedule 5 of the Housing (Scotland) Act 1988.[25] Normally, repossession is on grounds 11 or 12 for rent in arrears being 'lawfully due'.[26]

The tribunal will not make an order for repossession unless it thinks it is 'reasonable to do so'.[27]

Where there has been a delay in universal credit (UC) or housing benefit (HB), or the landlord has not properly carried out the pre-action protocol, the tribunal can refuse to award repossession.[28]

Pre-action protocol

The pre-action protocol only applies to cases where the ground for repossession is rent arrears.[29]

The Rent Arrears Pre-Action Requirements (Coronavirus) (Scotland) Regulations 2020 brought in pre-action requirements which all private sector landlords must now follow.[30] The requirements are that the landlord must:[31]
- provide the tenant with clear information about:
  – the terms of the tenancy agreement; *and*
  – the amount in arrears; *and*

- the tenant's rights in relation to proceedings for possession of a house (including the pre-action requirements); *and*
- how the tenant can accesses information and advice on financial support and debt management; *and*
• make reasonable efforts to agree with the tenant a reasonable plan to make payments of:
  - future payments of rent; *and*
  - the arrears; *and*
• reasonably consider:
  - steps being taken by the tenant which may affect the ability of the tenant to pay arrears within a reasonable time;
  - changes to the tenant's circumstances which are likely to impact on the extent to which the tenant complies with the terms of an agreed plan.

Notice to quit and notice of proceedings

When a landlord wants to evict a tenant, they must first serve them with a 'notice to quit'[32] and a 'notice of proceedings' (also known as an AT6 notice).[33]

The tribunal has the power to dispense with this if it deems it reasonable.[34]

The landlord must begin proceedings within six months of serving the AT6.[35]

Section 11 notice

Along with the notice of proceedings, the landlord must also serve a 'section 11' (Homelessness etc. (Scotland) Act 2003) notice to the local council where the property is situated.[36] This informs the local authority that the landlord is seeking repossession.[37] The landlord must have proof of sending a section 11 notice to the local authority.

Private residential tenancies

On 1 December 2017, a new type of tenancy – the private residential tenancy – came into force, replacing the assured and short assured tenancy agreements for all new tenancies.

These are covered in the Private Housing (Tenancies) (Scotland) Act 2016.

Grounds for eviction

There are 18 grounds for eviction.[38]

The tribunal can issue an eviction order where the client is three months or more in arrears and the tribunal believes it is reasonable to do so.[39] However, before issuing an order, the tribunal must consider:[40]

• whether the arrears are wholly or partly because of a delay or failure in the payment of a relevant benefit (eg, UC or HB); *and*
• the extent to which the landlord has complied with the pre-action protocol.

Pre-action protocol
A landlord in an action for repossession must comply with the pre-action protocol (see p241).

Advisers should check whether the pre-action protocol has been adequately followed by the landlord, as failure to do so can result in the action being dismissed.

Notice to leave
A tenant with a private sector tenancy must be served with a 'notice to leave'. A copy of the notice is set out in Schedule 5 of the Private Residential Tenancies (Prescribed Notices and Forms) (Scotland) Regulations 2017.[41]

The notice period for rent arrears is 28 days.[42]

If the client decides not to leave, the landlord must apply to the tribunal for an eviction order.

Application to the tribunal
The application to the tribunal (known as 'civil proceedings') depends on which type of tenancy the client has.

Civil proceedings applications are for issues not covered by a specific rule, but that arise from the relevant type of tenancy – eg, an application for a payment order for rent arrears. Civil proceedings applications can be submitted alone by the tenant or the landlord, or they can be submitted together with an eviction application by the landlord.

There are also some rules which apply across the board to all tenancy agreements.

Payment order and eviction order
When making an application to the tribunal, a landlord will more than likely make two applications: one for a payment order (for rent arrears) and the other for eviction (repossession and eviction).

The payment order is easier to deal with as there are several solutions available. It is up to the client or their representative to convince the tribunal that the order for eviction should not be given. This is at the discretion of the tribunal.

Application to the tribunal: common rules
Some rules apply to assured and short assured tenancies, and some apply to private residential tenancies. This section concentrates on the rules in common.

The rules common to all proceedings are in Part 1 of the Schedule to the First-tier Tribunal for Scotland Housing and Property Chamber (Procedure) Regulations 2017.

To begin an application for the client's eviction, the landlord must make an application to the tribunal.

All applications for eviction orders, for all tenancy types, are made to the tribunal in Form E and Form F.

The tribunal then looks at the application and decides what steps to take next.

The overriding objective of the tribunal

The overriding objective of the tribunal is to deal with the proceedings 'justly'.[43] This includes:
- dealing with the proceedings in a manner proportionate to the complexity of the issues and the resources of the parties;
- seeking informality and flexibility in proceedings;
- ensuring, so far as practicable, that the parties are on an equal footing procedurally and can participate fully in the proceedings, including assisting any party in the presentation of their case without advocating the course they should take;
- using the special expertise of the First-tier Tribunal effectively;
- avoiding delay, so far as compatible with the proper consideration of the issues.

Service to the client

Any communication served on the client must be by registered post, recorded delivery or email with the effective date being 48 hours after service, to allow time for delivery.[44]

Rejection or acceptance of an application

The tribunal can review the application and decide to accept or reject it.

An application can be refused if:[45]
- it is considered to be frivolous or vexatious;
- the dispute has already been resolved;
- the tribunal deems it not appropriate;
- there has already been an identical application.

Where accepted, the tribunal notifies all parties and gives them appropriate time to respond, usually at least 14 days.

Lay representatives, supporters and exclusions

A client may have a lay representative or a 'supporter' during the proceedings. Where this is the case, the tribunal should be notified before any hearing takes place.

The representative can participate in the hearing as though they were the client, with some exceptions.

A supporter cannot participate as much as a representative and they cannot represent the client. They can offer moral support and take notes.

The tribunal can order that a person is not to act as a supporter or lay representative of a client if:[46]

- it believes the supporter is an unsuitable person to act as a supporter/representative (whether generally or in the proceedings concerned); *or*
- it is satisfied that to do so is in the interests of the efficient administration of justice.

Ensure that if your client needs a representative or supporter that they have had some training on the procedures of the tribunal.

Directions from the tribunal

The tribunal can issue 'directions' to any of the parties about the conduct or proceedings of the case and can:[47]
- set and vary time limits;
- ask them to provide more information;
- require a party to lodge evidence.

Tribunal options

There are options open to the tribunal to try to resolve the situation before it proceeds to the hearing stage. This will be decided on a case-by-case basis.

Adjournment or postponement is also an excellent tool to buy more time to work out a solution for your client.

Case management discussion

The purpose of a case management discussion is to enable the First-tier Tribunal to explore how the parties' dispute may be efficiently resolved, including by:
- identifying the issues to be resolved;
- identifying what facts are agreed between the parties;
- raising with parties any issues it requires to be addressed;
- discussing what witnesses, documents and other evidence will be required;
- discussing whether a hearing is required;
- discussing an application to recall a decision.

The First-tier Tribunal can do anything at a case management discussion which it can do at a hearing, including making a decision.[48]

The tribunal has the powers to decide that it can proceed without a hearing, if it thinks that it has enough information and the parties are in agreement.[49]

Mediation

The tribunal can offer mediation between the parties to avoid having a full hearing. **Note:** there may be a charge for mediation.

If the parties both agree to the offer, the tribunal suspends the adjournment or postponement of the application pending the outcome.[50]

The tribunal cannot offer validation or recommendation of any particular mediation service or refer parties to a mediator.

Scottish Mediation is the professional body for mediators. It maintains the Scottish Mediation Register. Parties who want to use mediation can find a relevant mediator by accessing the register at scottishmediation.org.uk/find-a-mediator and by selecting 'Housing and Property' in the 'Types of Mediation' box.

Inquiries and giving evidence

The tribunal can ask the parties to appear at a hearing and answer questions or to provide evidence. This includes oral evidence at the hearing stage.

It may also ask the parties to lodge a list of documents referred to in the case and a list of any witnesses the client or creditor wishes to use, at least seven days before a hearing.[51]

All parties should receive a copy of any documents or evidence produced.

Hearings

When all other avenues have been explored and no agreement has been made, the case proceeds to the hearing stage.

Notice of a hearing should be notified to the client at least 14 days before the hearing is due.[52]

The hearing must be held in public unless the tribunal, on its own initiative or an application by a party, decides it is necessary to do otherwise in the interests of justice.

A party or their representative (but not a supporter) may conduct the party's case. They can make representations, call witnesses, give evidence on the client's behalf and cross-examine any witness called by another party.

During the hearing, the chair of the tribunal must introduce the parties to the tribunal members, explain the purposes of the hearing and ensure the parties to the hearing both understand and can participate in the hearing.[53]

Decisions

Where there are two or more tribunal members, the decision must be made by majority vote.[54] In the event of a tie, the chair has the casting vote.

The tribunal usually gives written reasons for its decision. Where there is no unanimous agreement, it must give a brief note of the opinion of the minority members.[55]

This may be useful to look at if your client is considering recall or appeal.

Dismissal, adjournment or postponement

The tribunal can dismiss the case where the tribunal decides the applicant has not complied with any orders or co-operated with the tribunal so that it cannot properly deal with the case.[56] This could be for not providing evidence or information about the application on time.

It can also decide to adjourn or postpone the case, either on its own or on application from either party.[57]

Where a party applies for an adjournment or postponement of a hearing, they must:
- if practicable, notify all other parties of the application for an adjournment or postponement; *and*
- show good reason why an adjournment or postponement is necessary; *and*
- produce evidence of any fact or matter relied on in support of the application for an adjournment or postponement.

The tribunal can adjourn or postpone the hearing to give a party more time to produce evidence if it is satisfied:[58]
- the evidence relates to a matter in dispute; *and*
- it is unjust to determine the case without the evidence; *and*
- where the party has failed to comply with directions for producing evidence, the party must have provided a satisfactory explanation for that failure.

Absence of client
Where the client does not respond or appear at a hearing, and if all relevant notices have been properly served, the tribunal can proceed with the application and take any decision it deems fit, including the award of the application.[59]

Recall
Where the client had good cause for not appearing or having representation at the hearing, they can apply to recall the decision. They can only make one application for recall.[60]

The application should be made within 14 days of the decision and state why the decision should be recalled and how it is in the interest of justice to do so. A copy must be sent to the other parties. The tribunal can extend this 14-day period if it believes it just to do so.[61]

The recall stops any further action or diligence taking place until a new hearing can be heard.

The landlords is asked if they wish to accept the request and, if not, they must inform all parties concerned within 10 days of receiving the notification for recall.

Once the tribunal has the landlord's reply, it can make a decision to:[62]
- grant the application and recall the decision; *or*
- refuse the application; *or*
- order the parties to appear at a case management discussion.

Review
A client can request a review within 14 days of the tribunal's decision, stating why a review of the decision is necessary. A copy of the application must be sent to all parties who can comment on the application.

The tribunal can accept or reject the application and it can review the application where it deems it fit to do so without a hearing.[63]

Appeal

A client can appeal a decision of the tribunal on a point of law only.

An application must be made in writing and identify the decision of the First-tier Tribunal to which it relates, identify the alleged point(s) of law and state the result they are seeking.[64]

Clients are advised to seek expert guidance or legal help in this matter.

Dealing with an eviction case

Rent arrears can be dealt with by an application for time to pay, the Debt Arrangement Scheme (DAS) and insolvency.

Remember, however, that an application to the tribunal will likely be in two parts: an application for payment of the arrears and one for repossession and eviction. The client must convince the tribunal not to award repossession when the arrears have been dealt with.

The first step is to contact the landlord and get their point of view and what they would like to happen. You could try to negotiate writing some of the debt off if the client restarts full payments or ask them to reduce the rent for a few months if the client is going through a difficult patch. You could ask them to defer payment of the arrears until the client's situation improves, or if the client is on benefits, arrange for the landlord to have a managed payment direct from the client's benefits.

Try to negotiate before the landlord decides to go to a tribunal.

Adjournment and postponement

If the case has already been called, you can ask for an adjournment or postponement to give you time to put a defence together and look at suitable options.[65]

Time to pay directions and orders

Time to pay directions (TTPDs) and time to pay orders (TTPOs) are a way to deal with arrears.[66]

Where your client has enough money to make an offer of repayment within a reasonable timescale, they can apply for time to pay, either before the decision is made (TTPD) or after the decision is made (TTPO).

Remember, this only deals with the rent arrears and not an action for repossession. The client must convince the tribunal that they should not allow the repossession to go ahead if the debt is being paid through a time to pay application.

A TTPD is received by the client at the same time as they receive notice of the case management discussion or hearing. The client can complete it and return it to the tribunal.

The application is sent to the landlord, and they can either agree or disagree to the application. If they agree, the time to pay application is awarded and there is no need for a hearing. If they disagree, the tribunal sets a hearing where it will be discussed and decided upon.

A TTPO needs a separate form and must be completed by the client. A copy of the TTPO form and guidance on how to apply can be found on the tribunal website.

See Chapter 11 for more detailed information.

Using the Debt Arrangement Scheme

Rent arrears can be included in the DAS. However, if it is advantageous for the client to make a separate arrangement and treat it as a priority debt with the landlord outside of the DAS, the client can exclude the arrears from the scheme.[67]

If they are included, this should be accepted by the landlord, and they should not pursue the client for the arrears outside of the DAS. See Chapter 6 for more detailed information.

When the case calls in the tribunal, it may be a good tactic to ask for an adjournment or postponement to allow time to make an application for a Debt Payment Programme (DPP). This allows you time to go over the client's whole situation and come up with a suitable strategy.

This alone does not stop an eviction, as there may be one application for the arrears and one for the eviction. The client must convince the tribunal that, as the arrears are being dealt with, it is unreasonable to grant an eviction order.

Using an insolvency option

This could be any of the three options open to clients (Minimal Assets Procedure, Full Administration Bankruptcy or protected trust deeds – see Chapter 6).

As with the DAS, the client must convince the tribunal not to award the eviction order. One argument is that the debt is not 'lawfully due' and so the ground for the eviction is wrong. In the end, it is up to the tribunal to decide.

Reasonableness

Before the tribunal grants an eviction order, it must be satisfied that it is 'reasonable' to do so.

Try to make a case that because the client has dealt with the arrears, it is not reasonable for the tribunal to grant an eviction order.

For assured tenancies, look at section 18(4) of the Housing (Scotland) Act 1988.

For a private residential tenancy agreement, look at Schedule 3 paragraph 12(4) of the Private Housing (Tenancies) (Scotland) Act 2016.

Making referrals

Shelter is an excellent place to refer a client for expert housing advice. You can signpost to Shelter's website[68] or arrange an appointment with one of their specialist advisers. The website is also an excellent source of information for advice workers on all forms of rent arrears.

The Legal Services Agency also takes referrals from debt advisers.[69]

Law centres are available throughout the country. Advisers should make contact with them and set up proper referral procedures.

3. Mortgage arrears

A 'standard security' is the Scots law equivalent of a 'legal mortgage' in England and Wales. It is the only effective form of fixed security that can be taken over land in Scotland. The property remains with the client as owner, while the creditor has fixed security over the property by a standard security registered on the land register through the Registers of Scotland.

Mortgage arrears should be treated as a priority debt.

What is a mortgage

Mortgages (or secured loans) are loans taken out through a bank or building society, usually to buy a property. They are paid back over a long period, typically up to 25 years and normally in monthly instalments. When the agreement is signed, a client gives the property as security. If a client does not make the repayments, the creditor can take back the property. To do this, they must take the client to court.

In Scotland, the process of buying property is through a secured loan and is governed by the Conveyancing and Feudal Reform (Scotland) Act 1970.

In this section, we use the terms 'secured loan' and 'mortgage' interchangeably.

Standard securities

The **'standard security'** is a legal document the client signs in favour of their lender giving their personal undertaking to pay back the loan on the terms agreed, with interest.[70] It gives the lender a security over the property.

The standard security is then registered in the Land Register of Scotland as a charge over the property in favour of the lender.

If the client cannot make their monthly mortgage payments, ultimately the lender has the right to enforce the standard security (referred to as 'calling up the standard security'), which eventually results in the client being removed from their property and the property being marketed and sold by the lender.

Common mortgage types

Mortgages can have different payment options which affect how much is paid and when it will be paid. Regulated financial advice should be taken by the client.

Capital repayment mortgages

Repayments for capital repayment mortgages go towards the amount borrowed (the capital) and the interest. Payments may vary each month depending on the rate of interest. See standard variable rate mortgages and fixed-rate mortgages below. Therefore, the whole loan should be paid off by the end of the mortgage period. This is the most common type of mortgage.

Interest-only mortgages

Interest-only mortgage repayments only pay off the interest. Payments may vary each month depending on the interest rate.

The capital is to be paid off at the end of the mortgage period in a lump-sum. This lump sum payment is normally paid from savings, pensions or an insurance policy taken out at the same time as the mortgage, such as an ISA or endowment policy.

The Financial Conduct Authority (FCA) is worried that there are many people with interest-only mortgages that are coming to the end of the loan term without them having the means to pay the capital part of the loan off. See p257 on the FCA guidance for more information.

Standard variable rate mortgages

This could be a capital repayment or interest-only mortgage.

Repayments towards standard variable rate mortgages may vary from month to month. If the lender increases its standard variable rate, monthly payments increase in capital repayment and fixed-rate mortgages.

Fixed-rate mortgages

Fixed-rate mortgages have a fixed interest rate for the entire mortgage or for a set period – eg, five years. The interest rate is set at the start of the term and does not change. This avoids variable payments and are popular for people who want to know how much they will pay each month.

Tracker mortgages

A tracker mortgage is a form of variable rate mortgage which tracks or follows a base rate (usually the Bank of England's base rate). The amount repaid can change each month. A tracker mortgage's payments may go up, but may also be reduced if the base rate goes down.

Shared ownership mortgages

Shared ownership schemes help people who cannot buy a home on their own. They buy a share in a home, usually a new-build development, at 25, 50 or 75 per cent. The rest of the property is owned by a housing association or the builder. The buyer pays a reduced rent (known as an 'occupancy payment') for the part of the home they do not own. The total cost of the reduced rent and mortgage repayments may be less than the cost of a 100 per cent mortgage.

Remember to count both the loan and the rental amount.

Islamic mortgages

There are three types of Sharia-compliant mortgages. Specialist advice should be sought.

- **Ijara:** repayments for this plan cover payments towards capital and rent payments. The buyer will have bought out the plan provider by the end of the term and they become the sole owner.
- **Murabaha:** the lender buys the property and sells it to the buyer at a slightly higher price. The price depends on the property's value, the deposit paid and the length of the mortgage. The deposit is at least 20 per cent of the purchase price. Repayments are fixed and the loan can be repaid at any time.
- **Diminishing Musharaka:** is a co-ownership agreement. The buyer and the bank own the property together. The buyer buys the bank's shares in the property over time, gradually increasing their stake in the property.

Loan for mortgage interest

A loan for mortgage interest is a loan secured on the property provided by the DWP to help a buyer make their mortgage payments. To claim a loan for mortgage interest a client must be entitled to universal credit, pension credit, income support, income-related employment and support allowance or income-based jobseeker's allowance.

Mortgage indemnity guarantee

Many mortgage lenders have a normal lending limit of 70–80 per cent of the property's value. If someone wants to borrow a higher proportion (eg, 95–100 per cent), the lender may ask the borrower to buy an insurance policy to protect themselves against a mortgage shortfall. This is the mortgage indemnity guarantee (MIG) (or indemnity insurance or building society indemnity). The insurance premium is usually paid as a lump sum at the time of purchase, or it may also be included in the monthly payments. Remember to check if there is a MIG in place.

Note: this insurance is intended to protect the lender, not the borrower. The only value to the borrower is that, without agreeing to pay the insurance premium, they may be refused the amount of mortgage.

The mortgage indemnity guarantee does not pay the full shortfall. The amount paid is a proportion of the shortfall relative to the lending risk. Therefore, there may still be a shortfall owing to the lender.

However, the insurance company can pursue the client for the money paid towards the mortgage shortfall. In some cases, the client may receive a demand for money from the insurer, even though the lender has agreed not to pursue the shortfall. Alternatively, some insurers appoint the lender to collect a client's liability on their behalf. In this case, the lender contacts the client to ask for payment of the entire shortfall. Commonly, the client can expect to receive a demand from the insurer and the lender for their respective proportions of the shortfall. These cannot be ignored and must be dealt with.

The FCA and regulated mortgage contracts

The FCA is the regulator for consumer mortgage lending. This includes how lenders deal with arrears and possession on regulated mortgage contracts.

A mortgage is a 'regulated mortgage contract' if it was taken out on or after 31 October 2004 and:
- the borrower is an individual – ie, they are acting as a consumer and not for business purposes;
- the loan is secured by a first mortgage on a property;
- the property is at least 40 per cent occupied (or is intended to be occupied) as a dwelling.[71]

Since 21 March 2016, secured loans which are not first mortgages are also regulated mortgage contracts if they meet the rest of the above criteria and:
- the loan was made before 21 March 2016 and was a regulated credit agreement when it was made and so covered by the Consumer Credit Act 1974; *or*
- the loan was made after 21 March 2016, but would have been a regulated agreement and covered by the Consumer Credit Act 1974 if it had been made before this date.

Mortgage prisoners

The FCA has introduced rules to help clients who are up to date with their mortgages, but who have been unable to switch to cheaper loan deals because of changes to lending practices during and after the 2008 financial crisis and the subsequent tightening of lending standards.[72] This group of borrowers are often referred to as 'mortgage prisoners'.

Mortgage lenders can relax the strict rules and provide 'more affordable mortgages' where:
- the new mortgage has a total lower expected cost and lower interest rate over the deal period (or whole term if there is no deal period) than the current mortgage; *and*
- the typical monthly payment over the new mortgage (during the deal period or if there is no deal period over the whole mortgage term) is lower than the monthly payment made in every one of the last 12 months under the current mortgage.

The rules apply where the client:[73]

- has a current mortgage; *and*
- is up to date with their mortgage payments; *and*
- does not want to borrow more, other than to finance any relevant intermediary, product or arrangement fee for the mortgage; *and*
- is looking to switch to a new mortgage deal on their current property.

The rules also apply to interest-only mortgages. The lender can extend a mortgage term but must warn the client if this would extend borrowing into retirement.

The modified 'affordability assessment' cannot be used when the client is looking to switch to a new mortgage on a new property. The new mortgage deal does not have to be with the same lender. While the new rules may help a considerable number of clients to obtain cheaper remortgages, they are of no assistance to those with arrears and are unlikely to help those in negative equity.

FCA guidance for lenders

The FCA has issued several guidance documents for lenders.

Note: at the time of writing, the FCA is in the process of replacing all the tailored support guidance with updated guidance in the CONC and *Mortgages and Home Finance: conduct of business sourcebook* (MCOB). This will come into force on 4 November 2024. See the FCA website and the online edition of this *Handbook* for details.

Tailored support guidance and forbearance

The FCA aims to ensure that clients affected by the pandemic continue to be offered the support they need and that this support is tailored to the client: called 'tailored support' by the FCA. This could potentially involve extended payment deferrals that must be reported on the client's credit reference file. This guidance applies with effect from 1 April 2021 and remains in force until varied or revoked. It applies in addition to the provisions of the MCOB, in particular MCOB 13 (see p258).

The FCA expects lenders to be flexible and not to take a 'one size fits all' approach but to consider short- and long-term options, including:
- providing appropriate forbearance (ie, refraining from exercising a legal right, especially enforcing payment of a debt) that is in the client's interests after consideration of their circumstances. Lenders should not repeatedly pursue the same forbearance option without reconsidering whether it remains appropriate or whether an alternative option should be explored;
- supporting clients through a period of payment difficulties and uncertainty, including by considering their other debts and essential living costs;
- ensuring they recognise and respond to the particular needs of vulnerable clients, especially those with 'protected characteristics' under the Equality Act 2010, such as physical or mental health disabilities;
- having systems, processes and adequately trained staff in place;

- reviewing arrangements regularly and, where a client's circumstances have changed, reconsidering what support they need.

Lenders are expected to offer clients the support to manage their finances, such as signposting to money guidance or referring them for debt advice.

Unless a client is unreasonably refusing to engage with a lender, the lenders should not start to repossess a client's property solely on the ground that any deferred payments remain unpaid. The lender's arrears and repossessions policy should specifically address this situation.

The FCA points out that the tailored support guidance continues to apply and lenders are still expected to consider appropriate forbearance arrangements for clients in financial difficulties and not to repossess a property unless all other reasonable attempts to resolve the position have failed. This is in line with the commitment made by signatories to the Mortgage Charter with effect from 26 June 2023 not to repossess a property within 12 months of a missed payment without the client's consent, except in exceptional circumstances.

The FCA has stated that the tailored support guidance is also applicable to support to borrowers who are struggling with payments because of the cost of living (see also p256).[74] So, if a customer indicates that they are experiencing or reasonably expect to experience payment difficulties due to the rising cost of living, firms should offer prospective forbearance to enable them to avoid, reduce or manage any payment shortfall that would otherwise arise. This includes customers who have not yet missed a payment.

The FCA amended its responsible lending rules in MCOB 11.6.3R from 30 June 2023 to support the implementation of the government's Mortgage Charter.[75] These changes mean that lenders do not need to undertake an affordability assessment as would usually be required under MCOB 11.6.2R when varying a mortgage agreement to enable a borrower to:
- reduce their capital repayments under a repayment mortgage (including to zero or paying interest only) for up to six months;
- fully or partly reverse a term extension within six months of extending the term.

Previously, MCOB 11.6.2R was only disapplied where the variation was made solely for the purposes of forbearance where the borrower was already in arrears or to avoid the borrower falling into arrears, but it is now more widely available. This allows borrowers a temporary, contractual reduction in their monthly mortgage repayments, but they should be made aware that this will involve higher monthly payments after the temporary period is over and higher overall costs over the remaining term of the mortgage. Lenders must ensure that borrowers are provided with sufficient information to enable them to make an informed decision. These new rules will be reviewed after 12 months.

Chapter 8: Housing debt
3. Mortgage arrears

Customers in vulnerable circumstances

The FCA guidance on the fair treatment of vulnerable customers lays out how the FCA wants lenders to behave.[76] It reminds firms that:

> 'a vulnerable customer is someone who, due to their personal circumstances, is especially susceptible to harm, particularly when a firm is not acting with appropriate levels of care and that characteristics of vulnerability may result in consumers having additional or different needs and may limit their ability or willingness to make decisions and choices or to represent their own interests. These consumers may be at greater risk of harm, particularly if things go wrong. We expect firms to provide their customers with a level of care that is appropriate given the characteristics of the customers themselves.'

To achieve good outcomes for customers, firms should:
- understand the needs of their target market/customer base;
- ensure their staff have the right skills and capability to recognise and respond to the needs of vulnerable customers;
- respond to customer needs throughout product design, flexible customer service provision and communications;
- monitor and assess whether they are meeting and responding to the needs of customers with characteristics of vulnerability and make improvements where this is not happening.

The guidance provides some examples of good practice for firms.

Guidance for firms supporting borrowers with the cost of living

In March 2023, the FCA issued its guidance for firms supporting existing mortgage borrowers impacted by rising living costs.[77] Finalised guidance comes into effect from 4 November 2024.

The guidance sets out the flexibility firms have when providing forbearance to those who need it, and the scope firms have to vary contract terms for other borrowers who want to reduce their monthly payments.

It covers areas such as:
- providing forbearance;
- contract variations for the purposes of forbearance;
- implications of forbearance arrangements;
- customers not requiring forbearance – but wanting to reduce their monthly payments (contract variations);
- interest rate switches;
- term extensions;
- variation to interest-only mortgages;
- exceptions to the requirement to provide advice.

Chapter 8: Housing debt
3. Mortgage arrears

Guidance for customers with interest-only mortgages

In 2018, the FCA urged action on interest-only mortgages. It estimates there are over 1.7 million interest-only mortgages in the UK, with many nearing maturity and needing to be paid off soon. It is worried that many customers will be unable to do so and is urging lenders to contact the customers and offer alternatives.

It has issued guidance to firms in *Dealing Fairly with Interest-only Mortgage Customers Who Risk Being Unable to Repay their Loan*.[78]

This gives examples of good practice and says lenders should:
- have a written strategy setting out the firm's policy and procedural framework for managing mortgage loans that may not be repaid in full at the end of the term;
- consider what options can be offered to interest-only customers, either during the mortgage term or at maturity, demonstrating why the firm offers some options and not others;
- provide procedural guidance for front-line staff on how to execute the firm's policy, with appropriate monitoring to ensure fair and consistent customer outcomes;
- collate enough management information to enable the firm to monitor its interest-only back book and review the performance of mitigation actions taken during the mortgage term or after maturity.

Customers should therefore have already been contacted about their interest-only mortgage and offered alternatives.

Actions to protect consumers should include:
- communicating early and frequently according to the potential risk of non-repayment within the firm's mortgage book, and communicating more regularly as customers approach the end of the mortgage term;
- giving customers enough time to consider maturity options, especially if the firm's range of options is limited or if customers must meet specific criteria to be eligible; customers may wish to consider other options and should be given enough time to do so;
- assessing affordability if a variation to an existing mortgage increases the monthly payment or where the revised terms extend the loan into retirement. (Principle 6 of the FCA's *Principles for Businesses* (PRIN) states that a firm must pay due regard to the interests of its customers and treat them fairly);
- considering MCOB 11.8.[79]

Some interest-only customers may be unable to change their mortgage or move to a different provider. Firms should be able to demonstrate how they have complied with Principle 6 in their treatment of such 'trapped' customers – eg, they should not unfairly charge them a higher rate of interest than other customers to exploit the fact that they are unable to exit the mortgage.

Lenders should be offering alternatives to the current loans such as:

- switching the mortgage to a full or part capital-repayment basis;
- extending the mortgage term, incorporating a switch to a full or part capital-repayment basis;
- extending the mortgage term to provide more time to repay the capital outstanding or to sell the property;
- accepting overpayments to reduce the end-of-term balance;
- combining part redemption and any of the above;
- extending the mortgage term on an interest-only basis.
- combining any of the above.

Advisers may also want to consider a move to mortgage to rent or a similar strategy for the client.

Consumer duty

The new 'consumer duty' sets higher and clearer standards of consumer protection across financial services. It requires firms to put their customers' needs first. This is known as a new Principle 12. Firms have been required to apply the duty to new and existing products and services from 31 July 2023. If the consumer duty applies, to set a higher and more exacting standard of conduct, Principle 12 replaces:
- Principle 6 – a firm must pay due regard to the interests of its customers and treat them fairly;
- Principle 7 – a firm must pay due regard to the information needs of its clients and communicate information to them in a way which is clear, fair and not misleading.

The rules can be viewed at fca.org.uk/publication/policy/ps22-9.pdf and the non-Handbook guidance at fca.org.uk/publication/finalised-guidance/fg22-5.pdf. The FCA has also published a 'Dear CEO' letter on implementing the duty in the debt advice sector.[80]

Key expectations of conduct under the consumer duty are explained further through cross-cutting rules.[81] The cross-cutting rules require firms to act in good faith, avoid causing foreseeable harm and enable and support retail customers to pursue their financial objectives.

Mortgages and Home Finance: conduct of business sourcebook

The FCA's *Mortgages and Home Finance: Conduct of Business Sourcebook* (MCOB) is useful to look at when dealing with a mortgage debt case if the loan is a regulated mortgage agreement.

Of particular use is MCOB 13 (arrears, payment shortfalls and repossessions: regulated mortgage contracts and home purchase plans). It covers important areas such as:

- dealing fairly with customers with a payment shortfall: policy and procedures (MCOB 13.3);[82]
- arrears: provision of information to the customer of a regulated mortgage contract (MCOB 13.4);[83]
- dealing with a customer in arrears or with a sale shortfall on a regulated mortgage contract (MCOB 13.5);[84]
- repossessions (MCOB 13.6).[85]

If the mortgage was made on or after 31 October 2004 (or for second secured loans, after 21 March 2016), it may be regulated by the FCA. If so, the lender is required by the MCOB to deal 'fairly' with borrowers in arrears and have a written arrears policy and procedures. This should include:
- providing clients with details of missed payments, the total amount of arrears, the outstanding balance due, any charges incurred to date, an indication of possible future charges and a copy of the current MoneyHelper's information sheet *Mortgage arrears or problems paying your mortgage*;[86]
- making reasonable efforts to come to an agreement with the client about repaying the arrears;
- liaising with an adviser or agency if the client arranges this;
- allowing a reasonable time for repayment, bearing in mind the need to establish, where feasible, a practical repayment plan for the client's circumstances (in appropriate cases, arranging repayments over the remaining term of the mortgage);
- granting the client's request for a change to the payment date or method of payment (unless the lender has a good reason for not agreeing to this);
- if no reasonable repayment arrangement can be made, allowing the client to remain in possession of the property to enable it to be sold;
- repossessing the property only where all other reasonable attempts to resolve the situation have failed.

The lender must take into account the client's circumstances and consider whether it is appropriate to agree to:
- extend the term of the mortgage;
- change the type of mortgage – eg, repayment mortgage to interest-only mortgage;
- defer interest payments;
- capitalise the arrears;
- make use of any government mortgage rescue initiatives.

If arrears have been capitalised and rescheduled over the remaining term of the mortgage, they are no longer arrears and so cannot be relied on as the basis for starting a repossession claim. If a client does not pay the full monthly contractual instalment, the lender must allocate the payment in a way that minimises the arrears (which should have the effect of minimising the default interest and charges).

The lender should also have given the client certain prescribed information as above. In addition, many mortgage lenders do not seek possession until payments of mortgage interest are three, or even six, months in arrears.

The repossession process

We use the term 'repossession' as it is used in common language. Although, strictly it is a 'calling up of the standard security'.

Pre-action requirements

In particular, lenders must provide borrowers with clear information about:[87]
- the terms of the standard security;
- the amount due, including arrears and charges;
- the details of any other debts due to the lender;
- make reasonable efforts to agree on a repayment plan, although if this is defaulted on, they can recommence repossession proceedings.

The creditor must signpost to debt advice and encourage the client to contact the local authority in whose area the security subjects are situated.[88]

The creditor cannot make an application if the client is taking steps which are likely to result in:[89]
- the payment of the arrears within a reasonable timescale; *and*
- any other obligation under the terms of the loan.

Lenders must provide evidence that they have complied with the pre-action requirements by completing Form 11C when they make an application to the court.

Once the pre-action requirements (and other necessary procedures) are complete, the creditor can proceed with court action.

If they have not, the application could be refused, and the lender must start again. This only delays the action.

Lenders must have regard of the Scottish government's guidance on repossession.[90]

Arrears letters

The first contact a client usually has is an arrears letter from the lender. If the client does not address the arrears by contacting the lender, the lender escalates the process.

Default notice

A 'notice of default' in Form B may be served on the client notifying them of the lender's intention to raise court action if the default is not dealt with. This must be addressed within one month.[91]

Calling-up notice and section 11 notice

Lenders must use Form A to begin proceedings. This gives the client two months to pay the full amount owed under the standard security.[92]

The calling-up notice must be served by recorded delivery or delivered in person. At the same time, the lender must serve a notice to the local authority that proceedings are beginning – this is known as a 'section 11 notice'. If this has not been served, the client can ask the court to refuse the application.[93]

Section 24 application and initial writ

An application to the court is made under section 24 of the Act and is by an initial writ.[94]

The sheriff may continue the case or not grant the application unless it is 'reasonable in the circumstances of the case' to do so and several factors have to be taken into account.[95]

Entitled residents

When making an application for repossession, the lender must also inform any 'entitled residents' of the proceedings.

Entitled residents can also make applications to the court to continue the action.[96]

If no such information was provided, they can have the proceedings halted.

Who is an entitled resident?[97]

An entitled resident is a person whose sole or main residence is the security subjects (in whole or in part) and who is:

(a) the proprietor of the security subjects (where the proprietor is not the client in the standard security);

(b) The non-entitled spouse of the client or the proprietor of security subjects which are (in whole or in part) a matrimonial home;

(c) the non-entitled civil partner of the client or the proprietor of security subjects which are (in whole or in part) a family home;

(d) a person living together with the client or the proprietor as husband and wife;

(e) a person living together with the client or the proprietor in a relationship which has the characteristics of the relationship between civil partners;

(f) a person who lived together with the client or the proprietor in a relationship described in paragraph (d) or (e) if–

   (i) the security subjects (in whole or in part) are not the sole or main residence of the client or the proprietor;

   (ii) the person lived together with the client or the proprietor throughout the period of six months ending with the date on which the security subjects ceased to be the sole or main residence of the client or the proprietor; *and*

   (iii) the security subjects (in whole or in part) are the sole or main residence of a child aged under 16 who is a child of both parties in that relationship.

Chapter 8: Housing debt
3. Mortgage arrears

Court hearing

All cases dealing with repossessing property must be heard in court.[98] Actions for recovery of heritable property are heard in the sheriff court using summary application at ordinary cause level. It is started by using an initial writ.

The sheriff can make any decision they see fit, but they must be sure that the lender has complied with the pre-action requirements and that it is reasonable (the 'reasonableness test').[99]

The sheriff should consider:[100]
- reasons for the default;
- the likelihood of the client fulfilling their obligations under the security within a reasonable time;
- any action taken by the lender to allow the client to fulfil those obligations;
- whether the client is taking part in the Debt Arrangement Scheme (DAS);
- whether the client and other residents can source alternative accommodation on repossession.

Advisers could argue in court that where the client enters into the DAS, repossession should not be granted while the scheme is in operation. This is at the discretion of the sheriff.

Court options

In court, the sheriff can make the following decisions.
- **Dismiss the case** – the sheriff throws the case out of court because the lender has not followed the correct procedure or does not have the right to repossess the client's home.
- **Continue the case** – the court sets another date for the case to be reviewed. This may happen if more information is required, or the court wishes to monitor a client's payments toward their arrears.
- **Sist the case** – this pauses the action without a further court date.
- **Grant an order for repossession** – the lender is given the right to evict the client.

At this stage, advisers could ask for the case to be continued or sisted if the client is looking at a Debt Payment Programme (DPP) under the DAS or informal payment arrangement and you need time to put an offer together. This is at the sheriff's discretion.

Order for ejection

Where the client has refused to move voluntarily, the lender can also apply for an order of ejection.[101]

Form for charge for removing

The next stage for those refusing to move is to serve a 'Form of Charge for Removing'.[102]

This gives the client 14 days (or longer in some cases) to remove themselves and their belongings from the property.[103]

If the client does not vacate the property, sheriff officers enforce the eviction. They have the right to remove clients from the property and change the locks.

Minute for recall

A minute for recall, rather than a reponing note, may be lodged by the client or an entitled resident. This means the case is heard again.

Minutes for recall can be made at any time before the decree has been fully implemented – ie, before the client is evicted.[104]

Recall can be applied for by the creditor, the client (only if they did not appear and were not represented in the proceedings) or an entitled resident (if they have not already made an application in the proceedings).[105]

Clients may want to seek legal advice on this.

Dealing with mortgage arrears

Negotiate with the lender

The first step is to contact the lender and try to negotiate some time so that you can see what their position is.

You can ask the lender to exercise forbearance as per the FCA guidelines.[106]

Most lenders are happy that you have become involved and are trying to sort the situation out.

The earlier you contact them the better. It is better to negotiate a settlement rather than rely on the courts.

Using guidance

Advisers should familiarise themselves with the FCA guidance about interest-only customers, mortgage prisoners and forbearance, the MCOB rules and other associated guidance (CONC). You can use this guidance to negotiate with the lender and ensure they comply with the rules.

Check for insurances

A client may have a mortgage payment protection policy. This covers mortgage repayments if the client is sick or has an accident which means they cannot work or lose their job by being made redundant.

Different policies provide different levels of protection. Some cover either illness or unemployment, while others cover both.

Interest-only payments

A large proportion of secured borrowing is repaid by monthly payments that combine interest with a repayment of capital. In such cases, a client can reduce the payments if the creditor agrees to accept payment of only the interest without any capital repayment. Creditors need to be persuaded that a request to make interest-only payments is not just a delaying tactic or an excuse for being unable to pay anything. If a client can afford to pay the interest which is accruing on an agreement, you are not asking for anything that is out of the ordinary or generous.

Payments towards the capital can be resumed if the client's financial circumstances improve in the future. Some creditors are prepared to wait until the property is sold for the capital to be repaid. Creditors must be satisfied either that the arrangement is temporary and the client will resume making the full contractual payments or they will be able to repay the capital in some other way.

Paying interest only is appropriate if the client cannot afford to pay both the interest and capital. Some mortgages allow for a 'payment holiday' of a couple of months. If this is not applicable and/or not appropriate, the lender might consider an interest-only arrangement as an alternative.

It cannot be used for endowment mortgages as the payments are already interest only.

Change from an endowment to a capital and interest mortgage

An endowment mortgage is a secured loan on which only interest is payable, accompanied by an endowment life assurance policy which is intended to pay off the capital borrowed either at the end of the agreed term or on the death of the borrower (whichever is the sooner).

For the borrower in debt, it is essential that the full amounts of both the endowment insurance payments and the interest on the loan itself are repaid on, or shortly after, the due date.

The creditor relies on the insurance company to repay the capital amount lent at the end of the loan period and, if payments to the insurance company stop, the creditor is likely to call in its loan on the basis that its security is at risk, unless an acceptable proposal for repayment of the capital at the end of the loan can be made. If, on the other hand, payments to the creditor are not kept up, the amount outstanding on the loan increases and is likely to become more than the amount that will be produced by the insurance policy at its maturity. Endowment mortgages are therefore less flexible than repayment ones.

To have the flexibility to capitalise arrears, extend the period of a loan or negotiate repayment of arrears over several years, an endowment mortgage needs to be changed to a repayment mortgage. The creditor does this automatically for some clients once the endowment premium is significantly in arrears.

However, to cease paying, surrendering or selling an endowment policy is a major financial decision and should not be taken without specialist advice from an independent financial adviser.

Reduced payments

A creditor can be asked to renegotiate the contract that has been made so that a client can afford the payments. There are three main ways in which payments can be reduced.
- Ask the creditor to reduce interest/charges, either for a period of time (eg, the next year) or for the rest of the loan, even if interest has already been added to the amount payable over the whole period of the loan.
- Ask the creditor to agree to reduce or write off the interest/charges that have already accrued on the loan so that the future payments are affordable by the client.
- Ask the creditor to allow repayments to extend over a longer period, thereby reducing the capital portion of the repayments. There must be sufficient equity to allow this – the amount of equity can be calculated by deducting the total amount of all loans secured on the property from the market value of the property.

Capitalise the arrears

If a client's mortgage arrears have built up, a lender can be asked to add the arrears to the total outstanding and for interest to be charged on the new capital amount. This can be included in the remaining period of the mortgage, or the repayment period may be extended as well. This is known as capitalising the arrears.

This strategy is useful when there is an improvement in the client's circumstances following a period in which arrears have built up. For example, if a client has recently become employed after a period of unemployment or returned to work after a long period of sickness, provided their payment record was previously satisfactory, most creditors will agree to capitalise the arrears.

Creditors only normally capitalise arrears if the property's market value is significantly greater than the amount of capital currently outstanding. They do not usually do so if it would lead to the capital outstanding being more than the value of the property.

Extend the mortgage period

If the client is several years into their mortgage, they could ask the lender to extend the mortgage term. This reduces the monthly payments. If the client has arrears, this may allow them to pay the new mortgage payment and something towards the arrears. They could also capitalise the arrears, as above, and extend the mortgage period.

Reduced payments or a payment holiday

The lender can be asked to renegotiate the mortgage so the client can afford the payments. They can be asked, for example, to charge a lower interest rate. This could be for a set period or the rest of the mortgage period. They can also agree to allow a payment holiday when the client is in a severe financial crisis.

Chapter 8: Housing debt
3. Mortgage arrears

Use pensions or other savings
If the client is over 55 and has a defined contribution pension, they could use some of their pension money to help pay the arrears. The client should also consider if they will need this money later in life. They may need to pay tax on some of the money they take from their pension, and it may also affect their benefits. It is strongly advisable that clients considering accessing their pension pots should get advice from an independent financial adviser or contact Pension Wise.[107] They can arrange for an appointment locally to discuss this (eg, at a local Citizens Advice bureau) or a phone or a face-to-face appointment.

Homeowners' Support Fund
The Homeowners' Support Fund runs two schemes which can help clients at risk of losing their homes.[108]
- **Mortgage to Rent** allows the house to be bought by a local council or housing association and carry out repairs to increase its rental value. The client can then stay in the home as a tenant paying rent to the new owners.
- **Mortgage to Shared Equity** allows the government to purchase up to 30 per cent of the equity in the home, which reduces overall mortgage repayments. The client is still responsible for maintenance and repair and can remain in their home.

Handing back the keys (voluntary surrender)
If a client cannot pay their mortgage, they should not hand the keys back to their mortgage lender. This counts as voluntary repossession and should always be the last resort. If the lender asks the client to give up their keys, they do not have to do this. The lender must have a court order before the client can be evicted.

When handing back the keys, the client is still responsible for costs associated with the property (eg, council tax and utilities) until the property is sold.

Using the Debt Arrangement Scheme
The client can apply for a DPP even if they have mortgage arrears. This is only suitable if they can continue to make their regular mortgage payments, as the programme only covers the arrears, and the client must be able to pay ongoing mortgage costs.

Remember that while this can deal with the arrears, it does not automatically stop the sheriff from granting repossession at the same time. The client's representative, or the client, must ask the sheriff not to grant repossession while the arrears are being paid. In this case, you could ask for a continuation or sist to buy the client time.

Using an insolvency option
Using insolvency is not an option for mortgage arrears as the inclusion of any debt owed does not stop the lender from repossessing the property.[109]

Insolvency can be a breach of the standard conditions in that if the client is insolvent, the lender can call up the security.[110]

Time order
The client can request the court to make a time order to reschedule the amount due over a longer period of time.

Time orders only apply to regulated mortgage contracts. They can only be granted if the court believes it is just to do so. See p105 for more information on time orders.

Recall the decree
If the client did not go to court for their court summons date and a repossession order was granted, they might be able to get the court's decision recalled (allowing the case to be heard again). The client must lodge a minute for recall. They will require help from a solicitor, adviser or lay representative.

The minute of recall can be applied for at any time before the repossession and eviction are carried out.

Mortgage shortfalls
Mortgage shortfalls exist when a client's home has been repossessed and sold but it does not make enough money to clear the debt. The lender is entitled to pursue the debt as an unsecured debt once court action has been taken. More information can be found in MCOB 12.4.[111]

As this is now a non-priority debt, it can be dealt with the same as other debts that the client may have, and a relative strategy is chosen for them.

The Mortgage Charter
Ninety per cent of all UK mortgage lenders have signed up to the UK government's 'Mortgage Charter'. This is a joint piece of work from the government, the FCA and mortgage lenders.[112]

In short, lenders have agreed the following.
- Anyone worried about their mortgage repayments can contact their lender for help and guidance, without any impact on their credit file, and we would encourage you to contact your bank, which is there to help.
- Lenders should provide support for customers who are up to date with payments to switch to a new mortgage deal at the end of their existing fixed rate deal without another affordability check.
- Lenders will provide well-timed information to help customers plan ahead should their current rate be due to end.
- Lenders will offer tailored support for anyone struggling and deploy highly trained staff to help customers. This could mean extending their term to reduce their payments, offering a switch to interest-only payments, but also a

range of other options like a temporary payment deferral or part interest-part repayment. The right option will depend on the customer's circumstances.

Taken together with the FCA guidance, there should be some room for negotiation with lenders for clients having difficulty paying their mortgages.

Complaints and the Financial Ombudsman Service

Complaints in the first instance must go through the lender's complaints procedure.

If the client is not satisfied with the result, they can escalate it to the Financial Ombudsman Service (FOS) to investigate. Note that you can only go to the FOS once you have received a final response from the financial institution you are complaining about or if it has not responded to your complaint within eight weeks. The FOS is free to use.[113]

Checklist

- Contact the lender and ask for forbearance as per the FCA guidance.
- Check that the rules and guidance in MCOB have been followed.
- Check that the lender has complied with the pre-action requirements.
- Compile a financial statement.
- Look at alternative mortgage packages.
- Look at the DAS or informal payment arrangement for the client.
- Consider a time order if applicable.
- Look at mortgage to rent or other schemes.

Notes

1. **Social housing sector**
   1 s14A H(S)A 2001
   2 scotland.shelter.org.uk/professional_resources/legal/security_of_tenure/eviction/pre-action_requirements_in_rent_arrears_cases#reference-6
   3 ss14 and 14A H(S)A 2001
   4 s14(4) H(S)A 2001
   5 See Sch 2 The Scottish Secure Tenancies (Proceedings for Possession) (Form of Notice) Regulations 2012 No.92 at legislation.gov.uk/ssi/2012/92/schedule/2/made
   6 s14 H(S)A 2001
   7 s36 H(S)A 2001
   8 Sch 1 r4.5 Summary Cause Rules
   9 Sch 1 r7.1 Summary Cause Rules
   10 Sch 1 Ch 2A Summary Cause Rules
   11 Sch 1 r8.2(3) Summary Cause Rules
   12 s16(1) H(S)A 2001
   13 Art 2 The Scottish Secure Tenancies (Repossession Orders) (Maximum Period) Order 2012 No.128
   14 Sch 1 r24.1 Summary Cause Rules
   15 Sch 1 Ch 24.1(9) Summary Cause Rules
   16 s14 H(S)A 2001

Chapter 8: Housing debt
Notes

17 r16 Act of Sederunt (Sheriff Court Rules) (Miscellaneous Amendments) 2011 No.193
18 Sch 1 r25.1 Summary Cause Rules
19 Sch 1 Ch 25 Summary Cause Rules
20 Art 4 Act of Sederunt (Actions for removing from heritable property) 2012 No.136
21 scotland.shelter.org.uk/professional_resources/legal/security_of_tenure/eviction/post_decree_eviction

2. Private rented sector
22 Reg 2 The First-tier Tribunal for Scotland Housing and Property Chamber and Upper Tribunal for Scotland (Composition) Regulations 2016 No.340
23 s32 H(S)A 2001
24 gov.scot/publications/form-at5
25 Sch 5 H(S)A 1988
26 Sch 5 H(S)A 1988 (grounds 11 and 12)
27 s18(4) Sch 5 H(S)A 1988
28 s4A(a) and (b) H(S)A 1988
29 s18 H(S)A 1988
30 Regs 3 and 4 The Rent Arrears Pre-Action Requirements (Coronavirus) (Scotland) Regulations 2020 No.304, amended by s8 H(S)A 1988 and Sch 3 Private Housing (Tenancies) (Scotland) Act 2016
31 The Rent Arrears Pre-Action Requirements (Coronavirus) (Scotland) Regulations 2020 No.304
32 edinburgh.gov.uk/downloads/file/24948/notice-to-quit-form-pdf
33 gov.scot/publications/form-at6
34 s19(1)(b) and Sch 5 H(S)A 1988
35 s19(7) and Sch 5 H(S)A 1988
36 s19A H(S)A 1998
37 s11 Homelessness etc. (Scotland) Act 2003
38 Sch 3 PH(T)(S)A 2016
39 Sch 3 para 12(1) PH(T)(S)A 2016
40 Sch 3 para 12(4) PH(T)(S)A 2016
41 legislation.gov.uk/ssi/2017/297/schedule/5/made
42 s54 PH(T)(S)A 2016
43 Sch 2 para 2 FTTSHPC(P) Regs
44 Sch r6 FTTSHPC(P) Regs
45 Sch r8 FTTSHPC(P) Regs
46 Sch rr10 and 11 FTTSHPC(P) Regs
47 Sch r16 FTTSHPC(P) Regs
48 Sch r17 FTTSHPC(P) Regs
49 Sch r18 FTTSHPC(P) Regs
50 Sch r19 FTTSHPC(P) Regs
51 Sch rr20, 21 and 22 FTTSHPC(P) Regs
52 Sch r24(2) FTTSHPC(P) Regs
53 Sch r25 FTTSHPC(P) Regs
54 Sch r26 FTTSHPC(P) Regs
55 Sch r26 FTTSHPC(P) Regs
56 Sch r27 FTTSHPC(P) Regs
57 Sch r28 FTTSHPC(P) Regs
58 Sch r28(4) FTTSHPC(P) Regs
59 Sch r29 FTTSHPC(P) Regs
60 Sch r30 FTTSHPC(P) Regs
61 Sch r30 FTTSHPC(P) Regs
62 Sch r30(9) FTTSHPC(P) Regs
63 Sch r39 FTTSHPC(P) Regs
64 Sch r37(2) FTTSHPC(P) Regs
65 Sch r28 FTTSHPC(P) Regs
66 The First-tier Tribunal for Scotland Housing and Property Chamber (Incidental Provisions) Regulations 2019 No.51; housingandpropertychamber.scot/news/time-pay-and-other-legislation-amendments
67 s8 The First-tier Tribunal for Scotland Housing and Property Chamber (Incidental Provisions) Regulations 2019 No.51
68 scotland.shelter.org.uk/housing_advice/eviction
69 lsa.org.uk/how-we-help/housing

3. Mortgage arrears
70 s9 CFR(S)A 1970
71 Art 61 The Financial Services and Markets Act 2000 (Regulated Activities) Order 2001 No.544
72 FCA Handbook, MCOB 11.9, which came into effect on 28 October 2019
73 FCA, MCOB 11.9
74 FCA, *Guidance for Firms Supporting their Existing Mortgage Borrowers Impacted by the Rising Cost of Living*, FG 23/2, March 2023
75 HM Treasury, *Mortgage Charter*, June 2023, available at gov.uk/government/publications/mortgage-charter
76 fca.org.uk/publication/finalised-guidance/fg21-1.pdf
77 fca.org.uk/publications/finalised-guidance/fg24-2-guidance-firms-supporting-existing-mortgage-borrowers-impacted-rising-living-costs
78 fca.org.uk/publications/finalised-guidance/fg13-7-dealing-fairly-interest-only-mortgage-customers-who-risk
79 handbook.fca.org.uk/handbook/MCOB/11/8.html
80 fca.org.uk/publication/correspondence/consumer-duty-letter-debt-advice.pdf

Chapter 8: Housing debt
Notes

81 FCA, *The cross-cutting rules set out how firms should act to deliver good outcomes for customers*
82 handbook.fca.org.uk/handbook/MCOB/13/3.html
83 handbook.fca.org.uk/handbook/MCOB/13/4.html
84 handbook.fca.org.uk/handbook/MCOB/13/5.html
85 handbook.fca.org.uk/handbook/MCOB/13/6.html
86 moneyhelper.org.uk/en/homes/buying-a-home/mortgage-arrears-if-you-have-problems-paying-your-mortgage
87 s24A CFR(S)A 1970
88 s24A CFR(S)A 1970
89 s24A(4) CFR(S)A 1970
90 Scottish government, *Home Owner and Debtor Protection (Scotland) Act 2010: guidance on pre-action requirements for creditors*, August 2010, available at gov.scot/publications/home-owner-debtor-protection-scotland-act-2010-guidance-pre-action-requirements-creditors/
91 Sch 6 Form B CFR(S)A 1970
92 s19 and Sch 6 CFR(S)A 1970
93 s11 Homelessness etc. (Scotland) Act 2003
94 s24 CFR(S)A 1970
95 s24(7) CFR(S)A 1970
96 s24B CFR(S)A 1970
97 s24C CFR(S)A 1970
98 Home Owner and Debtor Protection (Scotland) Act 2010
99 s24 (5)(b) CFR(S)A 1970
100 s24(7) CFR(S)A 1970
101 s5 CFR(S)A 1970
102 legislation.gov.uk/ssi/2011/158/schedule/made
103 s216 BD(S)A 2007
104 s24D(3) CFR(S)A 1970
105 s24D(2) CFR(S)A 1970
106 FCA, *Guidance for Firms Supporting their Existing Mortgage Borrowers Impacted by the Rising Cost of Living FG23/2*, 10 March 2023, available at fca.org.uk/publication/finalised-guidance/fg23-2.pdf
107 moneyhelper.org.uk/en/pensions-and-retirement/pension-wise
108 mygov.scot/home-owners-support-fund
109 s145(3)(f) B(S)A 2016
110 Sch 3(9) CFR(S)A 1970
111 handbook.fca.org.uk/handbook/MCOB/12/4.html
112 gov.uk/government/publications/mortgage-charter
113 financial-ombudsman.org.uk/consumers

Chapter 9

Diligence

This chapter covers:
1. Attachment and exceptional attachment (below)
2. Earning arrestment (p281)
3. Bank arrestment (p284)
4. Money attachment (p292)
5. Inhibition in execution (p295)
6. On the dependence (p297)
7. Adjudication for debt (p298)
8. Summary diligence (p299)

In Scotland, 'diligence' is the name for the action a creditor can take to recover a debt after court action.

Note: the Bankruptcy and Diligence (Scotland) Act 2024 will make changes to some rules. Check the online version of this *Handbook* for updates.

1. Attachment and exceptional attachment

The Debt Arrangement and Attachment (Scotland) Act 2002 introduced attachment and exceptional attachment to replace diligence of poindings and warrant sales. This 'new' diligence contains more protections for clients than the previous diligence, although it still bears many similarities to poindings and warrant sales. An integral part of the legislation is the requirement to provide helpful information to the client before starting this diligence, in the form of a Debt Advice and Information Package (DAIP) and debt advice. The intention is to avoid enforcement where possible.

Attachment and exceptional attachment make up around 1 per cent of all diligences carried out by creditors in Scotland, with non-earnings arrestments making up the majority of all diligences carried out by creditors.

Attachment

Part 2 of the Debt Arrangement and Attachment (Scotland) Act 2002 outlines the attachment of the client's 'corporeal moveable property'. This is property which

Chapter 9: Diligence
1. Attachment and exceptional attachment

is tangible (corporeal), is not fixed like land or buildings and can be handled and moved (moveable). Therefore, a client's car can be attached, as well as property within the car. It also includes property that is stored in a garden shed, a lock up or on business premises. A mobile home can be attached unless it is the client's sole or principal residence.

Property attached can be presumed to be owned by the client or jointly owned by the client and a third party in common with the client.

Property within a dwellinghouse cannot be attached and certain goods are exempt from attachment.

An attachment can only be actioned following the expiry of a charge for payment. The client must be provided with a DAIP which they must receive no later than the service of the charge for payment.

When attachment is used

Creditors rarely use attachments for personal debt as they can use other, more effective diligences – eg, bank and wage arrestment. The majority of attachments are executed against businesses but, regardless of whether it is a personal or business debt, the creditor must serve the client with a charge for payment after court action has happened. The charge for payment can only be served by a sheriff officer or messenger-at-arms.

Although summary diligence and summary warrant does not have a traditional court hearing, a charge for payment must still be served before the creditor can execute an attachment.

Times when attachment is not competent

It is not competent to execute an attachment on:[1]
- a Sunday; *or*
- a day which is a public holiday in the area in which the attachment is to be executed; *or*
- such other day as may be prescribed by Act of Sederunt.

The execution of an attachment cannot begin before 8am or after 8pm or be continued after 8pm, unless the officer has obtained prior authority from the sheriff for such commencement or continuation.

How the attachment is carried out

After the expiry of a charge for payment, the creditor can instruct sheriff officers to carry out an attachment. When the sheriff officers arrive at the client's property, they can open shut and lockfast doors – eg, a garage door or business premises doors. They then complete an attachment schedule: this shows all the property that has been attached and the value of the goods attached. A copy of the schedule is given to the client. The sheriff officer does not remove the property immediately unless they have a court order allowing them to do so.

Chapter 9: Diligence
1. Attachment and exceptional attachment

The sheriff officer must then report the attachment to the sheriff court within 14 days of it being carried out.[2] After the report is received by the sheriff, notice is then given to the client that the attached property will be collected for auction. The sheriff officer is then allowed to come on that day and remove the attached goods, which are sold at auction.

The client has 14 days from the date the attachment was executed to challenge the attachment or redeem their property from the sheriff officer.[3]

Goods exempt from attachment

Certain goods owned by the client cannot be attached. These include:[4]
- tools, books or other equipment reasonably required for the client's profession, trade or business and not exceeding in aggregate value £1,000;
- any vehicle, the use of which is so reasonably required by the client, not exceeding in value £3,000;
- a mobile home which is the client's only or principal residence;
- tools or equipment reasonably required for keeping the client's garden in good order;
- any money.

If a sheriff officer attaches any of these, the client can apply to have them removed from the attachment schedule on the grounds they are exempt.[5]

Unlawful acts after attachment

After goods have been attached (but not yet removed for auction), it is illegal for the client or any other third party to remove the goods from the place they were attached.[6] For example, an attached car cannot be moved to another property and kept there as if it was its new address.

The client cannot gift or sell the goods to someone else. They cannot wilfully damage or allow someone else to wilfully damage the goods. Where goods have been removed, gifted or sold to someone else or wilfully damaged, the client or third party that has done so may be guilty of an offence and could be fined or given a custodial sentence by the sheriff. The sheriff may also order a further attachment take place at the client's property.

If the goods are stolen or damaged in an accident, the client must inform the sheriff officers immediately and provide details of any insurance claims that are being made.

How long an attachment lasts

As a general rule, attachments cease if it has been six months since the sheriff officers executed that attachment or if sheriff officers have already removed the attached goods.[7] Then, if the goods have not been auctioned after 28 days, the attachments cease and if the goods have been removed, they are returned to the client.

The auction of the attached goods may be cancelled to allow the sums recoverable to be paid in accordance with an agreement between the creditor and the client. A sheriff officer cannot cancel the arrangements for such an auction on more than two occasions.

The auction
Generally, an auction is 'a public auction' unless it is impractical to do so. It should be held within 28 days of the goods being removed from the client's address.[8] If this does not happen, the attachment ceases to be valid and the goods are returned to the client.

The sheriff officer and a witness must attend the auction. When the goods are sold, the sheriff officer can take their fees and outlays from the monies 'ingathered'. The rest goes to the creditor and any amount over the debt total is returned to the client.

The creditor, a third party or the client can bid for the attached goods at auction.

The sheriff officer must send the court a report within 14 days of the auction outlining the outcome of the same.[9]

Redemption of attached goods

The client can, within 14 days of the date on which goods were attached, redeem (buy back) those goods.[10] They must pay the amount the goods have been valued at by the sheriff officers. When full payment of the value of the attached good is received by the sheriff officers, a receipt is given to the client which ends the attachment.

Challenging an attachment

There are several grounds where an attachment can be challenged.[11] Some of the common grounds used include:
- the fixed value of goods is too low;
- the release of a vehicle from an attachment;
- the attachment is invalid;
- the attached goods are jointly owned;
- the attached goods belong to someone else.

When a client takes the completed forms to the court, the sheriff clerk sets a hearing date and gives the client and the creditor an opportunity to make representations to the court. This also has the effect of postponing the auction until this is settled. The sheriff has the final say. There is no cost to the client to challenge an attachment, although if they lose and the creditor has costs associated with defending the action, they may ask the court to fix a hearing to allow expenses to be charged to the client.

The forms needed are in Schedule 1 (Appendix 1) to the Act of Sederunt (Debt Arrangement and Attachment (Scotland) Act 2002) 2002.

Fixed value of goods is too low
If the client believes the value fixed by the sheriff officer to any attached goods is too low, they can appeal this up to the date of the auction by completing Form 4. If the sheriff agrees with the client's assertion, the attachment ceases; if not the auction goes ahead.[12]

Release of a vehicle from attachment
A client can apply to the courts for the release of their attached vehicle.[13] This must be done within 14 days of the attachment and the car must be valued at £3,000 or less. The client can claim the sale would be **'unduly harsh'**. This is not defined in the Act, but it could be argued that the car is required for work or hospital appointments. If the attached vehicle is valued at more than £3,000, the sheriff can order the immediate sale of the car and state that £3,000 be returned to the client (to allow them to buy another car). If the car is not sold within 14 days of the order, it is returned to the client and excluded from the attachment. It cannot be attached again. A client must complete Form 11.

The attachment is invalid
At any time up until the auction, a client can make an application to the court to have the attachment declared invalid.[14] This can be on the grounds that there were procedural irregularities – eg, the attachment was carried out on a Sunday. The sheriff can also order that an attachment is invalid, without the client having made an application, if they are satisfied that the attachment has ceased to have effect (generally out of time) or the attachment was invalid due to procedural irregularities. Form 13 (Invalidity and Cessation of Attachment) should be completed.

The attached goods are jointly owned
Jointly owned goods can be attached by sheriff officers. The person who jointly owns the goods can (up to the date of the auction) pay the client's share of the value of the goods attached to the sheriff officers, which transfers ownership to them and releases the goods from the attachment. The client or the joint owner can also argue that attaching the goods would be 'unduly harsh' to the joint owner and, if accepted by the sheriff, the attached goods would be released from the attachment. In both instances, sheriff officers can execute a further attachment on the client. Form 20 is used when the claim is that the attachment would be unduly harsh to the joint owner.

Attached goods belong to someone else
If a person claims to own the goods attached (and before the auction occurs), they can challenge the attachment of those goods.[15] This can either be done when the

attachment is being carried out (and the sheriff officer is satisfied the goods they are about to attach belong to someone other than the client named on the attachment schedule) or by the owner using Form 18 to challenge the attachment of those goods when they have already been attached. If the sheriff is satisfied these goods belong to someone else, they are removed from the attachment schedule and sheriff officers can go back to the client's address to further attach other goods.

Exceptional attachment

Exceptional attachment order

An **'exceptional attachment'** is an order of the court allowing articles kept in a dwellinghouse to be attached. The order allows a sheriff officer to open shut and lockfast places and to attach, remove and auction the client's non-essential assets that are in the dwellinghouse at the time of attachment.

An exceptional attachment order:[16]
- authorises the attachment, removal and auction of the client's non-essential assets which, at the time of the attachment, are kept in any dwellinghouse specified in the application; *and*
- specifies a period during which the order is to be executed; *and*
- empowers the sheriff officer to open shut and lockfast places to execute the order.

Exceptional circumstances

Before a sheriff grants an exceptional attachment order to a creditor, they must be certain that there are exceptional circumstances for doing so.[17] They must consider:
- the nature of the debt (and, in particular, whether the debt incurred relates to any tax or duty or to any trade or business carried on by the client);
- whether the client resides in the dwellinghouse specified in the application;
- whether the client carries on a trade or business in that dwellinghouse;
- whether debt advice has been given to the client;
- whether a time to pay direction or order in relation to the debt has lapsed;
- any agreement between the client and creditor for the settlement of the debt;
- any declaration or representation made, or document lodged, by or on behalf of the client which relates to:
  – the existence of any non-essential assets owned by the client; *and*
  – where they exist, their value, or the client's financial circumstances.

Before deciding whether to make an exceptional attachment order, the sheriff may make:
- an order for a visit to the client by a person specified in the order for the purposes of giving debt advice to the client; *or*
- such other order as the sheriff thinks fit.

The sheriff must also be satisfied that:[18]
- the creditor has taken reasonable steps to negotiate (or seek to negotiate) a settlement of the debt; *and*
- the creditor has executed or reasonably attempted to execute a non-earnings arrestment and an earnings arrestment to secure payment of the debt; *and*
- there is a reasonable prospect that the sum recovered at auction would be at least equal to the total of a reasonable estimate of any chargeable expenses plus £100 (or other specified amount); *and*
- having had regard to the nature of the debt and whether the client resides in the dwellinghouse and carries out a business there and any other matters which the sheriff considers appropriate, it would be reasonable in the circumstances to grant the exceptional attachment order.

A creditor must normally try an earnings and a non-earnings arrestment before applying for an exceptional attachment order. However, in some circumstances this can waived.

Sheriff officer's power of entry

Unless the authorisation in an exceptional attachment order to open shut and lockfast places, a sheriff officer should not enter a dwellinghouse to execute the order unless there appears to be someone present who:[19]
- is aged 16 years or over;
- because of their age, knowledge of English, mental illness, mental or physical disability or otherwise, cannot understand the consequences of the procedure being carried out.

In addition, the sheriff officer must send a notice to the client at least four days before the intended date of entry, which explains what will happen and when.[20]

The creditor/sheriff officer can apply to the sheriff to dispense with the requirement to serve notice on a client. This is done when the creditor/sheriff officer believes the client will dispose of non-essential goods, so defeating the exceptional attachment.

Unlawful acts before attachment

When a client has received notice of an exceptional attachment order, it is unlawful for them or a third party (who is aware that the order has been made) to:[21]
- move any non-essential goods from the dwellinghouse, to sell, gift or give up ownership of any non-essential goods without the sheriff's permission;
- wilfully destroy or damage any non-essential items that would normally be attached in pursuance of the order.

Chapter 9: Diligence
1. Attachment and exceptional attachment

If non-essential goods are stolen before the exceptional attachment takes place but after the notice has been received, the client must inform sheriff officers straight away and provide details of any insurance claims that may be made.[22]

Valuation
Sheriff officers should value any goods at the price they are likely to fetch if sold on the open market.[23] If the sheriff officer considers it appropriate, they can arrange for an attached article to be valued by a professional valuer or other suitably skilled person.

If the goods are valued at a different value than the sheriff officer, the client is notified of the valuer's price.[24] This is often happens when paintings or jewellery are attached, and the sheriff officer is unsure of the value.

Goods exempt from an exceptional attachment order
Sheriff officers cannot take money from a client's home (although they may take it from business premises).[25] The exception is if the money is 'antique money', such as that kept by a coin collector, which may be worth more than the value shown on the money itself.

Sheriff officers cannot exceptionally attach:[26]
- basic items needed for family life, including clothes, work tools, essential furniture, housekeeping equipment, children's toys, bedding, household linen, floor coverings, lights or light fittings, home computers, radios, microwaves, TVs or telephones;
- rented or hire purchase/conditional sale goods which are still being paid off;
- if property belongs to other people (such as children, family members or a neighbour), proof must be shown. The owner can tell the sheriff officer that the item belongs to them and provide written evidence.

Schedule 2 to the Debt Arrangement and Attachment (Scotland) Act 2002 has a full list of all the goods which are exempt from being attached under an exceptional attachment order.

Redemption
After goods have been removed, the client only has seven days to redeem any attached items.[27] In the future, this could be extended to 14 days for goods that are not removed immediately.[28] Check the online version of this *Handbook* for updates. The client must pay the amount the goods had been valued at to the sheriff officers. Then the goods are released from the exceptional attachment schedule. If all goods on the exceptional attachment sche~redeemed, the auction does not take place. If there are still unredeemed goods, the auction is held as soon as possible after seven days have passed.

Goods of sentimental value

There is protection for the client against goods of sentimental value being attached during the execution of an exceptional attachment.[29]

Unlike for exempt goods, there is not a list of sentimental goods in the legislation. It is generally the sheriff officer's judgement, but a client can challenge any goods which have been exceptionally attached which they consider to have sentimental value, as long as it is worth no more than £150 – eg, a wedding ring.

Challenging an exceptional attachment

An attached article cannot be auctioned after its removal for seven days.[30] During this seven-day period, the client can challenge an exceptional attachment by applying to the court and asking that attached goods be released. This can be on the following grounds:
- the attachment of an item is not 'competent'. This means that the correct procedures have not been followed and the exceptional attachment order is not valid; *or*
- an auction of attached items would be 'unduly harsh'; *or*
- goods are of sentimental value and are worth less than £150; *or*
- the items were attached at a lot less, or more, than their true market value; *or*
- the value of the items is less than the likely costs of an auction.

Use Form 28 when challenging an exceptional attachment order.[31]

An 'appeal' is possible in respect of any decision in relation to proceedings concerning an exceptional attachment order.[32] This should be made to the sheriff clerk with the leave of the sheriff only on a point of law. The sheriff's decision on appeal is final.

Forms for exceptional attachments and attachments

A list of the forms can be found in Schedule 1 (Appendix 1) to the Act of Sederunt (Debt Arrangement and Attachment (Scotland) Act 2002) 2002. It shows the number of the form to be used, with a brief description of what it is. There is also a note of the rule within the Act which should be read at the same time.

Form Numner	Description	Rule Number
1	Warrant for intimation	5(1)
2	Certificate of intimation	5(4)
3	Attachment schedule	8(3)
4	Application for attachment to cease to have effect because the value fixed is too low	9(1)
5	Notice of theft of attached articles	10(1) and 32(1)

Chapter 9: Diligence
1. Attachment and exceptional attachment

6	Application for further attachment in same place and/or revaluation when articles moved, stolen, damaged or destroyed	11(1)
7	Application for consignation where articles have been damaged, destroyed, lost, stolen or disposed of	12(1) and 33(1)
8	Report of attachment	13(1)
9	Receipt for redemption of attached articles	14 and 35
10	Application for security of attached articles or sale of articles that are perishable or likely to deteriorate	15(1)
11	Application for (1) release of vehicle or mobile home from attachment (2) immediate sale of a vehicle	16(1)
12	Application for extension of duration of an attachment	17(1)
13	Application for an order declaring the attachment invalid or has ceased to have effect	18(1)
14	Notice of removal of attached articles and public auction	19(1)
15	Report of agreement resulting in cancellation of auction	20(1)
16	Application for an order for a new auction	20(2)
17	Report of auction	21(1)
18	Application in relation to articles belonging to a third party	23(1)(a)
19	Application in relation to articles belonging to a third party in common with the debtor	23(1)(b)
20	Application for attachment to cease as sale would be unduly harsh	23(1)(c)
21	Application in relation to articles belonging to a third party in common with the debtor that have been sold at auction	24(1)
22	Application for exceptional attachment order	25(1)
23	Form of service	25(2)(c)(i)
24	Declaration by debtor of financial circumstances	25(2)(c)(ii) and 26(1)
25	Notice of exceptional attachment order	28
26	Report of visit to give money advice	29(1)
27	Application for consent to move any article, to sell, make a gift or otherwise relinquish ownership	31(1)
28	Application for return of articles (1) removed where attachment not competent (2) where auction unduly harsh or (3) of sentimental value	34(1)

2. Earnings arrestment

An earnings arrestment was introduced by the Debtors (Scotland) Act 1987. It is the second most common form of diligence used in Scotland to recover debts, with 57,260 being served in 2022/23.

There are three types of arrestment:
- earnings arrestment;
- current maintenance arrestment;
- conjoined arrestment order.

Current maintenance arrestment

Since the introduction of the 'deduction from earnings order' (see p308) in 2016 for the collection of maintenance arrears, current maintenance arrestments are seldom used.[33]

Number of current maintenance arrestments executed

Year	Number
2011/12	16,025
2012/13	12,540
2013/14	19,495
2014/15	12,980
2015/16	15
2016/17	15
2017/18	20
2018/19	15
2019/20	5
2020/21	0
2021/22	25

Conjoined arrestment orders

A conjoined arrestment order (CAO) allows two or more creditors to share the proceeds of a diligence against earnings. The employer pays the sum deducted to the sheriff clerk of the court that grants the order, and the court divides that payment between the creditors conjoined in that order.[34]

How does it work

Before a creditor can arrest earnings, they must take appropriate legal action. This can be by issuing a claim, summons or writ to obtain a decree (court order) or obtaining a summary warrant.

After a decree or summary warrant has been awarded, the creditor must then serve a charge for payment on the client and wait until the charge has expired, which is normally after 14 days.

2. Earnings arrestment

The creditor must give the client a Debt Advice and Information Package (DAIP)[35] at least 12 weeks before arrestment takes place.[36]

A creditor who has obtained the decree or summary warrant can instruct the sheriff officers to arrest the client's earnings. This is done by serving an 'earnings arrestment schedule' on the employer, who is obliged by law to make the deduction and send the money to the court, where it is noted and passed on to the creditor.[37]

Earnings arrestment schedule

An earnings arrestment schedule is on Form 30. It states:[38]
- the name, designation and address of the creditor, the client, the employer and any person residing in the UK to whom payment under the arrestment is to be made; *and*
- the decree or other document constituting the debt and when, where and by whom it was granted or issued; *and*
- the date any charge for payment was served; *and*
- the debt outstanding and how it is calculated.

Attached to the earnings arrestment schedule is a copy of Schedule 2, which is a deduction from earnings calculation table.[39]

The sheriff officer should take all reasonably practicable steps to serve a copy of the schedule on the client. Failure to do so does not, by itself, render the arrestment invalid.

The schedule should be served by registered or recorded delivery letter or, if such a letter cannot be delivered, by any other competent mode of service.

The employer should notify the client of the date and amount of the first deduction.

No arrestment can be taken if the client earns less than £655.83 a month. The amount can change when the Diligence Against Earnings (Variation) (Scotland) Regulations 2023 No.27 are updated.[40]

An example of a monthly wage arrestment
Callum's net pay is £1,500.
£1,500 − £655.83 = £844.17 x 19% = £160.39.
The amount arrested is £160.39.

Employer's duty to provide information

Where an employer receives an earnings arrestment schedule, a current maintenance arrestment schedule or a copy of a CAO, they must send to the creditor (or for a CAO, the sheriff clerk), the following as soon as reasonably possible:[41]

- how often the client is paid – weekly, monthly or otherwise;
- the date of the client's next payday;
- the sum to be deducted on that payday and the net earnings from which deductions are to be taken.

The employer must also provide updates six-monthly and annually on 6 April, where the debt still exists and it is reasonable to do so.

If the client leaves that employment, the employer should notify the creditor or sheriff clerk as soon as possible that the client is no longer employed and provide new employment details if known. This information should also be sent to the client.

Creditor's duty to provide information

Six months after service of the order and then on 6 April thereafter, a creditor who is receiving payment from a client by an earnings arrestment, a current maintenance arrestment or CAO must send to the employer (or for a CAO, the sheriff clerk):[42]
- the sum owed by the client to the creditor;
- the amounts received by the creditor by virtue of the arrestment or order;
- the dates of payment of those amounts.

Client's duty to provide information

Where a client is no longer employed by an employer who is deducting sums due, they should give notice to the creditor (or for a CAO, to the sheriff clerk), that they are no longer employed by that employer and provide the name and address of any new employer. There is no sanction available to the creditor if the client does not provide this information.[43]

Applications for orders that an earnings arrestment is invalid

If the client believes that an earnings arrestment has been incorrectly served or miscalculated, they can apply to the court to recall it as invalid using Form 32.[44]

The court has the power to determine any dispute between the client, creditor or employer and make orders, including the reimbursement of any payment made in the operation of the arrestment which ought not to have been made or the payment of any sum which ought to have been paid in the operation of the arrestment but which has not been paid. This is requested by completing Form 33.[45]

When does an earnings arrestment end

The earnings arrestment stops if:
- the debt has been paid and is now extinguished; *or*

- the client is no longer employed by that employer; *or*
- the arrestment has been recalled; *or*
- the creditor abandons the arrestment;[46] *or*
- the client has a Debt Payment Programme (DPP) approved;[47] *or*
- the client has been sequestrated[48] or in a protected trust deed;[49] *or*
- a time to pay order has been made and granted;[50] *or*
- the client dies.

See Chapter 6 if you are looking to stop the earnings arrestment by applying for a DPP, or sequestration or Chapter 11 for time to pay order.

3. Bank arrestment

Arrestment is diligence that allows a creditor to attach a client's moveable property, such as goods or funds. Arrestment can only be used where the assets are owned by the client but are in possession of a third party.

Terminology
The creditor is known as the **'arrester'**.
The client is known as the **'common debtor'**.
The bank or building society is known as the **'arrestee'**.

Bank arrestments are a legal form of debt recovery that must be executed by a sheriff officer or messenger-at-arms. They can only be carried out if a creditor has obtained the 'authority of the court' to carry out the arrestment. The legislation which governs them is in the Debtors (Scotland) Act 1987 and the Bankruptcy and Diligence etc. (Scotland) Act 2007.

What is a bank arrestment

A bank arrestment is legally known as 'arrestment and action of furthcoming'. It is a two-part process.
- **Part 1**: on receiving a schedule of arrestment, the bank freezes any funds held in the client's bank account on the date and time that the arrestment is served (the arrestment), preventing the client from gaining access to those funds.
- **Part 2**: the funds are taken from the account and given to the creditor. This is known as the 'furthcoming'. Part 2 can only occur in two situations:
  - when a client signs a mandate authorising the bank to transfer the funds to the creditor. This can be done at any point after the arrestment; *or*
  - 14 weeks after the arrestment, when providing the client has not lodged any objection, or has a statutory moratorium in place, the funds are transferred automatically (by operation of law) to the creditor.

Chapter 9: Diligence
3. Bank arrestment

When can an account be arrested

A bank arrestment can only be actioned by the creditor if it has the 'authority of the court' to do so. The authority of the court depends on the type of debt involved.

Arrestments in execution (following decree)

For consumer credit debts (eg, personal loans and credit cards), the creditor must take the client to court and obtain a decree.[51] They must wait 14 days to allow for any appeals against the decree before applying for an 'extract of the decree'. Once this is issued, the creditor can instruct a sheriff officer to execute an arrestment on a bank account. They do not need to serve a charge for payment.

Summary warrant

Where debts are owed to HMRC or a local council for council tax, the process for executing a bank arrestment is different. This is because they obtained a court order called a 'summary warrant', which is issued in court without a hearing. These creditors must issue a 'charge for payment' before executing a bank arrestment and can only instruct the arrestment after the charge for payment has expired.

Summary diligence

In summary diligence, the process of registering the obligation with the courts in the Books of Council and Session acts as a substitute for the process of going to the court to get a decree. The client must be in default of the debt before the creditor can extract the debt from the register and execute diligence on it. Creditors do not need to serve a charge for payment. See p299 for more information about summary diligence.

Arrestment on the dependence

Arrestment on the dependence is an action taken by the creditor to freeze the debtor's assets which are in the hands of an arrestee (usually a bank or building society). The key difference is the arrestment takes place *before* the action is heard in court. Creditors must make a clear case why the diligence should be granted, but the decision to grant arrestment on the dependence rests with the court. See p297 for more information about diligence on the dependence.

The banks' role

Banks (the arrestee) are legally obliged to act upon the lawful instruction of a schedule of arrestment and must tell the creditor within three weeks of the arrestment being served by the sheriff officer if it has been successful. If a bank fails to disclose details of a successful arrestment to the creditor, it can be ordered by the court to pay the creditor the lesser of:

- the sum due by the client to the creditor; *or*
- the amount representing the protected minimum balance (PMB).

This amount reduces the debt owed by the client and the creditor cannot recover this sum from the client. The bank, however, does not need to disclose anything if the arrestment has been unsuccessful.

The date and time of '**execution of the arrestment**' is important, as only the funds in an account on this date and time can be arrested. The arrestment fails if no funds are in an account on this date.

Note that banks often charge a client's account when they action an arrestment. This can happen even if the arrestment fails and is not affected by any subsequent recall/restriction of an arrestment. Clients and advisers may have to negotiate refunds separately from any subsequent action they take against the bank arrestment.

Protected minimum balance

The PMB is an amount of funds within a bank account (or other financial institution) that is protected from arrestment.[52] Only funds over the regulated amount can be arrested. The PMB is currently £1,000. This amount is set by Scottish Ministers and is liable to change every April.

There is no limit to the amount of funds a creditor can take when it arrests a client's bank account. The full amount owed (including interest and charges), the creditor's legal costs and the costs of executing the arrestment can be seized. The client must be left with the PMB in their account.

The PMB applies to personal accounts only (including savings accounts). There is no PMB for business accounts.

If a client has multiple accounts with the same bank (or other financial institution), the £1,000 PMB applies to all the accounts together. If the client has multiple accounts with different bank/building societies, the £1,000 PMB applies to each account separately. Note that some banks with separate names are in the same banking group (eg, Halifax, Cheltenham and Gloucester and Bank of Scotland are all part of the Lloyds Banking Group) and separate accounts in the same banking group may be treated as being with the same bank. In that situation, the PMB can only be applied once.

Stopping a bank arrestment

Bank account arrestments can be stopped legally by being recalled or restricted. It is often necessary to raise an objection in court, but can be done by negotiation with the sheriff officer or the creditor.

Technically, only the following have the authority to recall or restrict and arrestment:

- sheriff officers, on the instructions of the creditors who authorised them to arrest the bank account; *or*
- a sheriff at the sheriff court.

Negotiating with a sheriff officer

It is worthwhile contacting the sheriff officer to negotiate the lifting of a client's bank arrestment before raising an objection through the court. An adviser's or their agency's relationship with sheriff officers often plays a part in how successful they are using these tactics. You can argue that the arrestment will cause hardship, that the client is vulnerable or has mental health issues. The sheriff officer may ask that a repayment plan is proposed, and if the client is employed will ask for their employer's details (often to action an earnings arrestment if the client defaults on a repayment plan). Note that a client's record of maintaining any previous arrangements will be looked at by the sheriff officers/creditor and, if they have had previous defaults, the negotiation is less likely to be successful.

If the arrestment was for council tax or another local authority debt, the adviser can contact the local authority directly and ask for the arrestment to be lifted on the grounds of hardship, especially if the arrestment means that other debts or priority payments cannot be met – eg, rent payments.

If an adviser is unable to get the sheriff officer or the creditor to agree to lifting or restricting the arrestment, they may need to raise an objection in court.

Raising a notice of objection in the sheriff court

Submitting a notice of objection in court is a formal legal process.[53] Forms are available at the local sheriff court or can be found in the Act of Sederunt (Sheriff Court Rules Amendment) (Diligence) 2009 No.107.

To submit a notice of objection, there are specific grounds the objection must be based on. These are:[54]
- the warrant the arrestment was executed on was invalid; *or*
- the arrestment has been executed incompetently or irregularly; *or*
- the funds attached are owed to a third party solely or in common with the debtor.

Notices of objection must be submitted within four weeks of the bank arrestment being executed.

The warrant the arrestment was executed on was invalid

This is rarely used as warrants are rarely invalid. However, if creditors have not served the client with a charge for payment (under the summary warrant process) or have served the charge for payment but not waited until it expires before actioning the arrestment, it can be argued that they had no valid warrant for arrestment and the action taken was invalid.

Chapter 9: Diligence
3. Bank arrestment

Under the summary diligence procedure, if there has been an error by the creditor in extracting the warrant from the Books of Council and Session (eg, the client had not defaulted on their agreement), it may be possible to argue that it was invalid, and a sheriff may lift the arrestment.

While a moratorium on diligence[55] is in place, it is not valid to serve a bank arrestment on a client's bank. If this does happen and the schedule was dated after the date the statutory moratorium was granted, you can object, citing section 197(3)(b) of the Bankruptcy (Scotland) Act 2016.

> *197(3) While a moratorium on diligence applies in relation to the person it is not competent–*
> (a) to serve a charge for payment in respect of any debt owed by the person, or
> (b) to commence or execute any diligence to enforce payment of any debt owed by the person,
> (c) to found on any debt owed by the person in presenting, or concurring in the presentation of, a petition for sequestration of the person's estate, or
> (d) where an arrestment mentioned in subsection (1) of section 73J of the Debtors (Scotland) Act 1987 has been granted in respect of funds due to the person, to release funds to the creditor under subsection (2) of that section.

The arrestment has been executed incompetently or irregularly

The other ground that could be argued is that an arrestment is incompetent or has been executed irregularly.

One argument in terms of incompetency is that the funds that were attached could not competently be attached – eg, the only funds going into the client's account are solely from benefits income.

Certain social security benefits are said to be 'inalienable', which means they cannot be attached.

Sheriff officers often argue this does not apply anymore since the PMB for bank arrestments came into force stating these protections were superseded by the PMB. However, their argument is flawed for a number of reasons.

With regards to Scottish benefits, the protection written into the legislation was done so after PMB for bank arrestment was introduced. Earlier legislation cannot have overwritten more recent legislation.

Further, in terms of the UK protections that were introduced in 1992, this area of law was not devolved to the Scottish parliament at the time the PMB was introduced, so it would not have been competent for the Scottish parliament to have amended UK laws in this area.

This can be an easier argument when the only deposits in the client's account are from benefits, although there is a counter argument from the banks that deposits lose their status when they go into an account, so identifying benefits-only income is impossible.

It can also be difficult if there is a mixture of benefits and other income. Technically, only the income that is not benefits should be arrested and only such income that is beyond the PMB as benefits should be treated as not being there, as they are inalienable from diligence.

This is a complex area of the law and, although recent caselaw in *Mackenzie v Edinburgh Council and Bank of Scotland*[56] is encouraging, it is always worth speaking to experienced colleagues or specialist advisers if you are unsure how to proceed.

An example of irregularly executing an arrestment is when a bank does not execute the arrestment on the date and time it is received, but waits until there are funds in the client's account – eg, a day or two after receiving the schedule of arrestment from sheriff officers. This is an irregular execution as bank arrestments can only arrest funds in an account on the date and time they are served. If there are no funds, they fail, even if funds are subsequently deposited in the account.

The funds attached are owed to a third party solely or in common with the debtor
This can arise where a client has a joint account with someone else and the funds are arrested. As a result, the joint account holder may lose their money because of the other person's debt.

This does not necessarily mean that it will be presumed 50 per cent of the money belongs to the other person, but will very much depend on who has been contributing to the account and for what purpose and to what extent.

It may also depend on, for example, where there is a joint debt like council tax, whether the other account holder was also liable for that debt (even if the bank arrestment did not name them specifically). These are factors that a sheriff will consider when deciding whether or not the funds arrested should be restricted.

Where it is not a joint account, this argument could still be used where someone else has been using the account – eg, if it can be shown that someone else's wages or benefits were paid into the account. Based on the facts of the case, a sheriff may lift the arrestment.

How to submit a notice of objection
A notice of objection is submitted to the sheriff clerk's office in the client's local sheriff court using Form 63F.[57] This must be submitted within four weeks of the date on the schedule of arrestment.

On receipt of the application, the sheriff clerk sets a hearing date when the application will be heard by the sheriff and notifies all the relevant parties, including the creditors and the bank.

There is no cost to raising an action under the Debtors (Scotland) Act 1987. Clients can either represent themselves or have a lay representative. They can also employ a solicitor, but this may incur a significant cost to the client (unless they qualify for legal aid).

Note that if the action is unsuccessful, the sheriff can order the client to pay the other parties' legal expenses in responding to the application.

Unduly harsh

Clients may feel that their bank arrestment is harsh. However, there is a difference between an action being 'harsh' and being 'unduly harsh'. Meeting the threshold of 'unduly harsh' has become problematic since the introduction of the PMB, as creditors argue that clients are left with money to meet their obligations. However, it does not mean that making an application citing the action as being unduly harsh should not be attempted.

Some common examples of situations where a bank arrestment may be considered unduly harsh include the following.

- **Earnings arrestment** – if a creditor is already arresting a client's wages and then arrests their bank account, this could be considered as unduly harsh. Note, though, that 'double diligence' is allowed under the law and is often used by local authorities when council tax becomes due for payment at the start of a new year.
- **Client's current commitments** – although the PMB is left in a client's account after the arrestment, if they have existing commitments such as rent/mortgage which will leave them with no money for food, heating or other essentials, it can be argued as being unduly harsh, especially if it impacts on the welfare and safety of children or others in the household.
- **Mixed income** – if a client has income from benefits (which is supposed to be alimentary in nature) as well as a small amount of earnings, it can be argued that this is unduly harsh as it has denied the client access to benefit income that legally parliament had intended to be protected from such diligences.
- It is too late to lodge a notice of objection with the sheriff court, the four-week period has passed and therefore the raising of an application using 'unduly harsh' on the same grounds is appropriate.

This list is not exhaustive and clients who do not meet any of the above may still have a valid case for arguing that the action of arrestment was unduly harsh. It is important to remember that when arguing that the action is unduly harsh, the focus should be on the factors that make it so, how it affects not just the client, but also their family, or anyone else who relies on them, as well as (with explicit consent) advising the court about any illness or disability that is impacted by the action.

How to object using 'unduly harsh'

An application to the sheriff court on the grounds that a bank arrestment is unduly harsh is made using Form 63G,[58] which is submitted to the sheriff clerk's office in client's local sheriff court.

There is no fee for making the application and the sheriff clerk should notify the relevant parties and schedule a hearing in front of the sheriff where all parties can be heard. Clients can either represent themselves or have a lay representative.

They can also employ a solicitor, but this may incur a significant cost to the client (unless they qualify for legal aid).

These actions are not quick processes, and it can take several weeks before the case is heard in court. During this time the client may need help with essentials such as food/housing and utilities as well sorting other creditor commitments, which will be impacted by the bank arrestment.

Bank arrestment stoppers

There are certain actions and debt options the client can choose which will strike down the bank arrestment and have the effect of returning the arrested money to the client's account. It will not mean any charges levelled by the client's bank would be returned or refunded. That would be a separate argument with the bank.

Time to pay order

If a time to pay order (TTPO) is successful, it strikes down the arrestment. More information on how and when to use TTPOs is in Chapter 11.

If considering a TTPO, advisers must ensure that the client can afford the offer they are making and that they have followed the debt advice process before making the application.

As a tactic to lift the arrestment, it can work, and it may buy the client time to repay the debt, but be aware of ongoing liability and other debts.

Example

Martha decided to do a TTPO for last year's council tax arrears. She then fell into arrears with this year's council tax. A summary warrant was issued and a charge for payment then served and the 14 days of charge have passed. Martha could get her bank account arrested for the newest debt while the TTPO was in effect for paying the old debt.

Statutory debt solutions

- **Minimal Asset Process bankruptcy, Full Administration Bankruptcy and creditor sequestration** – as all debts must be included in a bankruptcy/sequestration, a bank arrestment will be struck down when they are awarded.
- **Protected trust deed** – when a client's trust deed becomes protected and, as along as the debt is included, the bank arrestment is struck down. Advisers should be mindful that where the arrested amount is significant, it may vest with the trustee.
- **Debt Arrangement Scheme** (DAS) – although it cannot stop an arrestment which has already been served on the bank, it can stop the furthcoming from happening, providing this is done within the 14 weeks of the bank arrestment having been served – ie, no monies will be released to the creditor. When the DAS is completed, any monies captured in the arrestment will be returned to

the client. Advisers should be aware that with the nature of DAS this may take a considerable number of years.

4. Money attachment

What is a money attachment

A 'money attachment' is used to collect cash from commercial clients such as bars, clubs, shops or restaurants. It cannot be used to collect money in a dwellinghouse. A money attachment can be used by creditors once:[59]
- the debt is constituted by a decree or document of debt; *and*
- the client has been issued a charge for payment; *and*
- the period for payment specified in the charge for payment has expired without payment being made; *and*
- where the client is an individual, the creditor has, no earlier than 12 weeks before executing the money attachment, provided the client with a Debt Advice and Information Package.

A money attachment is not competent in relation to money:[60]
- kept within a dwellinghouse; *or*
- to which arrestment is competent.

What can be attached

A money attachment can attach any 'cash' or 'banking instrument'.[61]
   'Cash' means coins and banknotes in any currency.
   'Banking instrument' includes cheques, money orders, postal orders and promissory notes.[62]

When is a money attachment competent

There are strict time limits for when a money attachment can be carried out. It cannot be carried out on a Sunday or a public holiday, and not before 8am and after 8pm. These time limits can be extended by the sheriff.[63] In the future, attachment could be carried out on any day the premises are open for trade or business (whether to the public generally or not).[64] Check the online version of this *Handbook* for updates.

When making the attachment, sheriff officers must enquire as to the ownership of the money attached and try to ensure that the money is owned by the client.[65]

A sheriff officer must attach and remove from the premises any money found, but only to the amount owed plus interest and expenses.

Schedule and report

Sheriff officers must serve on the client a 'schedule of money attachment' and make a report of the attachment. The schedule must be signed by the officer of court (sheriff officer or messenger-at-arms) and specify the value of the money attached.[66]

A report should then be made to the sheriff 14 days after the attachment,[67] and a copy given to the client and the creditor.[68]

The sheriff can refuse to receive the report if it has not been duly signed within the relevant time period (14 days).

The creditor can then apply to the sheriff to make a payment order releasing the funds to them.

Where the application is opposed, the sheriff allows all parties to make representations or holds a hearing.

The client or a third party who claims ownership (whether solely or in common with the client) of any of the money attached may oppose the application.

This must be made before the expiry of the period of 14 days beginning with the day on which the application is made.[69]

If the sheriff agrees with the client, they can make an order declaring that the money attachment ceases to have effect and requiring the return of the money attached or, where the value of any such money has been realised, a sum equivalent to that value, to the client (or the person whose money it is).[70]

A money attachment ceases to have effect on the expiry of the period of 14 days beginning with the day on which the report of money attachment is made unless, within that period, the creditor applies for a payment order.[71]

Release of a money attachment

Unduly harsh

Where the sheriff is satisfied that the money attachment is unduly harsh to the client, the sheriff must make an order that the attachment has ceased to have effect and to return the money attached to the client.[72]

Applications for the release of money where it is considered to be unduly harsh can be made on Form 6.

Invalidity and cessation of attachment

A client or third party can apply to the court that the attachment is invalid due to the money being owned by a third party.

Before a payment order is made or the money attachment ceases to have effect, where the sheriff is satisfied that any money attached is not owned by the client, they must make an order:[73]

- declaring that the money attachment ceases to have effect; *and*

- requiring the officer of court to return the money attached or, where the value of any such money has been realised, a sum equivalent to that value, to the client or the person whose money it is.

Applications for declarations that the money attachment ceases to have effect can be made on Form 7.

Common ownership

Where the sheriff is satisfied that money attached is owned in common by the client and a third party, and that the disposal of the money would be unduly harsh to the third party, the sheriff can, on the third party's application made before the money's disposal, order that the money attachment is to cease to have effect in relation to that money.[74]

Applications for release of money where it is owned in common can be made on Form 11.

Invalidity and cessation of money attachment

Where, at any time before a payment order is made, or the money attachment ceases to have effect, the sheriff is satisfied that there has been a material irregularity in the execution of the money attachment, the sheriff must make an order such as:[75]
- declaring that the money attachment ceases to have effect; *and*
- requiring the officer of the court to return the money attached or, where the value of any such money has been realised, a sum equivalent to that value to the client or, as the case may be, the person whose money it is.

Forms

The forms in relation to money attachment can be found in the Appendix to the Act of Sederunt (Money Attachment Rules) 2009 No.382.

Time to pay

Applications for a 'time to pay order' may be competent, depending on whether there is a business or a personal debt. Seek expert advice on this.

The Debt Arrangement Scheme and insolvency

If the client has numerous debts, you may want to look at another solution such as the Debt Arrangement Scheme or an insolvency option, both for business and personal debt (see Chapter 6).

Checklist
- Have the proper procedures been carried out?
- Has the client received a copy schedule of the attachment and of the report of attachment?
- Does the client admit to owing the money attached?
- Is the attachment unduly harsh?
- Does the money belong to a third party?
- Does the money belong in common ownership?
- Can you recall the attachment?

5. Inhibition in execution

An **'inhibition'** is a form of diligence in Scotland aimed at preventing clients from disposing of land or property, or taking any further loans against it, without first paying the debt owed to the inhibiting creditor. It is usually used in conjunction with other forms of diligence.

What is an inhibition

An inhibition is a form of diligence that affects a client's land or buildings. It is a 'preventative' diligence in that it does not attach any money but merely prevents the client from disposing of their land or buildings. It does not allow the creditor to sell the property but prevents the sale of any property before the inhibition has been dealt with.

It is a personal diligence and covers all the client's land and property.

It is normally obtained after decree (or document of debt) and lasts for five years before it needs to be renewed.[76]

Register of Inhibitions

The Register of Inhibitions is part of the Registers of Scotland which includes many registers, such as the Land Register, Crofting Register and the Scottish Landlord Register.

The inhibiting creditor registers a copy of the schedule of inhibition served on the client and the sheriff officer's certificate of service in the Register of Inhibitions.[77]

Charge for payment

As an inhibition does not attach any property which can be sold to pay the debt (such as attachment), there is no need for the creditor to serve a charge for payment prior to executing an inhibition.[78]

Schedule of inhibition

The client is also served with a schedule of inhibition outlining the debt owed and how they can deal with it.

Where the client is an individual, a schedule of inhibition must be accompanied with a Debt Advice and Information Package.[79]

Once the schedule has been served, it is entered into the Register of Inhibitions and takes effect on the day that it is entered in the Register of Inhibitions.[80]

Inhibition on the dependence

A creditor can apply to the court (or tribunal) for an inhibition on the dependence of the action. See p297 for more information.

Discharge of inhibition

An inhibition is discharged when the client pays the debt due (including any interest), any expenses incurred in executing the inhibition and the expenses of discharging the inhibition.[81]

Dealing with an inhibition

As a debt adviser, there is not much that can be done to deal with an inhibition other than arrange for the client to pay the debt off, look at the Debt Arrangement Scheme (DAS) or an insolvency option.

One way to deal with it is to recall the original court decree and challenge the debt, asking for a 'decree of absolvitor'. This would be accepted as capable of lifting the inhibition.

Insolvency and the Debt Arrangement Scheme

An inhibition does not stop your client from applying for an insolvency solution or the DAS.

In an insolvency situation, the inhibition is struck down. However, the trustee may apply for their own inhibition as part of the insolvency process.

While the client is in the DAS, the inhibition continues, but the inhibiting creditor cannot pursue the debt where it is included in the Debt Payment Programme (DPP), and when the debt has been paid off, they should recall the inhibition.

Checklist

- Check that the client is liable for the debt sued for.
- Consider a recall of the decree if you can challenge the debt.
- Consider an application for a DPP under the DAS.
- Consider an insolvency option.
- Consider other ways to pay the debt off.

6. On the dependence

Diligence 'on the dependence' of an action is a way creditors can try to take court action against a client without them knowing about it – ie, diligence by surprise.

In simple procedure, it is known as 'provisional measures'. In this section, the term 'diligence on the dependence' is used to cover all court procedures.

The diligence is not complete; it freezes money or assets until the court holds a hearing and a decree (or equivalent) is granted. Full diligence can then resume.

It can be used for arrestments, attachments and serving inhibitions.

It prevents the client from disposing of assets and money before an upcoming action against them.

It was clarified by the Bankruptcy and Diligence etc. (Scotland) Act 2007 and is now covered in Part 1A of the Debtors (Scotland) Act 1987.

Diligence on the dependence of an action

A creditor can present a petition to the court asking to award diligence on the dependence of a future action.

The court can decide to hold a hearing (which the client can attend) or proceed without a hearing. In deciding whether to grant a warrant without a hearing, the court considers whether:[82]
- the creditor has sufficient evidence for the case to proceed;
- there is a real and substantial risk that enforcement of any decree in the action in favour of the creditor would be defeated or prejudiced by reason of:
  - the client being insolvent or verging on insolvency;
  - the likelihood of the client removing, disposing of, burdening, concealing or otherwise dealing with all or some of the client's assets;
- it is reasonable in all the circumstances.

The onus is on the creditor to satisfy the court that the order granting a warrant should be made.

Where the court makes an order granting a warrant for diligence on the dependence without a hearing, the court:[83]
- fixes a date for a hearing; *and*
- orders the creditor to notify that date to the client and any other person with an interest.

Where the court refuses to make an order granting a warrant without a hearing and the creditor insists on the application, the court:[84]
- fixes a date for such a hearing on the application; *and*
- orders the creditor to notify that date to the client and any other person appearing to the court to have an interest.

At the hearing, the client can put their case forward and state why diligence on the dependence should not be awarded. The onus is on the creditor to satisfy the court that it should be awarded.[85]

Service of summons following execution of diligence on the dependence

A summons must be served on the client within 21 days of the diligence being executed.[86] Otherwise, the diligence ceases to have effect.

Recall or restriction

The client and any interested person can apply to the court for an order recalling or restricting the warrant.[87]

Get expert advice if you come across an action for diligence on the dependence.

Expenses

A creditor is entitled to the expenses it incurs in obtaining warrant for diligence on the dependence, and where an arrestment or inhibition is executed in pursuance of the warrant, in executing the arrestment or inhibition.

Similarly, where a client opposes it and is successful, they can also claim their expenses.[88]

Prescription of an arrestment on the dependence

Where an arrestment has been made on the dependence and has not been pursued, it lapses in three years from the date it was last dealt with by the court.[89]

Checklist
- Check to see if the client admits the debt.
- Consider appearing at a hearing if it is called.
- Check to see if a recall may be appropriate.
- Consider all debt solutions.

7. Adjudication for debt

Adjudication for debt is a long established but rarely used diligence against property. It is exclusively a Court of Session process.

Adjudication for debt gives creditors a right or security over specific heritable (and some other) property owned by the client. It can be used alone or as a follow-on process from inhibition.

Adjudication for debt was scheduled to be replaced by land attachments in the Bankruptcy and Diligence etc. (Scotland) Act 2007, but, at the time of writing, this has not been completed and adjudication for debt still stands.[90]

The client has 10 years from the date of the decree for adjudication to repay the debt before the creditor can take action to transfer the ownership of the property to the creditor.

Before applying for adjudication, the creditor must have a decree for payment or a similar document of debt against the client.

Get expert advice if you come across this form of diligence.

Registration

Adjudication is a two-stage process.

A creditor already holding a decree for payment or relevant document of debt may raise an action for adjudication in the Court of Session.

After the expiry of one year and a day, adjudication gives the adjudging creditor a preference over other creditors, apart from those holding prior or equal ranking securities.

As mentioned above, a decree or a document of debt does not authorise adjudication in itself. To use this diligence, creditors must then apply to the Court of Session for a 'decree of adjudication'.

At the commencement of the Court of Session action, the creditor also usually registers a 'notice of summons of adjudication' in the personal registers which serves as an inhibition against the debtor in respect of the property that the creditor wishes to pursue.

Once the decree of adjudication has been granted and extracted, it is registered in the property registers to complete the diligence.[91]

Expiry of the legal

After the expiry of at least 10 years from the granting of the decree of adjudication, the creditor can move to the second stage of the process and apply to the Court of Session for a 'declarator of expiry of the legal'. This transfers ownership of the property to the creditor.

8. Summary diligence

Summary diligence is the Scottish legal term for debt enforcement procedures based on a 'document of debt' rather than a court decree. It allows a lender to execute diligence without having to raise court action and can be a fast-track way to collect a debt, bypassing the normal court processes.

A document of debt is described in section 221 of the Bankruptcy and Diligence etc. (Scotland) Act 2007 and includes 'a document registered for execution in the Books of Council and Session or in the sheriff court books'.[92]

Registration in the Books of Council and Session

In Scotland, it is normal procedure for a creditor to take a client to court, obtain a decree or similar and serve a charge for payment before commencing diligence. In some situations, this is not always necessary if a creditor has followed certain procedures and the client has specifically agreed to it.

The law in Scotland allows for a debt to be recorded on a personal bond, deed or similar document of debt and registered in the 'Books of Council and Session' in the Court of Session (or the sheriff court, but usually the Court of Session) and the extract of the document will contain a warrant to execute diligence in the event of non-payment.[93]

By registering a deed at the Court of Session, it then has the force of a decree of the court and can be used for enforcing a debt. It cannot be used for consumer debt but can be used by credit unions, for lease agreements and for loans not regulated by the Consumer Credit Act 1974.

Consent

This is a formal agreement between the lender and the client. Once signed, the client is bound by its terms.

If the document does not contain the client's consent, the lender may have to go to court to enforce the loan.

Diligence

Once the client is in default, the lender can extract the deed and enforce collection through all the usual diligence measures without having to go to court.

The lender though must still serve a Debt Advice and Information Package and a charge for payment before executing the following diligences:
- earnings arrestment;
- bank arrestment;
- registering an inhibition;
- sequestration, which is also an option once apparent insolvency has been constituted.

Dealing with a debt registered in the Books of Council and Session

Your client may be able to apply for a time to pay order once the charge for payment has been served if the debt is a personal debt rather than a business debt.

Other options open to the client may be limited to the Debt Arrangement Scheme (DAS) or an insolvency solution.

Chapter 9: Diligence
Notes

Checklist

- Check the agreement was properly registered and signed.
- Check it contains the words 'consent to registration for preservation and execution'.
- Contact the lender and see what their position is.
- Check eligibility for the DAS or an insolvency solution.
- Check to see if a full and final settlement could be an option.

Notes

1. **Attachment and exceptional attachment**
   1. s12 DAA(S)A 2002
   2. s17 DAA(S)A 2002
   3. s18 DAA(S)A 2002
   4. s11 DAA(S)A 2002
   5. s26 DAA(S)A 2002
   6. s21 DAA(S)A 2002
   7. s24 DAA(S)A 2002
   8. s24 DAA(S)A 2002
   9. s32 DAA(S)A 2002
   10. s18 DAA(S) 2002
   11. Sch 1 (Appendix 1) AoS(DAA(S)) 2002
   12. s23 DAA(S)A 2002
   13. s22 DAA(S)A 2002
   14. s26 DAA(S)A 2002
   15. s34 DAA(S)A 2002
   16. s47 DAA(S)A 2002
   17. s48 DAA(S)A 2002
   18. s47 DAA(S)A 2002
   19. s49(2) DAA(S)A 2002
   20. s49(1) DAA(S)A 2002
   21. s50 DAA(S)A 2002
   22. s50(3) DAA(S)A 2002
   23. s51 DAA(S)A 2002
   24. s54(3) DAA(S)A 2002
   25. s11 DAA(S)A 2002
   26. Sch 2 DAA(S)A 2002
   27. s56 DAA(S)A 2002
   28. s18(3) BD(S)A 2024
   29. s52 DAA(S)A 2002
   30. s55 DAA(S)A 2002
   31. Sch 1 App 1 AoS(DAA(S)) 2002
   32. s57 DAA(S)A 2002

2. **Earnings arrestment**
   33. ss51-56 D(S)A 1987
   34. ss60-66 D(S)A 1987
   35. aib.gov.uk/publications/debt-advice-and-information-package
   36. s47(3) D(S)A 1987
   37. s38 Act of Sederunt (Proceedings in the Sheriff Court under the Debtors (Scotland) Act 1987) 1988 No.2013
   38. Art 38 D(S)A 1987
   39. Sch 2 D(S)A 1987, amended by the DaE(V)(S) Regs
   40. DaE(V)(S) Regs
   41. s70A D(S)A 1987
   42. s70C D(S)A 1987
   43. s70D D(S)A 1987
   44. s50(1) D(S)A 1987
   45. s50(3) and (4) D(S)A 1987
   46. s47(B) D(S)A 1987
   47. s4(2) DAA(S)A 2002
   48. s72(2) D(S)A 1987
   49. s173 B(S)A 2016
   50. s9 D(S)A 1987

3. **Bank arrestment**
   51. s73A D(S)A 1987
   52. s73F BD(S)A 2007
   53. s73M D(S)A 1987
   54. s73M D(S)A 1987
   55. ss195-198 B(S)A 2016
   56. [2023] SC EDIN 21, 5 July 2023
   57. Act of Sederunt (Sheriff Court Rules Amendment) (Diligence) 2009 No.107
   58. Act of Sederunt (Sheriff Court Rules Amendment) (Diligence) 2009 No.107

Chapter 9: Diligence
Notes

4. Money attachment
59 s174 BD(S)A 2007
60 s174 BD(S)A 2007
61 s175 BD(S)A 2007
62 s175 BD(S)A 2007
63 s176 BD(S)A 2007
64 s19 BD(S)A 2024
65 s177 BD(S)A 2007
66 s179(2) and (3) BD(S)A 2007
67 s182(3) BD(S)A 2007
68 s182(4) BD(S)A 2007
69 s183(7)(b) BD(S)A 2007
70 ss183(11) BD(S)A 2007
71 s187(1) BD(S)A 2007
72 s185 BD(S)A 2007
73 s186 BD(S)A 2007
74 s191 BD(S)A 2007
75 s186 BD(S)A 2007

5. Inhibition in execution
76 s156 BD(S)A 2007
77 s148 BD(S)A 2007
78 s147 BD(S)A 2007
79 s147 BD(S)A 2007
80 s155 BD(S)A 2007
81 s157 BD(S)A 2007

6. On the dependence
82 s15E(2) D(S)A 1987
83 s15E(4) D(S)A 1987
84 s15E(6) D(S)A 1987
85 s15F(4) D(S)A 1987
86 s15G(2) D(S)A 1987
87 s15K(2) D(S)A 1987
88 s15M D(S)A 1987
89 s95A D(S)A 1987

7. Adjudication for debt
90 Part 4 BD(S)A 2007
91 AiB discussion document, *Abolition of Adjudication for Debt and the introduction of Land Attachment*

8. Summary diligence
92 s221 BD(S)A 2007
93 s3 Writs Execution (Scotland) Act 1877

Chapter 10

Non-diligence debt recovery

This chapter covers:
1. Introduction (below)
2. Direct earnings attachments (below)
3. Deductions from earnings orders (p308)
4. Third-party deductions (p313)

1. Introduction

Normally, a creditor can only force a client to pay their debts if they take the correct legal action. This requires them to get a court order or a tribunal decision. The action such creditors take to enforce payment of their debt is referred to as diligence. However, some creditors have fast-track powers that do not require them to go to court to recover the debt. Therefore, the action they take is not classed as diligence.

Money can be taken from a client's earnings without a creditor going to court or a tribunal, but only in certain circumstances. These are:
- **'direct earnings attachment' (DEA)** – used by the DWP, HMRC and local authorities (see below);
- **'deductions from earnings order' (DEO)** – used by the Child Maintenance Service (see p308).

Statutory moratorium
A statutory moratorium does not stop a DEA or a DEO as they do not count as diligence.

2. Direct earnings attachments

The DWP is responsible for recovering money owed to the state as a result of debt arising under the Social Security Administration Act 1992.

The Welfare Reform Act 2012, which became law in March 2012, allows DWP Debt Management to ask an employer to make deductions directly from their employee's earnings. This is done by asking them to operate a direct earnings attachment (DEA).

The legislation covering DEAs is found in the Social Security (Overpayments and Recovery) Regulations 2013 No.384, which came into force on 8 April 2013. DWP Debt Management began to use DEAs from this date, as part of a revised process to recover money owed to DWP.

Local authorities can use the same regulations as DWP Debt Management to implement a DEA, as can HMRC if there is an overpayment in tax credits. HMRC has passed the collection of these debts to DWP.

How a direct earnings attachment works

Before implementing a DEA, the DWP, HMRC or local authority contacts the client who owes them money to get them to agree a repayment arrangement. If the client ignores letters or if they cannot agree on a repayment, a DEA is implemented. A letter is sent to the client advising them that a DEA is being applied for.

A letter is also sent to the client's employer asking them to begin deductions from the client's salary. A DEA has effect from the next payday which falls on or after 22 days following the day it is given or sent. The 22 days allow the employer time to set up the DEA.

The payment should be sent to DWP Debt Management or local authority at the latest, by the **19th of the month following the first deduction** from the client's pay.[1] For example, a DEA deducted on 31 May must reach the creditor by 19 June and a DEA deducted on 1 June must reach the creditor by 19 July.

Example
A DEA notice to the employer is issued on 2 May.
If the employee is paid monthly – paid on the last working day of the month. The employer must implement the DEA from the first payday on or after 24 May. The first payment should therefore be taken from the wage paid on 31 May and must be received by the creditor (DWP, HMRC or local authority) by 19 June at the latest.
If the employee is paid weekly – Friday payday. The employer must implement the DEA from the first payday on or after 24 May. The first payment should therefore be taken from the wage paid on the Friday following this date and must be received by the creditor (DWP, HMRC or local authority) by 19 June at the latest.

An employer is also able to deduct an administration fee of £1 (maximum) for a DEA from their employee.[2]

If the employer ignores the DEA or fails to operate the DEA correctly, it can be fined up to £1,000. The client will still owe the overpayment.[3]

How deductions are made

The DWP or local authority has three options when applying for a DEA:[4]
- apply at a standard rate allowing a maximum of 20 per cent of net wages to be taken; *or*
- apply at a higher rate allowing a maximum of 40 per cent of net wages to be taken. (This is potentially used for fraudulent overpayments); *or*
- apply at a fixed rate.

The DEA must leave the client with no less than 60 per cent of their net income.[5] When the DEA is either on a standard or higher rate, a sliding scale is used. How much is deducted is based on a percentage and what the client's earnings are daily, weekly or monthly.

Deductions from earnings rates

Standard rate [6]

Daily earnings	Weekly earnings	Monthly earnings	Deduction rate to apply (%)
Up to £15	Up to £100	Up to £430	Nil
£15.01–£23	£100.01 to £160	£430.01–£690	3%
£23.01–£32	£160.01–£220	£690.01–£950	5%
£32.01–£39	£220.01–£270	£950.01–£1,160	7%
£39.01–£54	£270.01–£375	£1,160.01–£1,615	11%
£54.01–£75	£375.01–£520	£1,615.01–£2,240	15%
£75.01 or more	£520.01 or more	£2,240.01 or more	20%

Higher rate [7]

Daily earnings	Weekly earnings	Monthly earnings	Deduction rate to apply (%)
Up to £15	Up to £100	Up to £430	5%
£15.01–£23	£100.01 to £160	£430.01–£690	6%
£23.01–£32	£160.01–£220	£690.01–£950	10%
£32.01–£39	£220.01–£270	£950.01–£1,160	14%
£39.01–£54	£270.01–£375	£1,160.01–£1,615	22%
£54.01–£75	£375.01–£520	£1,615.01–£2,240	30%
£75.01 or more	£520.01 or more	£2,240.01 or more	40%

These amounts are updated every April.[8]

The following payments are classed as earnings for a DEA:[9]
- wages;
- salary;
- fees;
- bonuses;

Chapter 10: Non-diligence debt recovery
2. Direct earnings attachments

- commission;
- overtime pay;
- occupational pensions, if paid with wages or salary;
- compensation payments;
- statutory sick pay;
- payment in lieu of notice;
- most other payments on top of wages.

The following payments are *not* classed as earnings for a DEA:
- statutory maternity pay;
- statutory adoption pay;
- ordinary statutory paternity pay;
- statutory shared parental pay;
- any pension, benefit, allowance or credit paid by DWP, HMRC or local authority;
- a guaranteed minimum pension under the Pensions Schemes Act 1993;
- amounts paid by a public department of the government of Northern Ireland or anywhere outside the UK;
- sums paid to reimburse expenses wholly and necessarily incurred in the course of the employment;
- pay or allowances as a member of the armed forces, other than pay or allowances payable to them by you as a special member of a reserve force;
- statutory redundancy payments.

Direct earnings attachments and earnings arrestments

Other forms of arrestment, such as an earnings arrestment, are considered a higher priority than a DEA.[10] If other arrestments are applied, the DEA gives way to them.

If a priority arrestment leaves the client with less than 60 per cent of their earnings, the DEA should not be applied.[11] Student loans being deducted from the client's earnings also take priority.

If a DEA deduction can be taken, it must not leave the client with less than 60 per cent of their net earnings. If the full DEA deduction after other arrestments reduces net earnings to less than 60 per cent, a partial deduction can be made up to the protected earnings level.

Example
Yusuf is paid monthly and has a wages arrestment already active; a DEA is received by his employer.

Standard rate deduction
Net pay £3,600 monthly (60% = £2,160)
Wage arrestment (£600.25 plus 50% of earnings exceeding £3,563.83) £618.33

Net pay after wages arrestment	£2,981.67
DEA deduction at standard rate (20%)	£720
Wages arrestment and DEA total	£1,338.33
Leaves Yusuf with	£2,261.67

The DEA can be fully implemented as it leaves Yusuf with more than 60 per cent of his net wage.

Higher rate deduction

Net pay	£3,600 monthly (60% = £2,160)
Wage arrestment (£600.25 plus 50% of earnings exceeding £3,563.83)	£618.33
Net pay after wages arrestment	£2,981.67
DEA deduction at higher rate (40%)	£1,440
Wages arrestment and DEA total	£2,058.33
Leaves Yusuf with	£1,541.67
DEA deduction would be reduced to	£821.67
Leaving Yusuf with	£2,160

As the 40 per cent deduction brings Yusuf's net pay below 60 per cent, it cannot be fully implemented. However, it can be partially implemented up to the threshold level.

This would also apply if Yusuf had a DEA in place before a wages arrestment was actioned. A DEA will always defer to arrestment.

Direct earnings attachments and insolvency

If the client has a DEA and opts for a formal debt solution because of their circumstances, the DWP says it will not recover benefit overpayments.[12]

Recognised debt solutions include:
- Full Administration Bankruptcy (see p156);
- Minimum Asset Process bankruptcy (see p150);
- protected trust deeds (see p169).

In all cases, DEAs are lifted once the solution commences. The DWP writes to the employer advising them to stop the DEA. Any monies taken after this will be refunded to the client, even if the client has a fraudulent overpayment.

If the DEA was for a fraudulent overpayment that does not discharge, the DWP or local authority may begin the DEA when the client is discharged from their formal debt solution. It should, in theory, write to the client again and offer them the ability to make an arrangement before applying for another DEA.

Direct earnings attachments and the Debt Arrangement Scheme

Although the Debt Arrangement Scheme (DAS) is not insolvency, it is a statutory debt repayment programme and as such the DWP and local authorities will not recover overpayment of benefits if the client has entered into the DAS, as long as the debt is included in the scheme. When the DWP or local authority is informed of the inclusion of the overpayment debt in the DAS, they recall the DEA from the employer and any monies taken after this are refunded to the client.

Direct earnings attachments: local authority debt and new claims

Local authorities should recall the DEA when the client enters insolvency or the DAS. Issues have been highlighted when the client has a DEA and then applies for housing benefit. Many local authorities reduce a client's entitlement to these benefits based on a previous overpayment which is now part of their chosen insolvency option or DAS. This should not happen and should be challenged with the local authority. Where the debt is for a fraudulent overpayment, a DEA may begin again after discharge.

3. Deduction from earnings orders

Deduction from earnings orders (DEOs) are used to recover child support debts. Where a non-resident parent has arrears of child support payments, the Child Maintenance Service (CMS) can instruct their employer to make deductions from wages or salary and pay them to the CMS.[13] The CMS does not need a court order to do this and it is the first enforcement option that is likely to be used against an employed non-resident parent who cannot provide a good reason for the arrears, or who has failed to agree a method of payment with the CMS. If the full amount requested by the CMS cannot be deducted from earnings, the CMS may use other methods to collect and enforce the remainder.

A non-resident parent can also choose a voluntary deduction from earnings order as the method of making regular child support payments, even if there are no arrears.

How a deduction from earnings order works

A DEO takes child maintenance payments from a paying parent's earnings or pension. These deductions are sent to the CMS.

A copy of the DEO must be 'served' on the employer and the non-resident parent.[14] The employer must comply with it within seven days of receiving it, and can be fined up to £1,000 for providing false or misleading information, or deliberately withholding information from the CMS.[15]

Employers can manage DEOs online.[16]

If the client is self-employed or retired, money can be taken from their bank accounts.[17] This is called a 'deduction order'. The deductions can either be regular or be made as a lump-sum payment.[18]

The CMS can also take money from business, partnership or joint accounts.[19]

If the CMS cannot recover the arrears from the client's pay or bank account, they can ask the court for a 'liability order'. This allows the CMS to ask:
- sheriff officers to attach goods and sell them;
- for a court order to force the sale of the client's home.

If that still does not clear the arrears, the CMS can ask a court to consider:[20]
- taking away the client's driving licence or passport;
- sending the client to prison.

How deductions are made

The DEO states a 'normal deduction rate' and a 'protected earnings proportion'.[21]

The **'normal deduction rate'** is the amount deducted each payday, provided it does not bring the non-resident parent's net earnings below a certain amount (the protected earnings proportion). The normal deduction rate can include the current child support liability and an amount for any arrears, penalty payments and any fees due. There are no special rules on how quickly the CMS should aim to clear the liability, although often the maximum deduction rate of 40 per cent of net earnings is applied.

More than one normal deduction rate can be set, each applying to a different period.[22]

> **Earnings**
>
> **'Earnings'** include wages, salary, fees, bonuses, commission, overtime pay, occupational pension or statutory sick pay, any other payment made under an employment contract and a regular payment made to compensate for loss of wages.[23] Earnings do not include working tax credit, any social security benefit or disability benefit, a payment by a foreign government or the government of Northern Ireland, or a payment to a special member of a British reserved armed force.[24] **'Net earnings'** is the amount remaining after income tax, national insurance (NI) and contributions towards a pension scheme have been deducted.[25]

The **'protected earnings proportion'** is 60 per cent of net earnings.[26] Deductions must not reduce earnings below this level.

The CMS does not know the non-resident parent's net earnings or pay frequency, as it receives only gross income information from HMRC. The employer is therefore responsible for calculating the protected earnings proportion. The CMS provides employers with pay frequency options for weekly, fortnightly, four-weekly and monthly pay, from which the employer selects the normal deduction rate corresponding to the parent's pay frequency.[27] If the parent is paid at a different frequency, the CMS must cancel the DEO.[28]

> **Example: when an employer can deduct the full normal deduction rate**
> Emma's net earnings are **£1,200** a month.
> The minimum amount she must take home (**protected earnings proportion**) is **£720** a month.
> Net earnings of **£1,200** minus the protected earnings proportion of **£720** = **£480**
> The amount Emma owes in child maintenance (**normal deduction rate**) is **£150** a month.
> Emma has enough left for her employer to deduct the **full normal deduction rate** amount of **£150**.

> **Example: when an employer cannot deduct the full normal deduction rate**
> Craig's net earnings are **£500** a month.
> The minimum amount he must take home (**protected earnings proportion**) is **£300** a month.
> Net earnings of **£500** minus the protected earnings proportion of **£300** = **£200**
> The amount Craig owes in child maintenance (**normal deduction rate**) is **£250** a month.
> Craig does not have enough left for the employer to deduct the full normal deduction rate amount of **£250**.
> The employer should send **£200** to the CMS. The **shortfall of £50** is **carried forward to the next pay period.**

If an employer cannot deduct the full normal deduction rate, they must:[29]
- keep a record of the shortfall;
- carry forward the shortfall to the next period;
- send any deduction you have been able to make to the court or the CMS.

Employers then deduct the full amount of the shortfall *plus* the normal deduction rate owed for the next pay period but must still leave the client with the protected earnings proportion.

If the shortfall is carried forward for several weeks before being repaid, the employer should keep a record of the ongoing shortfall. The CMS or court may need to review a normal deduction rate if a client consistently cannot pay it.

The employer must ensure that the deduction leaves their employee with the amount of their protected earnings unless the deduction is for administrative costs. An employer can deduct an administration charge of £1 from their employee's wage.

When is money deducted

Money is deducted at the client's next pay date after the employer has received the DEO from the CMS. This is then sent by the 19th of the following month to the CMS.[30]

> **Example**
> Alex's DEO was received on 2 April. Alex is paid on the 25th of that month. The deduction will be made at this pay date and sent to the CMS by 19 May.
> The DEO was received on 25 April. Alex is not due to be paid until 25 May. The deduction will be made on 25 May and the money will be sent to the CMS by 19 June.
> If Alex is paid weekly, fortnightly or four-weekly, the same principles apply. The money must always be sent by the 19th of the month following the deduction.

Deduction from earnings orders and diligence against earnings

'Diligence against earnings' is a collective term for the ways creditors can deduct money directly from the client's salary to enforce the payment of a debt. The three methods are:

- **earnings arrestment (EA)** – earnings arrestment is used to make a deduction from the client's earnings for enforcement of a single debt. A creditor must be in possession of a decree (or relevant document of debt) and must have issued the client with a 'charge for payment for money', which must have expired, before proceeding with diligence against earnings. Where the debtor (client) is an individual, the creditor, must also have provided a Debt Advice and Information Package (DAIP);
- **current maintenance arrestment (CMA)** – a current maintenance arrestment is used to enforce a continuing maintenance obligation, such as a court-awarded divorce settlement or child maintenance payment. A CMA will only be used if the client has failed to keep up with their obligations and has fallen behind on the payments they are required to make. As with an EA, the order is served on the client's employer, and deductions are made directly from earnings.
The sum to be deducted under a CMA is calculated differently from those deducted under an EA. An EA and a CMA can be deducted at the same time. They are separate diligences;
- **conjoined arrestment order (CAO)** – an order granted by the court to enforce payment of two or more of the same type of debts, at the same time. For CAOs, the client's employer is required to make a deduction and pass it to the court to distribute the funds instead of paying it directly. The amount deducted is still the same as it would be for a single arrestment only the sum is divided on a pro-rata basis between the conjoined creditors. If a client has one EA and one

CMA, these will continue as separate payments and are not conjoined. In all the above diligences, the DAIP must be served on the debtor no earlier than 12 weeks before the arrestment is executed.

All of the above diligences take precedence over a DEO – except where the DEO is for current maintenance. This takes precedence over an arrestment for a civil debt. Employers often find this confusing when calculating how much should be deducted, the client should be left with at least 60 per cent of their net earnings after all deductions are made. See Chapter 9 for more information on diligence.

Deduction from earnings orders and statutory debt options

Bankruptcy and protected trust deeds

If the client is being made insolvent, a DEO ceases when the client is awarded sequestration or is granted a protected trust deed.

The client is still required to pay ongoing child maintenance after the date of sequestration or granting of a trust deed. Ongoing payments must be evidenced and included in the Common Financial Tool (CFT) calculation. Also essential is ensuring you add any monies being deducted via the DEO for arrears back into the income part of the common financial statement/common financial tool (see p116). Failure to do this can result in any disposable income being incorrect and any 'debtor contribution order' (DCO) having to be changed. It can also mean a client who you assumed qualified for minimum asset process bankruptcy no longer does. A DCO states the amount you need to pay during your bankruptcy and is set by the Accountant in Bankruptcy.

The employer cannot stop the DEO until they have received word from the CMS recalling or stopping the DEO.

The CMS has been known to be slow stopping deductions from a DEO and you may have to email and call several times to get the DEO stopped after your client is insolvent.

Unlike direct earnings attachments (DEAs), the client is refunded any monies paid to the CMS after they are insolvent.

All outstanding child support arrears discharge when the client is discharged. This differs from paying parents in England and Wales, who are still liable for any arrears when their insolvency ends.

Deduction from earnings orders and the Debt Arrangement Scheme

A Debt Payment Programme (DPP) under the Debt Arrangement Scheme (DAS) cannot protect a client from enforcement of child maintenance arrears. When applying for a DPP under the DAS, if a client has a DEO for arrears only, they can add this debt to their application. It is then up to the CMS to approve the DPP and remove the DEO. Any monies deducted must be added back into their CFT or Common Financial Statement to create an accurate picture of the client's financial situation. If, however, they have a DEO for both current maintenance and arrears, the approved debt adviser needs to find out the amount of arrears the client has from the CMS. They can then enter the arrears into the DPP and, if approved, the DEO must be adjusted to include current maintenance payments only. It is a standard condition of the DAS that ongoing child maintenance is paid. Failure to do so can result in the approved DAS being revoked.

4. Third-party deductions

People getting certain benefits can have deductions taken from their benefits and paid directly to a creditor or supplier under the third-party deduction scheme. Third-party deductions can only be made when it is considered to be in the interest of the client or the client's family. They should only be used by a creditor when all other recovery methods have been exhausted.

How third-party deductions work

Third-party deductions allow the client to pay their arrears (and some ongoing bills) straight from their benefit. Deductions can be taken from entitlement to universal credit (UC),[31] pension credit (PC), income support (IS), income-based jobseeker's allowance (JSA) and income-related employment and support allowance (ESA). In limited circumstances, deductions can be made from other benefits. See CPAG's *Welfare Benefits and Tax Credits Handbook* for further information.

Deductions can be made from the client's benefits and paid to third parties to pay **arrears** of:[32]
- housing costs for specified mortgage arrears;
- rent;
- gas or electricity;
- water charges;
- council tax;
- child support maintenance;
- certain loans.

Deductions can also be made to pay:
- county court fines;
- debts to the DWP.

The deductions are made when the benefits are paid. Further deductions may be taken to cover future bills in some circumstances. A client cannot just opt to pay their ongoing fuel costs via their benefits unless they already have arrears with that supplier.

Deductions to third parties can only be made if the client or their partner is liable to make the payments.[33] Deductions should only be made if there is evidence of liability – eg, the bill is in the client's name.

Third-party deductions can be used to pay multiple companies. However, if the total deductions are over 25 per cent of the benefit payment, it must be formally agreed. This is likely to change to 15 per cent from April 2025. Third-party deductions cannot be used to pay an old supplier – eg, a previous landlord or energy provider. Only current suppliers can be paid in this way.

If any third-party deduction will cause hardship, the client can write to the DWP's Debt Management department to ask for the deduction to be reduced, stopped or written off.

More than one deduction

More than one deduction can be made from **UC**. No more than three of the following deductions for third parties may be made from UC at any one time,[34] and the client must be left with at least one pence of UC:[35]
- housing costs;
- rent arrears;
- fuel;
- water charges;
- repayment of eligible loans;
- repayment of integration loans;
- council tax arrears;
- fines, costs and compensation orders.

Without the client's consent, the total amount payable for fuel and water charges combined cannot exceed an amount equal to 25 per cent (15 per cent from April 2025) of your standard allowance plus any child elements to which they are entitled.[36]

In practice, the DWP does not usually deduct more than 25 per cent of the client's standard allowance.[37] This maximum applies to the total of most deductions from UC, not just those for third parties. The total includes all those mentioned in the priority between deductions rules (see p315), as well as those for sanctions, benefit offences and to recover most overpayments of UC, JSA or ESA and advances of UC. If the total deductions would exceed 25 per cent (15 per cent from April 2025) of the client's standard allowance, the deductions mentioned in the priority between deductions rules are reduced (using the priority rules – see p315). However, deductions for ongoing costs (as opposed to arrears) of fuel or water charges are ignored when calculating the total. Deductions of more than the limit may still be made for housing costs, rent arrears or fuel debts, if the DWP considers it would be in the client's best interests.[38]

More than one third-party deduction can be made from **PC, IS, income-based JSA and income-related ESA**. The client must be left with at least 10 pence of benefit.[39]

Priority of debts

The debts covered by the scheme are rated in a priority order. This reflects the degree of risk to the individual or their family by the enforcement action that may result from non-payment.

For UC, an order of priority applies if the client's UC is 'insufficient' to meet all the deductions. The award of UC is 'insufficient' if the total amount of deductions would be more than 40 per cent of the standard allowance that applies to them. Deductions are paid in the following order of priority.

> *Priority order of debts for universal credit* [40]
> 1. Housing costs
> 2. Rent arrears (and related charges), if the amount of the deduction is 10 per cent of your standard allowance
> 3. Fuel
> 4. Council tax arrears
> 5. Fines
> 6. Water charges
> 7. Repayment of social fund payments
> 8. Recovery of hardship payments
> 9. Penalties instead of prosecution for benefit offences
> 10. Recovery of overpayments of benefits or tax credits caused by fraud
> 11. Civil penalties
> 12. Recovery of overpayments of benefits or tax credits not caused by fraud
> 13. Repayment of integration loans
> 14. Repayment of eligible loans
> 15. Rent arrears (and related charges), if the amount of the deduction is more than 10 per cent of your standard allowance

For IS, income-based JSA, income-related ESA and PC, if the client has more debts or current charges than can be met from their benefit, deductions are made in a similar order to those for UC (the first three in the list are the same as for UC).[41]

Deductions for child support are always payable.

If there are both gas and electricity arrears, the DWP chooses which one to pay first, depending on the client's circumstances.

Advisers should get advice from a benefits specialist if they are unsure.

How much can be deducted

Deductions from universal credit

If deductions to third parties are made from UC, they are usually made at a fixed rate of 5 per cent of the client's standard allowance, with the following exceptions.

Chapter 10: Non-diligence debt recovery
4. Third-party deductions

- Deductions for child support maintenance are made at a flat rate of £8.40 a week (£36.40 a month) for ongoing liability or £8.40 a week (£36.40 a month) for arrears.
- Deductions for rent arrears are made at a rate of at least 10 per cent but not more than 20 per cent of your standard allowance.

In practice, deductions of any kind from UC do not usually exceed 25 per cent of the client's standard allowance. If the client has more than one deduction, see p314 for how this limit applies. Third-party deductions cannot leave the client with less than one pence of UC.[42]

Deductions from other means-tested benefits

If deductions to third parties are made from **PC, IS, income-based JSA or income-related ESA**, the maximum deductions are shown below.

Type of arrears	Deduction for arrears	Deduction for ongoing costs
Housing costs	£4.55 for each housing debt (maximum of £13.65)	Current weekly cost
Rent arrears and hostel payments	£4.55	Nil (met by UC or HB)
Residential accommodation charges	Nil	The accommodation allowance (for those in local authority homes); all but £31.75 of your IS, JSA, ESA or PC (for those in private or voluntary homes)
Hostel payments	Nil	Weekly amount assessed by local authority
Fuel	£4.55 for each fuel debt (maximum of £9.10 payable)	Estimated amount of current consumption
Water charges	£4.55 (adjusted every 26 weeks)	Estimated costs
Council tax arrears	£4.55	Nil
Fines	Nil	£5 (lower amount £4.55)
Repayment of eligible loans	Nil	£4.55
Repayment of integration loans	Nil	£4.55
Child support maintenance	£8.40	£8.40
Repayment of tax credit overpayments and self-assessment tax debts	Nil	Maximum £13.65

The deductions

Rent/service charges arrears

If a landlord informs the DWP that a client on UC has rent/service charges arrears, an amount can be deducted monthly from ongoing UC payments until the balance is cleared. This is to prevent eviction and should only be used when other attempts at negotiating payment have failed.

There is a maximum and minimum deduction rate for rent arrears. The amount taken varies depending on other deductions that are being made. A rent arrears deduction can be a maximum of 20 per cent of the standard allowance or as low as 10 per cent of the standard allowance if other deductions are being taken. The amount of no less than 10 per cent and no more than 20 per cent will be reduced by any other deductions being made from the UC award. If there is insufficient UC in payment to take the full 10 per cent minimum, nothing is deducted.

Council tax arrears

Deductions for council tax arrears can be made from UC, IS, JSA, ESA or PC if the local authority gets a summary warrant or decree from a sheriff court and applies to the DWP for recovery to be made in this way. Deductions can be made for arrears and any unpaid costs or penalties imposed.

Council tax arrears cannot be deducted if the client already has 25 per cent of their standard allowance deducted. This is likely to change to 15 per cent from April 2025.

See CPAG's *Council Tax Handbook* for help with council tax arrears.

Utility arrears

If the client owes money to their current mains gas or electricity supplier, the company can request that an amount be deducted from the client's ongoing UC payments for the normal usage amount and arrears. This is to prevent disconnection of service. It stops when the arrears are cleared. If the client has a prepayment meter, they can only take an amount for arrears.

For UC, the amount deducted for arrears of gas, electricity and water is 5 per cent of the standard allowance. For IS, income-based JSA, income-related ESA and PC, an amount can be deducted each week and paid to the supplier in instalments – usually once a quarter.[43]

The amount allocated for normal usage is set by the supplier and cannot be more that 25 per cent of the client's standard allowance and child element unless the client agrees in advance. This is likely to change to 15 per cent from April 2025.

Court fines

Any court in Scotland can apply to the DWP for a fine, costs or compensation order to be deducted from UC, IS, JSA, ESA or PC.[44]

For UC, the maximum amount that can be taken is 5 per cent of the standard allowance. Court fines cannot be deducted if clients are already having 25 per cent (15 per cent from April 2025) of their standard allowance deducted.

Child maintenance

Deductions for ongoing child maintenance are not part of the third-party deduction scheme, although arrears for child maintenance are, and can be deducted from UC payments if the client is a non-resident parent and has no earned income. It can only be taken if the Child Maintenance Service requests the payment directly from the client's benefit. Child maintenance cannot be deducted if the client already has 25 per cent (15 per cent from April 2025) of their standard allowance deducted. This can be a complex area and advisers should get help from a benefits specialist if unsure.

Water Direct

Clients should be aware that even with a 100 per cent council tax reduction, they are still liable to pay at least 75 per cent of their water charges. Water Direct allows debts and current charges for water use to be paid through deductions to the client's benefits.

The scheme can protect a client from increasing debt through water and sewerage charges going to summary warrant. The scheme does not require court action and so avoids statutory additions from being added to the debt.

For more information, see p87.

Consent for deductions

The client's consent is required before deductions (including for arrears) are made for fuel costs and water charges from their UC if the total amount deducted for these payments exceeds 25 per cent (15 per cent from April 2025) of their UC standard allowance and child elements.[45] Otherwise, the DWP can make deductions from UC without consent.

Consent is also required before deductions are made from PC, IS, income-based JSA or income-related ESA for rent arrears, service charges for fuel and water, fuel costs (including arrears), water charges (including arrears) and repayment of integration loans in certain circumstances.[46]

Third-party deductions and insolvency

If a client decides to self-sequestrate or is sequestrated by a creditor and has third-party payment deductions applied to their benefits, they do not automatically stop. The DWP has said that third-party deductions remain the responsibility of the creditor for that debt, such as landlords for rent arrears, utility companies for fuel bill arrears or the courts for fines.[47] As all debts must be included in a bankruptcy, any debt for which a third-party deduction is being made must be included. The creditor, when they have been advised of the award of bankruptcy, should inform the DWP of the same and third-party deductions should stop. If you are dealing with a client who has third-party deductions from their benefits, it is good practice to write to the creditor(s) involved and request that the deductions stop.

Third-party deductions and the Debt Arrangement Scheme

Clients getting benefits can access the DAS if they meet the criteria. If the client has third-party deductions for anything other than ongoing rent, they should be included. It is the responsibility of the creditor to write to the DWP to stop these deductions and debt advisers should be mindful that creditors are not being paid twice – ie, through the DPP and by third-party deductions.

Notes

2. **Direct earnings attachments**
   1 Reg 22 SS(OR) Regs
   2 Reg 20(9) SS(OR) Regs
   3 Reg 30 SS(OR) Regs
   4 Reg 20 SS(OR) Regs
   5 Reg 17 SS(OR) Regs
   6 Sch 2 SS(OR) Regs
   7 Sch 2 SS(OR) Regs
   8 gov.uk/government/publications/direct-earnings-attachments-an-employers-guide/direct-earnings-attachment-a-more-detailed-guide#making-deductions
   9 Part 6 SS(OR) Regs
   10 Reg 29 SS(OR) Regs
   11 Reg 29 SS(OR) Regs
   12 DWP, *Benefit Overpayment Recovery Guide*, v3.20, January 2024, available at gov.uk/government/publications/benefit-overpayment-recovery-staff-guide/benefit-overpayment-recovery-guide

3. **Deduction from earnings orders**
   13 s31 CSA 1991
   14 s31(6) CSA 1991
   15 ss14A and 31(7) CSA 1991; CMS, *Make Child Maintenance Deductions from an Employee's Pay*, gov.uk/child-maintenance-for-employers
   16 childmaintenanceservice.direct.gov.uk
   17 s32A CSA 1991
   18 Reg 25A CS(C&E) Regs
   19 Part 3A CS(C&E) Regs
   20 Part IV CS(C&E) Regs
   21 Reg 9 CS(C&E) Regs
   22 Reg 9(d) CS(C&E) Regs
   23 Reg 8(3) and (4) CS(C&E) Regs
   24 Reg 8(4) CS(C&E) Regs
   25 Reg 8(5) CS(C&E) Regs
   26 Reg 11(2) CS(C&E) Regs
   27 Regs 10(1) and (2) and 11 CS(C&E) Regs, as substituted for '2012 rules' cases and other 'arrears only' cases by reg 4(4) CS(MOC&NCR) Regs
   28 Reg 10(3) CS(C&E) Regs, as substituted for '2012 rules' cases by reg 4(4) CS(MOC&NCR) Regs
   29 Reg 12 CS(C&E) Regs
   30 Reg 14(1) CS(C&E) Regs

Chapter 10: Non-diligence debt recovery Notes

4. **Third-party deductions**
   31 Guidance for third-party deductions from UC is available at gov.uk/government/publications/how-the-deductions-from-benefit-scheme-works-a-handbook-for-creditors/employment-and-support-allowance-jobseekers-allowance-income-support-and-pension-credit-third-party-payments-creditor-and-supplier-handbook
   32 Reg 60 and Schs 6 and 7 UC,PIP,JSA&ESA(C&P) Regs
   33 Sch 9 para 2(1) SS(C&P) Regs; Sch 6 UC,PIP,JSA&ESA(C&P) Regs
   34 Sch 6 para 3(1)(b) UC,PIP,JSA&ESA(C&P) Regs
   35 Sch 6 para 3(1)(a) UC,PIP,JSA&ESA(C&P) Regs
   36 Sch 6 para 3(3) UC,PIP,JSA&ESA(C&P) Regs
   37 The legal limit is actually 40 per cent. Sch 6 para 4 UC,PIP,JSA&ESA(C&P) Regs; DWP guidance, at gov.uk/guidance/find-out-about-money-taken-off-your-universal-credit-payment
   38 Sch 6 para 4 UC,PIP,JSA&ESA(C&P) Regs
   39 Sch 9 para 2(2) SS(C&P) Regs
   40 Sch 9 para 2(2) UC,PIP,JSA&ESA(C&P) Regs
   41 Sch 9 para 2(2) SS(C&P) Regs
   42 Sch 6 para 3(1)(a) UC,PIP,JSA&ESA(C&P) Regs
   43 Sch 9 para 6 SS(C&P) Regs
   44 F(DIS) Regs
   45 Sch 6 para 3(3) UC,PIP,JSA&ESA(C&P) Regs
   46 Sch 9 para 8(2) and (4) SS(C&P) Regs
   47 data.parliament.uk/DepositedPapers/Files/DEP2024-0442/086._Insolvency_V5.0.pdf

Chapter 11

Time to pay directions and orders

This chapter covers:
1. Time to pay directions (below)
2. Time to pay orders (p325)

The Debtors (Scotland) Act 1987 introduced two 'diligence stoppers': 'time to pay directions' and 'time to pay orders'.

Clients can use them to ask the court (or First-tier Tribunal for Scotland (Housing and Property Chamber)) for an extension of time to pay a debt.

This chapter uses the term 'court' to cover both the sheriff court and the First-tier Tribunal.

1. Time to pay directions

What is a time to pay direction

A **'time to pay direction'** (TTPD) is a court procedure *before* a decree is granted. It is covered in sections 1–4 of the Debtors (Scotland) Act 1987. It was introduced for clients who are willing but unable to repay their debts at the contractual amount.

It can only be used for a single debt, if the client has multiple debts, then an application for a Debt Payment Programme (DPP) under the Debt Arrangement Scheme (DAS), or insolvency may be a more suitable option (see Chapter 6).

Only individuals can apply. Limited companies, partnerships and limited liability partnerships are ineligible to apply for a TTPD, although individual partners can apply. If the decree is in the name of the partnership, the creditor can still take action against the partnership. Seek expert advice on this.

Sole traders can apply, even if the debt is registered in the name of the business, as there is no distinction between personal and business debts.

The client can apply to make payments weekly, fortnightly or monthly, or even by a deferred single payment of a lump sum. This may be an option if the client can raise funds within a reasonable period.

Chapter 11: Time to pay directions and orders
1. Time to pay directions

Diligence stopper

As well as extending the length of time a client has to pay a debt, it also acts as a 'diligence stopper'. This means that while the client is paying the agreed amount, the creditor cannot use any diligence against them.

While a TTPD is in place, a creditor cannot:[1]
- serve a charge for payment;
- commence or execute any of the following diligences:
  - an arrestment and action of furthcoming and sale;
  - an attachment;
  - an earnings arrestment;
  - a money attachment to enforce payment of the debt concerned.

What a time to pay direction does not do

A TTPD does not stop an inhibition.

If a creditor has made an application for a sum of money and for any repossession proceedings, the TTPD does not automatically stop the repossession part of the action. This is also true for hire purchase-type loans.

Stopping repossession is at the sheriff's discretion and advisers should remember that this has to be asked for separately.

When it cannot be granted

A TTPD cannot be used for debts:[2]
- over £25,000 (exclusive of any interest and expenses);
- where the decree contains a capital sum on divorce or on the nullity of marriage;
- in connection with a maintenance order;
- in connection with a liability order within the meaning of the Child Support Act 1991;
- in an action by or on behalf of the commissioners for HMRC for payment of any sum recoverable under or by virtue of any enactment or under a contract settlement;
- in an action by or on behalf of Revenue Scotland for payment of any sum recoverable under or by virtue of the Revenue Scotland and Tax Powers Act 2014 or any other enactment in respect of a devolved tax.

It is possible for a TTPD to be applied for rates, council tax and water rates debts. This was made a possible by an amendment in the Bankruptcy and Diligence etc. (Scotland) Act 2007. Some courts, however, still apply the old legislation. Where this is the case, advisers should make them aware of the amendments.

Chapter 11: Time to pay directions and orders
1. Time to pay directions

How to apply

A client can apply by making the relevant application to the court, either by returning the TTPD in the application/summons/writ or by making the application in person at the court hearing.

When considering an application, the court, 'where it is satisfied that it is reasonable in all the circumstances to do so', may grant a TTPD.

It can also take into account:[3]
- the nature of and reasons for the debt in relation to which decree is granted;
- any action taken by the creditor to assist the client in paying that debt;
- the client's financial position;
- the reasonableness of any proposal by the client to pay that debt;
- the reasonableness of any refusal by the creditor of, or any objection by the creditor to, any proposal by the client to pay that debt.

The client and/or the adviser should attend court when making the application.

Joint liability

Where the debt is joint and several, an application by one party does not prevent the creditor from taking action against the other party, but only to the effect of their pro rata share of the debt.

Therefore, both parties should apply if the debt is jointly owned.

The process

There are different processes for different court actions, but, generally, where an application for a TTPD has been made in response to a court application by the creditor, there is a form attached to the summons that allows the client to apply for a TTPD. If the client fills this in and returns it to the court, the creditor will be asked whether they agree to the application for time to pay.
- Where they agree, the case does not need to call in court and the time to pay is granted.
- Where the creditor disagrees, a court hearing is arranged, and the sheriff decides.

Forms

Forms for a TTPD are sent with the claim form.

If the client has any questions, they can approach the sheriff clerk or staff at the First-tier Tribunal for Scotland (Housing and Property Chamber) for help.[4] Sheriff clerks (and equivalents) can give advice on the proceedings and help the client complete and apply for time to pay applications.

Chapter 11: Time to pay directions and orders
1. Time to pay directions

Lay representation

Lay representation is allowed through the sheriff court (and tribunal) rules.

Advisers should prepare for the hearing and ensure they have a completed income and expenditure form as well as any other relevant documents and arguments that they intend to use.

Some advisers go with a two-year limit on the length of time that a TTPD is asked for, but there is no legislation that states this. It is up to the sheriff to decide whether they think it is reasonable.

Variation of a time to pay direction

If the client has a change in income or circumstances, it is possible, to apply for a variation.[5]

Lapse of a time to pay direction

If the client misses two payments and the third becomes due (or the aggregate of), the TTPD lapses and the creditor can continue diligence against the client.[6]

Effect of insolvency on a time to pay direction or order

If your client is currently in a TTPD/TTPO and they are sequestrated, apply for a trust deed or enter into the DAS, the time to pay ceases to have effect.[7]

Interest

Interest is usually payable at the judicial rate (8 per cent).

To claim the interest, before the last instalment of the debt (other than such interest) is payable under the direction, the creditor must state they are claiming such interest and specify the amount of the interest claimed.[8] Failure to do so means the interest is not recoverable.

Checklist for action

- Compile a full income and expenditure statement.
- Check whether a lump sum is available.
- Check the length of time it will take to pay the debt off.
- Check whether an application for a DPP or insolvency would be a better solution for the client.
- Try to contact the creditor to get them to accept the offer without the necessity of a court hearing.
- Be prepared to vary the amount offered if the creditor agrees to an increased offer.
- Explain the collection of interest to the client.

2. Time to pay orders

What is a time to pay order

A **'time to pay order'** (TTPO) is a 'diligence stopper'. It is similar to a time to pay direction (TTPD), but it applies post-decree.

In most cases, it can be applied for when a charge for payment has been served, or diligence has started.

A court or tribunal can grant a TTPO where it believes it is satisfied it is 'reasonable in all the circumstances to do so'. These circumstances are:[9]
- the nature of and reasons for the debt in relation to which the order is sought;
- any action taken by the creditor to assist the client in paying that debt;
- the client's financial position;
- the reasonableness of any proposal by the client to pay that debt;
- the reasonableness of the objection by the creditor to the offer by the client to pay that debt.

It can be applied for where:[10]
- a charge for payment has been served on the client; *or*
- an arrestment has been executed; *or*
- an action of adjudication for debt has been commenced.

A TTPO cannot be applied for:[11]
- where the amount of the debt outstanding at the date of the making of the application exceeds £25,000;
- where, in relation to the debt, a TTPD or a TTPO has previously been made;
- in relation to a debt including any sum recoverable by or on behalf of the commissioners for HMRC;
- in relation to a debt including any sum recoverable by or on behalf of Revenue Scotland under or by virtue of the Revenue Scotland and Tax Powers Act 2014;
- car tax due under the Car Tax Act 1983.

Or where:[12]
- articles belonging to the client have been attached and notice of an auction given under section 27(4) of the Debt Arrangement and Attachment (Scotland) Act 2002, but no auction has yet taken place;
- money owned by the client has been attached and removed;
- a decree in an action of furthcoming has been granted but has not been enforced.

Therefore, timing is important, and some diligence must be at an advanced stage before applying for a TTPO. Get expert advice on this.

The process

It is good practice to take an application to the court and have it checked. This can save time and also allow you to make contact with the court staff.

Once an application has been made and accepted by the court, an 'interim order' is made and all diligence is 'sisted' (paused) until a hearing is arranged. Creditors are informed of the application and have 14 days to reply.[13]

If the creditor does not reply within the timescale, the application is granted.

If the creditor does oppose it, a hearing will be held.

The creditor may also make a counter offer which the client can accept or refuse.

Effect of interim order on diligence

While an interim order granted under section 6(3) of the 1987 Act is in effect, it is not competent in respect of the debt:[14]
- to attach in execution of the decree any articles which have been attached by interim attachment;
- to give, in relation to any articles which have been attached, notice of an auction under section 27(4) of the Debt Arrangement and Attachment (Scotland) Act 2002;
- to execute a money attachment;
- to execute an earnings arrestment;
- to commence an action of furthcoming or sale, or to grant decree in any such action which has already been commenced, in pursuance of that arrestment;
- where a bank account arrestment is in place, and an action of forthcoming has been served, it is not competent to release these funds to the creditor;
- to commence an action of adjudication for debt.

The hearing

At the hearing, your client should be prepared to put forward their case.

They should have a fully completed income and expenditure form and be prepared to argue that the offer made is reasonable given their circumstances.

They should take a copies of any relevant paperwork with them for the sheriff and the creditors.

The sheriff (or tribunal) listens to the arguments from both sides and makes a decision on whether to grant the application or not.

Effects on future diligence

Once granted, the TTPO has the following effects on diligence.[15]
- Charge:
  – a new charge is incompetent;
  – an existing unexpired charge lapses;

– an existing unexpired charge remains effective to constitute apparent insolvency for the client.
- Arrestment (bank account):
  – a new arrestment and furthcoming is incompetent;
  – an existing arrestment may be restricted or recalled;
  – where an arrestment remains in effect, no further steps are taken to enforce it or an action of furthcoming;
  – the arrestment is recalled or restricted.
- Earnings arrestment:
  – a new arrestment will be incompetent;
  – an existing arrestment will be recalled.
- Conjoined arrestment order:
  – a new order will be incompetent because an existing earnings arrestment will be recalled;
  – the debt will be excluded from an existing order.
- Attachment:
  – a new attachment will be incompetent;
  – an existing attachment may be recalled;
  – an interim attachment may be recalled or restricted.
- Inhibition:
  – a new inhibition will be competent;
  – an existing inhibition will be unaffected.

Lay representation

Lay representation is allowed for any proceedings under the Debtors (Scotland) Act 1987 and also through the sheriff court (and tribunal) rules, depending on the type of civil action that has been raised. More information on lay representation can be found on the Scottish Courts and Tribunals Service website.[16]

Rules for lay representatives
Simple Procedure Rules – Part 2
Summary Cause Rules – Chapter 2 and Chapter 2A
Ordinary Cause Rules – Chapter 1A
Summary Application Rules – Chapter 1A
The First-tier Tribunal for Scotland Housing and Property Chamber (Procedure) Regulations 2017 SSI No.328 – regulation 10

Advisers should prepare for the hearing and ensure that they have a completed income and expenditure form, as well as any other relevant documents and arguments that they intend to use.

Some advisers go with a two-year limit on the length of time that a TTPO is asked for, but there is no legislation that states this. It is up to the sheriff to decide whether they think it is reasonable.

Lapse of a time to pay order

A TTPO lapses when the client has missed two payments and the third becomes due.

They cannot make another application for a TTPO.

Variation of a time to pay order

If the client has a change in income or circumstances, it is possible, just like in the Debt Arrangement Scheme (DAS – see p141), to apply for a variation.

Interest

Interest payments are collected separately to the payment of the sum due, once the original sum has been paid.

To claim the interest, the creditor must, before the date when the last instalment of the debt concerned (other than such interest) is payable under the direction, state that they are claiming such interest and specifying the amount of the interest claimed.[17]

Failure to do so means the interest is not recoverable.

Interest is payable at (normally) 8 per cent, the judicial rate.

Time to pay or the Debt Arrangement Scheme/insolvency

When considering whether to apply for time to pay through the court, first consider if the client has multiple debts and whether applying for a Debt Payment Programme (DPP) under the DAS or an insolvency option would be a better solution (see Chapter 6).

Time to pay order forms

Simple procedure – Form 5A[18]
Simple procedure for council tax – Form DSA2[19]
Ordinary cause – Form DSA2[20]
First-tier Tribunal for Scotland (Housing and Property Chamber) – Application for a Time to Pay Order[21]

Help, guidance and the necessary forms can be obtained from the sheriff clerk or the First-tier Tribunal.

Checklist for action
- Check whether the client is eligible to apply, as this depends on the stage of diligence.
- Compile a full income and expenditure statement.
- Check whether a lump sum would be available.
- Check the length of time it will take to pay the debt off.
- Check whether an application for a DPP or insolvency would be a better solution for the client.
- Try to contact the creditor to get them to accept the offer without the necessity of a court hearing.
- Be prepared to vary the amount offered if the creditor agrees to an increased offer.
- Explain the collection of interest to the client.

Notes

1. **Time to pay directions**
   1. s1 D(S)A 1987
   2. s1(5) D(S)A 1987
   3. s1(1A) D(S)A 1987
   4. s96(2) D(S)A 1987
   5. s3 D(S)A 1987
   6. s4(1) D(S)A 1987
   7. s12 D(S)A 1987
   8. s1(7) D(S)A 1987

2. **Time to pay orders**
   9. s5(2A) D(S)A 1987
   10. s5(1) D(S)A 1987
   11. s5(4) D(S)A 1987
   12. s5(5) D(S)A 1987
   13. s6(3) and (6) D(S)A 1987
   14. s8 D(S)A 1987
   15. S Cowan, *Scottish Debt Recovery: a practical guide* (2nd en), Sweet and Maxwell, 2018, para 4-27
   16. scotcourts.gov.uk/taking-action/lay-representation-in-civil-cases
   17. s5(7) D(S)A 1987
   18. scotcourts.gov.uk/media/diag5w1l/form-5a.pdf
   19. legislation.gov.uk/uksi/1988/2013/schedule/made
   20. legislation.gov.uk/uksi/1988/2013/schedule/made
   21. housingandpropertychamber.scot/time-pay

12

Chapter 12

Prescription and limitation

This chapter covers:
1. Introduction (below)
2. Short negative prescription (five years) (p331)
3. Long negative prescription (20 years) (p333)
4. Common debt types (p334)
5. Dealing with a prescription case (p336)

1. Introduction

Prescription and limitation are two different concepts in law. Both are governed by the Prescription and Limitation (Scotland) Act 1973 (the '1973 Act'). **'Prescription'** is the term for the principle whereby a right or liability is extinguished by a lapse of time. **'Limitation'** is different in that it refers to the period in which certain actions must be raised. **'Extinguished'** means that the right or liability no longer exists and the creditor has no debt to pursue.

The 1973 Act is complex legislation that directly impacts the advice that should be given to clients. A key aspect of the 1973 Act is 'negative prescription'. This deals with the lapse of time on rights and obligations and the effect this has on a creditor's right to pursue a debt.

This chapter looks at prescription and the rules for short (five years) and long (20 years) negative prescription.

Terms like 'statute barred' are used throughout the chapter. The meaning is the same as 'prescribed'.

Prescription (Scotland) Act 2018

In 2017, the Scottish Law Commission reviewed the 1973 Act to make the law around negative prescription clearer and easier to understand.[1] Subsequently, the Prescription Scotland Act 2018 (the '2018 Act') received royal assent in 2018. Its commencement and transitional regulations set out when various parts of the 2018 Act come into force to amend the 1973 Act.[2]
- The new section 11(3) and (3A) 'knowledge test' came into force on 1 June 2022.[3]

- The new section 13 came into force on 1 June 2022, enabling parties to enter into agreements to extend a five-year prescriptive period by up to one year.[4]
- All other provisions will come into force from 28 February 2025.

What is not covered by the Prescription and Limitation (Scotland) Act 1973

There are certain rights which do not prescribe either under short or long negative prescription. These include certain debts to the Crown – eg, payments of income tax and VAT.

Schedule 3 of the 1973 Act outlines imprescriptible rights and obligations. If a client has a debt which falls under any of the imprescriptible rights, they should be advised that this debt will not prescribe. If the client wants to challenge this, they should get legal advice as this is an area which cannot be dealt with by debt advisers.

2. Short negative prescription (five years)

Short negative prescription lasts five years. It usually covers most unsecured debts.

Schedule 1 of the Prescription and Limitation Act (Scotland) 1973 Act details which debts are covered by short negative prescription, and which are not. So, unless the creditor protects its claim by taking action or the client makes a payment or writes to the creditor to acknowledge the debt, it prescribes after five years have passed, meaning it is 'extinguished' (see p330).

Debts covered by the five-year prescription period

Most unsecured debts are covered by the five-year rule. These include (but are not limited to):
- credit cards;
- personal loans;
- store cards;
- overdrafts;
- catalogues;
- payday loans;
- rent arrears;
- benefit overpayments owed to Social Security Scotland.[5]

Chapter 12: Prescription and limitation
2. Short negative prescription (five years)

What the law says

For a debt to extinguish, specific criteria must be met. Section 6 of the 1973 Act outlines the following.

> *Negative prescription*
> 6. *Extinction of obligations by prescriptive periods of five years.*
>   (1) If, after the appropriate date, an obligation to which this section applies has subsisted for a continuous period of five years–
>   (a) without any relevant claim having been made in relation to the obligation, and
>   (b) without the subsistence of the obligation having been relevantly acknowledged,
>   then as from the expiration of that period the obligation shall be extinguished.

When does prescription start running

The legislation does not define the date prescription starts, rather it states that 'after the appropriate date' prescription is started. The issue of when prescription begins has been argued in court many times. Caselaw exists and can be useful.[6]

In general, for credit cards, loans and other consumer credit debts, the appropiate date is the date a **default notice** is served under the Consumer Credit Act 1974 ('CCA 1974').

Where the debt is not covered by the CCA 1974, it is when the creditor makes a demand for the total sum owed.

For rent arrears, it is usually when the last instalment was due or appropriate legal action commences.

Establishing when prescription begins to run can be complex. It is often not straightforward and can depend on a number of factors, including the type of debt and the terms of the contract the client entered into.

What is a relevant claim

The prescription period can be interrupted by a 'relevant claim' made by a creditor.

'Relevant claims' are when a creditor raises an action for the debt, or obtains a court order or raises a petition for the sequestration of the client. It can also include executing recovery action such as wage arrestments, attachment orders or serving a charge for payment or arresting the debtor's bank account.

Every time the creditor makes a relevant claim, it interrupts the running of prescription, which begins again from the start.

What is a relevant acknowledgement

What constitutes a **'relevant acknowledgement'** is the client making a payment to the debt or writing to the creditor to acknowledge the debt. This can include when a client is disputing the amount owed.

When there has been a relevant acknowledgement, the prescription period begins running again.

This also applies if the debt was joint and only one of the liable parties made a 'relevant acknowledgement' – prescription begins again, even if the other party did not make a payment or acknowledge the debt in writing.

Prescription can be interrupted when a client includes their debt in a Debt Payment Programme (DPP) under the Debt Arrangement Scheme (DAS) or gets a time to pay direction or order under the Debtors (Scotland) Act 1987 or a time order under the CCA 1974.

Prescription begins running again when the client comes out of the programme (when their DPP is revoked or the time to pay/time order is defaulted).

If they have completed the DAS or the time to pay and the debt is paid, the matter of prescription is no longer relevant.

Any fraud or error by the client that induces a creditor to not make a relevant claim can also interrupt the running of prescription – eg, the client pretending they are dead in order to stop a creditor raising an action in court.

3. **Long negative prescription (20 years)**

The long negative prescription period is 20 years. Debts which are not exempt from prescription or covered under the five-year rule are covered by the 20-year rule.

Debts covered by the 20-year prescription period

The types of debts covered by the 20-year rule include:
- debts constituted by court orders (this could include types of debt normally covered by the five-year rule);
- summary warrants;
- an order of a tribunal or an authority authorised by legislation to order that a debt is due (which includes benefit overpayments owed to HMRC or the DWP).

Note that when the Prescription (Scotland) Act 2018 comes fully into force in 2025, the long negative prescription period will not extend beyond 20 years, regardless of any further relevant claims made by the creditor.

Some types of debt are also not extinguishable, and this means they can never be written off – eg, VAT and income tax.

What the law says

For a debt to extinguish after 20 years, specific criteria must be met. Section 7 of the Prescription and Limitation (Scotland) Act 1973 outlines the following.

7. Extinction of obligations by prescriptive periods of twenty years

(1) If, after the date when any obligation to which this section applies has become enforceable, the obligation has subsisted for a continuous period of twenty years–

(a) without any relevant claim having been made in relation to the obligation, and

(b) without the subsistence of the obligation having been relevantly acknowledged,

then as from the expiration of that period the obligation shall be extinguished:

Provided that in its application to an obligation under a bill of exchange or a promissory note this subsection shall have effect as if paragraph (b) thereof were omitted.

When does prescription start running

For debts covered under the 20-year rule, prescription starts running from the date the debt becomes enforceable.

What is a relevant claim

Creditors covered by the 20-year rule (eg, by an order of a tribunal or an authority authorised by legislation to order that a debt is due – which includes benefit overpayments owed to HMRC or the DWP) can take court action to recover the debt they say they are owed. If they take court action, the prescription period begins again. This means clients can, in effect, have debts which are more than 20 years old.

Creditors originally covered under the five-year rule, on taking a client to court or getting a decree or petitioning for their sequestration, have 20 years to enforce any debt owed.

If a client is sequestrated, the debt may be discharged. If it does not discharge, the act of sequestrating begins the clock again for those debts.

What is a relevant acknowledgement

A **'relevant acknowledgement'** happens if a client makes payment to the debt or writes to the creditor acknowledging the debt. This sets the clock running again from the date the payment is made or the letter is sent to the creditor.

4. Common debt types

Benefit overpayments

The DWP is likely to try to take court action to recover a benefit overpayment within the following time limits.

If the DWP has decided that the overpayment should be recovered from a client, it has 20 years from the date of the decision to recover the overpayment and enforce it.[7]

If the DWP assess that the client has been overpaid a benefit, but has not yet decided that it should be recovered via court action from the client, it has five years from the date it assessed that the benefit was overpaid to decide this. If it decides it should be recovered before the five years has expired, it then has 20 years to recover the overpayment.

This is a complicated area and advisers may need specialist help to check whether an overpayment can still be recovered from a client.

Advisers should also be mindful of the DWP's ability to recover all overpayments without going to court through direct deductions and direct earnings attachments.

Sheriff court decree/decision

When a creditor has taken a client to court and has obtained a decree or court judgment (including a decision under simple procedure), it has 20 years to enforce it.[8] This is despite it falling off the client's credit file after six years.

Council tax

Council tax arrears are recovered under summary warrant and so come under the 20-year negative prescription rule.[9] This time limit runs from the date of the final demand or from the last time the debt was acknowledged by the client/clients (or an agent acting on their behalf). If there was a 'prolonged and unexplained delay' in recovery, it may be possible to challenge any new recovery action. Specialist or legal advice may be needed to pursue this.

Mortgage shortfall

If any balance remains after the sale or repossession of a client's home, the lender has 20 years to recover the capital amount owed and five years to recover any interest owed.[10]

Note that the lender/creditor only has five years from the date of sale or possession to decide and inform the client of their intention to pursue them for recovery of any shortfall.

Advisers should be mindful of the Financial Conduct Authority's rules under *The Mortgages and Home Finance: conduct of business sourcebook* (MCOB). MCOB 13 is concerned with how firms administer a regulated mortgage contract, administer a home purchase plan and administer a sale shortfall.[11]

Student loans

There are two types of student loans and different rules apply depending on when the client took out the loan. Student loan agreements are simple contract debts, and this gives the company pursuing five years from the date a client last paid or acknowledged the debt to go to court to enforce the agreement.

Old-style 'mortgage' student loans are Consumer Credit Act agreements. Payments cannot be automatically deducted from wages. Court action has to be taken before the debt can be enforced. This means that the time limits can apply if a client has not paid or acknowledged the debt for over five years.

Advisers should be aware that a client asking for the loan to be deferred may count as acknowledging the debt and start the prescription period again.

From September 1998, 'new-style' or 'income contingent' student loans include rules that say repayments will be automatically deducted directly from wages or through a client's tax return if they are self-employed. This means that the Student Loans Company can still take money for a loan after five years, as it does not have to go to court to do this.

5. Dealing with a prescription case

Although prescription can appear straightforward, it is a complex area of law. Advisers should always seek specialist help or support if they are unsure how to proceed as an improperly worded letter to a creditor may constitute a relevant acknowledgement and may interrupt prescription running, meaning it resets the prescription clock.

Contacting creditors

If a client believes their debt has prescribed, the next actions they take depend on how sure they are that the relevant period has passed.

If the client is certain the limitation period has passed, and they have not heard from the creditor, the client does not need to do anything.

If the creditor contacts the client, they can send a letter stating they believe the debt is now prescribed. This puts the ball in the creditor's court and forces them to provide evidence that the debt is not prescribed.

If the creditor can provide proof of payment or written acknowledgement of the debt, the client is still liable, and the debt is not prescribed.

If a client is not certain whether the relevant period has passed, they could check their credit file to see when the last payments were made for the debt. Remember, though, that just because a debt has fallen off or is not shown on a credit file, it is not proof that the debt has prescribed.

When a creditor actively contacts a client, advisers should not recommend that clients ignore the debt in the hope that the five-/20-year period will pass, as the creditor may start court action just before the limitation period has passed.

Model letters

There are several model letters available online that a client can use to challenge the liability of a debt they are being pursued for. It is important that they use the correct wording and do not in any way admit liability in the letter. It is preferable for the letter to be from the client directly and not written on their behalf – although an adviser can help a client compose the correct wording.

National Debtline has a sample letter template at nationaldebtline.org/sample-letters/time-has-run-out-recover-debt-s.

Defending at court

If a creditor takes a client to court over a debt which has passed the prescriptive period, the client must show the court that the relevant prescription period has passed and ask the court to cancel the creditor's case.

The client must complete any paperwork received from the court and return it before the deadline. Failure to do this leads to the court going forward with the court order, which starts the prescription clock again and allows the creditor to pursue diligence against the client.

The client may need to attend a hearing if the court requires more information.

Once the forms have been returned to the court, the creditor must provide evidence that the relevant prescriptive period has not passed. If it cannot, the court should dismiss the claim.

This can be complex to navigate and depends on the procedure under which the action is raised (simple procedure/ordinary cause). Advisers can get specialist help from the MATRICS team (consultancy@matrics.org.uk) if they are unsure how to proceed.

Payments after a debt has prescribed

If a client starts to make payments to a debt which has already prescribed, these payments *do not revive* the debt. The debt is still 'extinguished' and legally no longer exists. The client can request a refund of any monies paid.

Example

Umar had a bank loan which he stopped paying when he received a default notice 10 years ago. The bank sold the debt to another company that has been actively pursuing Umar and threatening him with court action. Unsure about his rights, Umar began making payments of £5 a month a couple of years ago.

In this instance, Umar did not revive the debt by making payments to the new debt owners and is entitled to a refund of all monies paid. This company should have known that the debt was extinguished when purchased from the original creditor.

Financial Conduct Authority

The Financial Conduct Authority's (FCA) *Consumer Credit Sourcebook* (CONC) provides guidance on whether a debt is being collected fairly. The FCA does not

Chapter 12: Prescription and limitation
5. Dealing with a prescription case

investigate individual complaints, but its rules can be used when a client is disputing a debt on the grounds of prescription. The FCA's rules and guidance apply to all debts no matter how old they are.

> **Key areas of guidance**
>
> **CONC 7.15.3**: in Scotland, a statute-barred debt ceases to exist and is no longer recoverable if:
> (1) a relevant claim on behalf of the lender or owner has not been made during the relevant limitation period; *and*
> (2) the debt has not been acknowledged by, or on behalf of, the customer during the relevant limitation period.
>
> **CONC 7.15.7**: it is misleading for a firm to suggest or state that a customer may be the subject of court action for the sum of the statute-barred debt when the firm knows, or reasonably ought to know, that the relevant limitation period has expired.
>
> **CONC 7.15.8**: a firm must not continue to demand payment from a customer after the customer has stated that he will not be paying the debt because it is statute-barred.

Not only will a statute-barred debt not be recoverable by the creditor, but the creditor must stop pursuing or threatening legal action for a statute-barred debt.

Financial Ombudsman service

If a creditor has dealt with an expired debt in a way which does not follow the FCA's guidelines, a complaint can be made. This should first be made to the creditor using its complaints procedure. If its response is not satisfactory, the complaint can be raised with the Financial Ombudsman Service, but only for events which occurred after April 2007.

Chapter 12: Prescription and limitation
Notes

Notes

1. Introduction
1. Scottish Law Commission, *Report on Prescription*, COM No.247, July 2017, available at scotlawcom.gov.uk/files/3414/9978/5138/Report_on_Prescription_Report_No_247.pdf
2. The Prescription (Scotland) Act 2018 (Commencement, Saving and Transitional Provisions) Regulations 2022 No.78
3. s5 PSA 2018
4. s13 PSA 2018

2. Short negative prescription (five years)
5. Not all benefit overpayments owed are covered by the five-year period, including DWP overpayments. See the section on overpayments for more information.
6. See, for example, *PRA Group Ltd v MacPherson* [2023] SC EDIN 21, available at advicescotland.com/wp-content/uploads/2019/01/Scottish.pdf

4. Common debt types
7. gov.uk/government/publications/benefit-overpayment-recovery-staff-guide/benefit-overpayment-recovery-guide
8. Sch 1 para 2 PL(S) Act 1973
9. Sch 1 para 2 PL(S) Act 1973
10. s8(2) PL(S) Act 1973
11. MCOB 13

Chapter 13

Messengers-at-arms and sheriff officers

This chapter covers:
1. Introduction (below)
2. What sheriff officers do (p341)
3. Sheriff officers' powers to enforce debts from other parts of the UK (p344)
4. Making a complaint about a sheriff officer (p344)

1. Introduction

Messengers-at-arms and sheriff officers are the officers of the court who carry out judgment enforcement. Messengers-at-arms are appointed by the Court of Session. They are not employed by the court, but independent contractors, normally acting on instruction from the pursuer. Sheriff officers are appointed by, and are responsible to, the sheriff principal.

The rules for messengers-at-arms and sheriff officers are in the Act of Sederunt (Messengers-at-Arms and Sheriff Officers Rules) 1991.

Messengers-at-arms

A messenger-at-arms is an officer of the Court of Session,[1] which is the supreme civil court in Scotland. A messenger-at-arms can travel anywhere in Scotland to serve documents and enforce orders of the Court of Session.

Qualification as a messenger-at-arms

A sheriff officer cannot become a messenger-at-arms unless they have been in practice as a sheriff officer for at least two years.[2] Within the five years before applying to the Court of Session for a recommendation for appointment as a messenger-at-arms, they must pass the relevant examinations. In special circumstances, the Court of Session may reduce the required period of practice.

Sheriff officers

A sheriff officer is an officer of the regional civil court. Scotland is divided into six regions called sheriffdoms, each of which has a sheriff principal responsible for the conduct of the courts.

The six sheriffdoms in Scotland are:
- Glasgow and Strathkelvin;
- Grampian, Highland and Islands;
- Lothian and Borders;
- North Strathclyde;
- South Strathclyde, Dumfries and Galloway;
- Tayside, Central and Fife.

Unlike a messenger-at-arms, a sheriff officer can only operate in the geographical area where they hold a commission.

Qualification as an officer of the court

A person cannot be an officer of court unless:[3]
- they are aged 20 or over and under 70 years; *and*
- they have trained for three years with a practising officer of court; *and*
- the officer of court with whom they trained has issued a certificate stating that the training has been completed satisfactorily and within five years before applying for a commission as a sheriff officer; *and*
- they have passed the relevant examinations; *and*
- they have attained the educational standard determined by the committee of examiners.

A sheriff officer must retire from practice as an officer of court when they reach age 70.

2. What sheriff officers do

A sheriff officer can visit homes or workplaces to serve you court papers and enforce court orders (including summary warrants) issued by the sheriff court. They can enforce court orders for:
- eviction;
- debt;
- property arguments;
- family matters (like adoption or divorce).

They can also carry out orders to:
- remove members of your family from your house (like an abused child or violent partner);

Chapter 13: Messengers-at-arms and sheriff officers
2. What sheriff officers do

- deliver a witness citation or other legal documents to you, if the court needs proof they were delivered.

Sheriff officers can also sometimes work as debt collectors, but they cannot at the same time use the powers available to them as a sheriff officer.

Entering a home or workplace

A sheriff officer has the power to enter a home or workplace to carry out their order, but only if the court gives them permission to do it.[4]

Sheriff officers can be asked to show the document that says they are allowed to enter.

It might not always be clear from the document that the sheriff officer has the right to enter a home or workplace. It might have a phrase like 'grants warrant for all lawful execution' on it. This means they are allowed to enter.

For evictions and debt enforcement, a sheriff officer usually writes in advance to advise they are coming.

They are not usually allowed to attend at night unless they have a warrant that allows them to enter – eg, if someone is in danger or a child has to be removed for their protection.

Forcing entry

If a sheriff officer has permission from the court to enter a home or workplace but is denied entry, they are allowed to use 'necessary reasonable force' to gain access.[5]

This includes:
- forcing open a door;
- breaking a lock;
- breaking a window.

If someone tries to stop the sheriff officer from entering a house or workplace, they could be charged with breach of the peace.

If no one is at home or at the workplace when a sheriff officer visits, they can only force entry if they are:
- carrying out an eviction; *or*
- making sure certain work has been carried out; *or*
- getting back property.

Checking an officer's identity

You have the right to ask for a sheriff officer's identity if they attend a home or workplace.[6]

Every sheriff officer has a red identity booklet which contains:
- their photograph; *and*

- the crest of the Scottish Courts and Tribunals Service; *and*
- the signature of the sheriff clerk for the area they work in.

A sheriff officer must show you their identity booklet if asked for it.

Eviction

Sheriff officers generally enforce eviction orders between 8am and 8pm.[7] However, they can come in the middle of the night if given special permission from a court order or if it is to secure someone's safety. Where required, sheriff officers are entitled to use necessary and reasonable force (eg, provided they have the correct warrant, they can force a door or break a lock or a window) to enter the property and remove:
- the tenant(s);
- the tenants' possessions;
- anyone else living in the property.

The landlord should inform the tenant of the eviction date by sending them a letter (called a 'Form of Charge for Removing'). This letter must be served on the tenant by the sheriff officer and generally give the tenant 14 days to vacate the property.

If the tenant fails to leave the property within this time, the sheriff officer informs the tenant of when they will arrive to evict them. Generally, the sheriff officer gives the tenant 48 hours' notice.

If someone tries to stop the sheriff officer carrying out an eviction, they could be charged with breach of the peace.

Exceptional attachment

The court may decide that some belongings can be taken and sold to help pay a debt.

When this happens, the sheriff officer might carry out an 'exceptional attachment'. This means they have permission to enter a home or workplace and take non-essential possessions. They cannot take possessions that are seen as essential for everyday life – eg, clothing, beds, sofas, computers and cookers.[8]

A sheriff officer must advise in advance that they are coming to take possessions with an exceptional attachment.

Although they can force entry into a home or workplace, they cannot take anything if nobody is in the property.

They also cannot take anything if there is someone in the property, but they:
- are under 16 years old; *or*
- cannot speak or understand English; *or*
- do not understand the situation because of physical or mental disability.

3. Sheriff officers' powers to enforce debts from other parts of the UK

Sheriff officers have the power to enforce a debt in Scotland from elsewhere in the UK, but only if the party has a document known as a 'Certificate of Money Provisions' from the court which issued the judgment.[9] The certificate must then be sent to the Keeper of the Registers of Scotland for registration in the Register of Judgments. After registration, the party is provided with an official extract copy of the certificate bearing an execution which will enable the creditor to proceed using the services of a sheriff officer.

Bailiffs from elsewhere in the UK have no power of enforcement in Scotland.

Creditors from elsewhere in the UK must go through a court process and instruct a sheriff officer to enforce the action.

4. Making a complaint about a sheriff officer

You should write to the firm that employs the sheriff officer if you believe that they have:
- behaved in an unreasonable or disreputable way; *or*
- exceeded their powers.

If you are not happy with the firm's response or do not want to complain to the firm directly, you can write to the sheriff principal. They can be contacted through the sheriff clerk at your local sheriff court.

You can find details of your local sheriff court on the Scottish Courts and Tribunals Service website.[10]

You can also complain to the Society of Messengers-at-Arms and Sheriff Officers.[11] It has its own disciplinary procedures but often handles complaints from the sheriff principal's office. Its address is Society of Messengers-at-Arms and Sheriff Officers, Forth House, 28 Rutland Square, Edinburgh EH1 2BW (telephone: 0131 292 0321).

Notes

1. **Introduction**
   1. scotcourts.gov.uk/the-courts/supreme-courts/about-the-court-of-session
   2. r4 AoS(MASO) Rules
   3. r3 AoS(MASO) Rules

2. **What sheriff officers do**
   4. s49 DAA(S)A 2002
   5. mygov.scot/sheriff-officer-powers-rights/entering-your-home-work
   6. mygov.scot/sheriff-officer-powers-rights/proof-of-identity
   7. s217 BD(S)A 2007
   8. Sch 2 DAS(S)A 2002

3. **Sheriff officers' powers to enforce debts from other parts of the UK**
   9. smaso.org.uk/faqs

4. **Making a complaint about a sheriff officer**
   10. scotcourts.gov.uk/the-courts/sheriff-court/find-a-court
   11. smaso.org.uk

Chapter 14

Business debts

This chapter covers:
1. Introduction (below)
2. Types of small business (p348)
3. Stages of debt advice (p354)
4. Checklist (p374)

1. Introduction

This chapter looks at how the debts and strategies covered elsewhere in this *Handbook* may need extra consideration when advising someone who is, or has been, running a small business (ie, self-employed clients).

A small business (small- to medium-sized enterprise – also known as an SME) is defined by the government as an organisation with fewer than 250 employees and a turnover of less than €50 million or a balance sheet total of less than €43 million. A breakdown of the different organisation sizes is in the table below. These figures are currently being reviewed.[1]

Defining an SME

Turnover or balance sheet total	Headcount	Business size
Less than or equal to €50 million or €43 million	less than 250	medium
Less than or equal to €10 million or €10 million	less than 50	small
Less than or equal to €2 million or €2 million	less than 10	micro

The chapter also examines how a self-employed client's circumstances can affect the level of support that non-business specialist debt advisers can provide.

This chapter should be used in conjunction with the rest of the *Handbook*. It is not a guide to business credit or business viability. These are both specialist areas in their own right.

Chapter 14: Business debts
1. Introduction

Giving advice to self-employed clients

When dealing with self-employed clients, you need to look at their overall situation, both from a personal debt position and a business perspective.

This is so that you can fully consider how a client's circumstances can affect your advice. Remember, you are not a chartered accountant, insolvency practitioner or a business specialist. Your role is simply to identify the debt issues the client has presented with and look at the whole picture. A client's circumstances may change over the time you are advising them; thus your advice may also need to reflect any changes. Do this even if a self-employed client says that they have personal debts only.

It is worthwhile taking the time to ask the client about their business – what is it precisely that they do? What service do they offer? How is the business run – do they keep daily records of all business transactions and expenses – if so, what is their recording method? Knowing a bit about the client's business will help you to help them.

Additionally, do they have an accountant to do their business books or does the client do it themself? Do they make the most of the expenses offset using the HMRC guide?[2] Do they understand the implications of being self-employed? Some clients may be full-time employed and have a self-employed business on the side to generate extra income. Some clients may only be self-employed at certain times of the year and employed at other times of the year.

Experience as a money adviser will tell you that clients do not always have a clear picture themselves on either the personal debt side or the business side.

Organisations should have a policy (or guidelines) that sets out the level of support debt advisers are expected to provide self-employed clients. If your organisation does not have such a policy or guidelines, you need to raise this with your organisation.

The policy should take into account the level of an adviser's knowledge in this area and the technical support available within their organisation. It should also recognise that three key factors usually affect the type of help that self-employed clients need to deal with their situation.

These three key factors are:
- how the client is set up in business (their trading status);
- whether the client has stopped trading;
- whether the client has any complex business debts (such as a business premises lease or a tax dispute).

The remainder of this chapter assumes that your organisation's policy provides some support to self-employed clients. The chapter shows how these key factors can affect the scope and type of advice that debt advisers may be able to offer a self-employed client. It also explains when a signpost or referral to a specialist service is usually required.

Chapter 14: Business debts
2. Types of small business

This chapter is not intended to challenge any organisation's policy. Advisers should refer to their own guidelines and always seek specialist advice if they are uncertain about advising a self-employed client.

Business Debtline provides free business debt advice for self-employed people and small businesses. It can advise clients who are still trading, and clients who have ceased trading and who have complex debt situations. Advice is available by webchat via its website at businessdebtline.org/Scotland or by calling 0800 197 6026.

2. Types of small business

Most self-employed clients that debt advisers deal with run their businesses on their own. However, their situations can vary greatly. For example, a client who says they 'just work for themselves' may be set up as a sole trader or director of a limited company. It is important to identify how a client is set up in business (their trading status) because this affects which debts they are liable for and when specialist advice is needed.

Trading status also affects the type of financial statement a client must complete. There should be one for the business and one for the client.

If a client is unsure of their trading status, they could ask their accountant or bookkeeper for information. If this is not available, signpost the client to specialist business advice.

Sole traders

Giving advice to a sole trader

A sole trader is a person who is self-employed and runs their business on their own (without any business partners). Sole traders can use their own name for their business or use a separate business name.

Sole traders do not register their business with Companies House and their business name should not end with 'Ltd' or 'limited'.

Sole traders are legally responsible for their business. They are personally liable for any debts created through running their business and personally own any business assets.

Typical sole traders might include plumbers, electricians, gardeners, beauty therapists, taxi drivers, food delivery services and salespeople who work on a purely self-employed basis.

Sole traders should be registered with HMRC and provide a self-assessment for tax purposes every year. They can register as self-employed at gov.uk/register-for-self-assessment.

A sole trader will not have wages but will take 'drawings' from the profit of the business. The client may not necessarily understand this difference – ie, they will simply pay themselves monies from the business bank account. While these 'drawings' can be taken at any point, it is important to note that these are not deductible in working out the profits for the business and the client will have to pay tax on the profits through the self-assessment system.

A sole trader and their business are one and the same. If the business struggles to pay its debts, the client's income and assets may be at risk. Therefore, consider the client's overall situation.

If a client is still trading

You may be able to give advice about dealing with personal debt emergencies, such as council tax enforcement agents (sheriff officers) and, if it has been established that the advice will not negatively impact the client's business, provide basic advice about dealing with personal creditors.

At the time of writing, individuals could still apply for a 'statutory moratorium' (see p199) to protect themselves from enforcement action such as an earnings arrestment (if employed) or a bank arrestment or attachment or a creditor applying to have them declared bankrupt – the duration of the statutory moratorium protection at the time of this review was six months.

You may also be able to advise the client about the implications of continuing to trade, such as the risk to assets and further indebtedness.

Specialist advice is needed if the client has any business debts or complex business issues, such as a disputed tax debt. The client also needs specialist debt advice before deciding how best to proceed with their debts. A specialist adviser looks at the client's overall situation (at home and in the business) and discusses how any action the client takes could affect their ability to continue trading. For example, a sole trader plumber who relies on trade credit for their business supplies may struggle to meet the credit limits imposed by bankruptcy or the Debt Arrangement Scheme. The client needs to be prepared to inform the supplier about this if they borrow more than the limit imposed by the legislation. Such a disclosure could put the client's supply at risk.

If a client has ceased trading

Check whether the client has any complex business debts, such as an ongoing liability for a business lease. If any complex debts are identified, the client needs specialist advice. Specialist advice might also be needed if the client has a disputed tax debt or has failed to submit tax returns (see TaxAid[3]).

Providing the client does not have any complex business advice needs, you can usually give the client full debt advice. You should check whether the client has told their creditors, suppliers and HMRC that they have stopped trading and give advice on that if needed.

If the client has ceased trading and is no longer self-employed, they must inform HMRC.[4] If not advised, HMRC will assume that the individual is still self-

Chapter 14: Business debts
2. Types of small business

employed and so self-assessments returns will still be required to be submitted – failure to submit self-assessments can lead to penalties and fines being imposed.[5]

Partner in a business partnership
Giving advice to a business partner

The legal definition of a 'partnership' in the UK is: 'a partnership is a relationship resulting from a contract or agreement, oral or written. The implementation of that agreement creates the partnership relationship. If it is not implemented, it is not effective.'[6]

A business partnership can exist when two or more people carry out a business together to make a profit. A partnership is sometimes also called 'a firm'. There is no limit on the number of partners a partnership may have. See gov.uk/hmrc-internal-manuals/partnership-manual/pm120100.

A partnership can also be entered into informally. A written agreement is not needed for a partnership to exist, and the Partnership Act 1890 applies in the absence of a written agreement. The partners share equally in the profits and losses of the business unless otherwise agreed.

A partnership can trade using the partners' names or a separate business name. Partners do not register the partnership with Companies House. Their business name should not include 'Ltd', 'limited', 'LLP' or 'limited liability partnership' or any other use of wording that infers a status it does not have.

A partnership set up formally through a written partnership agreement should cover how any profits in the business are shared out between the partners and how the partnership can be ended. Unless the partnership rules state otherwise, contracts can be entered into by any of the partners. The partnership agreement can be useful if there is a dispute between the partners.

If there is no written agreement it can be difficult to identify whether a business partnership exists. If you are unsure whether a business is being run as a partnership, get specialist advice.

Usually, partners personally own a share of the partnership's assets and are jointly and severally liable for the debts accrued by the partnership. However, each partner always has sole liability for their own income tax and national insurance contributions.

Unless an agreement states otherwise, a partner is not liable for debts accrued by the partnership before they joined.

Unless the other partners and creditors agree otherwise, a client who has left a business partnership continues to be liable for the debts accrued when they were a partner.

Unless suitable notice is given to creditors and the client's name is removed from the partnership's paperwork, a client could be held liable for partnership debts that are accrued after they leave the partnership. The client also needs to check the terms of any written partnership agreement.

A client must do all they can to limit their personal liability for any existing or future partnership debts. If a client is considering leaving a business partnership or disputes liability for a partnership debt, signpost the client to specialist advice.

If a client is still trading

Give advice about dealing with personal debt emergencies, such as council tax enforcement agents, and also provide basic advice about dealing with personal creditors. You may also be able to advise the client about the implications for continuing to trade, such as the risk to assets and further indebtedness. Since partnerships can be complex, it is often best to seek specialist advice.

Specialist advice is required if the client has any business debts or any complex business issues, such as a disputed tax debt. The client also needs specialist debt advice before deciding how best to proceed with their debts.

A specialist adviser looks at the client's overall situation (at home and in the business) and also discusses how any action that the client takes could affect whether the client and the partnership can continue in business. The client also needs to be aware that some strategies, such as protected trust deeds, do not usually offer the same protection for partnership debts and the partnership itself may also have to enter into a trust deed.

In some cases, separate strategies may be required to deal with the partnership's debts. Specialist advice is required. Advisers should have contacts for reputable firms of insolvency practitioners or accountants who can advise clients where specialist advice is required and can then refer them on – check what your organisation's policy is for referrals.

If a client has ceased trading

Check whether the client has any complex business debts, such as an ongoing liability for a business lease. If any complex debts are identified, the client needs specialist advice. Also check whether the client notified their creditors, suppliers and HMRC that they had stopped trading with the partnership and complied with the terms of any partnership agreement. If you are unsure whether the client has exited the partnership appropriately, always signpost the client to specialist advice with the client's consent. It is important to do that because specialist advice may help the client to limit their personal liability for any existing or future partnership debts.

Providing there are no complex debt needs and the client has exited the partnership appropriately, you can give full advice about dealing with the client's debts.

Chapter 14: Business debts
2. Types of small business

Director of a limited company

Giving advice to a director of a limited company

A limited company is a separate legal entity and must be registered with Companies House. A limited company's name must usually end in either 'limited' or 'Ltd'.

A limited company can be set up as a private company (in which shares are owned by and transferred between a limited number of people) or as a public company (in which shares can be bought and sold on the stock market). The most common type of limited company business debt advisers deal with is a private company.

A limited company is owned by its shareholders and run by its directors. Many small companies are run by just one person, who is both the director and shareholder.

Since a limited company is a separate legal entity, it can own assets and is liable for its own debts. A limited company will need to comply with company law, as well as important documents lodged with Companies House (the memorandum of association and articles of association and accounts). Dealing with limited companies can be complex. Advisers should signpost clients to specialist advice if there is an issue with the limited company. (An insolvency practitioner might be useful in this situation.)

A director of a limited company has duties and responsibilities to the limited company. A director is not usually liable for the limited company's debts unless:
- the director gave a personal guarantee; or
- the company was dissolved (struck off) or liquidated, and, following an investigation, it was decided that the director had acted inappropriately in their role.

A director could have acted inappropriately in their role for many reasons. Here are a few examples:
- acting fraudulently towards the company's creditors;
- taking money from the company for their own use at the expense of the company's creditors;
- increasing a company's debt by continuing to trade a company while it was insolvent when there was no reasonable chance it could trade out of its difficulties.

The case of *Antuzis v DJ Houghton Catching Services Ltd*[7] confirmed the principle that directors entering into contracts in bad faith can be held personally liable.

If a director disputes liability for a limited company debt or liability is unclear, signpost the client to specialist advice.

A director will be an employee of the business and will normally receive a wage or 'dividends', or a mixture of both. It is important to clarify how they are paid.

If a client is still trading

The status of a limited company as a separate entity should usually allow you to give advice to directors on their personal debts. However, because personal and business finances often become merged for these clients, there are some common issues that you need to consider.

Personal debt issues for a director of a limited company often indicate problems with the limited company. For example, it may indicate that the client is using personal credit to prop up the business. Explore the reasons for the client's personal indebtedness. If the client's debts are caused by the limited company's performance, signpost the client to a specialist adviser.

Ensure the client has checked whether they have given any personal guarantees for the limited company. If they have, they need to consider how certain strategies may affect the limited company. This can be particularly important if a guarantee exists but has not been called in. Signpost the client to specialist business advice if that is the case.

Suggest to the client that they also get specialist business debt advice before deciding how to proceed with their personal debts. The client must consider whether any action they take to deal with their personal debts could affect their ability to continue acting as a director.

Insolvency practitioners are usually a good source for help. Get to know a few of them and ask them for advice.

If a client has ceased trading

Check whether the client has closed the business or resigned as a director. Signpost to a specialist business adviser for advice on leaving or closing the business if that is needed. Has the client submitted an application for 'striking off' to Companies House – to apply to strike off a limited company, the client must send Companies House Form DS01. The form must be signed by a majority of the company's directors.

They should deal with any of the company's assets before applying – eg, close any bank accounts and transfer any domain names. Applications for 'striking off' can be refused and this is invariably due to debts due to outstanding creditors – eg, HMRC who can object to the application. Alternatively, the other way to close is through a formal liquidation process. This, however, can be expensive and cost up to £5,000 (with VAT) for a straightforward liquidation.

For insolvent companies, this is known as a creditors' voluntary liquidation (CVL). The process can only be entered into under the guidance of a licensed insolvency practitioner. The client should always be referred to an insolvency practitioner in these cases, for further advice and guidance.

Ensure the client has checked whether they have given any personal guarantees for the limited company debts. If a personal guarantee relates to a complex business debt, such as an ongoing business lease, the client needs specialist advice.

Providing the client has no complex business debts that require specialist help, you can give the client full advice on their personal debts. Advisers could also seek the advice of an insolvency practitioner or the client's accountant.

Member of a limited liability partnership

A limited liability partnership (LLP) is a separate legal entity run by its members. An LLP must be registered with Companies House and have some characteristics of a partnership and some of a limited company. The liability of a member of an LLP to pay towards the debts of the LLP is usually limited to the value of the assets that the member puts into the business. Solicitors and accountancy businesses commonly use LLPs.

Debt advisers rarely deal with LLPs. Specialist advice is usually needed if the client is trading as a member of an LLP or wants to stop trading as a member of an LLP. Advisers could also seek the advice of an insolvency practitioner.

Client with a franchise agreement

A franchise is a business agreement. It allows a client to run a branch of an existing business using the established business's name. A client who has bought a franchise can usually decide how to set up their business – eg, as a sole trader, a partner in a business partnership, or director of a limited company.

Debt advisers rarely deal with franchises. Specialist advice is needed if there is any doubt about a client's liability or if the client wants to end the franchise agreement. Advisers could seek the advice of an insolvency practitioner.

Member of a co-operative

A co-operative is a business owned and controlled collectively by the people working for the business. Debt advisers rarely deal with co-operatives. Specialist advice may be needed as it can be difficult to establish a co-operative member's individual liability for any business debts. Advisers could seek the advice of an insolvency practitioner or accountant.

3. Stages of debt advice

This section highlights factors to consider in the debt advice process, as outlined in Chapter 3, when advising a client who is either running or has previously run their own business as a sole trader, a partner in a business partnership or as a director of a limited company.

Create trust

Self-employed clients may pose extra challenges for advisers in this area.

Being self-employed often requires independence and self-confidence. This can sometimes make it more difficult for a self-employed client to ask for help because they are usually the person who sorts out any problems. Self-employed clients are often emotionally, as well as financially, invested in their business. If the business is struggling, some clients may feel a sense of personal failure. That is in addition to the usual problems that clients face when dealing with serious debt, which can make asking for and accepting help more difficult.

Some self-employed clients may feel protective of their business and reluctant to share information about the business or its debts. Explain that you are asking for this information to ensure the client gets the advice they need. That helps the client to get the best outcome for dealing with their situation and to protect their business when possible.

Ensure that a self-employed client is given the appropriate level of responsibility for carrying out tasks needed to deal with their situation. Be aware that some self-employed clients may feel deskilled and disempowered if an adviser takes over simply because they, or their business, is in financial difficulty.

List creditors and minimise debts

List creditors

Consider the client's overall situation. Gather information about any personal and business debts for which the client is liable. If the client is a director of a limited company, check whether the client has given any personal guarantees for any limited company debts and whether any guarantees have been called in.

Minimise debts by ceasing to trade

You should not attempt to advise a limited company (or limited liability partnership) on ceasing to trade. That is an area that requires specialist advice.

If a client runs a business but is seriously in debt, they should consider whether to continue trading. The client needs to consider whether the business can improve its situation and trade out of its financial difficulties or, if the situation is unlikely to change, will trading on just increase indebtedness? If the business is a limited company, continuing to trade when there is no realistic chance that the insolvent company can trade out of its difficulties could be deemed an offence at a later stage (and the director(s) could be held liable).

Deciding whether to trade on is a complex area and specialist help should always be sought from a specialist business adviser, such as Business Debtline or the business's bookkeeper or accountant. Again, a friendly insolvency practitioner may be able to help here.

To help with the process, you can assist the client in drawing up a business financial statement. The business financial statement is similar to the personal financial statement drawn up for the client, except that it deals with the income and outgoings of the business.

If the business financial statement shows that nothing is available for the client to take as an income from the business, and that is unlikely to change, this usually indicates that trading needs to stop. However, the client must obtain specialist advice before taking such a major step. This is because several issues, such as liability for tax or payments due under a business lease, could make the difference between viability and insolvency.

Business assets

Self-employed clients also need to look at any available assets to the business and consider how this affects the business's viability. The types of assets that a business has vary from business to business. You can help the client to prepare a list of assets by examining their circumstances.

Consider the approximate resale value of equipment or machinery. This amount will be different from amounts shown in professionally produced accounts, where the 'book value' may be based on the original cost of an item and its theoretical life.

Check whether the business has work in hand and consider the contractual status of any agreement. For instance, a painter and decorator may have agreed in the autumn to paint the exterior of an existing customer's house the following spring. If the customer loses their job during the winter, without any binding agreement, the work may not go ahead.

Lease agreements

Valuing a lease for business premises is complex and can only be accurately assessed by a professional. Leased business premises are not valued in the same way as domestic premises. The shorter the period that the lease has left to run, the less likely it is to be of any value. Also, if no one is prepared to take over the lease, that might create a liability rather than an asset because the tenant remains liable for the rent until the lease expires. Also, the client may remain liable for rent payments under the lease even when they have arranged for the lease to be 'assigned' to someone else, if that person fails to pay.

Items like cars and vans should be valued at the price likely to be obtained at auction rather than a price an optimist might expect to get from a private sale. Various used car price guides are available online and from newsagents that give a trade price for reasonably modern cars and vans – eg, parkers.co.uk. These can be used as a guide.

Debts owed to the business

Check whether the business has any debts owed to it and assess the likelihood of the business being paid. Draw up a list of payments that the business expects to receive. Consider signposting the client to specialist business advice on recovering monies owed to the business.

Assets owned by the business

A realistic value for any business premises that are owned should be sought. Ideally, a specialist, such as a local estate agent, should do this. However, because there is likely to be a fee for the valuation of business premises, a client's estimate of value may have to be accepted in some cases. Business premises are particularly susceptible to a fall in value caused by developments in the local area. For instance, the opening of a new supermarket could cause the collapse of a local general store (due to reduced trade) and a corresponding fall in the value of the business premises. Circumstances outside of the business's control can reduce the value of its assets and the protection that the assets would otherwise have provided from financial problems.

If a client is trading as a partner in a business partnership

This section gives an overview of issues to consider if a partner in a business partnership wants to cease trading. This is a complex area of advice. Clients should be signposted to specialist advice to help make sure that they do all they can to limit their personal liability for any partnership debts.

The decision to stop trading may not rest solely with the client if they are a partner in a business partnership. If the client wants to stop trading but the other partners do not, the client should make sure that they formally end (sever) any written partnership agreement. This will help limit the client's liability for partnership debts to those accrued during the period they were a partner.

If a partnership has been set up informally and there is no partnership agreement to set out how the client can leave, the Partnership Act 1890 applies. The client should seek legal advice so that an agreement can be drawn up to end their links to the partnership.

Other ways to determine if a partnership exists is to look at the bank accounts and see whose name they are in. Previous tax returns can also help here.

A client should also seek legal advice to see if there are any viable ways to limit their liability for the partnership's debts and protect themself from future claims. For example, a client could ask the partnership creditors and the remaining partners if they agree in writing that the client is not liable for any debts that subsequently come to light and relate to the period the client was a partner.

A client who wants to leave a business partnership should also give the partnership's creditors notice that they have left the partnership. The client's name should be removed from the partnership's paperwork.

Sometimes informal business partnerships exist between people with personal relationships, such as married or cohabiting couples. In these cases, ending the personal relationship can prompt a need to end the business partnership. Without a written partnership agreement, either party can usually enter into contracts on behalf of the partnership, for which both partners are jointly and severally liable.

Although the same advice applies to these clients, it should be recognised that the couple's previous relationship may complicate matters. In some cases, it may also limit the amount of information that is available to the client. This is often the case when one partner has made most of the business decisions and the other partner sees themselves as a 'sleeping partner'. The sleeping partner may be unaware of their joint and several liability for the partnership debts.

Minimise other debts

Banks may secure business borrowings against a person's home.

Sometimes the security is not enforceable if the agreement was entered into as a result of undue influence or misrepresentation by the creditor or another client. This may occur if a person, who is not the borrower, is asked to agree to a charge (security) being made on a property that they either jointly own or have an interest in (perhaps because they live with the owner).

In one case, it was decided that a charge was not enforceable when a client's wife had signed it but had not been recommended to take separate legal advice and had been told that her husband's business would be closed down by the bank if she did not do so.[8] The law is complex in this area.

If undue influence or other wrongdoing occurred when the security was signed, specialist or legal advice should be obtained.

The debts owed by a self-employed person may include tax debts. If a client is unsure whether they have taken into account all the allowances available to them personally and to the business, signpost them to an accountant or bookkeeper for specialist advice. You will also need to refer the client for specialist help (eg, from TaxAid[9]) if they have failed to submit tax returns.

List business income and expenditure

In addition to the personal financial statement, a business financial statement is also needed to assess the position of self-employed clients who are sole traders or partners in a business partnership. Read further on for information about the types of business financial statement available and for dealing with other types of self-employed clients.

The business financial statement uses information about how the client's business has performed in recent months to estimate what income the client is likely to get from the business in the future. The statement takes information about the business's income and expenditure (running costs) over a set period to work out an average of the profit or loss that the business produced during this time. This information is used to estimate the amount that a self-employed client can expect to take from their business as income, after allowing for income tax and national insurance (NI) liability. The net business income figure (or loss) should be included in the client's personal financial statement.

Business income

Only income for the business should be included in the business financial statement. Personal income, such as benefit income or employed income, is covered in the personal financial statement. Unless the client's business is seasonal, you usually need details of the income received by the business during the last three months. This should be based on actual payments received by the business (not on invoices issued by the business). The income figure should not include an amount due for work the business has completed unless payment for the work has been received.

If the client's business is seasonal, a longer analysis of business income may be needed (up to a maximum of the last 12 months). You must explore how a client's business usually fluctuates to decide what period the business financial statement should cover. Specialist advice may be needed.

Advisers should also check whether the self-employed client's business has received any Covid-related government payments, such as bounce-back loans, to cover business income reductions caused by the pandemic. This type of payment will need to be listed, but you should be aware that any one-off payments could distort what the financial statement shows as available to the client. Specialist advice is usually needed in this situation.

Business expenditure

Look at the business's expenditure figures (running costs) for the same period of time that has been chosen to assess the client's business income.

Make sure that you include all relevant expenditure for the business – eg, banking facility and overdraft charges, lease or rental charges (for property and equipment), utility bills (including telephones and waste disposal), payments to suppliers, VAT payments, staff costs (including wages and employers' costs) and accountancy fees. Only include expenditure for the business in the business financial statement. The client's personal and household costs are covered by the personal financial statement.

Be careful not to double count expenses that are shared by the business and the client personally – eg, electricity costs for a sole trader client who trades from home or travel costs for a client who uses a single vehicle for business and personal transport. Double counting (when the full cost, or part of the cost, is added to both the business and personal financial statement) reduces the client's available income and creates an inaccurate assessment of their financial position.

Shared expenses need to be divided between the client's business and personal statements based on the client's individual circumstances. A client needs to work out how much of the cost covers business use and add this proportion to the business financial statement. The remainder of the cost should be included in the personal financial statement. Sometimes, it can be difficult to separate shared costs. Useful advice is available to help work out how much of the client's shared costs should be included in the business statement at gov.uk/expenses-if-youre-self-employed. Signpost the client to specialist advice if needed.

Maximise income

The scope for improving the income of a person running their own business can be greater than that of an employee. Specialist business advice can improve profitability, for example, through better marketing, reducing production costs and overheads or by diversification. Check whether any specialists can help the client in this area. Business rescue specialists such as insolvency practitioners can advise on this.

In addition, grants and other facilities, such as low-interest loans, may be available to small businesses. More information can be found at gov.uk/business-finance-support or gov.uk/business-finance-support/funding-circle-uk.

The payment of tax may use up a substantial proportion of income for self-employed clients. Ensure that all relevant individual tax allowances, reliefs and expenses that a business can offset against tax are being claimed. You can also signpost clients to a useful tool at gov.uk/simplified-expenses-checker to check whether simplified expenses could save the business tax. Since this can be a complex area, the client may need to speak to their bookkeeper or accountant.

Business rates can be a major expense for clients with a business lease. Check for any exemptions or discounts with the local authority.

Some self-employed people miss out on benefits because they incorrectly assume that they are not entitled to claim benefits because they are in business.

- Self-employed clients may be able to claim universal credit (UC). Minimum income floor rules usually apply unless the business is in a start-up period. A UC claim is assessed monthly, so there is no need for a projection apart from when the claimant is in their first assessed month.
- A self-employed client may be able to claim council tax reduction, council tax discounts and disability benefits.
- If they do not come under the UC system, a self-employed client may be able to claim housing benefit, although this is rarely available for clients under pension age.
- If the relevant NI payments are up to date and the client cannot work because of sickness, they may be able to claim 'new-style' employment and support allowance.

Since a self-employed client's income can be prone to fluctuations and eligibility rules vary among benefits, a client will likely benefit from specialist welfare benefits advice. The Turn2us website, turn2us.org.uk, provides a personalised benefits check for self-employed clients. Most self-employed clients will come under the 'minimum income floor' rules for UC. For further information, see gov.uk/government/publications/universal-credit-and-self-employment-quick-guide/universal-credit-and-self-employment-quick-guide or citizensadvice.org.uk/scotland/benefits/universal-credit/on-universal-credit/how-universal-credit-payments-work-if-youre-self-employed.

Draw up a financial statement for a self-employed client

Creating a personal financial statement for a client running their own business is generally similar to that of an employed person, except that expenses may need apportioning and the amount of income may be less predictable. Both of these things should be made clear on the personal financial statement.

How to calculate the amount of income that a client can take from the business depends upon the client's trading status and any special rules that may apply to the type of business that the client carries out.

Sole traders and partners in a business partnership

For sole traders and partners in a business partnership, a business financial statement is required to calculate the income (drawings) the client can take from the business. The business financial statement forms part of the overall assessment of the client's financial position. It uses information about how the client's business has performed in recent months to estimate what income (net of income tax and NI) the client will likely get from the business in the future.

It is important to complete a business financial statement if needed, and not to simply use the amount that a client says the business can pay them. This helps to provide a more accurate view of how the business is performing. It also protects against a client giving figures that are based on what they would like their business to be able to provide, rather than what the business can afford to pay.

It is not unusual for a client who is struggling to pay their debts to be surprised at the drawings figure produced by a business financial statement. Some clients may need time to digest this information and assess how it affects their next actions. If a client's business cannot provide any drawings or is running at a loss, specialist advice is needed. Specialist debt advice organisations can provide templates for a business financial statement. The Business Debtline website[10] provides interactive statements for both sole traders and partners of a business partnership. Both statements can be saved and printed by the client. It is important that the correct business financial statement is selected based on the client's trading status. That is because, for a partner in a business partnership, the statement needs to look at how the business is performing and calculate the client's own share of any business profit or loss.

Consider any special tax rules that may apply

When dealing with clients who are sole traders or partners in a business partnership, you should always consider how any special tax rules affect the business financial statement they are using. This commonly affects clients who receive a self-employed income as a foster carer, from letting residential property or who are covered by the Construction Industry Scheme. You need to check that the business financial statement you are using takes into account any special tax rules that apply. If not, a signpost to specialist help is usually needed.

Directors of a limited company

Do not attempt a business financial statement for a limited company. The director of the limited company should obtain monthly drawings figures from the company's bookkeeper or accountant. These figures can be used as income on a personal financial statement.

They may also receive income as dividends, and this information should be obtained from their accountant.

Check that the figure provided by the client is net of any tax liability.

Deal with priority debts

This section gives information about common business priority debts. It is important to look at a client's individual circumstances when deciding how to classify their business debts. In some cases, a debt that is usually considered a non-priority debt may be essential to the running of a business. For example, if an unsecured overdraft is used as cash flow for a business and there is no alternative credit available, the overdraft facility may need to be treated as a priority. Seek specialist advice if you are uncertain how to classify a business debt.

Services

If a business has ceased trading and utility debts on commercial premises are outstanding, the gas and electricity bills may need to be treated as a priority. This is because energy suppliers can disconnect home premises for non-payment of commercial bills if the supplies are in the same name and provided by the same supplier. If a client is trading from home (or was previously and still has the same supplier), gas and electricity arrears are priority debts.

Clients with a commercial energy contract have less protection than domestic customers. If a client trades from part of the same building that they live in (eg, they run a shop and live in a flat above the premises), if possible, they should separate the supply to the two premises before arrears accrue to avoid the risk of disconnection of the domestic premises.

Water companies cannot disconnect the supply to residential premises and can only disconnect a supply to the premises to which the water was supplied. It is not entirely clear how this affects mixed-use premises. Ofwat has issued guidance stating it believes the disconnection of mixed-use premises could be illegal and reminds customers of their right to take court action if this happens. In practice, companies rarely disconnect mixed-use premises.

Water companies can disconnect the supply to a separate non-domestic premises. The environmental risk of a business being without water could lead to its closure. More information can be found on the Scottish Water website.[11]

Non-domestic rates (business rates)

If the client has a lease for a business premises, they are liable for the business rates for as long as the lease exists. This applies even if the premises are empty, although there are some time-limited exemptions. Check for any exemptions with the local authority in your area.

Non-domestic rates are collected and enforced similarly to council tax, except that, for instance, tools of the trade are not exempt. This means that enforcement agents (sheriff officers) can take control of a client's property (including at their home address) once a summary warrant has been issued.

Another difference is that attachment of earnings orders and deductions from benefits are not allowed for business rates.

More information on non-domestic rates in Scotland can be found at mygov.scot/non-domestic-rates-guidance.

Tax, national insurance and VAT debts

Income tax arrears

HMRC says it wants to work with clients to find a way for them to pay off their tax debts as quickly as possible but in an affordable way, such as a time to pay arrangement (an instalment payment plan).[12] In appropriate cases, HMRC says that it may be able to offer a short-term payment deferral for a set period of time during which HMRC would undertake no collection activity. Where clients are unwilling to discuss a payment plan or fail to respond to communications, HMRC says it will consider using its enforcement powers to collect outstanding tax debts.

Most income above certain fixed limits is taxable. Employees are taxed by direct deduction from their income by their employer (the 'pay as you earn' (PAYE) scheme). PAYE taxpayers rarely owe tax on their earned income unless mistakes have been made in the amounts deducted. Self-employed people receive their earnings before tax is deducted and are responsible for paying their own tax directly to HMRC. Arrears are, therefore, more likely to occur with self-employment.

The legal position

Income tax is payable under the Taxes Management Act 1970 and the Income and Corporation Taxes Act 1988 and subsequent Finance Acts and regulations.

Recovery of debt can be by court action, or, more likely, by summary warrant. A summary warrant is a type of court order granted by the sheriff court for certain types of debts that are owed to local authorities and HMRC. They are issued to recover taxes and water and sewage charges and authorise sheriff officers to carry out formal legal debt recovery.

Special features

There are many ways of reducing tax liability, unless it is deducted under PAYE. Self-employed people, in particular, require detailed advice on completing their tax returns and any arrears that HMRC may be claiming. Self-employed people should obtain specialist help either from an accountant, Business Debtline (businessdebtline.org) or TaxAid (taxaid.org.uk) if they wish to challenge the amount of any arrears claimed.

A good source of basic information for the self-employed client is the Low Incomes Tax Reform Group (litrg.org.uk).

It may also be possible to negotiate remission (write-off) of a tax debt if the client's circumstances are unlikely to improve – eg, if they are permanently unable to work because of ill health or if they have no hope of increasing their income because of their age. This, however, is entirely at the discretion of HMRC. The tax is not permanently written off, but you will not receive further demands unless your circumstances improve unexpectedly.

If the business is continuing to trade, however, it is vital that the client pays any ongoing tax on time and makes arrangements to repay any tax debt, otherwise HMRC can take control of essential goods without a court order and so close down the business.

National insurance contributions

NI contributions are a compulsory tax on earnings and profits above certain levels (set annually).

The legal position

NI contributions are payable under section 2 of the Social Security Act 1975, as amended by the Social Security Contributions and Benefits Act 1992.

Special features

Employed people pay class 1 NI contributions directly from their wages and so do not build up arrears. Class 2 contributions can be paid by self-employed earners on a voluntary basis. In addition, self-employed people may have to pay class 4 contributions, calculated as a percentage of their profits above a certain level (set annually). After the year end, HMRC sends out demands to self-employed people from whom it has not received the required class 2 contributions.

National insurance classes

The class you pay depends on your employment status and how much you earn.

National insurance class	Who pays
Class 1	Employees under state pension age earning more than £242 a week from one job – they are automatically deducted by your employer.
Class 1A or 1B	Employers pay these directly on their employee's expenses or benefits.

Class 2	Self-employed people earning profits of £12,570 or more a year. From the 2024/25 tax year, class 2 contributions are only paid on a voluntary basis.
Class 3	Voluntary contributions – you can pay them to fill or avoid gaps in your NI record.
Class 4	Self-employed people earning profits of £12,570 or more a year.

If a self-employed person has also employed someone else, they may be liable for class 1 NI contributions for the employee, as well as class 2, and perhaps 4, contributions for themself.

Demands for payment should be distinguished from the notice sent to people whose contribution record is insufficient to entitle them to use it towards a retirement pension or bereavement benefits. In such cases, HMRC sends a notification giving the opportunity to make up the deficit for a particular year with voluntary (class 3) contributions. This is not a demand for payment.

It is vital that the client pays any ongoing contributions on time and makes arrangements to repay any arrears, otherwise HMRC can take control of essential goods without a court order and so close down a business. In addition, if contributions remain unpaid, the client's eventual entitlement to contributory benefits, including retirement pension, will be affected.

Value added tax

Value added tax (VAT) is a tax charged by HMRC on most transactions of businesses with an annual taxable turnover of more than a certain limit, set annually. A business must be registered for VAT unless its turnover is below the limit.

The legal position

VAT is payable under the Finance Act 1972, the Value Added Tax Act 1994 and subsequent regulations and amendments. Its scope and level are reviewed each year and changes are often made to the Act following the Budget.

Special features

VAT is a tax on the value added to goods and services as they pass through the registered business. So, although VAT is payable on purchases, this amount can be offset against the tax on the business's own sales. For example, if the total purchases in a year were £100,000 and the total sales were identical, there would be no value added and no tax payable.

A debt adviser generally encounters VAT debts after a business has ceased trading and the partner or sole trader is left responsible for VAT. Some goods are exempt and the calculation of the amount of VAT is complicated. In most cases, seek help from an accountant specialising in VAT. If VAT is overdue, a surcharge, which is a percentage of the VAT owed, is added to the debt. This amount can be appealed.

Rent arrears

A landlord can recover rent arrears through the sheriff court or tribunal and institute the normal diligence procedures:
- serving a charge for payment; *and*
- carrying out an arrestment of funds or moveable property owned by the tenant in the hands of third parties (including banks); *and*
- executing an attachment of goods, equipment or money owned by the tenant.

Where it is a company, it can also issue a statutory demand on the business and instigate winding up proceedings.

Some lease agreements may have a reference to 'summary diligence' (see p299), and this allows them to institute diligence without a court hearing.

If your client struggles to maintain the rent payments, the first option is to discuss this with the landlord. They may be agreeable to a payment plan as the reality is that for them to evict you could lead the premises to be empty for a considerable time in the current economic climate, thus the landlord having no income from the premises – the cities and towns of Scotland are full of empty business premises in our high streets. A more pragmatic approach is required.

Landlord hypothec

Under common law, your landlord has a right known as the 'landlord's hypothec'.[13] This gives them security over moveable property that you own, which is kept on land or in buildings that you rent from them. It does not allow your landlord to take these items from you.

In practice, the landlord's hypothec will not benefit your landlord unless you become insolvent. If this happens, the landlord should be paid first out of any money raised by the sale of items covered by the hypothec.

The landlord's hypothec is only security for rent that is due but unpaid. Your landlord's rights under the landlord's hypothec only continue for as long as that rent remains unpaid. However, the right does not apply to:
- items kept in a home, a mobile home, a croft or on agricultural land; *and*
- property owned by someone other than you; *and*
- property a third party obtains from you in good faith.

Be sure to check the wording of any lease. If in doubt, seek a legal opinion.

The premises lease

Many businesses lease their work premises. In some cases, the unexpired part of a business lease can be a valuable asset that can be realised if the client decides to cease trading or trade from other premises. Professional advice should always be sought on the valuation of such leases. If a lease is to be 'assigned' to another person, legal advice should be sought. The permission of the landlord is required. In certain circumstances, if the new tenant fails to pay their rent, the earlier tenant can still be held responsible. To protect against this future liability, it is sometimes better to agree to surrender a lease, even if it may be sellable for a premium.

A landlord may be prepared to accept the surrender of a lease (which ends the tenant's contractual obligations, such as rent and therefore business rates) if it is clear that they are unlikely to get any more money from a particular tenant. If a client has ceased trading and is likely to remain unemployed for some time, and has responsibility for a lease, you could approach the landlord directly.

Explain that the client is unlikely to meet their contractual obligations and, in some cases, landlords agree to a surrender. You should ensure that you are not dealing with a lease that is of value (perhaps because it forms a small part of a redevelopment site or because the rent has been fixed at a low rate for many future years) before the client gives it away. Specialist advice should be obtained.

Other leases

Many businesses have equipment like photocopiers, electronic scales or games machines that are held on a lease. First, check whether or not the lease is a regulated agreement under the Consumer Credit Act 1974. Many lease documents are complex and specialist help may be required.

A business equipment lease runs for a number of years, during which time the owner of the goods (which may be a finance company) simply charges the rent to use them. At the end of the period, there is no automatic transfer of the goods to the lessee but, in practice, items are often not taken back by lessors. A lease usually contains a provision for early settlement. However, in many cases, this figure is likely to be almost as high as continuing to pay rent until the end of the lease period.

Business leases are complex and, since the sums of money involved can be substantial, expert advice should always be obtained before reaching any agreement with a lessor about early settlement. Trading standards departments may be able to provide such advice.

VAT debts

VAT is a type of tax. Businesses with a turnover of an amount set each year by the government do not have to register for VAT, although they can choose to register voluntarily. All other businesses must register for VAT, unless HMRC grants an exemption from registering. VAT-registered businesses must file returns at a frequency agreed with HMRC to show the difference between the VAT they pay to other suppliers (input tax) and the VAT they charge their customers (output tax).

Chapter 14: Business debts
3. Stages of debt advice

On 1 April 2019, most VAT-registered businesses needed to sign up to Making Tax Digital.[14] These businesses must keep digital records and use HMRC-compatible software to produce and submit their VAT returns. From 1 April 2022, all VAT-registered businesses must sign up for Making Tax Digital unless they have an exemption from doing so. Exemptions are based on:
- your age; *or*
- a disability; *or*
- you running your business from a remote geographical location; *or*
- you objecting to using computers on religious grounds; *or*
- any other reason why it is not reasonable or practical.

If a VAT return or payment is late, HMRC may be able to add a surcharge. This can increase the amount owed. Changes were made to these rules from January 2023. This is a complex area. If a client disputes any surcharges or penalties that HMRC has applied, signpost them to specialist advice. Also, if the VAT return is outstanding, HMRC can estimate the amount due and issue its own assessment. The amount estimated by HMRC is payable immediately.

Local HMRC officers who collect VAT vary greatly in their approach to struggling or failed businesses. In general, they consider themselves to be collectors of a tax that has already been paid by a third party to the client and of which the client is only a custodian. While this may bear little relation to the realities of running a small business, this attitude means officers can be more aggressive in the recovery of VAT.

Once payment is outstanding, the HMRC officer at a local office usually uses the threat of enforcement action to take control of goods to force payment. This may initially consist of a visit, phone call or letter to state that enforcement action will be used. An enforcement notice giving seven clear days before action will then warn that immediate payment is required and enforcement agents will be used in default. A warrant to take control of goods is then signed by an HMRC officer. A court order is not needed.

The warrant is usually used by a firm of private enforcement agents with an HMRC officer in attendance. HMRC can obtain a warrant to force initial entry, but this is rare. However, most business premises are accessible to the public (including enforcement agents), so negotiation is essential. A client who is still trading should always try to give the enforcement agents some money and treat this debt with utmost priority. Taking control of goods can provoke or escalate the collapse of a business, both by removing necessary stock or equipment and reducing confidence in the business.

If you have a client with unpaid VAT, you should:
- contact HMRC, explain the position and request a short time to organise the client's affairs; *and*
- get an accountant to check the amount claimed, particularly if it is an assessed amount; *and*

- explain the seriousness to the client. Use a small business adviser if necessary to look at the viability of the business and its credit control procedures.

HMRC can use other methods to collect the debt, such as court action, including the summary warrant procedure, to recover arrears of VAT.

HMRC also uses bankruptcy as a means of collection. Any threat of bankruptcy must be taken seriously.

More information can be from a qualified accountant or the HMRC guidance manual.[15]

Income tax debts

Self-employed people and businesses are responsible for making a return to HMRC on which tax bills are based. Under the self-assessment system, taxpayers calculate their own tax and make a payment for each relevant tax year. A small business should always get specialist help in claiming all the allowances against tax to which it may be entitled, and in treating its profits and losses in the most tax-efficient way.

In addition to the tax due on its profits, a business may also owe tax and NI contributions on wages paid to employees.

The assessment process is outside the scope of this *Handbook*. If necessary, you should get specialist help to check the amount of tax demanded. TaxAid is a useful source of help or the Low Incomes Tax Reform Group.[16]

If the client fails to file a tax return, HMRC makes its own 'determination' of how much tax is due and this can be enforceable immediately. It can only be overturned by filing a return and time limits apply. HMRC can impose penalties for late filing of returns and/or non-payment of tax. If there is no tax to pay when the return is filed, the penalty is not reduced and is, therefore, still payable by the client. They can appeal the penalty on the grounds that they had a 'reasonable excuse' for the failure. It is still important to file returns, however late, because HMRC has a policy that payment arrangements are not accepted until returns are up to date.

> *What may count as a reasonable excuse?*
> A **'reasonable excuse'** is something that stopped you from meeting a tax obligation that you took reasonable care to meet. Examples include the following.
> – Your partner or another close relative died shortly before the tax return or payment deadline.
> – You had an unexpected stay in hospital that prevented you from dealing with your tax affairs.
> – You had a serious or life-threatening illness.
> – Your computer or software failed just before or while you were preparing your online return.
> – Service issues with HMRC's online services.[17]

Chapter 14: Business debts
3. Stages of debt advice

- A fire, flood or theft prevented you from completing your tax return.
- Postal delays that you could not have predicted.
- Delays related to a disability or mental illness you have.
- You were unaware of or misunderstood your legal obligation.
- You relied on someone else to send your return, and they did not.[18]

You must send your return or payment as soon as possible after your reasonable excuse is resolved.

What does not count as a reasonable excuse?

The following will not be accepted as a reasonable excuse.
- Your cheque bounced or payment failed because you did not have enough money.
- You found the HMRC online system too difficult to use.
- You did not get a reminder from HMRC.
- You made a mistake on your tax return.

If a tax bill is unpaid, HMRC may be able to use the following types of enforcement:
- a debt collection agency or sheriff officer;
- petition for the client's bankruptcy or put the business into administration or liquidation.

HMRC also has the power to use the summary warrant procedure, and subsequent diligence measures, speeding up the recovery process.

As with VAT, HMRC is likely to be particularly strict if the money owed includes tax already collected by a business from employees and not passed on to HMRC. HMRC will still consider starting bankruptcy proceedings, even if this is unlikely to lead to a payment being made. Any threat of bankruptcy must be taken seriously. They will first have to make the client apparently insolvent through a charge for payment or statutory demand.

If the sheriff court process is used, the client can ask for time to pay in the usual way. This is not available when the summary warrant procedure is used for business (company) debts.

It is possible to negotiate a time to pay arrangement with HMRC. Although it is generally easier to negotiate after the client has ceased trading, as with all negotiations, the outcome depends on the client's circumstances. HMRC's guidance *How to Pay a Debt to HMRC with a Time to Pay Arrangement* is available at gov.uk/guidance/find-out-how-to-pay-a-debt-to-hmrc-with-a-time-to-pay-arrangement. It explains the process and the information a client usually needs to provide to HMRC.

A client may also be able to set up an online time to pay arrangement for their self-assessment tax bill through their Government Gateway account without speaking to HMRC. To do this, a client must have filed their latest tax return and be within 60 days of the payment deadline. The client must also owe less than £30,000 and plan to pay their debt off within the next 12 months or fewer.

Choose a strategy for non-priority debts

The impact of a debt strategy on a client's ability to continue trading depends on several factors and varies from business to business. The type of impact can depend on the client's business status and may also be affected by the type of business they run – eg, if the business needs a certain type of licence to trade, some strategies may put this at risk (ie, if they are in the licensing trade). You will also need to consider whether any agreements essential to the business, such as a premises lease, could be terminated by the creditor if the client enters a particular debt strategy. If there is any doubt about how a debt strategy could affect a client's business, signpost the client to specialist advice.

Bankruptcy and protected trust deeds

Bankruptcy and protected trust deeds (PTD) are discussed in Chapter 6. Bankruptcy may often be the most satisfactory way out of the large debts that can arise after the failure of a business. Bankruptcy does not necessarily mean a sole trader must cease trading, particularly if there are no assets of significant value.

However, remember that although discharge from bankruptcy may occur after one year, a person's credit rating is affected for considerably longer (a notification of bankruptcy remains on an individual credit file with all credit reference agencies for six years unless they are subject to a Bankruptcy Restriction Order (BRO) and, if the client wishes to run a business that will require credit in the future, bankruptcy can be an obstacle to securing credit. Someone with an otherwise viable business but serious debts may be better advised to consider a PTD.

In most cases, if a partner in a business partnership applies for individual bankruptcy, the business partnership may be dissolved as this could be written into the partnership agreement.

If all partners wish to go bankrupt, then a joint partnership application may also have to be made.

The sequestration of the estate of a partnership is:
- by debtor application made by the partnership where the partnership is apparently insolvent; or
- by debtor application made by the partnership with the concurrence of a qualified creditor or qualified creditors; or
- on the petition of:
  - a trustee acting under a trust deed; or
  - a qualified creditor or qualified creditors, if the partnership is apparently insolvent.

A 'qualified creditor' means a creditor who, at the date of the presentation of the petition, or as the case may be at the date the debtor application is made, is a creditor of the debtor in respect of relevant debts which amount (or of one such debt which amounts) to not less than £5,000. 'Qualified creditors' means creditors who, at the date in question, are creditors of the debtor in respect of relevant debts which amount in aggregate to not less than £5,000.[19]

The whole point of joint and several liabilities of partners is to enable a creditor to pursue any one partner for the whole of the debt due by the firm to them. You should seek help and advice if this arises.

However, if the trustee finds that the bulk of assets revealed to them by the client are, in fact, 'partnership' assets which, being assets of a separate legal person, do not vest in the trustee by virtue of their appointment, they should send a notice to all creditors advising them:
- that as the trustee of the estate of the individual partner they cannot realise or otherwise deal with the partnership assets; *and*
- that they have no title to petition the courts for bankruptcy of the partnership to secure protection for those assets, but creditors of the partnership may; *and*
- point out that, unless action is taken by a partnership creditor, those partnership assets are at risk and may disappear.

The other partners, and the partnership itself, may then face recovery action from their creditors.

In these circumstances, it would then be open to the trustee(s) of the individual partners to petition for the bankruptcy of the partnership.

If the business is a limited company, creditors can apply to have the company wound up, appoint an administrator or liquidate the company.

A client cannot act as a director of a limited company or member of a limited liability partnership while they are subject to a bankruptcy order unless they get permission from the court.

Business debt solutions in Scotland

Depending on the type of business that the client has/had, there may be different solutions open to them.
- If the client is a sole trader, you could look at the usual debt solutions, the Debt Arrangement Scheme (DAS) or insolvency and treat the debt as totally personal.
- If the client is a member of a partnership, you may need to look at personal debt solutions and deal with the partnership separately.
- If the client is a limited company, you may need to consider solutions for the client as an individual if there are personal guarantees in place, and other solutions for the company such as winding the company up, administration or liquidation.

- Different solutions may need to be looked at where the business continues to trade and advisers should seek advice on this.
- Advice could be sought from an insolvency practitioner or accountant.

Business Debt Arrangement Scheme

In Scotland, it is possible for certain types of business' to use the DAS.

Business DAS is a statutory debt management tool introduced by the Scottish government to help partnerships, trusts or unincorporated body of persons which are in debt to repay their creditors.

A Debt Payment Programme (DPP) under Business DAS allows the business to pay off debts over an extended period of time, while giving them protection from creditors taking action against them to recover their debts.

There are five parties involved in Business DAS.

- **The client:** this has to be a partnership, trust or unincorporated body of persons which has debts and has agreed to a DPP with an insolvency practitioner.
- **DAS-approved insolvency practitioner:** provides debt management advice to the client and applies for a DPP on behalf of a client.
- **Creditor:** someone who is owed money and has agreed or is obliged to accept payments under the programme.
- **DAS administrator:** responsible for the approval of a DPP, the approval of money advisers and payments distributors and maintaining the DAS Register and eDEN.
- **Payments distributor:** distributes the money gathered to creditors.

Similar to individuals and couples, Business DAS must be applied for through the help of a DAS-approved adviser. Note that, due to the nature of Business DAS, this adviser must be a qualified insolvency practitioner.

However, there are exclusions to Business DAS. These include:
- limited or public companies;
- businesses not formed under Scots law;
- those established or carrying on business outside of Scotland.

The Business DAS application is similar to a normal DAS application, but with a few differences:
- all debts must be included and all assets must be declared;
- insolvency practitioners in a Business DAS must review the DPP viability every 12 months and must apply for revocation where it is no longer viable;
- all Business DAS cases must be completed within five years and no payment breaks are allowed;
- no offer of composition may be made in business DAS.

Advisers should have a referral agreement with insolvency practitioners to make an appropriate referral.

# **Chapter 14:** Business debts
Notes

4. Checklist

Checklist
- Check what type of business it is.
- Check whether the client is still trading.
- Check liability for debts.
- Separate business from personal debts.
- Compile two financial statements.
- Consider a referral to a qualified professional – eg, a tax accountant or insolvency practitioner.
- Help the client choose a suitable strategy.

Notes

1. Introduction
1. gov.uk/government/publications/fcdo-small-to-medium-sized-enterprise-sme-action-plan/small-to-medium-sized-enterprise-sme-action-plan
2. gov.uk/expenses-if-youre-self-employed

2. Types of small business
3. taxaid.org.uk; telephone: 0345 120 3779
4. gov.uk/stop-being-self-employed
5. gov.uk/self-assessment-tax-returns/penalties
6. *Dickenson v Gross* [1927] 11 TC 614
7. [2021] EWHC 971 (QB), 23 April 2021

3. Stages of debt advice
8. *Royal Bank of Scotland v Etridge* [2001] UKHL 44, reported as [2002] HLR 4
9. taxaid.org.uk
10. businessdebtline.org
11. scottishwater.co.uk/business-and-developers/licensed-providers/connections-and-disconnections
12. taxaid.org.uk/guides/taxpayers/tax-debt/time
13. s208 BD(S)A 2007
14. gov.uk/government/publications/making-tax-digital
15. gov.uk/government/collections/vat-manuals
16. litrg.org.uk/tax-guides
17. gov.uk/government/collections/hm-revenue-and-customs-service-availability-and-issues
18. gov.uk/appoint-tax-agent
19. s7 B(S)A 2016

Chapter 15
Debt and mental health

This chapter covers:
1. Introduction (below)
2. Mental health conditions (p376)
3. Issues for clients and advisers (p378)
4. Data protection and sensitive personal data (p380)
5. Debt and Mental Health Evidence Form (p380)
6. Mental health and capacity to contract in Scotland (p382)
7. Key requirements and guidance (p384)

1. Introduction

Mental health can impact a person's ability to manage money, as it affects how they feel, think and act, and can influence their decision-making, planning, spending behaviours, coping strategies and communication.

According to the Royal College of Psychiatrists, an estimated one in four adults living in the UK experience a mental health problem every year.[1] When combined with financial difficulties, mental health problems can affect not only the individuals concerned, but also the organisations with which they have relationships (eg, debt advice agencies). Debt advisers and creditors are not trained to diagnose mental health problems and often do not understand the implications of mental health on a client's ability to cope or engage with them.

Many mental health conditions have no physical signs, and fluctuations in the severity and effects of an illness are common. In many cases, a creditor will not be aware that a person has a mental health issue until they have missed payments and the collections process has reached an advanced stage.

A lack of understanding of mental health issues, combined with process-driven procedures in large agencies, can lead to a lack of individualised support. Advisers should gain at least a basic awareness of mental health conditions so they can recognise when a client may need extra support. And once a creditor is aware of a client's mental health issue, it should have practices and systems in place to take account of the situation, and should respond fairly and appropriately. Creditors should both assist people to make informed borrowing choices and themselves make informed and responsible lending decisions.

> **Useful guidance**
> The Financial Conduct Authority's *Consumer Credit Sourcebook* (CONC) provides information on common potential causes of limited mental capacity[2] and specific indications that should alert a lender to a client's condition:[3]
> – CONC 2: Conduct of business standards: general
> – CONC 7: Arrears, default and recovery (including repossessions)
> – CONC 8: Debt advice

2. Mental health conditions

Debt advisers are not trained to diagnose mental health problems. However, being aware of common mental health conditions may help you to recognise when a client is in crisis and focus on symptoms and experiences of mental health problems rather than specific diagnoses. See CPAG's *Mental Health and Benefits Handbook* for an overview of mental health symptoms and treatments and how to discuss them. It is available free online at cpag.org.uk/handbooks.

The main mental illnesses can broadly be split into two categories: neurotic and psychotic.

The difference between **neurotic behaviour** and normal behaviour is intensity. Neurotic thoughts and behaviours can be so extreme that they interfere with a client's life, personally and professionally.

Everyday situations are made worse because of these thoughts and behaviours, leading the client to blame themselves for being pessimistic and feeling negative. They may feel constantly irritated, sad, guilty, self-conscious, vulnerable or another negative emotion.

Neurotic behaviours may stem from mental health issues. A person with a neurotic personality may be more likely to have a condition such as generalised anxiety disorder, depression, obsessive-compulsive disorder, social phobias or post-traumatic stress disorder.

A **psychotic illness** can cloud a person's judgement, cause them to react emotionally, disrupt clear thinking, change the way they view reality and negatively affect the way they behave. It can lead to hallucinations or delusions.

Some people may experience a psychotic episode for a short period and, for others, it may be a long-term problem. Some people may not find it distressing, while for others it will significantly change their day-to-day life.

Severe psychotic symptoms can lead people to have problems staying in touch with reality or dealing with daily life, but usually the symptoms can be treated. People may experience psychosis as part of a mental illness such as severe depression, schizophrenia, bipolar disorder, paranoid personality disorder, post-natal psychosis, delusional or paranoid disorder.

Note: not everyone with a mental health condition has a formal diagnosis, and those with a diagnosis might not agree with it. Diagnoses can also change over time. It is more useful for advisers to be aware of the symptoms, triggers and effects of clients' mental health problems than specific diagnoses.

Common causes, triggers, symptoms and the effects of medication

The causes and triggers of mental illness can be as many and varied as the symptoms a client has. The effect of medication on a client who has a mental health condition can also affect how they engage with you and your organisation.

Common causes

A mental health condition (neurotic or psychotic) may develop from one or a combination of the following common issues:
- childhood abuse/neglect;
- social isolation;
- homelessness;
- unemployment;
- long-time caring for a family member;
- a long-term physical health condition;
- significant trauma – eg, from an accident or crime.

For psychotic disorders only, other causes are:
- susceptibility to a genetic hereditary condition;
- body chemistry;
- drug misuse.

Triggers

A trigger is something which can affect a person's emotional state, sometimes significantly, and can cause overwhelming distress. A trigger may affect a person's ability to remain in the moment, bring up specific thought patterns or influence their behaviour. Common triggers include:
- stress;
- lack of communication within families;
- isolation;
- pressure to succeed/deliver;
- belief that you are what you achieve;
- unrecognised grief following many forms of loss;
- substance misuse;
- a particular place or type of environment.

Symptoms of mental illness

The signs and symptoms of mental illness differ according to the type and severity of condition. A symptom can also sometimes be mild and at other times more severe. A client may be focused and involved in one meeting but be unable to engage at the next.

Some common symptoms of mental illness are:
- a change in thinking or perception;
- reduced level of social functioning – eg, stops going to work, never returns calls, does not turn up to social events;
- changes in sleep patterns – eg, too much or too little;
- personal neglect – eg, unwashed hair, dirty clothes;
- feelings of hopelessness;
- suicidal thoughts;
- low mood;
- catastrophising;
- undue worry;
- self-harm.

Effects of medication

Medication can help to stabilise a mental condition, but may have side effects for the person taking it. These may prove challenging for a client and their adviser, and more time may be needed in a meeting, or a different approach may be required from the agency's standard protocols.

Some common side effects of medication taken for a mental health condition are:
- feeling flat and disconnected;
- weight gain – this can increase feelings of not being worthwhile or feeling 'less' than others;
- agitation and/or violence – anti-psychotic medications may cause this, as can medications for Alzheimer's disease;
- stomach upsets/nausea and indigestion – this can be a common side effect of depression or anti-psychotic medications;
- hyper-salivation/sweating, shaking – also common with anti-psychotic medication.

3. Issues for clients and advisers

Although all the clients we see have a degree of vulnerability, clients who have mental health conditions are often particularly vulnerable. They may not react or engage in the same way as a client who does not have a mental health condition. The limitations of the agencies may be difficult for them to understand, as it can often feel that they never talk to the same person or they have to repeat their story several times, which can be exhausting and distressing, or that staff can seem unsympathetic.

Clients with mental health conditions will often unconsciously practise avoidance, including missing appointments or deadlines. They may not return telephone calls or answer emails, or they may have problems focusing during an appointment or lack the motivation to deal with their debt issues. Medication can also make the client easily agitated.

All of these issues can make the job of a debt adviser more challenging. Some of the following techniques can help both you and your client.

Interviewing clients

Interviewing a client with mental health problems can be challenging. It is important to use the regular interviewing techniques that you would use with any other client, but also to be aware of specific techniques that may help to support this particular client.

General interview techniques

Mental health problems are common. Be respectful, avoid patronising your client and go through your regular interviewing techniques. You should be aware of your own prejudices and work to rise above them. The client may have difficulties in seeking help or attending a meeting with an adviser. It is important to be aware of this and provide support when needed.

Specific interview techniques

There are some interview techniques which may be particularly useful when working with a client with mental health problems.
- Using closed questions can help to focus the client – eg, 'Have you got a letter about that?'
- Encourage positivity, while being aware of the client's possible sensitivity to being discounted or upset.
- It is important to be clear of any time sequence, so ask when an event took place.
- To help the client to understand information, you could deliver it in small chunks or as a list.
- Help the client to rehearse what they might say or do in particular circumstances – eg, dealing with a creditor phone call.
- Record telephone numbers, sequences of actions or information the client would find useful.
- Be specific about what you can and cannot do. Manage expectations.
- Advisers/agencies may want to follow up with confirmation of advice in writing, which sets out the actions agreed by both the client and the adviser.

Chapter 15: Debt and mental health
5. Debt and Mental Health Evidence Form

Dealing with a client in crisis

It can be very upsetting if a client is distressed and considering self-harm or has suicidal feelings. It is normal for an adviser to feel shocked, worried or upset in this situation. Remember to listen, be supportive and try not to judge the client. See the advice on p392 for help with dealing with clients with suicidal feelings.

Use the following pointers when talking with a client in crisis.
- Be honest. Tell the person why you are worried for them.
- Ask questions. Be direct, but in a caring, supportive way.
- Do not panic. It won't help the person if you panic. Stay calm and supportive.
- Listen and empathise. Use active listening techniques. Try to see their point of view.

Hearing about suicide can be tough. It is vital to look after your own physical and mental wellbeing. Talk to people you trust about how you feel, to avoid feeling overwhelmed and be able to stay focused on supporting your client.

4. Data protection and sensitive personal data

Certain information that a client gives an adviser is defined as 'sensitive personal data' by the Data Protection Act 2018 (DPA 2018). Before you can record this type of information, you need to obtain the 'explicit consent' of the client to do so. You must ensure you follow your responsibilities under the DPA 2018 by ensuring that the client has received an explanation of how their information will be processed and that they have given explicit consent for this to happen. This explanation must include why their data is being collected, how it will be recorded, used, shared, stored and deleted, and when this will take place. You must also explain to the client that they can withdraw their explicit consent at any time and the process for doing so.

If an adviser or agency breaches the DPA 2018, they can both be sanctioned by the Information Commissioner's Office. This can include a hefty fine for serious continual breaches.

5. Debt and Mental Health Evidence Form

The Debt and Mental Health Evidence Form (DMHEF) was launched in 2008 by the Money Advice Liaison Group. The form collects external evidence on a client's mental health situation.

The client (or someone formally authorised to act on their behalf) must give their consent for the DMHEF to be completed. They can also request for it to be done. The DMHEF can only be completed by health and social care professionals, with the client's assistance, who then share it with creditors when they need to evidence a client's mental health. Creditors can use the form to help them decide what support to give to the client or what action to take.

The DMHEF is currently in its fourth version. It is simpler and shorter to complete than previous versions. On the reverse side of the form there is an optional space for the health or social care professional to add further information about the client – eg, how their condition may affect their ability to manage money.

Health and social care professionals are not legally required to complete the DMHEF; it is their choice to do so, including which questions they complete. In Scotland, health and social care professionals may request a charge for completing the DMHEF, while in England and Wales they cannot charge to fill in the form. In practice, most health and social care professionals will not request payment to complete the DMHEF.

There are two particular issues with using the DMHEF.[4]
- The form does not specifically address the question of whether or not the client was able to understand the contract they originally entered into. This is relevant to the enforceability of the contract and, therefore, the client's liability for the debt. This is a matter that advisers should consider first of all (see p382).
- The client must give their written consent to the form being used. However, a third party authorised to act on behalf of the client can complete and sign the consent form.

The DMHEF and guidance notes for advisers and creditors are available to download from moneyadvicetrust.org/advice-services/dmhef.

Who can use the Debt and Mental Health Evidence Form

The DMHEF can be used by:
- creditors, to aid them in deciding which action they should take;
- debt advisers, to aid in negotiations with creditors;
- clients with mental health problems, with support from debt advisers.

When to use the Debt and Mental Health Evidence Form

Before the DMHEF is started, creditors or debt advisers should consider whether the evidence needs to be collected. If it is required, they should check if alternative evidence may be available which provides the same information. This could be copies of prescriptions, patient letters or other information which may confirm the client's situation.

If a creditor decides the DMHEF should be used, they should give instructions and support to the client to make sure they get help completing the form.

UK Finance and the Credit Services Association have advised their members to accept any suitable evidence and only ask for the DMHEF as a last resort.

6. Mental health and capacity to contract in Scotland

A client is considered legally competent to enter into a contract with a creditor if they are shown as having 'the capacity to contract'. '**The capacity to contract**' is defined as the client being of sound mind. For legally binding agreements, a client may not have the capacity to enter into an agreement for a number of reasons, including being underage, mentally impaired or intoxicated.

In Scotland, the definition of incapacity, in relation to when a person cannot make decisions on their own behalf, is contained in Part 1, section 1(6) of the Adults with Incapacity (Scotland) Act 2000.

Nature of a contract

A contract is binding when the following six essential aspects have been fulfilled:
- offer;
- acceptance;
- legal capacity;
- intention;
- consensus;
- legality.

If one of these is invalid, the contract will be void (meaning that no contract ever existed) or voidable (a contract is in force until declared void by one of the contracting parties).

Capacity to contract

In the case of general contracts, a person with mental incapacity is bound to the contract in the same way as someone with no mental incapacity. The exception will be if the person with a mental incapacity (or a person authorised to act on their behalf) can show that they did not understand what they were doing. If this can be shown, the contract is void.

In Scottish law, it is not necessary for the creditor to have known of this incapacity at the time the contract was taken out.

There is an exception to this rule existing in law, and that is when the person is contracting for 'necessaries'. The meaning of the term 'necessaries' depends on the facts of the individual case. Things that are relevant include the particular circumstances of the person, the actual need and what the purchased item will be used for. Food, lodging, clothing, medicine, medical attention and education are all generally recognised as necessary.

There is a common law (law made through court rulings) presumption that even a person who has mental incapacity may be held liable and expected to pay a reasonable price for necessaries. This presumption also appears in statute law contained in section 3 of the Sale of Goods Act 1979.

> *Section 3: Capacity to buy and sell*
> (1) Capacity to buy and sell is regulated by the general law concerning capacity to contract and to transfer and acquire property.
> (2) Where necessaries are sold and delivered to a minor or to a person who by reason of mental incapacity or drunkenness is incompetent to contract, he must pay a reasonable price for them.
> (3) In subsection (2) above 'necessaries' means goods suitable to the condition in life of the minor or other person concerned and to his actual requirements at the time of the sale and delivery.

A client who enters into an agreement while incapacitated mentally cannot be bound by that contract (excluding necessaries), although the burden of proof is on the person trying to avoid being bound by the contract. This is because there is a presumption of capacity.

The issue could be more complicated when the client has entered a contract while incapacitated, such as a credit card. The effect is the agreement is void – ie, it did not exist. However, should the client recover mental capacity (either fully or for a period) and make additional transactions using the credit card, they may be held responsible for these. As a matter of good practice, when someone is incapacitated and enters any agreement or transaction and then recovers, they should immediately rescind the agreement or transaction with their creditor.

Contract law is very complex, and this is mainly due to the fact that it is based on caselaw that develops over a substantial period of time rather than through government legislation in a single Act. Mental health issues are more relevant today than ever before. This is primarily due to the increase in personal debt and the cost of living crisis with the resultant problem debt that emerges for a number of socially patterned groups, including those with mental health difficulties.

To be able to help clients in this area, debt advisers must be aware of the legal position, approach creditors from the correct perspective, build relationships with other professionals, and keep up to date with pending changes in the field of debt and mental health.

Debt advisers who are unsure how to proceed should approach a more experienced debt adviser or contact the MATRICS team.

Adults with Incapacity (Scotland) Act 2000

The Adults with Incapacity (Scotland) Act 2000 ('the Act') sets a framework for safeguarding the welfare and managing the finances of adults who lack capacity. Its main aim is to protect adults with limited capacity to make decisions while aiding them in making decisions about their own lives whenever possible. The Act allows someone else to make decisions on behalf of a person who lacks the capacity to make their own decisions.

The Act applies to anyone over the age of 16 who, due to a mental disorder or brain injury, is considered to lack the capacity to make some or all decisions for themselves. This also includes anyone unable to communicate their decision due to physical disability.

7. Key requirements and guidance

The Financial Conduct Authority (FCA) states that clients with limited mental capacity can be particularly vulnerable to detriment and requires that all organisations under its regulation establish clear and effective procedures to identify particularly vulnerable clients and support them appropriately.[5] This includes advice agencies.

The FCA position on mental capacity is informed by the Adults with Incapacity (Scotland) Act 2000.[6] It expects both creditors and advice agencies to comply with the law and its regulatory frameworks.

Financial Conduct Authority guidance

The FCA's *Consumer Credit Sourcebook* sets out the legal framework in Scotland for safeguarding the welfare and managing the finances of adults who lack capacity due to mental disorder or inability to communicate.[7]

Creditors should document the steps they take to assist people to make informed borrowing decisions and to ensure they make informed and responsible lending decisions.[8] The guidance recommends that creditors present clear, jargon-free information to explain credit agreements in user-friendly formats[9] and gives guidance on the treatment of customers with limited mental capacity.[10]

Other guidance

A creditor may not be in a position to know whether a client has some form of limited mental capacity, and not be able to assess their level of understanding of any explanations – eg, if there is no face-to-face interaction or the internet is used for transactions. Additionally, not every client with a mental health problem is automatically vulnerable or unable to manage their money.

On its website, the Money Advice Liaison Group (MALG) has two linked resources that address these issues, each with 12 steps for treating potentially vulnerable customers fairly:
- *Lending, Debt Collection and Mental Health* (published by the Royal College of Psychiatrists and the Money Advice Trust); *and*

- *Vulnerability: a guide for advice agencies* (published by the University of Bristol and the Money Advice Trust).

See malg.org.uk/resources/malg-mental-health-and-debt-guidelines for these guides and MALG's publication endorsed by the *Consumer Credit Sourcebook*:[11] *Good Practice Awareness Guidelines for Helping Consumers with Mental Health Conditions and Debt.*

The guidance includes the following.
- Creditors, debt collectors and advisers should have procedures in place to ensure that people with mental health problems are treated fairly and appropriately.
- If a creditor has been notified of a mental health problem, an adviser should be allowed a reasonable period to collect evidence and send it to the creditor. This could be extended, if the relevant evidence was not collected by the end of one month.
- If creditors sell debts once a mental health issue has been advised, they should monitor the debt purchaser to ensure compliance with the guidelines.
- If there is an imminent or serious threat of enforcement action being taken in these circumstances, advisers should consider whether a mental health crisis moratorium ('breathing space') application is appropriate.
- If a client has a serious mental health problem, creditors should only start court action or enforce debts through the courts as a last resort and only when it is appropriate and fair for lenders to do so.
- Creditors should consider writing off unsecured debts when a client's mental health problems are long term and unlikely to improve, and if it is highly likely they will be unable to pay outstanding debts.
- Disability benefits should be recognised as specifically awarded for meeting mobility and care needs. It is the client's decision whether to include any of these benefits as disposable income in the financial statement.

Note: these guidelines only apply to managing debt problems and not to the stage when the debt was incurred. However, the guidelines suggest that creditors may wish to 'flag' the files of clients who have explained the effect of a mental health problem on money management and debt issues. In addition, a client and someone holding a power of attorney for them could voluntarily add information about their mental health problems to their credit reference file so that creditors who carry out a search as part of a credit application are aware of the position. This can be done by a 'notice of correction'.

If creditors and advisers need more information about particular mental health terms, North East London and East London and The City University Mental Health NHS Trusts and Mental Health Literacy produced a useful mental health glossary.[12]

Chapter 15: Debt and mental health
Notes

Notes

1. **Introduction**
   1. rcpsych.ac.uk/mental-health/mental-illnesses-and-mental-health-problems/debt-and-mental-health
   2. CONC 2.10.6G
   3. CONC 2.10.8G

5. **Debt and Mental Health Evidence Form**
   4. See C Trend, C Fitch and A Sharp, 'Debt and mental health: tools of the trade', *Adviser* 160

7. **Key requirements and guidance**
   5. CONC 8.2.7
   6. CONC 2.10.2G
   7. CONC 2.10.2
   8. CONC 2.10.12G
   9. CONC 2.10.14G
   10. CONC 7.10
   11. CONC 7.2.3G
   12. See malg.org.uk/wp-content/uploads/2017/03/Mental-health-glossary.pdf, and mentalhealthliteracy.org/schoolmhl/wp-content/uploads/2018/02/mental-health-glossary.pdf

Chapter 16

Debt and vulnerability

This chapter covers:
1. Introduction (below)
2. What is vulnerability (below)
3. Client vulnerability (p389)
4. Building useful relationships (p391)
5. Clients with suicidal feelings (p392)
6. Vulnerability and financial capability (p392)
7. Safeguarding (p395)
8. Actions and considerations (p395)
9. Tools and support (p396)

1. Introduction

People can find themselves in vulnerable circumstances at any time. The Financial Conduct Authority's recent Financial Lives Survey[1] shows that 27.7 million adults in the UK now have characteristics of vulnerability such as poor health, experiencing negative life events, low financial resilience or low capability. Not all people with these characteristics will suffer harm, but they may limit people's ability to make reasonable decisions or put them at greater risk of harm.

2. What is vulnerability

Defining vulnerability is a challenging task as it exists within a spectrum of risk. All clients are potentially at risk of becoming vulnerable, but having characteristics of vulnerability (see p388) increases this risk.

The Adult Support and Protection (Scotland) Act 2007 is the legislation to protect adults who are at risk of harm or neglect.

Financial Conduct Authority definition

The Financial Conduct Authority (FCA) defines vulnerability as follows.[2]

Most customers seeking advice on their debts under credit agreements or consumer hire agreements may be regarded as vulnerable to some degree by virtue of their financial circumstances. Of these customers some may be particularly vulnerable because they are less able to deal with lenders or debt collectors pursuing them for debts owed. Customers with mental health and mental capacity issues may fall into this category.

Energy UK definition

Energy UK defines vulnerability in its policy booklet as follows.[3]

A customer is vulnerable if for reasons of age, health, disability or severe financial insecurity, they are unable to safeguard their personal welfare or the personal welfare of other members of the household.

Many of the UK's energy suppliers have come together to develop and sign a vulnerability commitment to customers.[4]

DWP definition

The DWP describes vulnerability as people identified as having complex needs and/or requiring additional support to help them access DWP benefits and use its services. This could be a claimant, customer, client or any other type of DWP service user. Complex needs means any difficult personal circumstances and/or life events which affect an individual's ability to access DWP benefits.

Vulnerability levels

There are three stages of vulnerability that advisers should be aware of. Clients can move through each stage many times in their lives; some may never move, while others may move backwards as well as forwards.

- **Potentially vulnerable:** a client who is at risk of becoming vulnerable if their circumstances change – eg, they are solvent, but their employer is threatening redundancy.
- **Vulnerable:** a client who is more likely to experience financial or other types of harm, loss or disadvantage – eg, they are elderly and have no support.
- **Particularly vulnerable:** a client who needs a different approach or extra help from an adviser or a third party – eg, they have an addiction.

It is important to be aware that actions taken by a debt adviser can improve or worsen the client's situation. Because of this, advisers have a responsibility to ensure that vulnerable clients are safeguarded and supported.

Vulnerability characteristics and drivers

Characteristics of vulnerability include:
- communication difficulties – eg, learning difficulties, English not being the client's first language or dyslexia; *and*
- reduced physical or mental capacity.

The FCA has identified four key drivers which can lead to increased risk of client vulnerability.[5]
- **Health:** conditions or illnesses affecting a client's ability to carry out day-to-day tasks, whether physical or mental, severe or long term.
- **Life events:** such as bereavement, job loss or relationship breakdown.
- **Resilience:** low ability to withstand emotional or financial shocks.
- **Capability:** low knowledge of financial matters or low confidence in managing money, or low capability in other relevant areas such as literacy or digital skills.

3. Client vulnerability

A client in vulnerable circumstances may find it difficult to engage with financial services. They can be less able to represent their own interests and may have different and complex needs.

Gambling

Gambling-related vulnerability affects a client's decision-making and can lead to poor outcomes.

Clients affected by harmful gambling may lack perspective and have low interest in anything apart from gambling. They may take excessive risks and make poor judgements. With this comes heightened stress and anxiety.

They may experience related conditions such as mental health, alcohol or drug problems. This leaves them vulnerable to over-indebtedness, arrears and problem debt. They may risk repossession of their property. They can end up with reduced access to financial services or be excluded. This can leave them open to being victims of fraud, scams or financial abuse.

The Gambling Commission runs the National Gambling Helpline (tel: 0808 802 0133). Its website has tools to manage gambling activity and lists free multi-operator and national self-exclusion schemes (see gamblingcommission.gov.uk/public-and-players/safer-gambling).

Age-related vulnerability

Older people may have specific age-related vulnerability – eg, physical disability, memory problems, bereavement, a lack of financial resources and/or loneliness. If they are from a less affluent background, they may have had a lifetime of exposure to poorer life chances, leaving them at even greater risk.

Mental capacity

Mental capacity is a client's ability to understand, remember and consider information presented to them and make an informed decision based on it. It differs from mental health, as a mental health condition may not affect the capacity to make an informed decision. Vulnerability is a much broader concept. Capacity can fluctuate – a client may have capacity one day but not the next. This is often seen in clients with addictions or suffering from dementia.

Data Protection Act 2018

Advisers must recognise their legal duties under the Data Protection Act 2018 (DPA 2018) to ensure they can correctly collect, respond to and store information about their clients. The DPA 2018 is the UK's implementation of the General Data Protection Regulation (GDPR).

The key elements are as follows.
- **Collect relevant information:** advisers should record relevant details about a client's situation; this can be used to identify vulnerability. Explain to the client why the information is being collected, to improve trust and rapport.
- **Adviser's legal duty:** the adviser's organisation must have a policy on what information needs to be collected and how it will be used, stored and disposed of under the DPA 2018.
- **Explicit consent:** information on a client's vulnerability is 'special category data' (sensitive data). The client must give their explicit consent for this data to be recorded. Explain why this information is being collected, how it will be used and who it will be shared with. The client can withdraw their consent at any time.
- **Data processing:** information held about the client must be adequate, relevant and not excessive. It must be up to date and not kept longer than needed. The adviser must review the information with the client, especially if their situation changes, and update case notes accordingly.

Challenges when working with vulnerable clients

Vulnerable clients may have additional needs that limit their ability to make decisions and choices, or to represent their own interests. This can leave them at greater risk of harm if things go wrong.

Engagement may be an issue due to a client's lack of motivation or because they struggle with their mental health. Advisers should check in with clients during an interview to ensure they are engaged, work to build rapport with active listening skills and reflect back to encourage engagement.

Clients' conditions may fluctuate and change, requiring advisers to be flexible in their approach. It is useful for advisers to identify the help and support the client may need. For clients with multiple needs, a referral or multiple agency working may be necessary.

Clear communication can help break down barriers and help the client to share personal information.

4. Building useful relationships

Clients

Seeking debt advice can be a challenging and emotional situation for clients. Advisers can build positive relationships with clients in a number of ways.
- When talking with a client, use simple, clear language and check beforehand if they wouldd like support from a third party at the meeting – eg, a family member, friend or interpreter.
- If possible, plan ahead by writing a list of questions to help navigate the interview.
- Aim to meet in a quiet space, with enough time to go through all the questions fully.
- Check whether the client prefers contact at a particular time of day – eg, some vulnerable clients do not sleep well and may feel better at certain times of the day.
- Avoid overloading clients with information and only move on in the discussion when everything is understood and clear.
- Consider what type of support your client may need. You may need to suggest options, as they may not know themselves or feel too overwhelmed to make any decisions.
- Check that the client understands what will happen based on any decisions they make. Some vulnerable clients may just want to 'sort' their debt now without considering the consequences, so you may have to repeat information and check they understand it more often.
- Let clients know that they can come back to you for further explanations of any aspects they do not understand.

Creditors

Creditors are expected to understand the client's needs and ensure their staff have the training to recognise and help support the needs of vulnerable customers, in line with the Financial Conduct Authority's *Consumer Credit Sourcebook* (CONC). They must respond to vulnerable people's needs in their product design, customer service and communication. They should also monitor and assess that they are meeting the needs of vulnerable people and make improvements if not.

If a creditor is not co-operating with you, your client or agency, remind the creditor of their responsibilities under the CONC. If you or your client are still not satisfied, you can make a complaint to the Financial Ombudsman Service.

5. Clients with suicidal feelings

Some advisers are uncomfortable talking about suicidal feelings. It is okay to ask questions if you are worried about a client. Talking about suicide has not been shown to be harmful. Being direct and empathetic with the client gives them permission to open up and lets them know they are not a burden. It can often be a relief to talk about how they feel. Even though having these conversations can be beneficial, take care of the questions you ask and only explore what is relevant. If you are having these conversations, make sure you have plans in place to support someone afterwards if they feel vulnerable.

Do not overreact or assume that all suicidal feelings need urgent medical attention. While these experiences and feelings are serious and indicate that the person having them is in a vulnerable place, they may have their own support and safety measures in place to manage them. Make sure you listen to what they have to say before taking any next steps.

Advisers may want to consider doing training on dealing with clients with suicidal feelings. They should check with their line managers about available courses in their area.

NHS Inform has support for people with suicidal thoughts at nhsinform.scot/suicide. See CPAG's *Mental Health and Benefits Handbook* for information about advising clients with suicidal feelings and safeguarding. It is available free online at cpag.org.uk/handbooks.

6. Vulnerability and financial capability

Advisers can assess an individual's financial capability through four areas: managing money, planning ahead, choosing products and staying informed. Those at most risk of harm or damage are below average in all four of these areas. Clients who are more likely to face challenges with financial capability are those who are single, unemployed, below the age of 35, social tenants and/or without educational qualifications.

These clients often lack confidence in managing money and can find it difficult to communicate concerns they have about their finances.

This may be for many reasons, including that they have:
- variable income;
- little or no savings;
- restricted access to financial products and services;
- behaviours and preferences that lead to increased costs of mainstream products that lead to choosing higher-priced everyday products;
- low confidence, which undermines their choices;
- failed to recognise a problem or get help at the right time.

Clients who have lower than average financial capability may:
- choose the wrong financial products;
- pay a high price unnecessarily;
- be treated unfairly by their chosen provider;
- get into unmanageable or problem debt.

Credit products

Clients on benefits or a very low income tend to use credit products to cover day-to-day expenses. They potentially face the highest risk of detriment. They might think they cannot access mainstream forms of lending and mainly focus on the affordability of repayments, which are usually low weekly amounts.

Common credit options are listed below.
- **Home credit:** often seen as friendly, flexible and non-judgemental. There are fewer home credit companies on the market now, but interest is usually very high.
- **Catalogues:** used mostly for white goods (eg, fridges and washing machines) and clothing. Clients might not consider this to be borrowing.
- **Rent-to-own:** often used because the borrower believes they are more likely to be approved (usually for white goods). Numerous firms operate in the UK, predominantly on Facebook and other social media. You can check the Financial Conduct Authority register at fca.org.uk/firms/financial-services-register to see if they are authorised.
- **Unlicensed lender:** also known as a 'loan shark', this type of lender will often take advantage of familiarity and vulnerabilities to maintain their position. The Scottish Illegal Money Lending Unit provides information and support at stopillegallending.co.uk or telephone 0800 074 0878.
- **Credit unions:** clients are often referred to these by support services, as approval is likely even to those with poor credit scores and clients will often be able to save while repaying their loan. This can be an expensive way to borrow, as interest rates are often higher than for high street banks, although they can be considerably lower than for other types of credit products.

Financial abuse

Financial abuse is when a person controls another person's ability to acquire, use and maintain financial resources (whether cash, assets or other finances). It is a form of domestic abuse and can leave the abused person feeling isolated, lacking in confidence and trapped.

Financial abuse can take different forms and can happen to anyone of any age. Abusers can be partners, ex-partners, family members or others, such as carers or friends.

Sometimes (but not always), financial abuse will be recognised by the police as coercive or controlling behaviour, which is also a criminal offence. Victims do not have to be living with the person for the coercive or controlling behaviour offence to apply. In many cases, financial abuse can continue, or even start, after couples separate.

Financial abuse is often part of wider economic abuse (see Chapter 17).

If a person uses another person's funds, property or any resources without their authorisation and in an improper manner, it is financial abuse.

> **Types of financial abuse**
> Financial abuse may include:
> – theft – ie, money or possessions stolen, borrowed or withheld without permission;
> – wrongfully controlling access to money or benefits;
> – preventing someone from buying goods, services or leisure activities;
> – absorbing money into a care home or household budget without the person's consent;
> – deliberately overcharging for goods or services or asking a person for money under false pretences;
> – carrying out unnecessary work and/or overcharging;
> – postal, telephone and internet scams where there was human interaction and a person lost money;
> – unlicensed money lending (loan sharks) – ie, being offered a loan on very bad terms;
> – misuse of a person's assets by professionals;
> – altering ownership of property without consent;
> – exerting undue influence on a person to give away their assets;
> – pressure in connection with wills, property, inheritance, possessions or benefits;
> – putting undue pressure on a person to accept lower cost/lower quality services to preserve more financial resources to be passed to beneficiaries on death;
> – misuse of powers of attorney.

Common signs of financial abuse

Debt advisers should be aware of common signs of financial abuse, especially when dealing with a vulnerable client – eg:
- personal items which are missing;
- an unexplained lack of funds;
- money being withdrawn from accounts without explanation;
- someone managing the client's financial affairs being evasive or uncooperative;
- the client's family or friends show an unusual interest in their assets;
- rent is unpaid or the client is facing eviction;
- a client with high financial resources living in poor living conditions;
- unusual/unrecognised entries on the client's credit report.

Identifying abuse and protecting vulnerable clients

When attempting to identify whether abuse is taking place and protect a vulnerable client, it is important to stay calm and listen to what the client has to say, and avoid sounding shocked or angry. You should reassure the client that they are doing the right thing by telling someone what is happening. Avoid putting pressure on the client for information and do not judge them. Advisers must not promise to keep secrets or attempt to confront an abuser.

You should report the issue to the relevant person within your organisation. Write up a factual account of what the client told you as soon as possible.

7. Safeguarding

Safeguarding refers to protecting clients in vulnerable circumstances who may be at risk of abuse or neglect by another person. Services should work together to identify people at risk and to help protect them. The Adult Support and Protection (Scotland) Act 2007 is the legislation to protect adults who are at risk of harm or neglect.

Advisers have a responsibility to safeguard vulnerable adults and to follow the correct procedures when abuse is identified. Advisers must be aware of their internal safeguarding policy and notify the appropriate agencies if abuse is identified or suspected.

Clients in an abusive situation must be taken seriously, granted confidentiality and treated with respect. It may also be appropriate to discuss how to communicate with them. They may not want letters coming to their home if their abuser lives with them.

8. Actions and considerations

When dealing with vulnerable adults, the first priority is ensuring their safety and protection. Some actions against a client may be considered a criminal offence, requiring the police to be notified for their safety.

While confidentiality is important, this may not be possible if there is a risk to the client or someone else. It will depend on the level of risk and the capacity of the client to understand the decision.

An adviser's role is not to find evidence of abuse; it is to support the vulnerable adult and log relevant information to aid in an effective formal investigation.

Chapter 16: Debt and vulnerability
9. Tools and support

9. **Tools and support**

The Royal College of Psychiatrists and the Money Advice Trust have developed a series of drills, set out below, to help advisers identify and support clients in vulnerable circumstances. Public Health Scotland runs Scotland's Mental Health First Aid (SMHFA) courses – see smhfa.com/find-a-course.aspx for details.

Advisers should prioritise their wellbeing alongside their clients', and seek support from colleagues, line managers or appropriate external agencies if they feel overwhelmed or ill-equipped to handle a situation.

TEXAS	**When your client tells you about themselves**
Thank	Thank the client.
Explain	Explain how the information gathered from the client will be used.
EXplicit	Obtain explicit consent.
Ask	Ask the client questions to get a better understanding of their circumstances.
Signpost	Signpost or refer to internal or external specialist help when appropriate.

BRUCE	**For clients experiencing a mental capacity limitation**
Behaviour	Look for clues of a limitation in the client's behaviour and speech.
Remembering	If they are struggling to remember the advice, ask what might help, write it down or see if someone can help them.
Understanding	Ask them to summarise their understanding. Fill any gaps by repeating advice or using different explanations by simplifying or rephrasing.
Communication	How would they prefer to communicate? Try to accommodate this. Allow enough time and pause regularly.
Evaluation	Discuss each option simply, writing down any pros and cons.

IDEA	**This technique is useful when talking to a client about their vulnerability**
Impact	How does it impact on your personal and financial situation?
Duration	How long have you been living with this?

Chapter 16: Debt and vulnerability
9. Tools and support

Experience	Have you experienced this before, does it fluctuate?
Assistance	Is there anything we should know about the support you are receiving which could help us support you better?

BLAKE	**This technique is to help advisers when dealing with a suicidal client**
Breathe (to focus)	To help deal with the shock and fear when dealing with a suicidal client, take a moment to breathe and focus your thoughts.
Listen (to understand)	Listen carefully and assess the risk of harm to the client.
Ask (to discover)	If you need more information, ask questions.
Keep safe (from harm)	If the client is at risk of imminent harm, the emergency services should be contacted.
End (with summary)	Everything that has been discussed and agreed should be summarised when suitable.

SPIDER	**This technique can be useful for causing minimal distress when you have to deliver bad news to a client**
Set the scene	Thank you for calling, we need to talk about…
Perspective	How are you feeling and what are you planning to do next?
Invitation	Invite questions: Can you talk through this today or would you like to talk another time?
Deliver	Use simple, clear language. I'm sorry this news is disappointing. I'll explain it, and we can go through the options.
Empathise	Listen carefully and give the client space to express their feelings.
Recap	Summarise the information and check understanding. If they are not ready to make a decision, rearrange the meeting and offer reassurance.

RED FLAGS	**Vulnerability indicators to look out for**
Potentially vulnerable	Signs include difficulty, distress, or life events that might lead to a vulnerable situation.
Vulnerable	More likely to experience harm, loss or disadvantage compared to others.
Particularly vulnerable	Heightened or imminent risk of detriment (a more serious or negative impact). Offer support quickly to avoid significant harm.

Chapter 16: Debt and vulnerability
Notes

Individual factors	Illness, disability, contact with health or social care workers and getting certain benefits (like personal independence payment).
Wider circumstances	Excessive or unusual expenditure, life events (eg, bereavement) or income shocks (eg, unemployment).
Organisational actions	Something 'has been done' causing difficulty (eg, a change in communication method) or things that 'haven't been done' (like no consideration of a third party trying to help).

CRISIS	Ways to support a client in crisis, and yourself
Calm	Be calm and take appropriate action.
Listen	To a concerned third party. Check if the client is available. If not, don't share data, note their observations, explain your plan and take action.
Acknowledge	Refer to BRUCE, SPIDER or BLAKE cards for support.
Ask	For support, debrief and take time out if you feel upset or worried.
Protect	Anyone in an abusive situation must be taken seriously, given support and referred to those who can protect them.
Signpost	Or refer to those who can help – eg, Samaritans (telephone 116 123) for suicidal or despairing people, 24 hours a day.

Notes

1. Introduction
1 FCA, *Financial Lives 2022: key findings from the FCA's Financial Lives May 2022 survey*, 2023, fca.org.uk/publication/financial-lives/financial-lives-survey-2022-key-findings.pdf

2. What is vulnerability?
2 CONC 8.2.8
3 energy-uk.org.uk/news/vulnerability-commitment-good-practice-guide-published
4 See energy-uk.org.uk/our-work/vulnerability-commitment
5 FCA, *FG21/1 Guidance for firms on the fair treatment of vulnerable customers*, 2021, fca.org.uk/publication/finalised-guidance/fg21-1.pdf

Chapter 17

Economic abuse

This chapter includes:
1. Introduction (below)
2. What is economic abuse (below)
3. Who is affected by economic abuse (p400)
4. Financial abuse versus economic abuse (p400)
5. Identifying economic abuse (p401)
6. The adviser's role (p402)
7. Economic abuse and debt (p406)
8. Financial Abuse Code (p410)

1. Introduction

Economic abuse rarely happens in isolation and usually occurs alongside other forms of abuse, including physical, sexual and psychological abuse. Ninety-five per cent of cases of domestic abuse involve economic abuse.[1]

This type of abuse intends to create economic instability and/or make a person (often the partner of the abuser) economically dependent on another person, which limits their freedom. Without access to money and the things that money can buy, it is difficult to leave an abuser and find a safe place. Someone experiencing this type of abuse can become trapped in a relationship with the abuser, unable to resist the abuser's control and at risk of further harm. In this way, economic safety underpins physical safety.

2. What is economic abuse

Economic abuse is a recognised form of domestic abuse. It often occurs in the context of intimate partner violence and involves the control of a partner or ex-partner's money and finances, as well as the things that money can buy.

Economic abuse can include exerting control over income, spending, bank accounts, bills and borrowing. It can also include controlling access to and use of things like transport and technology that allow clients to work and stay connected socially, as well as property and daily essentials like food and clothing. It can include destroying items and refusing to contribute to household costs.

Economic abuse is often invisible. The abuser seeks to control and isolate the victim-survivor through controlling or coercive behaviour such as:
- retaining their salary or giving them an 'allowance';
- forbidding them from accessing work and education;
- restricting access to their private and shared bank accounts;
- convincing or forcing them to take on debt on behalf of the abuser.

In England and Wales, economic abuse is defined in the Domestic Abuse Act 2021. Although it is not defined in the Domestic Abuse (Scotland) Act 2018 in the same way, it can be relied on when prosecuting a perpetrator. The 2018 Act criminalises 'coercive control', which is a pattern of abuse tactics of which economic abuse is one such tactic. This can be evidenced when prosecuting the perpetrator. The 2018 Act only applies to 'romantic relationships', whereas the English legislation applies to a broader section – ie, family.

The Scottish Women's Rights Centre has a useful economic abuse legal guide and factsheets at scottishwomensrightscentre.org.uk/professionals-legal. There are also a variety of resources available at the Surviving Economic Abuse website, survivingeconomicabuse.org.[2]

3. Who is affected by economic abuse

Although women experience the majority of economic abuse, it crosses all social boundaries and kinds of relationships. It can be committed by friends, family members, neighbours, work colleagues and carers, and can affect more than just the victim, such as children and other family members.

Abusive relationships do not differentiate based on sexuality, age, religion, ethnic background or income. Those with high educational attainment and high income can also be affected: it could happen to anyone.

4. Financial abuse versus economic abuse

'**Financial abuse**' is the use or misuse of financial resources to exert control over another person, restricting their freedom and dignity. It is often part of a pattern of coercive control characterised by belittling, threatening, intimidating and domineering behaviour.

Although the terms 'financial abuse' and 'economic abuse' are often used interchangeably, economic abuse has a wider meaning than controlling access to money and finances.

'**Economic abuse**' encompasses controlling behaviour that may restrict a person's access to:
- education and training;
- employment;
- essential services such as benefits, food and clothing;
- travel – eg, removing or restricting access to their driving licence or passport.

This list is not definitive.

5. Identifying economic abuse

Economic abuse is often difficult to identify. There could be many reasons for unusual spending or for a client answering questions in a certain way, but there are some key signs that may help identify that a client is vulnerable to economic abuse or already a victim, including the following:
- a surplus in their budget but they are struggling financially;
- little or limited knowledge about their financial situation;
- cannot answer key questions about their income and expenditure;
- may have income paid into their partner's account rather than their own;
- no access to their own bank account or are dependent on a joint account;
- no understanding of, or unaware of, borrowing in their name;
- says their partner forced them to take out a credit card or loan or forced them to use credit against their wishes;
- no access to key documents related to their financial situation;
- appears withdrawn, fearful, distressed or scared;
- says their partner deals with all the finances, and may have unexplained sudden transfers of assets to a family member or someone outside the family;
- have unexplained withdrawals from a cash machine at a time when the account holder could not have accessed the account;
- all bills being in one party's name and all assets in the other's.

Advisers may also want to look out for clients who choose to accept their partner's advice rather than theirs or allow their partners to do all the talking in an interview situation.

Clients regularly missing, cancelling appointments or continually not acting on advice, when it is in their own best interests, may be an indicator that they may not want to upset an abusive partner.

Economic abuse can cause emotional issues and feelings of isolation. It can lead to clients feeling anxious or guilty about buying/having things for themselves and they can regularly blame themselves for the abuse.

Advisers should make themselves aware of the tactics and methods abusers can use to gain and keep control of a client's finances – eg:

- having or having had control of all household finances;
- misinforming the client about their right to occupy their home or claim a share of the equity;
- telling them they have no rights in relation to their matrimonial home;
- refusing to pay bills leading to debt;
- preventing the client from working, or forcing them to work and/or taking or controlling access to their wages;
- restricting their access to other income, including welfare benefits;
- extending borrowing or taking out secured loans on jointly-owned property.

Post-separation economic abuse

Economic abuse can continue beyond a relationship breakdown. It does not require physical proximity – eg, it can include withholding child maintenance payments or sending money via bank transfers with abusive references.

Some abusers get their benefits paid into the abused person's account as a way of justifying further contact after separation. To get around this, contact CPAG, which has an arrangement with the DWP to deal with this issue on a case-by-case basis. See cpag.org.uk/unwanted-payments-abusers-benefit-your-account for more details.

6. The adviser's role

Debt advisers are in an ideal position to identify economic abuse. Their involvement can be critical in spotting warning signals and supporting clients to regain control of their finances and rebuild their lives. For example, you can help the client write a note to add to their credit file, which could stop further applications for credit in their name by their abuser.

The Domestic Abuse (Scotland) Act 2018 recognises that abuse can also occur after separating from an abusive partner. This is crucial in relation to economic abuse, as the abuse can start, continue or escalate after physically separating from an abusive partner and can, for example, include:
- deliberately and unreasonably delaying legal proceedings to increase legal fees;
- misusing and sabotaging joint financial products.

This behaviour can be used as evidence against the abuser. Clients should discuss this with their solicitor or support worker, or contact Scottish Women's Aid for further support.

While advisers should not shy away from raising economic abuse as an issue, there may be instances where referral to other agencies is appropriate. It is important to know your limitations and when it is appropriate to refer onto another more qualified organisation.

Try to encourage meaningful partnership working through which information is shared, to avoid the client having to repeat their story.

> **Agencies that may be able to help**
> – Scottish Women's Aid: womensaid.scot
> – Scotland's Domestic Abuse and Forced Marriage Helpline: sdafmh.org.uk
> – LGBT+ Helpline Scotland: lgbthealth.org.uk/services-support/lgbt-helpline-scotland
> – Men's Advice Line (for male victims of domestic abuse): 0800 801 0327 and mensadviceline.org.uk
> – AMIS (Abused Men in Scotland): abusedmeninscotland.org
> – Saheliya (for black, minority ethnic, asylum seeker, refugee and migrant women and girls aged 12+): saheliya.co.uk
> – Scottish Women's Rights Centre: scottishwomensrightscentre.org.uk
> – Women's Support Project: womenssupportproject.org.uk
> Other local resources may be available.

Supporting a client who is experiencing economic abuse can be challenging, as it may feel like the ways in which they can be helped are limited. However, by understanding the position that the client is in, discussing their options with them and advocating on their behalf, advisers are playing a crucial role in helping them move forward. An adviser's support may also help the client gain the confidence to speak to another agency about the abuse.

Economic abuse and physical abuse often go hand in hand. The client's safety is paramount: check that it is safe for your agency to contact them. Ensure you establish the client's safe contact methods and if there are any immediate concerns, take advice from your local women's aid or manager.

As a responsible adviser, you need to understand your agency's safeguarding policies and be mindful of your own wellbeing while supporting your client.

Supporting clients – key principles

Surviving Economic Abuse, in partnership with Money Advice Plus, has produced a helpful 'conversation kit' for debt advisers.[3] The guide outlines eight principles advisers should be aware of when dealing with a client who may be experiencing, or is a survivor of, economic abuse.

Principle 1: be patient

A client may not have access to the documents normally needed to support them fully. While this can seem frustrating, and you may feel that there is little you can do to help with these gaps in information, being patient with your client may give them the space they need to explain why they do not have the information or documents required.

Principle 2: try to understand the client's spending

An abuser's control could transform unnecessary spending into priority spending for a client – eg, they may be insistent that certain expenses are met to the detriment of essential spending like rent. Avoid blaming the client for unusual spending, as this may make them less likely to share further information.

Principle 3: understand why clients may not disclose abuse

It is important to understand why some clients may not disclose their experiences of economic abuse.

They may be:
- ashamed about the situation they are in;
- afraid of the abuser finding out that they have spoken to an adviser;
- worried about being judged in the response they receive;
- concerned that it will negatively affect the support they are offered;
- unaware that a debt adviser can support them if they are experiencing economic abuse;
- coming to terms with the abuse they are experiencing.

The client may have lived with the abuse for a long time. It may seem 'normal' to them, and they may be unaware they are experiencing a type of abuse.

Principle 4: create the right environment for the client to talk

There are certain things advisers can do to make it easier for clients to talk about the abuse they are experiencing and to let them know that they are there to support them, including creating a safe environment.
- Remember that they will need to speak to you when their abuser is not around. Ask if it is a convenient time for them to talk and if it is safe for them to do so, or if another time would be better.
- Would they prefer a telephone or video call, or would they like to make an appointment to speak with you in person?
- Is there a code word that the client would like to use to indicate when they are not able to speak?
- Would the client like you to pretend to be someone else if the telephone was to be suddenly taken by the abuser?
- If leaving the client a message/sending a text, check it is safe to do so.

Principle 5: ask the question

If you suspect that a client may be experiencing economic abuse and they have not yet disclosed this directly, it may be appropriate to ask more questions about their situation. Ensure that the environment is right for them to talk and assure them they are supported.

Asking some softer questions (eg, 'how are things at home?') can open conversation around the topic and may be better than direct questioning, which may make the client feel threatened.

Principle 6: listen

Active listening skills help to create an environment in which a client can speak openly. It also helps ensure that you learn as much information as possible to be able to support them appropriately.

Remember to give space and time for the client to explain their situation. If your appointment slot is not long enough to cover all the facts, you should arrange a mutually convenient time to continue the conversation.

Principle 7: respond appropriately

It is important to avoid judging your client – eg, expressing shock or horror at what you hear. The client may have had judgemental responses previously, which may have made it harder for them to talk.

Responses that judge the actions of the client and indicate that they need to be better at budgeting can also reinforce things that the abuser may say to belittle them. Advisers have an opportunity to counter these messages and help rebuild their client's confidence with money. This can, in turn, encourage them to reach out for help from other sources.

It is also important to give a professional response that shows understanding and lets the client know there are things you can do to help relieve the financial pressure they are under and help them regain control of their finances.

Remember that the abuser is controlling their behaviour and that an adviser can help empower them to regain control, rather than tell them what to do.

Principle 8: offer support

By being there, empathising and listening, you are already providing support to the client. There may also be other ways in which you can offer practical help that eases the day-to-day financial burden the client is experiencing.

Discuss with the client the options they have for establishing a more secure economic position, including reducing their outgoings and increasing their income. But remember that the abuse the client is experiencing may mean that some options normally suggested could put them at risk of further harm.

For example, some changes to banking could lead to the bank sending a letter to their address, or an address the abuser has access to. The client will be the best judge of their own safety, so never push them to pursue any action.

Client ID

It is good practice to look at getting new documents in the client's name only, to prevent the perpetrator from taking out new debt. It is also useful to run new credit checks.

Future safeguarding – digital breakup tool

Refuge has a digital tool to help clients distance themselves and their information from their perpetrators. You can browse the tool at refugetechsafety.org/digitalbreakup.

7. Economic abuse and debt

According to a joint report by The Co-operative Bank and Refuge,[4] a large proportion of UK debt could be the direct result of economic abuse perpetrated by a current or former partner.

Coerced debt

Coerced debt is where a person is forced into taking out financial products for someone else's benefit.

Clients may have been made to carry out financial transactions or take out credit in their name by the abuser. For example, the abuser might:
- make the client take out a loan, mortgage or credit card against their wishes or in their name;
- use other sources of credit in the client's name, such as car finance agreements;
- put bills in the client's name, including utility or mobile phone contracts.

Advances in technology, particularly online banking, alongside lenders' willingness to increase credit, can make it easier to carry out economic abuse.

Online banking is commonly used by perpetrators to closely track their partner's accounts and monitor their spending. Perpetrators can set up text alerts on their partner's accounts, impose spending limits and take money out of their accounts using an online banking app without the client's permission.

The impact of coerced debt

An abuser can use debt as a lever to gain power and control over another person, causing financial instability and dependency on the abuser.

A common indicator that a client is experiencing economic abuse is where all the assets have been placed in the abuser's name and the debts in the client's name.

In the short term, the client will have to deal with the stress of this situation and may have little or no opportunity to leave the relationship due to lack of funds. In the long term, it will affect their ability to get credit, save for a deposit to move to a safe place or travel to employment opportunities.

Challenging coerced debt

Some people may wish to challenge the liability of credit agreements they have been coerced into signing. This is not the right option for everyone and will depend on the client's circumstances.

It can be very difficult to have coerced debt recognised by the courts and/or lenders, as they often assume that 'couples' are a financial unit. A client will usually be responsible for repaying the money owing on any credit agreements that are in their name.

There is no general exception for people who have experienced economic abuse and have been coerced into taking out credit.

However, there are some elements of law that may make it possible to challenge the liability for coerced debt in some cases.

- **Consumer credit law**: all organisations providing credit must follow consumer credit law. If they do not, a challenge could be made on this basis.
- **Lender obligations**: the Financial Conduct Authority (FCA) requires all credit providers to treat customers fairly. Challenges can sometimes be made if a lender has not upheld these obligations. These include properly assessing that a customer can afford credit repayments and checking that the customer has not been forced into taking out credit.
- **Contract law**: a contract with a lender may be invalid in cases of economic duress, undue influence or misrepresentation.
- **Fraud**: challenges to the liability of a credit agreement can also be made if the credit was taken out in the client's name without their knowledge. This is known as fraud, and it is a criminal offence. Laws exist to support people who have had credit fraudulently taken out in their name. Clients should report fraud to the lender and the police. It is possible to negotiate with creditors to achieve partial or total write-off and a credit repair where there is agreement that the debt has been obtained fraudulently.

Consumer credit law

Consumer credit is regulated by the Consumer Credit Act 1974 (CCA 1974), amended in 2006. This law protects consumers because it places legal obligations on lenders. If lenders do not meet these obligations, a credit agreement may be unenforceable.

Terms of a credit agreement

The CCA 1974 prescribes terms that must be in all credit agreements. These include:
- a statement of the total amount borrowed (not including charges);
- the rate of interest and if it is variable;
- a notice of cancellation in a required form (if it is cancellable);
- details of how it is to be repaid, and the amount and frequency of payments.

Check the credit agreement carefully to make sure that these terms are included. If any of these terms are not included, you may be able to challenge the agreement.

Note: what terms need to be included can often depend on the date that the agreement was taken out, as the rules change over time. Depending on when the credit agreement was taken out, the lender may also be legally obliged to include other terms in the agreement.

Request for information

The lender must give the customer certain information related to credit agreements in their name.

If requested, they must share with the customer a 'true copy' of the agreement, related documents, and a statement of account. Lenders sometimes provide a 'reconstituted agreement', which has not been signed, instead of a 'true copy'. An agreement may be invalid if it is not signed. However, a court may rule in the lender's favour if they later provide a signed agreement.

Unfair relationships

It is possible to challenge the liability of a credit agreement based on an unfair relationship between the client (as a consumer) and the lender.

A court may find there to be an 'unfair relationship' if the lender has mis-sold a customer a financial product for personal gain – eg, by deliberately misleading them.

The relationship with the abuser will not normally be considered where the court is ruling on an unfair relationship in relation to a credit agreement.

If the court decides that the relationship between the lender and the customer is unfair, they can alter the terms of the credit agreement, reduce the amount owed, make the lender refund any money paid or remove any obligation on the customer to repay.

Lender obligations

All firms that provide financial products and services to customers in the UK are regulated and supervised by the FCA.

The FCA sets out a firm's obligations when providing credit. All firms must comply with these rules. The rules include considering the interests of customers and treating them fairly; communicating information clearly to customers; and taking reasonable care to ensure that customers are given suitable advice.

Failure to assess affordability

Another responsibility that lenders have is to assess a customer's ability to repay the money they have requested to borrow. This is known as an 'affordability assessment' and lenders must do this before any credit agreement can be entered into.

This assessment looks at the risk to the lender as well as the client's ability to repay. The lender will consider whether the repayments would affect the client's wider financial situation or cause financial distress.

If the lender did not do an affordability assessment, or it was insufficient, raise a complaint with the lender, in the first instance, or the Financial Ombudsman Service (FOS).

Undue influence

In cases of coerced debt, most challenges will be made on the basis of 'undue influence' – ie, if a person has taken unfair advantage of their influence over another person. Unfortunately, this can be difficult to prove.

Undue influence does not apply if the lender has:
- advised a customer to take independent legal advice regarding credit agreements in their name; or
- explained to them in private what their responsibilities are and the consequences of not meeting them.

However, a credit agreement with a lender could be voided if there are obvious signs of economic duress or undue influence from a third party, such as a partner, and the lender ignores these signs. For example, there may be a telephone recording of the application, in which the borrower is being coached through the process.

There are also certain situations when the lender is expected to know there is a risk of undue influence. This is called 'constructive knowledge' and applies, for example, if a customer has agreed to act as a guarantor to someone else's borrowing. In these situations, the lender is put 'under notice' of undue influence. This means that the lender must takes steps to ensure that the client is acting of their own free will. In practice, this usually means that the lender must tell the customer to seek independent legal advice.

Challenging the liability of a credit agreement that is in a customer's name is difficult and it will only be possible in a small number of cases. It is not the right course for every debt client. Other debt solutions may be possible, including asking the lender to write off the debt, asking for a repayment plan or one of the statutory debt options available in Scotland, including the Debt Arrangement Scheme and bankruptcy.

When negotiations do not go your way and your client wants to challenge the decision not to write off the debt, you can complain to the FOS. For more information and case studies, see financial-ombudsman.org.uk/consumers/complaints-can-help/complaints/complaints-involve-domestic-economic-abuse.

8. Financial Abuse Code

Members of UK Finance (the trade association for the UK banking and financial services sector) developed the *Financial Abuse Code,* working with charities, victim support and government departments.

First launched in 2018, the Code was created to increase financial firms' awareness and understanding of financial abuse and how to spot it. Three years on from publication, the UK Finance Vulnerability Committee agreed to revisit the Code to ensure that it reflects their deeper understanding of victim-survivors' needs, and to ensure that it is aligned with the Financial Conduct Authority's *Guidance for Firms on the Fair Treatment of Vulnerable Customers*.[5]

Participating firms include Barclays Bank, Clydesdale Bank, Yorkshire Bank, TSB, Lloyds, Halifax and the Bank of Scotland.

Fear of not being believed is a major barrier to victim-survivors disclosing abuse. The act of disclosure can be very challenging for some: it is an important moment for them, and how staff respond to being told about abuse can make a significant difference, which in turn can affect what the victim-survivors do next.

Some of the recommendations in the Financial Abuse Code include:
- review internal data sharing to minimise the number of times customers have to disclose the same information to one organisation;
- support the customer to access appropriate help from elsewhere in the organisation – this may include specialist teams;
- provide guidance material for people affected by financial abuse as part of the assistance for customers – this could be material produced in-house or from organisations that support victims of abuse;
- provide a straightforward process to help victims regain control of services that have been compromised by an abuser accessing them fraudulently or under duress – eg, by using their partner's online banking or their card in an ATM;
- forbearance measures should include referral and signposting to free advice. The customer may also need independent legal advice;
- to manage these requirements, it is recommended that organisations have a clear policy on dealing with financial abuse in intimate partner relationships.

For further information on these recommendations, see UK Finance's website.[6]

Notes

1. Introduction
1 Surviving Economic Abuse, *Impact Report 2022-23*, 2023, impactreport.survivingeconomicabuse.org

2. What is economic abuse
2 See also the *Introduction to Economic Abuse* at malg.org.uk/wp-content/uploads/2020/02/Introduction-to-Economic-Abuse-presentation-MALG-Feb-20.pdf

6. The adviser's role
3 See survivingeconomicabuse.org/im-supporting-someone/resources-for-professionals/conversation-kit-for-money-and-debt-advisors

7. Economic abuse and debt
4 The Co-operative Bank and Refuge, *Know Economic Abuse: 2020 Report*, 2020

8. Financial Abuse Code
5 See ukfinance.org.uk/system/files/2023-11/Financial-Abuse-Code-FINAL.pdf
6 ukfinance.org.uk/system/files/2022-12/Financial-Abuse-Code-2021_Updated_2022.pdf

Chapter 18
Debt when someone dies

This chapter covers:
1. Liability for debts (below)
2. The executor (p413)
3. The estate (p414)
4. Checklist (p416)

1. Liability for debts

People have conflicting beliefs about debt after someone dies. Some believe that any debts end with the person who has died, while some believe that the deceased's relatives are liable and must pay the deceased's debts. The reality lies somewhere in the middle.

For practical advice when someone dies, see *What to Do After a Death in Scotland*, available on the Scottish government website.[1]

General liability

Debts do not end when someone dies. Instead, they must be paid off by the executor of the estate, using the money and other property left behind when the debt owner dies. Any assets in the deceased's estate are first used to pay the funeral expenses and any costs incurred when they were dying, known as 'deathbed expenses'. The rest is used to pay off debts, then the beneficiaries of the estate.

If there is not enough money to pay off the deceased's debts in full, the estate is effectively insolvent. Money cannot be paid to beneficiaries in the will until all remaining debts are paid.

If someone in financial difficulty dies, their spouse, partner or family member may be concerned that they will be responsible for their debts. This is not the case as no one else is required to pay their debts unless they are jointly liable for the debt – eg, if they had a joint loan or they were guarantor.

A debt adviser should look at all the debts and check liability.

Sole liability

Debts solely in the name of the person who died either need to be written off if the person did not have any assets or be repaid through the deceased's estate. The deceased's partner does not normally become responsible for the debt.

Therefore, checking liability for every debt is important as creditors may attempt to claim the debt from a spouse or partner.

Joint liability

If the person who died had a debt which is joint and several, the other person listed in the agreement can be pursued for the full amount owing – eg, council tax debt. This is also the case if the person who died took out a joint personal loan or where someone acted as the guarantor for the loan. Utility companies may argue that others living in the deceased's home were beneficial users and should pay the debt, but this is not correct and should be challenged. Seek expert advice on this.

The family home

If the deceased owned a home, funds from the sale of it must be used to pay off any debts secured over the home first, such as a mortgage. If there is any equity left over once that is done, it will then be used to pay off ordinary unsecured debts, such as credit cards and loans, and then the beneficiaries of the estate. Estates dealing with property should be referred to a solicitor.

Where the property is in joint names, seek expert advice.

2. The executor

An executor is a representative of the deceased; they must pay off any debts or taxes from the person's estate and any remaining funds are then distributed to beneficiaries. An executor may be named in the will. If no one is named as executor, the solicitor or the sheriff clerk will arrange for the court to appoint an executor called an 'executor dative'. They are usually the deceased's surviving spouse or civil partner or another person entitled to inherit from the estate.

The executor's role is to administer the estate until it is completed. They must:
- make an inventory of the deceased's estate;
- 'ingather the estate' (this means creating a list of all the deceased's estate consisting of assets and liabilities and everything the deceased owned, less any debts due);
- pay inheritance tax if due (inheritance tax is payable if the estate exceeds the limit set by HMRC).[2]

When reviewing a deceased person's debts, the first step should be to work out what debts are left and what kind of debts they are. Papers and financial statements will need to be checked to compile a list of everything owed. If there is a guarantor for any debts, they remain responsible for any debt covered by the agreement if the estate does not pay it.

Confirmation

Confirmation is a legal document provided by a court which gives the executor authority to uplift money or property belonging to the deceased from the holder, such as a bank, and distribute it according to law. An application to obtain confirmation is lodged with the sheriff court. The application for confirmation must include an inventory of the deceased's property at the time of death. Confirmation is only possible if the inventory includes at least one item of money or property in Scotland.

There are two types of confirmation:
- small estates – where the total value of the estate is less than £36,000;
- large estates – where the total value of the estate is over £36,000.

The forms used and fees to be paid are different depending on the type of estate. If the estate is small, the sheriff clerk can help prepare the inventory. For a large estate, legal advice is recommended.

3. The estate

An estate is everything owned by the deceased. It may be made up of:
- money, including cash, money in a bank account and money from life insurance policies;
- money owed to the deceased;
- shares and investments;
- property;
- personal belongings such as a car, jewellery or other items of value – eg, antiques.

Any debts owed by the deceased are paid out of the estate before any money is paid to the beneficiaries.

Dealing with the estate

The executor must ingather the estate. They make a list of all the deceased's estate consisting of assets and liabilities, referred to as the 'inventory of estate'. The inventory should contain everything the deceased owned, less debts due and bring out a final amount due to be distributed.

Once ingathering has started, the executor can start paying off the debts due, including funeral costs. The debts must be paid off in an order of priority.

Chapter 18: Debt when someone dies
3. The estate

Debts such as funeral and administration expenses are 'privileged' and will be paid first. Any tax due to HMRC is payable; this is important as if the executor fails to pay the correct tax, they become personally liable for any shortfall. Legal advice is strongly recommended.

The estate should not be distributed until six months has passed since the date of death to allow anyone with a claim on the estate to make their claim known.

There is a service that you can use, called 'Tell us once', where you can enter the client's details once and this will be shared with HMRC, DWP, Social Security Scotland, the local council and others. You can find more information at gov.uk/after-a-death/organisations-you-need-to-contact-and-tell-us-once.

Hierarchy of debts

The priority for payment of unsecured debts becomes relevant when there are insufficient funds in the deceased's estate to cover all outstanding debts.

The order of priority for payment of debts on death in Scotland is as follows.[3]

- Deathbed, funeral and administration expenses from the deceased's estates are 'privileged debts' and are payable before all other debts.
- 'Preferred debts' will be paid next. This will include contributions to pension schemes and payments owed to the deceased's employees, if applicable.
- 'Ordinary debts' are paid finally. These are all other debts which are not secured.

Impact on debt solutions already in place

Insolvency

If the deceased was in bankruptcy or a protected trust deed and the trustee has not been discharged, the trustee will wind up the estate. They can cash in any life policies belonging to the deceased and use them to pay outstanding debts and costs of winding the estate up. The trustee has a legal responsibility to pay the funeral and deathbed expenses, but their fees and expenses get priority treatment for payment from the estate.[4]

Debt Payment Programmes

Under the Debt Arrangement Scheme, the Debt Payment Programme (DPP) is revoked on the client's death.[5] All interest, penalties, charges and fees are reapplied and must be dealt with by the executor. If the client was in a joint DPP, it will be revoked. The revocation will have no effect for 14 days. The partner in the joint DPP must apply for a new DPP, but only for the debts for which they are liable.

Creditors

Creditors need to be contacted to inform them of the death, and to reduce the stress of creditors demanding payment on the deceased's family. They must be informed that the client is going through the legal process of dealing with the person's estate. Good practice is to send a copy of the death certificate to all creditors.

A creditor owed over £5,000 can apply for the sequestration of the deceased's estate by petitioning the court.[6] Unless the apparent insolvency of the deceased was established four months prior to death, the creditor must wait six months after the death of the person before they can present a petition for sequestration.

Where there is no estate

If there is no estate, the deceased's partner or family cannot be held liable for debts if they were not taken out jointly or if they did not act as a guarantor.

Creditors should be contacted and informed of the death. They can be sent a copy of the death certificate. They must also be informed that there is no money in the estate and asked to confirm that the account is closed.

Where there is some estate

If the deceased's estate cannot cover the debts in full, the estate is technically insolvent and the executor will cease dealing with the deceased's property. The executor, once aware the estate is insolvent, can apply for the estate to be sequestrated. Anyone who is entitled to be appointed as an executor can apply for sequestration of an insolvent estate.

The executor will make an application to the Accountant in Bankruptcy. The application of sequestration proceeds in the same way as a normal sequestration using the BASYS system (see Chapter 6), either by the executor using an accredited money adviser, or by passing the case to an insolvency practitioner.

The executor is only liable to pay the deceased's debts up to the extent the funds in the estate allow them to. For example, if the total debts are £10,000 and, after paying funeral and deathbed expenses, the estate is only worth £3,000, the executor is only responsible for paying £3,000. In these cases, the estate should be made bankrupt or alternative solutions such as offers of composition can be made.

4. Checklist
- Identify the executor.
- Identify debts which are the sole liability of the deceased.
- Identify which debts are jointly liable.
- Identify which debts can be written off.
- Pay off privileged debts first.
- Consider whether bankruptcy is an option.
- Help the surviving partner or family member choose a relevant debt solution.

Notes

1. **Liability for debts**
   1 gov.scot/publications/death-scotland-practical-advice-times-bereavement-revised-11th-edition-2016-9781786522726

2. **The executor**
   2 See gov.uk/inheritance-tax

3. **The estate**
   3 thegazette.co.uk/wills-and-probate/what-to-do-when-someone-dies-executor-duties
   4 s129(1) B(S)A 2016
   5 Reg 14 The Debt Arrangement Scheme (Scotland) Amendment Regulations 2013 No.225
   6 s7 B(S)A 2016

Chapter 19

Benefits and other payments

This chapter covers:
1. Introduction (below)
2. How to use this chapter (p420)
3. A–Z of benefits and tax credits (p422)
4. A–Z of other financial help (p440)

1. Introduction

When advising a client about their debt and expenditure, it is also important to advise them about maximising their income. You can do so by checking that:
- they receive all the benefits to which they are entitled, and they are paid the correct amount; *and*
- their tax liability is as low as possible; *and*
- all possible sources of income have been explored.

If you are not a welfare rights specialist, you should consider consulting with colleagues who are, signposting the client to a website considered appropriate by your agency or referring cases to someone who can undertake this work.

As a debt adviser, you need a working knowledge of benefits. CPAG publishes books and online resources to help advisers navigate the benefits system – see cpag.org.uk/welfare-rights. CPAG also runs benefits training for non-benefits advisers – see cpag.org.uk/training for details. Materials and tools are also available on the Money and Pensions Service website at debtquality.org.uk. This chapter assumes general advice knowledge, but cannot explain all the ways in which income can be maximised. Instead, it describes some common ways of increasing income for people in debt.

The rules of entitlement to benefits are in detailed regulations. Many terms are not described fully here and if you are unfamiliar with them, consult CPAG's *Welfare Benefits and Tax Credits Handbook*, which is fully referenced to the law, including caselaw.

The criteria for entitlement are strict and must be met. In particular, these include the following.

Chapter 19: Benefits and other payments
1. Introduction

- **Claims.** Most benefits must be claimed, either online, on a paper form or by making a telephone claim to the DWP, HMRC, the local authority or Social Security Scotland (SSS). Satisfying the rules of entitlement is not enough; if a claim is not made for a benefit, the client cannot receive it.
- **Time limits.** There are strict time limits in the benefit system. If your client has been given a deadline to do something connected with their benefits, you should help them to meet it, or contact the authority that pays the benefit immediately if this is not possible. Although extensions are sometimes available, you should not assume that one will be granted, or that there will be flexibility for your client if they miss a deadline.
- **Backdating.** Some benefits can be backdated, but the rules vary and some important basic benefits, like universal credit (UC), are difficult to backdate.
- **Appeals.** There is a right to appeal most benefit decisions, including whether or not to award benefit. For many DWP benefits, clients must apply for a decision to be reconsidered (known as a 'mandatory reconsideration') before they can appeal. Appeals must be made in writing. This is usually done online or by using an official form. They must be submitted within a maximum of 13 months. For SSS benefits, clients must apply for a 'redetermination' before they can appeal. Appeals can be made by phone, in writing or for some benefits only, online. Appeals must be made within a maximum of one year of clients being notified of the redetermination. Errors by the authority paying the benefit can be common, but if the client does not appeal an incorrect decision, they may lose out.
- **Residence and immigration tests.** Most benefits have residence, presence and immigration tests. A client who is a 'person subject to immigration control', sponsored or an asylum seeker has limited access to most of the benefits in this chapter. Specialist immigration advice should always be obtained for such clients. In addition, most means-tested benefits have residence tests. These mainly affect European Union nationals. Refer to CPAG's *Benefits for Migrants Handbook* for more information.
- **Changes in circumstances.** A client must notify the authority that pays their benefits about any changes of circumstances that might affect their entitlement or the amount – eg, if they are claiming a benefit on the basis of being out of work and then get a job. If they do not do so, they may have been overpaid.
- **Overpayments.** If your client has been overpaid an amount of benefit or tax credits, they may have to pay it back. For some benefits, these overpayments must be paid back even when they were due to an error by the authority that pays the benefit. The rules vary for different benefits and there are important rules about appealing an overpayment or asking for recovery to be 'waived'.
- **Deductions from benefits.** Deductions can be made from benefits for a wide variety of charges or debts – eg, for fuel or rent arrears. Some deductions can be reduced or paused in certain circumstances.

Chapter 19: Benefits and other payments
2. How to use this chapter

The benefits system is complex, and there are many ways of categorising benefits. It can be helpful to think of benefits as falling into three types.
- **Contributions-based benefits** – eg, contribution-based jobseeker's allowance (JSA), contributory employment and support allowance (ESA) and retirement pension. Typically, these are based on national insurance contributions and are not means tested. If a client has worked or been self-employed in the past, they may qualify for a contribution-based earnings-replacement benefit.
- **Benefits that depend on a person's circumstances** – eg, adult disability payment and child benefit. These are paid because the client has certain needs or falls into a certain category – eg, they have a disability or a child.
- **Means-tested benefits or tax credits** – eg, UC, pension credit and housing benefit. A client may also have an existing award of income-related ESA, income-based JSA, income support or tax credits, but no new claims can be made for these benefits because they are being replaced by UC. Means-tested benefits top up a client's benefit and/or other income to a certain level, sometimes referred to as the 'safety net'.

2. How to use this chapter

The table on pp421–22 lists common circumstances and the benefits it may be possible to claim in those circumstances. A client may be eligible for several benefits, so you should check all the headings that could be relevant.

The A–Z of the most common benefits (see p422) outlines the main eligibility criteria for each benefit. This chapter cannot describe fully the entitlement conditions for every benefit. It is a guide to which benefits you should consider that may be appropriate for a client.

Other sources of financial help that may be available to clients are listed on pp440–47.

For more detailed information, see CPAG's *Welfare Benefits and Tax Credits Handbook*.

Which benefits and tax credits can a client claim

The table gives a non-exhaustive overview of the possible benefits and tax credits to which a client may be entitled depending on their circumstances. More than one circumstance may apply to a particular client (eg, they may have a child, a disability, a mortgage and work part-time), in which case you should refer to all relevant headings.

Chapter 19: Benefits and other payments
2. How to use this chapter

Circumstance	Potential benefits and tax credits
Bereaved	Bereavement support payment
	Funeral support payment
	Statutory parental bereavement pay
Carer	Carer's allowance or carer support payment
	Universal credit with a carer element
	Income support (existing awards only)
	Young carer grant
Responsible for a child	Child tax credit
	Universal credit with a child element(s)
	Child benefit
	Guardian's allowance
	Scottish child payment
	Statutory maternity pay
	Statutory paternity pay
	Statutory shared parental pay
	Statutory adoption pay
	Maternity allowance
	Health benefits
	Best Start grant
	Best Start foods
Disabled	Personal independence payment
	Adult disability payment
	Disability living allowance
	Child disability payment
Pensioner	Attendance allowance
	Pension age disability payment
	Industrial injuries benefits
	Retirement pension
	Pension credit
	Universal credit (in some cases where your partner is not yet pension age)
	Winter fuel payment
	Pension age winter heating payment
Pregnant	Statutory maternity pay
	Maternity allowance
	Health benefits
	Best Start grant
	Best Start foods
Paying rent	Universal credit
	Housing benefit (existing awards and certain types of housing only)
	Discretionary housing payments

Chapter 19: Benefits and other payments
3. A–Z of benefits and tax credits

Sick and unable to work	Contributory employment and support allowance
	Income-related employment and support allowance (existing awards only)
	Statutory sick pay
	Universal credit
Unemployed and seeking work	Contributory jobseeker's allowance
	Income-based jobseeker's allowance (existing claims only)
	Universal credit
Unemployed and not seeking work	Universal credit
	Income support (existing claims only)
Working, but on a low income	Universal credit
	Working tax credit

3. A–Z of benefits and tax credits

Unless otherwise stated, all the benefits referred to in this section are claimed from and paid by the DWP. For more information and the current rates, see CPAG's *Welfare Benefits and Tax Credits Handbook*.

Adult disability payment

Adult disability payment (ADP) has replaced personal independence payment (PIP) for new claims from people living in Scotland. People getting PIP or working-age disability living allowance (DLA) who live in Scotland are gradually being transferred to ADP.

ADP is a benefit for people who have care and/or mobility needs as a result of a physical or mental disability or health condition. It is for working-age clients but can often continue to be paid after pension age. It is paid by Social Security Scotland (SSS).

ADP has two components – a daily living component and a mobility component. Each component has two rates – a standard rate and an enhanced rate.

Entitlement to ADP is determined by testing the difficulty a client has performing a specified list of activities. Points are given for each activity and benefit is awarded once a specified number of points is reached. Clients may be asked to take part in an assessment consultation which usually takes place over the phone.

To qualify for ADP, a client must usually have met the conditions for 13 weeks and be expected to meet them for at least a further 39 weeks. However, a client who is terminally ill (ie, who has a progressive disease that can reasonably be expected to cause their death) is normally awarded the enhanced rate of both components. This can be backdated to the date they were first judged to be terminally ill if they claim ADP within 26 weeks. If they claim later than this, ADP can be backdated for 26 weeks.

An award of ADP always makes a household better off. It is not means tested, taxable or based on national insurance (NI) contributions. Entitlement to ADP may mean that a client becomes entitled to a means-tested benefit or to an increased amount of a benefit that is already being paid. Someone who spends time caring for the client may also be able to claim carer's allowance (CA) or carer support payment (CSP) (see p425) and/or get the carer element of universal credit (UC) (see p437). If a client is under 19 and gets the enhanced rate of the daily living component of ADP during a qualifying week in September, they will be entitled to child winter heating payment. Child winter heating payment is an annual payment which is paid automatically by SSS.

ADP cannot be backdated unless the client is terminally ill.

Attendance allowance

Attendance allowance (AA) is a benefit for clients who are pension age or over when they first claim and who have a mental or physical health condition or disability. To get the lower rate of AA, they must usually need:
- frequent help with personal care throughout the day; *or*
- continual supervision throughout the day to avoid danger to themselves or others; *or*
- repeated or prolonged attention at night to help with personal care; *or*
- for another person to be awake for a prolonged period or at frequent intervals at night to avoid danger to the client or others.

If a client meets one of the daytime conditions *and* one of the night-time conditions, they will be paid the higher rate of AA.

Clients must satisfy these conditions for at least six months before they can get AA. However, people who are terminally ill (ie, who have a progressive disease from which they could reasonably be expected to die within 12 months) should be awarded the higher rate of AA immediately.

An award of AA always makes a client better off. It is not means tested and does not count as income when calculating means-tested benefits and tax credits. Entitlement to AA may actually increase a client's entitlement to a means-tested benefit, or mean that they are entitled to a means-tested benefit that they could not get before. An award of AA could also mean that a client's carer could claim CA or CSP (see p425) and/or get the carer element of UC (see p437) for looking after them.

AA cannot be backdated. It is not taxable.

AA is going to be replaced by pension age disability payment in Scotland. It is being piloted in some areas from October 2024, followed by a gradual roll-out across the country starting in early 2025. Pension age disability payment will be paid by SSS.

Bereavement support payment

Bereavement support payment replaces the 'old' bereavement benefits (bereavement payment, widowed parent's allowance and bereavement allowance) for people whose spouse, civil partner or (in some cases) co-habiting partner died on or after 6 April 2017. If the death was before 6 April 2017, clients may be entitled to the 'old' bereavement benefits.

To qualify, the client's late spouse, civil partner or cohabiting partner (where applicable) must either have paid sufficient NI contributions or been an employee and died as a result of an industrial accident or disease. In addition, the client must be under state pension age.

There are two rates of bereavement support payment:
- the standard rate, comprising an initial lump sum and a monthly amount; *and*
- the higher rate, payable to pregnant women and those with dependent children, comprising a higher initial lump sum and a higher monthly amount.

Bereavement support payment is paid for a maximum of 18 months after the death and must normally be claimed within 12 months of the death. It is automatically backdated for up to three months, to the date of death.

The initial lump sum is disregarded as capital for means-tested benefits for the first 12 months and the monthly allowance is disregarded as income for means-tested benefits and tax credits.

Best Start grants and food

The Best Start grants and Best Start food are paid by SSS. The Best Start grant is a package of three payments.
- The pregnancy and baby payment is a grant to help with the costs of being pregnant or having a new baby if clients are on a low income or if they are under 18 and are pregnant or have a child. It can be claimed from after the 24th week of pregnancy until six months after the birth in most cases. A higher amount is paid for a first child and a smaller grant is paid for any subsequent children.
- The early learning payment is a one-off grant to help with the costs of having a pre-school child. It can be claimed from a child's second birthday up until the child is three and a half. Clients must have a low income or be under 18 to qualify.
- The school age payment is a one-off grant to help with the costs of having a school-age child. It can be claimed from 1 June in the year that the child could first start school until the last day of February in the following year.

Best Start foods is a prepayment card available to claimants who are pregnant or responsible for a child aged under three. Claimants must be receiving a qualifying benefit or be aged under 18. The prepayment card is credited with a higher amount for a child aged under one and a lower amount for pregnant women or children aged one or two.

Carer's allowance and carer support payment

CA is being replaced by CSP for carers in Scotland. CSP is paid by SSS. CSP was introduced for new claims in pilot areas on 19 November 2023 and is being gradually rolled out in the rest of Scotland during 2024.

CA and CSP are benefits for clients who are providing regular and substantial care (35 hours a week or more) for someone who is in receipt of:
- AA (or pension age disability payment when available);
- the middle or highest rate of the care component of child disability payment (CDP) or DLA;
- either rate of the daily living component of ADP or PIP;
- armed forces independence payment, or constant attendance allowance paid with an industrial injuries disablement benefit or a war disablement pension.

This includes caring for a partner, family member, friend or neighbour.

Clients who claim CA or CSP may be entitled to an extra amount, called a 'carer premium' in a means-tested benefit or a 'carer element' in UC. This is the case even if CA or CSP is not paid because of special rules on 'overlapping benefits'.

Note: a claim for CA or CSP can mean that the cared-for person receives less in means-tested benefits and so a detailed better-off calculation may be needed. Clients should usually be referred for specialist advice before claiming CA or CSP.

CA and CSP are not means tested, but clients cannot get either benefit if they have earnings above a set limit. CA and CSP are taken into account in full as income for means-tested benefits and tax credits. CA and CSP are taxable.

If you get CA or CSP and live in Scotland, you get a carer's allowance supplement once every six months. This is paid by SSS to increase the amount of money that carers get. The supplement is expected to be paid until CSP is fully rolled out in Scotland. There is a qualifying date for each six-monthly payment. If you are receiving CA or CSP on that date, you will automatically be paid the supplement.

Carers aged 16, 17 or 18 can get a young carer grant if they provide an average of 16 hours' care per week to a disabled person. The disabled person must be getting one of the same qualifying benefits as for CA or CSP. The young carer cannot get the grant if they were entitled to CA or CSP on the date of the claim. The grant is paid once a year and cannot be claimed if another person has claimed a young carer grant for caring for the same person. The young carer grant is paid by SSS.

Chapter 19: Benefits and other payments
3. A–Z of benefits and tax credits

Child benefit

Child benefit is a benefit for clients who are responsible for a child under 16 or a 'qualifying young person' aged 16 to 20 who meets certain conditions, such as being enrolled on a course of full-time, non-advanced education or on approved training.

To be responsible for a child or qualifying young person, the client must live with the child or contribute to the cost of supporting them of at least the child benefit rate.

Child benefit is not means tested, and can be paid in addition to other benefits and tax credits. Child benefit is not taxable, unless a client or their partner individually earns more than £60,000 a year. Child benefit is claimed from and paid by HMRC.

Child benefit is not affected by the 'two-child limit'.

Child disability payment

CDP is a benefit for children and young people in Scotland with disabilities or long-term health conditions. It is paid by SSS.

CDP has replaced DLA for children and young people living in Scotland.

CDP has two components.

To qualify for the '**care component**', the child must need:
- help with personal care for a significant portion of the day; *or*
- frequent help with personal care throughout the day; *or*
- continual supervision throughout the day to avoid danger to the child or others; *or*
- frequent or prolonged supervision at night to avoid danger; *or*
- prolonged or repeated attention at night.

Children qualify for the '**mobility component**' if:
- they are unable or virtually unable to walk; *or*
- the exertion needed to walk would lead to a danger to their life or deterioration in their condition; *or*
- they have no legs or feet; *or*
- they are both blind and deaf; *or*
- they have a severe visual impairment; *or*
- they are terminally ill; *or*
- they have a severe mental impairment, have severe behavioural problems and are entitled to the highest rate of the care component (see p427); *or*
- they need guidance or supervision on unfamiliar routes.

CDP care component is paid at three different rates and the mobility component at two different rates. Which rate is awarded depends on which needs the child has from the list above. Children can get the care component or the mobility component or both. They can receive the higher rate of the mobility component from age three, the lower rate of the mobility component from age five and any rate of the care component from age three months.

The child must satisfy the conditions above for at least 13 weeks before the start of the award and be likely to continue to satisfy them for at least the next 26 weeks. However, a child who is terminally ill (ie, who has a progressive disease that can reasonably be expected to cause their death) should be awarded the higher rate of both components. CDP can be backdated to the date they were first judged to be terminally ill if they claim CDP within 26 weeks. If they claim later than this, it can be backdated for 26 weeks.

An award of CDP for a child will always make a family better off. It is not means tested and does not count as income when calculating means-tested benefits and tax credits. If a client's child gets CDP, this may mean that the client becomes entitled to a means-tested benefit, or a higher amount of benefit that is already being paid. The client may also be able to claim CA or CSP (see p425) and/or get the carer element of UC (see p437). If a client's child gets the highest rate of the care component of CDP during a qualifying week in September, they will be entitled to child winter heating payment. Child winter heating payment is an annual payment which is paid automatically by SSS.

CDP cannot be backdated unless the child is terminally ill. It is not taxable.

Child tax credit

Note: child tax credit (CTC) is affected by the introduction of UC (see p437). It is no longer possible to make a new claim for CTC, although a client may be able to get it for the first time if they already receive working tax credit (WTC). It is not possible to be entitled to CTC and UC at the same time. A claim for UC causes CTC to be terminated.

CTC is paid to clients who are responsible for a child or qualifying young person (see p426). A client counts as responsible for a child if the child normally lives with them. CTC is affected by the 'two-child limit', meaning that your client may not get CTC in respect of third or later children born after 5 April 2017.

CTC is paid in addition to child benefit and can also be paid alongside most other benefits. People entitled to income support (IS), income-based jobseeker's allowance (JSA), income-related employment and support allowance (ESA) or pension credit (PC) automatically get maximum CTC, but it counts as income for housing benefit (HB), except for people who are have reached the qualifying age for PC (see p433).

CTC is claimed from and paid by HMRC and is means tested. The means test for tax credits is different from that for benefits, and is based on annual income. CTC is not taxable.

Disability living allowance

DLA has been replaced by CDP for children and young people living in Scotland. Some adults who claimed DLA in the past continue to receive it and in the future may move on to ADP or a new benefit called Scottish adult disability living allowance which is expected to be introduced in 2025. No new claims can be made for DLA in Scotland. DLA is not covered in this *Handbook*.

Employment and support allowance

Note: ESA is affected by the introduction of UC (see p437).

ESA is a benefit for clients who cannot work because of an illness or disability. Employees usually claim statutory sick pay (SSP) for the first 28 weeks of illness rather than ESA. Self-employed and unemployed people claim ESA straight away.

There are two types of ESA.
- **Contributory ESA (sometimes called 'new-style ESA')**, which is paid if a client satisfies the NI contribution conditions. It is not means tested. It is only paid for 52 weeks, except if the claimant is in the 'support group' (see below). Contributory ESA is *not* being replaced by UC.
- **Income-related ESA**, which is means tested and has no NI contribution test or maximum duration. It is possible to receive contributory ESA topped up with income-related ESA. Income-related ESA is being replaced by UC and a client cannot make a new claim for it.

A basic allowance of ESA is paid during an initial 'assessment phase' of 13 weeks. The amount paid could be higher if, for example, it includes disability premiums. The client's ability for work is then assessed by the DWP under a 'work capability assessment'. A small number of people are automatically treated as having limited capability for work and do not have to undergo this assessment – eg, people who are terminally ill, those receiving or recovering from certain types of chemotherapy and hospital patients.

After the initial assessment phase, clients who pass a medical assessment go on to the 'main phase' of ESA. Clients are put into either:
- the 'work-related activity group' and must attend work-focused interviews and undertake work-related activity. They may get an extra amount of ESA called the work-related activity component, but few claimants can now get this; *or*
- the 'support group' and have no work-related requirements. They also get an extra amount of ESA called the support component.

Clients in the work-related activity group may have their benefit reduced by a sanction if they do not attend a work-focused interview or carry out work-related activity. There is a right to appeal this and it is always worth considering whether a sanction could be challenged. Clients whose income-related ESA has been reduced by a sanction may qualify for hardship payments.

The general rule is that people cannot get ESA if they are working. Clients can do some limited work (called 'permitted work') while on ESA, but they must notify the DWP and they can lose their ESA entitlement if they earn more than a certain amount. Clients affected by these rules may need specialist advice.

Contributory ESA is not means tested, but it is affected by any income from certain pensions and is subject to the 'overlapping benefit' rules. It can be 'topped up' with income-related ESA or with UC.

Income-related ESA is a 'passporting' benefit, which means that it can help the client to get maximum HB, help with health costs, free school meals for their children, budgeting loans and Scottish benefits such as funeral support payment. Extra amounts of income-related ESA, called premiums, can be paid depending on the circumstances of the client and their partner.

Contributory ESA is taxable; income-related ESA is not.

Funeral support payment

Funeral support payment is a one-off grant to help with the costs of a funeral. It replaced the social fund funeral payment in Scotland and is paid by SSS.

The client must be responsible for the funeral arrangements, it must be reasonable for them to have accepted responsibility and they must be receiving a qualifying benefit, such as UC or PC for example. Some of the assets of the person who has died can be deducted from the funeral support payment. Clients can claim a funeral support payment at any time from the date the person died until six months after the funeral.

Guardian's allowance

Guardian's allowance is a benefit paid to a client who is responsible for a child who is effectively an orphan. Clients can be paid it if they are entitled to child benefit for a child:
- whose parents have died; *or*
- where one of the child's parents has died and either the whereabouts of the other parent is unknown, or the other parent has been sentenced to a term of imprisonment of two years or more or is detained in hospital by a court order.

Guardian's allowance is not means tested, does not count as income for other benefits and tax credits, and can be paid in addition to child benefit. It is claimed from and paid by HMRC.

Health benefits

In Scotland, most NHS services are free, including prescriptions and eye and dental checks.

Clients might have to pay for some other services, such as NHS dental treatment and glasses and contact lenses. They might be exempt from these

Chapter 19: Benefits and other payments
3. A–Z of benefits and tax credits

charges or be able to claim a reduction on low-income grounds. They can be exempt either because they are getting a qualifying benefit or because they are in one of the exempt groups.

Clients can get free NHS dental treatment, vouchers for glasses and contact lenses and certain fares to hospitals if they receive:
- UC and either have no earnings or have earnings below a certain amount;
- IS;
- income-related ESA;
- income-based JSA;
- the guarantee credit of PC;
- CTC and they are not eligible for WTC – eg, because they do not work enough hours to qualify;
- CTC *and* WTC;
- WTC that includes a disability or severe disability element and they have income below an income threshold.

Clients who do not get any of the above benefits might be able to get help under the NHS low income scheme. They should apply directly to the NHS Business Services Authority by completing an HC1 form. This form should be available from community pharmacies, GP practices, Citizens Advice Bureaux and Jobcentre plus offices.

There are different rules for exemption from NHS dental treatment, help with glasses and contact lenses and help with travel costs. For example, dental treatment is free for women who are pregnant or who have given birth in the last 12 months as well as for young people aged under 26 years old. Young people aged 16 to 18 in full-time education can get help with the cost of glasses and contact lenses.

Housing benefit

Note: HB is affected by the introduction of UC (see p437).

HB is a means-tested benefit, claimed from and paid by local authorities to tenants to help with the cost of their rent. HB can be paid to people in and out of work.

Clients in private rented accommodation may not have their full rent covered by their HB if their rent is more than a local housing allowance for their area. This is based on the number of bedrooms a client is allowed under the rules and the local housing allowance rates set by the rent officer.

Clients in local authority or housing association accommodation may not have their full rent covered by their HB if they are living in a property that has more bedrooms than they are allowed (known as the 'bedroom tax').

Clients in any type of housing could find that their HB does not cover their full rent if:

Chapter 19: Benefits and other payments
3. A–Z of benefits and tax credits

- their household income from benefits is above a certain amount (known as the 'benefit cap'); *or*
- their rent includes non-eligible charges, such as fuel, water or some service charges; *or*
- if a non-dependant (eg, a relative or friend) lives with the client.

Clients entitled to IS, income-based JSA, income-related ESA or the guarantee credit of PC are usually entitled to HB, but they must make a separate claim. Clients not on a means-tested benefit can also qualify for HB if their income is sufficiently low and they have capital below a certain amount (£16,000 for most clients). There is no capital limit for clients who get the guarantee credit of PC.

Most working-age clients can no longer start a new claim for HB. If they want to start getting help with housing costs, they must claim UC instead. However, people already getting HB can continue receiving it until they are asked to move to UC, and pensioners and people living in certain types of housing (eg, supported accommodation and some types of temporary accommodation) *can* still make new claims for HB.

Claims for HB can be backdated for a maximum of one month if a client can show good cause for claiming late. Clients or their partners not in receipt of IS, income-based JSA or income-related ESA who are at least pension age can get HB backdated for up to three months without needing to show a good cause.

Clients whose HB does not cover the whole amount of their rent can apply for a discretionary housing payment (DHP) to help make up the shortfall (see p441). DHPs are paid from a cash-limited budget and are not guaranteed.

HB and DHPs are not taxable.

Income support

Note: IS is being replaced by UC (see p437). It is not possible to make a new claim for IS. Clients already getting IS can continue to do so until they are asked to claim UC instead.

IS is a means-tested benefit that provides basic financial support for clients on a low income who are not expected to look for work.

IS pays a basic amount for the client and their partner, if they have one. Some people who have been getting IS since before 2004 may also receive amounts for their children. IS is a 'passporting' benefit – ie, it can help the client get maximum HB, help with health costs, free school meals for their children, budgeting loans and Scottish benefits such as funeral support payment. Extra amounts can be paid depending on the circumstances of the client and their partner – eg, premiums for carers or because of a disability.

IS is not taxable.

Industrial injuries disablement benefit

Industrial injuries disablement benefit (IIDB) is for clients who:
- have a personal injury while working as an employee – eg, from an accident at work; *or*
- have a prescribed industrial disease contracted during the course of their employment – eg, asbestosis.

Clients must be assessed as having a degree of disablement resulting from a loss of faculty – eg, a reduced ability to walk because of arthritis. Clients can get IIDB if they are still in work. It can be paid on top of contributory ESA and other non-means-tested benefits. IIDB is not taxable. It generally counts as income for the purposes of calculating means-tested benefits, but is disregarded as income for tax credits.

Jobseeker's allowance

Note: income-based JSA is affected by the introduction of UC (see p437).

JSA provides basic financial support for people who are expected to look for work. There are two types of JSA.
- **Contribution-based JSA (sometimes called 'new-style JSA')**, which is paid for six months to those who have recently paid NI contributions. Contribution-based JSA is *not* being replaced by UC.
- **Income-based JSA**, which is means tested with no requirement to have paid NI contributions. Income-related JSA is being replaced by UC and a client cannot make a new claim for it.

Income-based JSA pays a basic amount for the client and their partner, if they have one. Some people who have been getting income-based JSA since before 2004 may also receive amounts for their children. Income-based JSA is a 'passporting' benefit – ie, it can help the client get maximum HB, help with health costs, free school meals for their children, budgeting loans and Scottish benefits such as funeral support payment. Extra amounts can be paid depending on the client's circumstances – eg, if they are caring for someone or have a disability.

Contribution-based JSA pays a basic amount for the client and is only paid for six months. Contribution-based JSA can be 'topped up' with income-based JSA or UC.

Clients may have their JSA reduced by a sanction if they do not comply with certain 'jobseeking conditions' (eg, attending interviews) and for other things, such as losing a job because of misconduct, giving up work without a good reason or for not participating in specified training or employment schemes. There is a right to appeal, and it is always worth considering whether a sanction could be challenged.

Clients can apply for hardship payments if their JSA is not paid because of a sanction and they are considered to be in a vulnerable group – eg, carers, and people who have a disability or children.

JSA is taxable.

Maternity allowance

Maternity allowance (MA) is a benefit for women who are pregnant or who have recently given birth. It is normally claimed by women who do not qualify for statutory maternity pay (SMP) – eg, self-employed women, those not currently in work or those who have not worked for the same employer for long enough to get SMP. To qualify for MA, the client must have been employed or self-employed for at least 26 of the 66 weeks before the week in which the baby is due, and have had average weekly earnings of at least £30 a week in 13 weeks of this 'test' period.

MA is not taxable.

Pension credit

PC is a benefit for people on a low income who are at least pension age. A client's pension age depends on their date of birth. Pension age is currently 66 (as of 2024) and will eventually go up to 68.

PC is made up of a guarantee credit and a savings credit.

The guarantee credit is the basic amount paid for the client and their partner. It is means tested, but there is no limit on how much capital a client can have.

Extra amounts of guarantee credit can be paid depending on the client's circumstances – eg, if they are caring for someone or have a disability. PC is a 'passporting' benefit – ie, it can help the client get maximum HB, free school meals for their children, budgeting loans and Scottish benefits such as funeral support payment.

The savings credit is an additional amount of PC, paid to clients who have qualifying income (eg, retirement pension) over a certain amount. However, savings credit is being phased out and is only available for people who reached pension age before 6 April 2016.

PC is not taxable.

Personal independence payment

PIP is being replaced by ADP in Scotland. Clients cannot make a new claim for PIP in Scotland. People living in Scotland who are getting PIP will be transferred to ADP without having to make a claim.

Scottish child payment

Scottish child payment is a benefit for lower income families in Scotland who are responsible for children under the age of 16. It is paid by SSS.

Chapter 19: Benefits and other payments
3. A–Z of benefits and tax credits

To be responsible for a child, clients or their partners must be getting child benefit for the child, the child must be included in their or their partner's award of UC, CTC or PC or the client or their partner must be a kinship carer for the child. There is no limit on the number of children that you can get Scottish child payment for.

Scottish child payment is not means tested but clients must be receiving a means-tested benefit or tax credit to qualify. The qualifying benefits are:
- UC;
- CTC;
- WTC;
- IS;
- PC;
- income-based JSA;
- income-related ESA.

Scottish child payment does not count as income for means-tested benefits and tax credits. It is not based on NI contributions and it is not taxable.

Social fund payments

Most social fund payments have been replaced in Scotland by benefits paid by SSS, such as Best Start grant (see p424) and funeral support payment (see p429). The following payments are still available from the social fund in Scotland.
- **Budgeting loans.** These are for specified types of expenses, such as an item of furniture or household equipment. They are discretionary, so a loan is not guaranteed. The client must have been getting a qualifying benefit (IS, income-based JSA, income-related ESA or PC) for at least 26 weeks. The amount paid is determined by a formula based on the size of the client's family and the amount of any outstanding budgeting loan debt. Loans are repaid through weekly deductions from benefits, but are interest free. The loan must usually be repaid within two years. **Note:** clients getting UC cannot apply for a budgeting loan and must apply for a budgeting advance of UC instead (see p439).
- **Winter fuel payment.** This is a lump-sum payment to help pay fuel bills, although it can be spent on anything the client wants. Clients must be at least pension age (see p433) and must be getting a means-tested benefit to qualify. It is usually paid automatically. The winter fuel payment is going to be replaced by the pension age winter heating payment in Scotland. The pension age winter heating payment will be paid by SSS.

State retirement pension

Clients who reach pension age on or after 6 April 2016 can get the new state pension. Clients who reached pension age before 6 April 2016 may be entitled to an 'old' retirement pension, known as category A, category B and category D retirement pensions.

The amount of state pension a client receives depends on their NI contribution record. State pension is paid at a basic weekly rate, which can be increased if a client has chosen to defer the pension.

A client must claim state pension on the approved form, by telephone or online. State pension can be backdated for a maximum of 12 months from the date they would have been first entitled. Any claim made after this date can be treated as an application to have the pension deferred. Clients should consider the financial implications before choosing to either have their pension backdated for 12 months or have it deferred.

State pension is not means tested, but is taken into account as income for other benefits and tax credits. It is taxable.

Statutory adoption pay

Statutory adoption pay (SAP) is paid to clients who are (or have recently been) employees and who take adoption leave.

A client's average gross weekly earnings must be at least the NI 'lower earnings' limit. They must have worked continuously for their employer for 26 weeks by the end of the week in which they are notified that they have been matched for adoption.

SAP is claimed from the client's employer and is paid in the same way as the client's normal pay. The employer must be given relevant notice and information within a strict time limit. SAP is paid for 39 weeks. It is not means tested, but counts as earnings for means-tested benefits. The first £100 of a client's weekly SAP is ignored for tax credits; anything above £100 is counted as employment income.

SAP is taxable.

Statutory maternity pay

Statutory maternity pay (SMP) is paid to clients who are (or have recently been) employees and who take maternity leave.

A client's average gross weekly earnings must be at least the NI lower earnings limit. She must have worked continuously for her employer for 26 weeks up to and including the 15th week (called the 'qualifying week') before the week in which her baby is due.

SMP is paid for a maximum of 39 weeks. For the first six weeks, clients get a higher rate equal to 90 per cent of average weekly earnings and a further 33 weeks at the lower rate. These are the minimum amounts of maternity pay; the client's employer might offer more generous contractual maternity pay. Clients who do not qualify for SMP may be able to claim MA (see p433). Entitlement to SMP does not depend on the client returning to work.

SMP is claimed from the client's employer and is paid in the same way as her normal pay. The employer must be given relevant notice and information within a strict time limit. SMP is not means tested, but counts as earnings for means-tested benefits. The first £100 of a client's weekly SMP is ignored for tax credits; anything above £100 is counted as employment income.

SMP is taxable.

Statutory parental bereavement pay

Statutory parental bereavement pay (SPBP) is paid to clients who are employees and are taking leave following the death of a child or a stillbirth. It is paid for up to two weeks for deaths and stillbirths occurring on or after 6 April 2020.

To qualify for SPBP, the client must have been continuously employed by the same employer for at least 26 weeks. Their earnings must be at the NI lower earnings limit. The client must give their employer notice of the period over which they want the payment to be made. The payment can cover two consecutive weeks or two separate weeks, but must be paid within 56 weeks of the child's death.

Statutory paternity pay

Statutory paternity pay (SPP) is paid to clients who are (or have recently been) employees and are taking paternity leave because their partner has just given birth. They do not have to be male. Clients can also get SPP if they are adopting a child and their partner is claiming SAP. Clients may also qualify for statutory shared parental pay (SSPP – see below).

A client's average gross weekly earnings must be at least the NI lower earnings limit. They must have worked continuously for their employer for 26 weeks up to and including the 15th week (called the 'qualifying week') before the week in which the baby is due.

SPP is claimed from the client's employer and is paid in the same way as normal pay. The employer must be given relevant notice and information within a strict time limit. SPP is paid for a maximum of two weeks which do not have to be consecutive weeks. It is paid at either a standard rate or 90 per cent of average weekly earnings, whichever is lower.

SPP is not means tested, but counts as earnings for means-tested benefits. The first £100 of a client's weekly SPP is ignored for tax credits; anything above £100 is counted as employment income.

SPP is taxable.

Statutory shared parental pay

A client can get SSPP if they qualify for either:
- SMP or SAP; *or*
- SPP and they have a partner who qualifies for SMP, MA or SAP.

If the eligible partner ends their maternity/adoption leave and pay (or MA) early, the other partner can take the remainder of the 39 weeks of pay (up to a maximum of 37 weeks) as SSPP.

The client's average gross weekly earnings must be at least the NI 'lower earnings limit'. They must have worked continuously for their employer for 26 weeks up to and including the 15th week (called the 'qualifying week') before the week in which the baby is due.

SSPP is claimed from the client's employer and is paid in the same way as normal pay. The employer must be given relevant notice and information within a strict time limit. A mother must take a minimum of two weeks' maternity leave following the birth (four if she works in a factory). SSPP is paid at either a standard rate or 90 per cent of average weekly earnings, whichever is lower.

SSPP is not means tested, but counts as earnings for means-tested benefits. The first £100 of a client's weekly SSPP is ignored for tax credits; anything above £100 is counted as employment income.

SSPP is taxable.

Statutory sick pay

SSP is paid to employees who are sick and unable to work for at least four consecutive days. SSP is not paid during the first three days of illness. Clients cannot get ESA while they are entitled to SSP, but can claim UC to top up any SSP if their income and capital are sufficiently low.

Clients must have average earnings of at least the NI lower earnings limit to qualify.

SSP is claimed from the client's employer and is paid in the same way as their normal pay. It is paid at a standard rate for a maximum of 28 weeks for each episode of illness. If a client is still off work sick after SSP has expired, they may then qualify for ESA (or UC). SSP is not means tested, but it counts as earnings for means-tested benefits and tax credits.

SSP is taxable.

Universal credit

UC is a means-tested benefit for people on a low income who are under pension age (or who have a partner under pension age). UC can be claimed by workers, by jobseekers and by people whose ability to work is limited by their health or circumstances.

UC has been gradually introduced from October 2013 and is replacing the following means-tested benefits and tax credits:
- IS;
- income-based JSA;
- income-related ESA;
- HB (for most people);

Chapter 19: Benefits and other payments
3. A–Z of benefits and tax credits

- CTC;
- WTC.

People already getting these benefits and tax credits can continue getting them for a time – eg, until their circumstances change and they lose entitlement, or until they are written to by the DWP/HMRC and asked to move to UC under the 'managed migration' process.

To qualify for UC, the client must usually:
- meet certain residence rules and not be a 'person subject to immigration control';
- not be a student (with some exceptions);
- have a low enough income and have capital below £16,000;
- agree to meet certain work-related requirements, including attending work-focused interviews, and preparing for and looking for work.

Note: there are special exceptions for people moving to UC under 'managed migration'. For more information, see CPAG's *Welfare Benefits and Tax Credit Handbook*.

The amount of UC a client can get is calculated using a standard allowance plus a number of 'elements' including child element(s), housing costs element, carer element and elements connected with health/disability. The client's earnings, other income and savings are taken into account when calculating their UC amount. Their UC payment can be further reduced by, for example:
- the benefit cap, 'bedroom tax' or local housing allowance rates (like HB – see p430);
- the 'two-child limit', which means that your client may not get a child element in respect of a third or later child born after 5 April 2017.

UC is paid monthly in arrears. New UC claimants can apply for a repayable 'advance' to tide them over until their first payment. Repayments are deducted from future benefit payments and the rate of repayment is difficult to reduce. It is therefore essential to have details of any advance repayments when drawing up the client's budget.

Clients in Scotland can ask for their UC to be paid twice monthly rather than monthly and for their housing costs element to be paid directly to their landlord. These are called the 'UC Scottish choices'. These are similar to the DWP's 'alternative payment arrangements', although the DWP can also split a single UC payment between two partners. The alternative payment arrangements are discretionary and are only available in exceptional circumstances though. Clients cannot set up one of the Scottish choices if they already have a similar alternative payment arrangement in place.

Clients who need help with expenses such as buying new furniture or household equipment may be able to apply for a 'budgeting advance'. Budgeting advances must be repaid, usually by deductions from future payments of UC.

UC replaces income-related ESA for people whose ability to work is limited by health or disability. A client's ability for work is assessed by the DWP using a 'work capability assessment'. A small number of people are automatically treated as having limited capability for work and do not have to undergo this assessment – eg, people who are terminally ill.

A work capability assessment can lead to one of three outcomes:
- a client is found to have 'limited capability for work and work-related activity'. They do not have work-related requirements and may receive an extra amount of UC; *or*
- a client is found to have 'limited capability for work'. They can still have some work-related requirements (eg, work preparation activity) and do not usually get an extra amount of UC; *or*
- a client is found 'fit for work' and can be given a range of work-related requirements.

Most UC claimants have work-related requirements. Clients may have their UC reduced by a sanction if they do not comply with their work-related requirements, without good reason. There is a right to appeal this, and it is always worth considering whether a sanction could be challenged.

Clients whose benefit has been reduced by a sanction may qualify for a hardship payment if they can demonstrate that their reduced level of income is causing hardship.

UC is a qualifying benefit for free school meals (see p442), help with health costs (see p429) and some Scottish benefits such as Best Start grant (see p424), Scottish child payment (see p433) and funeral support payment (see p429).

It is not taxable.

Working tax credit

Note: WTC is affected by the introduction of UC (see p437). It is no longer possible to make a new claim for WTC unless the client is already entitled to CTC or making a renewal claim. It is not possible to be entitled to WTC and UC at the same time. A claim for UC causes WTC to be terminated.

WTC is paid to a client who is, or whose partner is, in full-time paid work. The client must be:
- a lone parent with a dependent child and working at least 16 hours a week; *or*
- a member of a couple with a child, one partner who works at least 16 hours a week, and the other disabled, in hospital or in prison, or entitled to CA/CSP; *or*

- a member of a couple with a child. The couple must work 24 hours between them, with one partner working at least 16 hours a week. If only one partner works 24 hours, they will qualify; *or*
- disabled and work at least 16 hours a week; *or*
- aged 25 or over and work at least 30 hours a week; *or*
- aged 60 or over and work at least 16 hours a week.

WTC is claimed from and paid by HMRC. It is means tested, and counts as income for the purposes of means-tested benefits. It is claimed and assessed at the same time as CTC.

WTC is not taxable.

4. A–Z of other financial help

Charities

There are thousands of charities that can provide payments to individuals in need. Some are open to everyone and others are for certain groups only, such as armed service personnel or people with specific disabilities. Many have a committee that considers applications and meets on a cyclical basis.

Some charities expect a person to have exhausted other statutory provisions before approaching them. Turn2us has a website (turn2us.org.uk) with an A–Z of all the charities that can provide financial help and, in many cases, applications for support can be made directly from the website.

The Directory for Social Change publication *The Guide to Grants for Individuals in Need* provides a list of local and national charities, advises on the most appropriate charity and gives guidance on how to make a successful application. See dsc.org.uk/publications.

Most charitable payments are ignored for means-tested benefits and tax credits if they are made regularly. Most that are made irregularly are treated as capital and so only affect the benefit if they take the client above the capital limit.

Child maintenance

Clients may be able to get child maintenance for their children if they are not living with their other parent. Child maintenance may be paid voluntarily, following a court order or following an application to the Child Maintenance Service. See CPAG's *Child Support Handbook* for full details.

Child maintenance is disregarded as income for all means-tested benefits and tax credits.

Civil compensation for damages

Personal injury claims can be made against an individual or organisation if they have been negligent in causing damage, either by doing something or by failing to do something. Injury caused by negligence can be an issue in road traffic accidents or accidents at work, in the street or other public places. Damages for personal injury can be substantial, but can be reduced by the amount of social security benefit paid as a consequence of the injury.

If the injury occurred at work, the client should contact their trade union, if a member. Other clients may need to be referred to a solicitor. More information is available from:
- the Law Society of Scotland on 0131 226 7411 or at lawscot.org.uk;
- the Association of Personal Injury Lawyers on 0115 943 5400 or at apil.org.uk;
- the Motor Accident Solicitors Society on 0117 925 9604 or at mass.org.uk.

Council tax reduction

If a client needs help paying their council tax, they may qualify for council tax reduction. There is a national council tax reduction scheme in Scotland which is administered by local authorities. See CPAG's *Council Tax Handbook* for more information.

Discretionary housing payment

A discretionary housing payment (DHP) can be made by a client's local authority to help them with rent or with certain other housing costs. To apply for a DHP, they must be entitled to help with their rent through universal credit (UC) or housing benefit (HB).

DHPs can be made because UC or HB does not cover a client's full rent – eg:
- due to the local housing allowance or bedroom tax;
- due to deductions being made from their benefit because they live with a non-dependant;
- because they are affected by the benefit cap.

The client can also apply for a DHP towards certain one-off costs – eg, if they need rent in advance or a deposit for a new home, or if they have moving expenses.

Payments are discretionary, which essentially means that they are made on a case-by-case basis. They are made from a cash-limited budget allocated to the local authority. A client might be refused a DHP for budgetary reasons even if they make a strong application, or they might be successful but only receive assistance for a short period.

The Scottish government gives funding to local authorities so that DHPs can be used to mitigate the effects of the bedroom tax and the benefit cap. Clients who are affected by the bedroom tax or the benefit cap should apply for a DHP as they should be able to get one.

The client's local authority may have a paper application form and/or an online application form for DHPs.

Equal pay rules

Equality legislation provides that a woman should not be paid less than a man for work of equal value or for the same work. If a woman is in debt, it is always worth checking whether these rules might help increase her income. If a client is being paid less than others doing similar work because of their age, gender, disability, race, religion and belief, or sexual orientation, it could constitute unlawful discrimination. Specialist help is necessary to pursue a claim. For further details, contact the Equality Advisory and Support Service on 0808 800 0082, or see equalityadvisoryservice.com.

Food banks

Clients who are without any means to obtain food may be able to get help from a food bank. Most food banks operate on a referral basis. To find a local one, see trusselltrust.org/get-help/find-a-foodbank. Many foodbanks limit the number of times that a client can use them in a set period. Some food banks can also issue 'fuel bank' vouchers to top up gas and electricity prepayment meters.

Free school meals

Children are entitled to free school meals if their family receives:
- income support (IS), income-based jobseeker's allowance (JSA) or income-related employment and support allowance (ESA);
- UC, child tax credit (CTC) or both CTC and working tax credit (WTC) if their annual income is below a threshold.

Also entitled are 16–18-year-olds who receive the above benefits and tax credits in their own right, and asylum seekers in receipt of asylum support.

In addition, in Scotland, free school meals are provided to all children during the first five years of primary school. Also, all children in early learning and childcare can get a free meal on the days that they go in. The Scottish government has pledged to expand free school meals to all Primary 6 and 7 children in receipt of Scottish child payment at some point during 2024/25.

Guarantee pay

If an employer fails to provide work for an employee (ie, lays them off), in most cases, they must pay guarantee pay for five days of lay-off in any period of three months. The right to guarantee pay can be enforced through an employment tribunal. Specialist help should be obtained. A client who is dismissed for seeking to enforce this right is entitled to claim unfair dismissal to an employment tribunal, regardless of the length of their service.

Guarantee pay is taken into account as earnings for means-tested benefits.

For further details, see the guidance on guarantee pay at gov.uk/lay-offs-short-timeworking/guarantee-pay.

Help to Save

Help to Save is a UK-wide government scheme offering a top-up to working people on low incomes who open a special type of savings account and pay into it regularly. To be eligible, a client must be:
- getting UC with a minimum amount of earnings; or
- getting WTC at more than a nil rate; or
- be eligible for WTC and get CTC at more than a nil rate.

The most a client can pay into their account each calendar month is £50, which is £2,400 over four years. In those four years, they can earn up to £1,200 from their savings. See gov.uk/get-help-savings-low-income for more information.

A client can withdraw money from a Help to Save account at any time, but it will affect the amount of bonus they can get.

Scottish Welfare Fund

Clients who need financial help after an emergency or an unexpected event, might be able to get a grant from the Scottish Welfare Fund. Grants are also available to help clients set up or maintain their home or to help families experiencing exceptional pressure.

There are two types of grant – crisis grants and community care grants. They are grants, not loans, so they do not have to be paid back. To be eligible, claimants must have a low income or be unable to access their money. Usually claimants can only get a maximum of three crisis grants in any 12-month period. There are no limits on the number of community care grants they can get as long as they meet the eligibility criteria.

The Scottish Welfare Fund is a national scheme that is administered by local authorities. It is a discretionary scheme and councils may only be able to pay out high-priority claims if the budget is running low. Grants can be paid in cash, in kind, or in prepaid cards or vouchers.

Mortgage interest loans

From 6 April 2018, repayable loans replaced the previous benefit support for mortgage interest on certain loans secured on a client's home. Clients getting IS, income-based JSA, income-related ESA or pension credit (PC) can qualify for a loan. The loans can cover the interest on mortgages or other payments used to purchase a home, or the interest on a loan to pay for specified repairs or improvements.

Chapter 19: Benefits and other payments
4. A–Z of other financial help

A client should be advised to seek independent financial and legal advice before taking out a loan for mortgage interest.

The loans attract interest, which will continue to accumulate until the loan is paid or written off.

Clients may still be able to get an amount for housing costs included in their benefit for service charges, ground rent, co-ownership schemes or certain types of rent.

National minimum wage

Most employees are entitled to be paid at a rate equivalent to at least the national minimum wage. A client who is entitled to the minimum wage and is being paid less than this can complain to the Acas helpline or to an employment tribunal. For more information, visit gov.uk/national-minimum-wage or contact the helpline on 0300 123 1100.

Notice pay

An employee is entitled to be paid during their notice period if they work during that period or cannot work because of illness, pregnancy or childbirth, or because they are on adoption, parental or paternity leave or holiday, or the employer does not wish them to work. An employee who is dismissed without being given the correct notice is entitled to be paid their normal wages 'in lieu' of notice, unless the dismissal is due to gross misconduct. Notice rules are laid down in the law and these depend on length of service. Some employees may be entitled to a longer period of notice under the terms of their contract with the employer. The contract may be written or unwritten.

For further details, see gov.uk/handing-in-your-notice.

Payments for war injury

There are a number of different schemes providing benefits for those disabled, or for the dependants of those killed, in either the First World War or any conflict since 3 September 1939. Some of these schemes only cover members of the armed forces, but there are others that apply to auxiliary personnel, civil defence volunteers, merchant mariners and civilians. Who qualifies and what payments they can receive are complicated. For who may be eligible, see gov.uk/government/organisations/veterans-uk or contact the Veterans helpline on 0808 191 4218.

Private and occupational pensions

Clients who are members of an employer's (occupational) pension scheme or a private pension plan may be entitled to take benefits from these plans before the normal retirement age if, for example, they become permanently incapable of work. Benefits available from pension schemes should be closely examined and independent financial advice should be sought before making a decision to take benefits early from a private scheme.

Redundancy pay

An employee who has two years' continuous service, is not in an excluded occupation, and who loses their job through redundancy, might be entitled to statutory redundancy pay. If a statutory redundancy payment has not been made or is not for the correct amount, the employee can apply to an employment tribunal. There is a strict three-month time limit from the date of termination for making such an application. A client in need of advice in this situation should be referred to an employment law adviser.

Some clients may be entitled to a larger redundancy payment under the terms of their contract.

For further details about redundancy pay, see gov.uk/redundancy-your-rights.

School clothing grants

In Scotland, local authorities pay school clothing grants to low-income families. Policies vary but the grants must be at least £120 per child of primary school age and at least £150 per child of secondary school age. The eligibility criteria for school clothing grants are usually similar to the criteria for free school meals (see p442) on the basis of low income.

School transport

Local authorities have a duty to provide free transport for a pupil under 16 if they attend the 'nearest suitable school' and live at least two miles away (if they are aged under eight) or three miles away (if they are eight or older). In addition, children must be given free transport if there is not a safe walking route, irrespective of how far from the school they live.

Social work

Local authority social work departments have statutory duties to provide a range of practical and financial help to families, children, young people, older people, people with disabilities and asylum seekers.

Special funds for sick or disabled people

A range of help is available from local authority social work departments for people with an illness or disability to assist with things like paying for care services in their own home, equipment, holidays, furniture and transport needs.

Chapter 19: Benefits and other payments
4. A–Z of other financial help

Student support

For details, see Chapter 21 of this *Handbook*, and also CPAG's *Benefits for Students in Scotland Handbook*, which is available free online at cpag.org.uk/handbooks.

Tax allowances

The personal allowance is a basic allowance that is available to most people resident in the UK.

Clients may also be entitled to a married couple's allowance if they are married or in a civil partnership, and either they or their spouse or civil partner were born before 6 April 1935.

Those who are married or in a civil partnership and were born after 5 April 1935 may be entitled to a transferable tax allowance or 'marriage allowance'. This allows any underused personal allowance up to a set limit to be transferred from one to the other partner in the marriage or civil partnership.

A client who is registered blind can claim a blind person's allowance for the whole tax year. This is in addition to the personal allowance. Any unused allowance can be transferred to their spouse or civil partner. If both spouses and civil partners are registered blind, they can claim an allowance each.

A backdated claim can be made for up to four years for any allowances, so check whether the client has not received an allowance to which they are entitled.

Tax rebate

A client who is unemployed or is laid off may be entitled to a tax rebate at the end of the tax year. However, this is reduced or may be cancelled out if they receive a taxable benefit. In some cases, if HMRC has delayed paying the tax rebate, it must pay interest on it.

Tax reliefs

Tax reliefs are amounts that are deducted from taxable income in recognition of money that is needed to be spent by the taxpayer in working. They can be claimed in addition to a personal allowance and can be backdated for up to six years. Tax reliefs for self-employed people should be calculated by a specialist adviser.

For employed people, it is possible to claim relief on any money that is spent to enable a job to be done, but which is not paid for by the employer. The expenses have to be 'wholly, exclusively and necessarily' incurred in order to do the work.

Items for which tax relief can be claimed include:
- membership of professional bodies;
- special clothing for work;
- using heating/lighting or the telephone at home for work;
- buying tools.

Another form of tax relief is the 'rent-a-room' scheme. This enables someone to let out a main room in their home and not pay tax on the rental income, provided the rent stays below a certain level. Even if the client cannot benefit from this scheme, there are other forms of tax relief that may be applicable if they let out property. Specialist advice should be obtained.

Trade unions

Many trade unions have hardship funds for members or ex-members. Unions may also be involved in various benevolent funds and charities associated with particular industries. If a client has been a member of a union, it is worth enquiring about possible lump-sum payments or, in some cases, ongoing support.

Warm Home Discount

Warm Home Discount is a one-off credit or discount of £150 on annual energy bills. A client may be able to get a Warm Home Discount if they get the guarantee credit of PC or they are on a low income, get other qualifying means-tested benefits and meet their energy supplier's criteria. Note that not all energy suppliers take part in the scheme. For further information, visit gov.uk/the-warm-home-discount-scheme and see the relevant energy supplier's website.

Chapter 20

Court fines

This chapter covers:
1. Introduction (below)
2. The Crown Office and Procurator Fiscal Service (below)
3. Non-payment of court fines (p450)
4. Debt solutions (p452)
5. Checklist for action (p452)

1. Introduction

A sheriff court or justice of the peace court can order your client to pay a fine. This could be for a road traffic offence, for not having a television licence or for another offence such as theft, minor assault or breach of the peace. Some fines are given out after prosecution at court, others are issued as an alternative to prosecution.

2. The Crown Office and Procurator Fiscal Service

The Crown Office and Procurator Fiscal Service (COPFS) is the body which decides if a case is to be prosecuted in court or if the accused can be offered alternatives.
COPFS staff:
- consider cases reported to COPFS and decide whether there is enough evidence to take further action;
- decide, based on the public interest, whether to prosecute a case or take alternative action, such as offering a fine.

If your client has been reported to the procurator fiscal in connection with an alleged offence, the procurator fiscal may, in certain circumstances, offer them the opportunity to have the allegation dealt with outside of court without getting a criminal conviction.

When deciding whether to offer a fine, COPFS uses its *Prosecution Code* to decide whether to proceed with court action or offer an alternative.[1]

Alternatives to prosecution

COPFS looks at every individual case to decide whether:
- to prosecute; *or*
- not to prosecute; *or*
- not to prosecute at the moment; *or*
- to issue a warning; *or*
- to offer a fixed penalty notice (road traffic offences); *or*
- to offer a fiscal fine.

Alternatives to prosecution are sometimes known as 'conditional offers'. You can find more information at copfs.gov.uk/the-justice-process/scotland-s-criminal-justice-system.

Fixed penalty notices

Fixed penalty notices can be issued as an alternative to prosecution where the offence is low priority. This could be, for example, for some parking offences, anti-social behaviour or breach of the peace. If the fine is paid, there is no prosecution.

Fiscal fines

Where the offence is low priority, COPFS may offer a 'fiscal fine'. The offer may be to allow the offender to pay a sum of money as an alternative to prosecution. In most cases, the fine can be paid by instalments.

Your client has 28 days to accept or reject the offer. If they do not reply, they are deemed to have accepted it.

The offer letter specifies the clerk of court to whom payment should be made. Enforcement action will be taken if the fine is not paid.

If your client does nothing, they are assumed to have accepted the offer and are liable to pay the fiscal fine, compensation offer or combined offer in full at the instalment rate provided in the offer letter.

If the offer is accepted and the fine paid, the client cannot be prosecuted for the alleged offence.

Fines can also be collected by civil diligence – namely arrestment, attachment, and money attachment – as if they were following an extract decree.[2]

The Scottish Courts and Tribunals Service (SCTS) is responsibile for collecting all fiscal penalties issued by COPFS or Police Scotland.

Fines issued after prosecution

Court fines issued after prosecution can be referred to a solicitor, although clients could try to negotiate a payment with a fines enforcement officer (FEO) first, if it is not too late.

Fines enforcement officers

FEOs are employed by the SCTS and are responsible for giving information and advice about paying fines and for making sure that fines are paid in the way stated in enforcement orders.

The sheriff or justice of the peace usually sets the payment rate when the fine is issued. If your client is having difficulty keeping up with payments, they can ask the FEO to change the rate of payment.

The FEO will ask your client to complete a 'declaration of income' form and supporting information should be provided to allow the FEO to decide whether to reduce payments and/or allow more time to pay.[3]

See scotcourts.gov.uk/taking-action/pay-a-fine/contact-the-fines-enforcement-team for more information.

3. Non-payment of court fines

If your client decides not to pay the fine, the fines enforcement officer (FEO) has several options.

First, they may obtain an enforcement order from the court allowing them to continue with diligence against your client.

Enforcement orders

An enforcement order (EO) can be made when a fine is imposed or when the court is granting further time to pay a fine. It allows the FEO to proceed with diligence in the event of non-payment.[4]

An EO gives the FEO the authority to enforce fines administratively. This cuts the amount of court time spent dealing with fines enforcement.

The EO sets out the payment terms and whether the fine is to be paid in full by a set date or by instalments. The EO allows the FEO to agree realistic payment plans with fine payers.

The EO encourages the offender to stay in contact with the FEO during the lifetime of the order. It also allows the FEO to take certain action against the offender if needed. The FEO can quickly identify offenders who are not paying and take the most suitable enforcement action. At the same time, they are available to support those who need advice and are genuinely struggling to pay.

An EO gives the FEO the options to:
- make a seizure of vehicle order (SVO) (see below); *or*
- make an arrestment of funds order (AFO) (see below); *or*
- make a deductions from benefits order (see p452); *or*
- refer back to the court (see p452); *or*
- make a variation (see p452).

Seizure of vehicle order

The FEO can make an SVO. This orders that a motor vehicle be:
- immobilised (clamped); *and if the client cannot pay the fine and clamping costs within 24 hours*
- impounded (taken into storage).

If your client still does not pay the fine and costs, the court can sell (or sometimes destroy) the vehicle.

The FEO must give your client seven days' notice in writing that they will ask the justice of the peace or sheriff for an order to sell the vehicle. Your client can then make written representation to the court as to why it should not be awarded.

Eventually, if your client has not paid the fine and costs, the FEO can apply for a court order to sell the vehicle. If this happens:[5]
- the money from the sale is paid towards the fine; *and*
- any additional money is paid towards the expenses of the seizure of vehicle order; *and*
- after the fine and expenses have been paid, any remaining money is paid to your client.

Arrestment of funds order

When the court makes an EO, it also grants a warrant for diligence. This warrant gives the FEO the power to carry out the following types of diligence if your client defaults:[6]
- arrestment of earnings; *and*
- arrestment of funds in accounts held at any bank or other financial institution.

There is no direct appeal against an AFO, and it is not subject to normal time to pay applications.

When an AFO is applied, the client's funds are frozen by the financial institution.

If the arrestment is successful, the client can sign a mandate in the prescribed form allowing the bank to release money to the court. The court then pays the money towards the fine.

Alternatively, after a period of 14 weeks starting on the date of service of the AFO, the bank must automatically release the funds to the court.

There is more about AFOs at scotcourts.gov.uk/taking-action/pay-a-fine/arrestment-of-funds.

Deduction from benefits order
Deductions can be made from some benefits (such as universal credit, jobseeker's allowance and pension credit), with or without the client's consent. There is a maximum amount allowed to be deducted.[7]

Refer back to court
Where a fine has not been paid, the FEO can refer the case back to court to be dealt with. When the case is referred back, the court can:[8]
- revoke the enforcement order and deal with the offender as if the enforcement order had never been made; *or*
- vary the enforcement order; *or*
- confirm the enforcement order as previously made; *or*
- direct the FEO to take specified steps to secure payment of, or towards, the relevant penalty in line with the enforcement order; *or*
- make such other order as it thinks fit.

Variation
Where a client already has an agreement to pay a fine but cannot keep up with the agreed arrangements, they can apply to the FEO for a variation.[9]

4. Debt solutions

As court fines are criminal fines, they are exempt from insolvency solutions, and cannot be entered into a Debt Payment Programme under the Debt Arrangement Scheme. Your client could contact the fines enforcement officer to arrange a suitable repayment plan and treat this as a priority debt.

Remember: court fines do not discharge in any insolvency solution.

5. Checklist for action

- Treat a fine as a priority debt.
- Check the details of the fine.
- Check whether it is an alternative to prosecution.
- Advise of the consequences of non-payment.
- Work out a reasonable and sustainable financial statement.

Chapter 20: Court fines
Notes

- Contact the fines enforcement officer and consider extending the repayment period.
- Look for charity grants etc. to pay the fine.
- Make appropriate referrals.

Notes

2. **The Crown Office and Procurator Fiscal Service**
   1 copfs.gov.uk/publications/prosecution-code
   2 s221(1) CP(S)A 1995
   3 s226A(2) CP(S)A 1995

3. **Non-payment of court fines**
   4 s226B CP(S)A 1995
   5 s226D CP(S)A 1995
   6 s226F CP(S)A 1995
   7 s226E CP(S)A 1995
   8 s226G CP(S)A 1995
   9 s226C CP(S)A 1995

Chapter 21
Student debt

This chapter covers:
1. Advising students (below)
2. Tuition fees (p455)
3. Student loans (p455)
4. Bursaries and grants (p458)
5. Educational trusts and endowments (p461)
6. Help with housing costs (p461)
7. Council tax (p462)
8. Overdrafts (p463)

1. Advising students

When advising students and ex-students about debt, you may need to adopt different strategies and be aware that students expect to owe money before and at the end of their studies. Most creditors (banks and the Student Loans Company) have structured repayment programmes for student debt once the student starts earning. Such debts should not adversely affect the student's creditworthiness (see p458).

Some students can cope with increased debt, accepting that a certain level of indebtedness is inevitable. For others, it can have a more negative impact. The stage at which the student presents may affect their emotional state, as many wait until the situation can no longer be dealt with without external assistance before seeking help. The impact can be that the student may be experiencing poor mental and physical health, relationship problems and difficulties with their course – eg, low marks and missed deadlines. Some students may feel forced to withdraw from their course completely.

Student funding arrangements are different in Scotland than in the rest of the UK. Generally, tuition fees for Scottish students at Scottish colleges or universities ('home students') are paid by the Scottish government (see p455). To cover living costs, there are repayable student loans (see p455) and non-repayable grants and bursaries (see p458).

Home students

In general, to count as a 'home student' and get tuition, loans, bursaries and grants, students must have a 'relevant connection' with Scotland. This means they must be 'settled' in the UK and 'ordinarily resident' in Scotland on the first day of the first academic year of the course. They must also have lived in the UK for the three years immediately before this date.[1]

Students who are in Scotland to study, but otherwise would be living elsewhere, are not ordinarily resident in Scotland.

Get advice from Student Awards Agency for Scotland if you are unsure.

2. Tuition fees

Since 2008, full-time home students who are 'ordinarily resident' in Scotland and study for a first degree in a Scottish college or university have their fees paid by the Scottish government.[2] The Student Awards Agency for Scotland (SAAS) pays fees directly to the college or university. These are non-repayable, but students must apply every year. If they do not have a funding arrangement in place, they may need to pay the tuition fees (£1,820) themselves.

Scottish undergraduates studying elsewhere in the UK can apply to SAAS for a tuition fee loan of up to £9,250.

Part-time students with an annual income below £25,000 can apply for a part-time fee grant. See the SAAS website for more information.

Tuition fees for most full-time postgraduate diplomas and masters are also non-repayable if the student ordinarily lives in Scotland.

3. Student loans

What is a student loan

Student loans are low-interest loans for students to cover living costs. See p456 for when and how they are repaid. Student loans are partly means-tested.

Plan 4 loans

There are five student loan plans in the UK. Plan 4 loans relate only to students funded by the Student Awards Agency for Scotland (SAAS). The information in this section relates to plan 4 loans. For information about other plans, see CPAG's *Debt Advice Handbook*.

The Student Loans Company (SLC) pays loans to students from across the UK and collects their loan repayments.

Chapter 21: Student debt
3. Student loans

SAAS assesses student finance applications and pays bursaries for students from Scotland. SAAS does not pay student loans, although it asses the loan amount an applicant is eligible for and sends this information to the SLC.

Students must apply each year they study for a student loan.

Interest is applied to student loans from the start of the loan until it is fully repaid. Interest is currently charged at 6.25 per cent a year.

Who can get a student loan

Eligibility for a student loan depends on the applicant's course and college or university. Usually, they must be under 61 on the first day of the course. How much is paid is partly based on the student's household income.

Students must also meet the residency conditions (see p455).

If an applicant is studying to be a paramedic, nurse or midwife at a Scottish university, they get a bursary to cover their expenses instead of a loan (see p461). See p460 if the student was previously 'looked after' by a local authority.

The amount of student loans

Student loans for 2024/25 are in the table below. From 2024/25, students get a special support loan of £2,400, in addition to the student loan for maintenance. The special support loan is for course costs such as study and travel costs.

Maximum student loan 2024/25 (including the £2,400 special support loan)

Household income	Dependent student under 25 – maximum student loan	Independent student under 25, or student 25 or over – maximum student loan
Below £24,000	£9,400	£10,400
£24,000 to £33,999	£9,400	£9,900
£34,000 or over	£8,400	£8,400

Payments are made directly to the student's bank account. They can choose to be paid over term time or over 12 months. They cannot be paid over 12 months if they are on a one-year course or in the final year of their course.

Repayment of a student loan

Generally, students do not make any repayments while studying. Repayments start in the April after they have completed or otherwise leave the course and earn over a certain amount (known as the 'salary threshold'). The salary threshold is adjusted each year. The salary threshold is £31,395 in 2024/25. If a client's income falls below the salary threshold, payments stop and only begin again when the salary threshold is met.

Chapter 21: Student debt
3. Student loans

The repayment rate is 9 per cent of any income earned above the salary threshold. If income changes, either falling or rising, the repayment amounts automatically change to reflect this.

Example monthly repayments 2024/25

Annual income before tax	Approximate monthly repayment
£31,395	£0
£32,000	£4
£35,000	£27
£37,000	£42
£40,000	£64

Repayments are normally made by deductions from salary through the PAYE system. If the client is self-employed, repayments are made through the self-assessment tax process. They must tick the box on the self-assessment return stating they have a student loan and budget for student loan payments when they submit their self-assessment tax return to pay HMRC at the end of January.

Clients can choose to pay off their student loans sooner by:
- paying extra each month;
- making an extra one-off payment;
- paying it off in full.

Cancelling a student loan

The SLC can cancel any remaining student loan plus any interest if the client:[3]
- dies before paying the loan off; *or*
- permanently cannot work due to a disability and gets a disability-related benefit (eg, adult disability payment); *or*
- took out their first student loan before 1 August 2007, it is cancelled when the client turns 65 or 30 years after they became eligible to repay as long as the client is up to date with repayments; *or*
- took out their first student loan after 1 August 2007, it is cancelled 30 years after they became eligible to repay as long as they are up to date with repayments

Getting a student loan cancelled if the client permanently cannot work due to a disability

A written request for a loan to be cancelled must be sent to the SLC. It must include the customer reference number and copies of letters from:

– a doctor, consultant or psychiatrist stating the client is permanently unfit for work, dated within the last six months; *and*

– Social Security Scotland or the DWP showing the client gets a disability-related benefit such as adult disability payment or industrial injuries benefit.

If the client themself cannot report that they are unfit to work, information and evidence can be accepted from a third party. The SLC can only communicate directly with the third party if they have power of attorney. If no one has power of attorney, the SLC writes to a third party care of the customer's address.

Non-payment of student loan repayments

If a client fails to make repayments when they are due, the SLC can start recovery by employing a debt recovery agency to collect the debt. It can also apply for a court order to make the client repay the total loan in a single payment. This would be enforced as a civil debt whether the client is in the UK or living abroad, and can lead to further costs and diligences for the client.

Credit rating

Student loans are different from other types of borrowing because they do not appear on a clients credit file and their credit rating is not affected. However, any repayments made (or due to be made) are listed as outgoings in affordability calculations in future credit applications.

Old 'mortgage style' student loan details are however passed onto credit reference agencies. This can happen even if the loan is deferred or an arrangement to pay the loan back has been made.

Arrears on repayments to all types of student loans are registered with credit reference agencies and affect a client's credit score.

Refunds

At the end of the tax year, clients can apply for a refund of the overpaid amount plus interest if:
- their total annual income is below the salary threshold;
- they started making repayments too soon;
- they have repaid more than needed to because their employer put them on the wrong repayment plan;
- they have paid more than the total amount they owe.

See gov.uk/repaying-your-student-loan/getting-a-refund for how to request a refund.

4. Bursaries and grants

Bursaries and grants are money students do not need to pay back. They are means-tested based on either the student's parents' income or their own household income or circumstances if they are an independent student. They are paid on top of a student loan.

Young students' bursary and independent students' bursary

These bursaries top-up student loans for students from lower-income households.

Young students' bursary

Students may be eligible for a young students' bursary if they are from a family with an income of less than £34,000 a year and they:
- are under 25 on the first day of the first academic year of the course (for an autumn start course, this is 1 August); *and*
- have not supported themself financially outside of education for three years; *and*
- are not married, in a civil partnership or living with a partner; *and*
- have no dependent children.

The amount they receive depends on the student's and their family's income. In 2024/25, a maximum of £2,000 is paid if the student's and their family's combined income is under £21,000 a year.

Independent students' bursary

Students who do not meet the young student criteria above are classed as independent students. Students classed as independent are eligible for £1,000 if their household income is below £21,000 a year.

Estranged students' bursary

The estranged students' bursary operates in the same way as the independent students' bursary. It is an extra £1,000 in addition to the maximum loan for maintenance and the special support loan. It can be paid to students under 25 at the start of the course who no longer have contact with their parents. There must usually be a permanent breakdown in the relationship. Parental income is not assessed for this bursary. Evidence of estrangement from a professional must be provided.[4]

Disabled students' allowance

Students with a disability or learning difficulty can claim for extra expenses that arise because of the course. Income is not assessed and the allowance is not repayable. They can also apply for travel costs if they cannot use public transport because of their disability.

Chapter 21: Student debt
4. Bursaries and grants

Disabled students' allowance	Maximum rate 2024/25
Non-medical personal help	£20,520 a year
Consumables – eg, printing	£1,725 a year
Equipment, software and accessories	£5,160 per course

Care-experienced students' bursary

Students who have previously been looked after by a local authority in the UK may be eligible for a care-experienced students' bursary.[5] This is a non-income-assessed grant of £9,000 in 2024/25. It is paid instead of the student loan/bursary package.

From 2024/25, students can get a special support loan of £2,400, in addition to the care-experienced students' bursary. The special support loan is for course costs such as study and travel costs. It is repayable.

Students can be paid their care-experienced bursary payments over term time or over 12 months. It cannot be paid over 12 months if is for a one-year course or in the final year of a course.

Summer accommodation grant

Students who were in local authority care may get a grant of £1,330 if they rent accommodation, or £665 if they stay with friends or family (2024/25), to help with accommodation costs during the long vacation.[6] Income is not assessed and the grant is not repayable. It is usually a one-off payment in advance.

Dependants' grant

A dependants' grant is an income-assessed, non-repayable grant students can claim for a spouse, civil partner, partner, or adult dependant who they care for. The maximum amount in 2024/25 is £2,640. The maximum amount is paid if the adult dependant's income is under £1,160 a year.

Childcare fund

The discretionary childcare fund helps with the cost of registered or formal childcare. It is administered by colleges and universities. They decide who is eligible and how much the payments will be. However, eligible lone parent students can get a lone parents' childcare grant from this fund to help with the cost of registered or formal childcare costs. Depending on the costs of childcare, the maximum amount is £1,215 in 2024/25. Income is not assessed and the grant is not repayable. It is administered by colleges and universities.

Lone parents' grant

Lone parent students can get a lone parents' grant, worth £1,305 in 2024/25 if they have at least one dependent child. Unearned income is assessed (although benefit income is disregarded) and the grant is not repayable.

Higher education discretionary fund

Colleges and universities administer discretionary funds to help with living costs, and decide how much the payments will be. Students are expected to apply for a full student loan before asking for help. The funds are for students in financial difficulties. This can include help in the summer vacation for continuing students.

Paramedic, nursing and midwifery student bursaries

Paramedic, nursing and midwifery students may be able to get their tuition fees paid, as well as a bursary and grants for living costs.[7] Students on paramedic, nursing or midwifery diplomas or degrees can get a non-means-tested paramedic, nursing and midwifery bursary of £10,000. In the first year, an extra £60 initial expenses allowance is paid. For nursing and midwifery students, in the fourth year, the bursary is reduced to 75 per cent. Paramedic students get £10,000 for each of the three years of their course.

5. Educational trusts and endowments

Some charitable trusts provide funds, usually small amounts, to students. For example, Family Action has an educational grants programme (family-action.org.uk/what-we-do/grants/educational-grants). Student Awards Agency Scotland (SAAS) has a register of education endowments at saas.gov.uk/full-time/register-of-education-endowments, which lists Scottish trusts that may be able to help. Lead Scotland also has a list of trusts that provide educational grants at lead.org.uk/charitable-trusts-providing-educational-grants-for-individuals.

Carnegie Trust can help with tuition fees in certain circumstances where these are not covered by SAAS. Read more at carnegie-trust.org/award-schemes/undergraduate-tuition-fee-grants.

6. Help with housing costs

Full-time students cannot usually get help towards their rent from universal credit or housing benefit. There are some exceptions if the student is:
- on a part-time course; or
- disabled; or

- responsible for children; or
- under 21 and taking a non-higher education course such as Highers; or
- receiving a state pension; or
- leaving the course temporarily because of illness or caring responsibilities; or
- living with a partner who is not a student.

See CPAG's *Benefits for Students in Scotland Handbook* for more information. This is available free online at cpag.org.uk/handbooks.

7. Council tax

Some dwellings are exempt from council tax. If the dwelling is exempt, there is no council tax to pay for anyone who lives there or for a non-resident owner. There are two main ways in which students are exempt from paying council tax.
- The accommodation they live in may be exempt.
- They may not be liable to pay any council tax.

If neither of these applies, they may be able to reduce their council tax bill.
- They may be able to get a discount.
- They may be able to get a council tax reduction or a second adult rebate.

Educational institutions may provide local authorities with lists of full-time students attending courses and, if requested, they must issue a letter to a student establishing their status. Some institutions have been known to charge for this letter and you should argue that this is inappropriate. Students should inform council tax offices of their status to obtain an exemption or reduction.

For more information about students and council tax, including the definition of full-time students, see CPAG's *Benefits for Students in Scotland Handbook* at cpag.org.uk/handbooks.

Students eligible for council tax reduction

Part-time students are eligible for council tax reduction. Full-time students are not eligible unless:[8]
- they are a qualifying young person for child benefit purposes; or
- they are aged under 22 on a course of further education which they started when they were under 21; or
- they are a full-time student in higher education, or aged 19 or over in further education and:
    - they get universal credit, income support, income-based jobseeker's allowance or income-related employment and support allowance; or
    - they are a lone parent; or

- they have a child and their partner is also a full-time student; *or*
- they are a disabled student; *or*
• they have reached pension age.

8. Overdrafts

Student overdrafts have some features that are different to other overdrafts. Most banks offer full-time undergraduate students and some postgraduates special interest-free overdrafts up to a set limit. However, these are usually subject to certain residency requirements and credit checks and, in most cases, banks do not allow a student to open a new account if one already exists with a competitor. Packages vary – eg, students in different academic years may have different overdraft limits.

These special features notwithstanding, strategies where issues arise are usually the same as for other overdrafts.

Note that most banks allow students terms that continue for a period after graduation. The length of time varies between banks and can often be extended by negotiation. This is preferable and you should negotiate this option rather than agreeing to overdrawn accounts being 'converted' into graduate loans. Most banks offer preferential graduate terms – eg, lower mortgage rates for limited periods.

Notes

1. **Advising students**
   1 The Education (Fees) (Scotland) Regulations 2022 No.156); The Student Support (Scotland) Regulations 2022 No.157

2. **Tuition fees**
   2 The Education (Fees) (Scotland) Regulations 2022

3. **Student loans**
   3 Reg 8 The Repayment of Student Loans (Scotland) Regulations 2000

4. **Bursaries and grants**
   4 saas.gov.uk/guides/estranged-students
   5 saas.gov.uk/full-time/support-for-care-experienced-students
   6 saas.gov.uk/full-time/support-for-care-experienced-students/care-experienced-accommodation-grant
   7 saas.gov.uk/full-time/funding-paramedic-nursing-midwifery

7. **Council tax**
   8 Reg 20 CTR(S) Regs

Appendix 1
Glossary

Accountant in Bankruptcy
An executive agency of the Scottish government responsible for administering personal bankruptcies and recording corporate insolvencies in Scotland.

Acquirenda
Any property or right acquired or received by a client within four years after the date of sequestration or protected trust deed.

Additional respondent
Used in simple procedure actions, a person who is not named as a respondent in the claim form but who enters the case later.

Alternative dispute resolution
Ways clients can solve problems without having to go to court, like using mediation, arbitration and conciliation.

Apparent insolvency
When a person cannot pay their debts as they fall due. This can be evidenced by a failure to pay a charge for payment or statutory demand.

Arbitration
A way of resolving a dispute without going to court. A third party (the arbitrator) looks at both sides and decides on a resolution.

Arrestment
The legal process through which a creditor can take possession of goods that are owned by a client but are in the possession of a third party.

Arrestment on the dependence
An order freezing client's funds or goods held by a third party (typically money held in a bank account) in advance of the sheriff making a decision in a civil court case.

Appendix 1: Glossary

Assets
Goods belonging to a client which can be sold for the benefit of their creditors.

Attachment
Can be used to enforce payment of a debt by means of valuing, removing and selling the client's corporeal moveable property.

Award of sequestration
The order issued by a sheriff declaring a person to be bankrupt and sequestrating their estate. The award vests the client's estate in the trustee.

Bankruptcy
A formal insolvency process where a trustee is appointed to realise and distribute the bankrupt's estate for the benefit of creditors. Also known as sequestration in Scotland.

Bankruptcy Restriction Order
Restrictions placed on a debtor where there has been misconduct before or after the date of sequestration. The restrictions are imposed by a sheriff or the Accountant in Bankruptcy and remain in force after the date of discharge for periods varying between two and 15 years. They are published in the Register of Insolvencies.

Business Debt Arrangement Scheme
A statutory debt management tool to help partnerships, trusts or an unincorporated body of persons to pay off their creditors over an extended period. It also provides protection from creditors taking action against them to recover their debts.

Certificate for Sequestration
A formal document confirming that a client cannot pay their debts and is apparently insolvent.

Charge for payment
A formal demand for a debtor to pay the money they owe to their creditor. The amount includes the original debt plus any interest or charges. The client has 14 days to pay the charge for payment.

Charge for removing
A formal document served by a sheriff officer advising a client about eviction from their home. Generally, the clients then has 14 days to leave the property.

Appendix 1: Glossary

Common Financial Statement
Used by advisers in Scotland to create a uniform approach to preparing financial statements.

Common Financial Tool
Used by the Accountant in Bankruptcy to assess household income and expenditure to set a contribution across all statutory debt solutions.

Condescendence
A written statement setting out the factual and legal grounds of action of the pursuer in a civil action.

Continuation (of an action)
An order made by a sheriff to continue the case to another date – ie, a temporary postponement.

Corporeal movable property
Anything that can move or be moved – includes money, furniture, clothing, farm livestock, crops etc.

Court of Session
Scotland's highest civil court.

Courtroom supporter
A person who accompanies a party in court to provide moral support. They are sometimes referred to as a 'lay supporter' or 'McKenzie friend'.

Credit reference agencies
Agencies providing lenders with information (a 'credit reference file' or 'credit report') about potential borrowers, which lenders use to make their decisions.

Credit union
A financial co-operative, owned and controlled by its members, which provides savings, loans and aservices to its members. The Financial Conduct Authority oversees and regulates credit unions.

Creditor
Any person, business or organisation which is owed money by another.

Creditor petition
An application by a creditor, through the court, for the sequestration of a client's estate.

Appendix 1: Glossary

DAS Administrator
The Accountant in Bankruptcy overseeing the Debt Arrangement Scheme (DAS). Its responsibilities include maintaining the DAS Register and approving debt advisers, payments distributors and Debt Payment Programmes.

DAS Register
An online public register which holds information about those applying for the Debt Arrangement Scheme (DAS) and those who already have a Debt Payment Programme under a the DAS.

Debt Advice and Information Package
A booklet which provides information to clients to help them deal with their creditors. A creditor is required by law to provide this before using most types of diligence.

Debt Arrangement Scheme
A statutory debt payment plan to help those who want to pay what they owe over an extended period, free from the threat of enforcement action by creditors through diligence or bankruptcy. It freezes interest, fees and charges on the debts included.

Debt Payment Programme
A proposal under the Debt Arrangement Scheme allowing a client to pay their debt over an extended period. It can be for any amount of money or for any reasonable length of time. Monies are ingathered and distributed by an appointed payments distributor.

Debt packager
Commercial business providing debt advice and generating income by referring customers to debt solution providers and receiving a fee. They must be approved by the Financial Conduct Authority.

Debtor application
When a person applies for their own bankruptcy.

Debtor contribution order
The fixed amount a client pays in contributions towards their bankruptcy usually over a 48-month period. This is set by the Accountant in Business using the Common Financial Tool.

Debtor discharge
The date that the client is formally discharged from their bankruptcy or protected trust deed.

Appendix 1: Glossary

Decree
A money judgment issued by the sheriff court. It is an order to pay the amount claimed by a creditor. The total may include interest and court expenses.

Decree by default
A final order granted to a party against another party who has failed to appear, to lodge a document or do something required by the court or rules of court.

Decree in absence
A final order granted to the pursuer in a civil action where the defender has not lodged a notice of intention to defend or has not lodged defences and does not appear or have someone appear on their behalf in court.

Decree absolvitor
A court judgment in favour of the defender. This usually means that the same action cannot then be re-raised.

Deductions of earnings order
Used by the Child Maintenance Service to take child maintenance payments from a paying parent's earnings or pension. This is not classed as diligence

Default notice
A formal letter (notice) sent by a creditor when a client is in arrears on a consumer credit contract. The notice should give the client 14 days to pay the arrears. A creditor must serve a default notice before they can take any further legal action.

Defender
A person against whom a civil action is raised.

Diligence
The technical term for enforcement in Scottish law. It is the steps a creditor can take to get their money back after they have taken court action against a client or entity.

Diligence against earnings
A collective term for the ways creditors can deduct money directly from a client's salary to enforce the payment of a debt. The three methods are: earnings arrestment, current maintenance arrestment and conjoined arrestment orders.

Direct earnings attachment
Where an employer is asked to deduct benefit overpayments from an employee's pay. This is not diligence.

Appendix 1: Glossary

Dividend
The distribution of funds to creditors in a bankruptcy. This could repay the debt in full or in part.

Exceptional attachment order
A form of diligence in which a creditor attaches moveable property belonging to a client which is inside the client's home (eg, jewellery), which is then removed and sold at auction.

Executor dative
A person appointed by the court to gather and distribute the estate or property of a deceased person.

Extract/extract decree
A written instrument signed by a clerk of court containing a statement of a decree or order of the court and, if necessary, a warrant to charge the named person and to execute all competent diligence against person or property.

Financial Conduct Authority
A government body which regulates the financial services industry in the UK. Its role includes protecting consumers, keeping the industry stable and promoting healthy competition between financial service providers.

Fiscal fines
Can be offered as an alternative to prosecution in cases which would otherwise have proceeded in the lowest-level criminal court. If the accused accepts a fiscal fine, they cannot be prosecuted for the alleged offence.

Full Administration Bankruptcy
A form of bankruptcy where a client has debts of more than £3,000 and does not meet the criteria for Minimum Asset Process bankruptcy.

Gratuitous alienation
The voluntary disposal of a client's asset by the client to another person for no value or less than full value.

Heritable estate
Property in the form of land and houses, as distinct from moveable property such as jewellery or an animal.

Inhibition
A personal diligence against a client, preventing them from selling, transferring or otherwise disposing of their property. It also prohibits the client from securing new loans against the property.

Appendix 1: Glossary

Initial writ
The document by which ordinary civil proceedings in the sheriff court are usually initiated.

Insolvency
A state in which a person or business cannot pay their debts.

Insolvency practitioner
Someone who is licensed and authorised to act in relation to an insolvent individual, partnership or company. Most insolvency practitioners are accountants or insolvency specialists working in firms of accountants. They must hold a licence and have passed the insolvency examinations.

Interim attachment
A process (similar to diligence on the dependence) which restricts the clients's ability to deal with a limited range of moveable assets in their possession while a court action progresses.

Interim order
A temporary court order made until a final order is made.

Judgment
The decision of a court setting out its reasons for the decision.

Justice of the peace
Lay magistrates who sit with a legally qualified adviser to deal with summary criminal cases.

Lay representative
Someone authorised by a client to help prepare and conduct a civil legal action. They can do anything involved with the preparation or conduct of a case that a party can do. A lay representative is not a legal representative.

Legal representative
An advocate, a solicitor, a trainee solicitor or a person otherwise entitled to conduct proceedings in the sheriff court.

Limitation period
A procedural bar from bringing certain types of action after the expiry of a time limit. In certain cases, the court can allow an action to proceed even after the limitation period has expired.

Lodge
To deposit documents and other evidence to the sheriff clerk *before* a hearing, for their use at that hearing.

Appendix 1: Glossary

Messengers-at-arms
Officers who execute civil and criminal processes of the Court of Session and High Court of Justiciary.

Minimal Asset Process
A simplified sequestration process for people with few assets and who meet the relevant criteria at the date of making the application for bankruptcy. Anyone awarded a bankruptcy through this route will (as long as they cooperate with their trustee) receive a discharge automatically after six months.

Money attachment
A diligence used to collect cash from commercial clients such as bars, clubs, shops or restaurants. It cannot be used to collect money in a dwellinghouse.

Moveable estate
Personal estate encompassing all assets, but excluding land and buildings.

Offer of composition
An offer made to creditors seeking agreement to accept payment or part payment of debts owed by the client. Where creditors agree, the debt is discharged.

Ordinary cause
Used in sheriff court procedure when the debts being recovered are for £5,000 or more. It is a complex and expensive process to raise and to defend

Party litigant
A person who represents themself in civil court proceedings without representation from a solicitor.

Pause
To temporarily suspend the progress of a simple procedure action case.

Personal insolvency
The awards of bankruptcy in Full Administration Bankruptcy and Minimal Asset Process or entering a protected trust deed.

Petition for sequestration
The formal application to court by a creditor, creditors or a trustee under a trust deed for the bankruptcy of a client's estate.

Prescription (negative)
A substantive rule of Scots law which extinguishes certain rights and obligations after the applicable time. This means that after that period, the right or obligation ceases to exist, and is not simply unenforceable. In Scotland, the obligation to pay

Appendix 1: Glossary

a debt prescribes five years after the debt becomes enforceable unless, within that time, the creditor has made a relevant claim or the client has relevantly acknowledged the claim. Prescription following a decree is extended to 20 years.

Procurators fiscal
Legally qualified civil servants who receive reports about crimes from the police and others and decide what action to take in the public interest, including whether to prosecute.

Protected minimum balance
The minimum amount protected from arrestment (currently, £1,000).

Protected trust deed
A voluntary formal debt solution entered into by a client. It transfers their estate to a trustee to be realised for the benefit of their creditors. A trust deed may be protected if a majority in number or a third in value of creditors do not object to its terms. Once protected, the terms of the trust deed become binding on all the creditors and prevent them from pursuing their debt or making the client bankrupt.

Provisional order
An order which protects or secures a claimant's position before a hearing in a simple procedure action.

Qualified creditor
A creditor who is owed at least £5,000 is able to petition for the client's bankruptcy.

Recall
The process of bringing an action back to court to be heard by a sheriff.

Recall of sequestration
A process to end the bankruptcy and restore as far a possible the client, or any persons affected by the bankruptcy, to the position they would have been in if the bankruptcy had not been awarded.

Register of Inhibitions
A public record holding information on individuals who cannot competently enter into property transactions – eg, sell their owned property.

Register of Insolvencies
A publicly accessible statutory register which holds information on the insolvency of individuals and businesses in Scotland. It also holds information on anyone who has been granted a statutory moratorium.

Appendix 1: Glossary

Scottish Public Services Ombudsman
The organisation that handles the final stage for complaints about devolved public services in Scotland including councils and the Scottish government and its agencies and departments.

Sequestration
Sequestration is the term used in Scottish law for entering bankruptcy.

Sheriff clerk
Responsible for the organisation of work of the sheriff court. In the courtroom, they call out the case name and record the decision of the sheriff. In the sheriff clerks' office, they give advice on procedures and help fill out some court forms.

Sheriff court
This court deals with the majority of civil and criminal cases in Scotland. It has jurisdiction over all civil cases with a monetary value of up to £100,000.

Sheriffdom
The court system in Scotland is divided into six areas called sheriffdoms. A sheriff principal sits as the administrative head of each sheriffdom.

Sheriff officer
An officer of the sheriff court responsible for serving documents and executing orders of the sheriff court.

Sheriff
A legally qualified judge. Sheriffs deal with many debt-related cases, including those involving compensation, contract disputes, bankruptcy, company liquidation and evictions.

Sheriff principal
These judges are the heads of each of Scotland's six sheriffdoms. They are responsible for ensuring the efficiency of the sheriff courts in their sheriffdom. They also sit in the Sheriff Appeal Court.

Simple procedure
A sheriff court process to provide a speedy, inexpensive and informal way to resolve disputes.

Sist
In Scottish law, sist can mean two things: when someone intervenes in legal proceedings as a third party (eg, as a trustee) or an order that stops or suspends legal proceedings for a time.

Appendix 1: Glossary

Statutory moratorium on diligence
Provides a period of protection during which creditors cannot take any formal recovery action (diligence) against a client for debts owed.

Summary cause
A simplified procedure applicable to civil cases in the sheriff court with a limit of £5,000 in the case of monetary claims. Certain actions to recover heritable property must also be by summary cause.

Summary warrant
An expedited court process which some public sector bodies can use to enforce debts. There is no court hearing. Instead, the creditor presents a list of names and certifies that the legislative requirements necessary to use the process have been met. Currently, creditors using summary warrant can only enforce debts using arrestment, earnings arrestment or attachment.

Time order
A request to the court for more time to pay a credit agreement. Clients can only apply for a time order if their credit agreement is regulated by the Consumer Credit Act 1974.

Time to pay direction
Can be used by the client to ask the court (or tribunal) for an extension of time to pay a debt owed. It is applied for before a decree or decision is awarded.

Time to pay order
Similar to a time to pay direction (above), but it applies post-decree.

Trigger figures
Spending guidelines set by the Common Financial Tool. They represent levels of expenditure among households in the bottom quintile of the income distribution in the UK.

Trustee
A person who administers a bankruptcy or trust deed. In bankruptcy, a trustee can be the Accountant in Bankruptcy or a private insolvency practitioner. In trust deeds, the trustee must be an insolvency practitioner.

Trustee discharge
The date the trustee is discharged from liability (other than from fraud) after finalising the administration of the insolvent estate.

Appendix 1: Glossary

Vest (seised)
A person is seised or vested in property when it becomes that person's property by legal right or authority. For example, when a client is sequestrated, their property 'vests' with their trustee.

Warrant
A formal, written authority by the court to cite a person to appear before it or authorising certain actions such as searching premises or evicting occupiers. It is also used to signify a document evidencing a right of some kind – eg, in a title to heritable property.

Writ
The document that usually initiates and sets out the details of the claim and legal remedies sought in ordinary civil actions in the sheriff court.

Appendix 2
Useful organisations

Trade bodies

Consumer Credit Trade Association
Tel: 01274 714 959
Email: info@ccta.co.uk
ccta.co.uk

Credit Services Association
Tel: 0191 217 0775
Email: info@csa-uk.com
csa-uk.com

Energy UK
Tel: 020 7930 9390
energy-uk.org.uk

Finance and Leasing Association
Tel: 020 7836 6511
Email: info@fla.org.uk
fla.org.uk

Insolvency Practitioners Association
Tel: 020 8152 4980
insolvency-practitioners.org.uk

Lending Standards Board
Tel: 020 7012 0085
Email: contactus@lstdb.co.uk
lendingstandardsboard.org.uk

UK Finance
ukfinance.org.uk

Ombudsmen and regulatory bodies

Accountant in Bankruptcy
Tel: 0300 200 2600
Email: aib@aib.gov.uk
aib.gov.uk

The Adjudicator's Office
Tel: 0300 057 1111
gov.uk/government/organisations/the-adjudicator-s-office

Financial Conduct Authority
Tel: 020 7066 1000
Consumer helpline: 0800 111 6768/0300 500 8082
Firms helpline: 0300 500 0597
fca.org.uk

Financial Ombudsman Service
Tel: 0800 023 4567/0300 123 9123
Email: complaint.info@financial-ombudsman.org.uk
financial-ombudsman.org.uk

Information Commissioner's Office
Tel: 0303 123 1113
ico.org.uk

Ofgem (Office of Gas and Electricity Markets)
Tel: 020 7901 7000
ofgem.gov.uk

Appendix 2: Useful organisations

Energy Ombudsman
Tel: 0330 440 1624
enquiry@energyombudsman.org
energyombudsman.org

Organisations giving advice or representing advice networks

AdviceUK
A membership organisation for advice centres.
adviceuk.org.uk

Business Debtline
Tel: 0800 197 6026
Webchat: businessdebtline.org
businessdebtline.org

Citizens Advice Scotland
Helpline: 0800 028 1456
cas.org.uk

CPAG in Scotland
Advice line (for advisers only): 0141 552 0552
cpag.org.uk/scotland

Law Centres Network
Tel: 020 3637 1330
lawcentres.org.uk

MATRICS Consultancy
Tel: 0845 123 2326
Email: consultancy@matrics.org.uk

Money and Pensions Service
Advice line: 020 7943 0500
MoneyHelper advice line: 0800 138 7777
Email: contact@maps.org.uk
moneyandpensionsservice.org.uk

Money Advice Scotland
Email: info@moneyadvicescotland.org.uk
moneyadvicescotland.org.uk

Money Advice Trust
Advice line: 020 7489 7790
contactus@moneyadvicetrust.org
moneyadvicetrust.org

National Debtline
Tel: 0808 808 4000
Webchat: nationaldebtline.org/get-help
nationaldebtline.org

Shelter Scotland
Helpline: 0808 800 4444
Webchat: scotland.shelter.org.uk/about_us/contact_us/online_chat
scotland.shelter.org.uk

Student Awards Agency Scotland
Tel: 0300 555 0505
Webchat: saas.gov.uk/contact-us
www.saas.gov.uk

TaxAid
Tel (advisers): 0300 330 5477
Helpline (clients): 0345 120 3779
Email: help@taxaid.org.uk
taxaid.org.uk

Appendix 3

Statement of Undertaking and Statement of Truth

When making an application for a Minimal Asset Process or a Full Administration Bankruptcy, the client must sign a Statement of Undertaking and a Statement of Truth to confirm they have understood the process and their legal obiligations.

The client and adviser may complete the Statement of Truth, Statement of Undertaking and Certificate for Sequestration electronically as long as an averring statement is provided by the client. This statement must include the client's full name, address and date of birth as well as a short statement giving the adviser authorisation to submit an application on their behalf.

Statement of Undertaking
A statement of undertakings confirms the following:
I confirm that:
1. I have received money advice from the money adviser detailed in the money advice declaration section of this form. I agree to them acting on my behalf throughout the bankruptcy application process.
2. I have made a full disclosure of all assets which I owned or in which I had an interest in on my bankruptcy application date.
3. I will notify my trustee if I inherit, win or otherwise acquire any further assets during the period of 4 years after my bankruptcy award date.
4. I will immediately inform my trustee of any change of address or change in my financial circumstances during the period of 4 years after the date of bankruptcy.
5. I understand that I have a legal obligation to co-operate with my trustee and to provide any financial information or documents which may be required.
6. I understand that until I am discharged I may not, either alone or jointly with another person, obtain credit (which includes where goods are hired to me under a hire purchase agreement or agreed to be sold to me under a conditional sale agreement) either: (a) of £2000 or more; or (b) of any amount, where, at the time of obtaining credit, I have debts amounting to

Appendix 3: Statement of Undertaking and Statement of Truth

£1000 or more without informing the person from whom I obtain it of my bankruptcy

7. I understand that, until I am discharged I am subject to certain restrictions on the appointments I may take up or offices I may hold, including that I may not be a member of parliament or a justice of the peace.

8. I understand that until I am discharged I may not act as a director of a limited company or be involved directly or indirectly in the promotion, formation or management of a limited company without the leave of the court.

9. I understand that after 12 months from my bankruptcy award date (or normally after 6 months for Minimal Asset Process (MAP) cases) the Accountant in Bankruptcy may discharge me and that my discharge may be dependent on my compliance with this statement of undertakings.

10. I understand that I may be required by my trustee to undergo financial education and that my discharge may be dependent on completion of this financial education.

11. I understand that any assets which vested in my trustee on my bankruptcy award date, and which have not been sold, realised or ingathered by my trustee, will continue to vest in my trustee notwithstanding my discharge.

12. I understand that any assets which were acquired by me during the period of 4 years after my bankruptcy award date and which would have vested in my trustee if they had been part of my estate on my bankruptcy award date will vest in my trustee and that any such assets which have not been sold, realised or ingathered by my trustee, will continue to vest in my trustee notwithstanding my discharge.

13. I understand that if my bankruptcy is converted from MAP to Full Administration my discharge may not be granted until the total Full Administration bankruptcy application fee is paid. Statement of Undertakings

14. I understand that my circumstances will be assessed for the purpose of a client contribution order and that my discharge may be dependent on compliance with that order. I understand that my on-going liabilities, e.g. utility payments, may not be included in the sequestration and I may still have a duty to pay them.

Appendix 3: Statement of Undertaking and Statement of Truth

The Statement of Truth

I, _____(insert name) agree to be made bankrupt, if I meet the bankruptcy criteria as defined in the Bankruptcy (Scotland) Act 2016, and certify that the information I have supplied in this application form is true, complete and accurate to the best of my knowledge and belief.

I understand that by becoming bankrupt, I may be required to make regular contributions from my income if I am financially able to do so and that my assets may be sold to repay my debts.

I have read and understood the warning below. Note for completion – If you are signing as executor, or entitled to be appointed as executor, on the estate of a deceased client, you are agreeing and certifying in relation to the estate of the deceased client being made bankrupt.

In relation to the warning below, the reference to bankruptcy restrictions does not apply.

Signature _____

Date _____

Appendix 4
Abbreviations used in the notes

Art(s)	Article(s)
CA	Court of Appeal
Ch	Chapter
Civ Comm	Civil Division Commercial Court
EWHC	England and Wales High Court
FCA	Financial Conduct Authority
HLR	Housing Law Reports
para(s)	paragraph(s)
QB	Queen's Bench Reports
r(r)	rule(s)
reg(s)	regulation(s)
s(s)	section(s)
Sch(s)	Schedule(s)
TC	tax case
UKHL	United Kingdom House of Lords

Acts of Parliament

B(S)A 2016	Bankruptcy (Scotland) Act 2016
BD(S)A 2007	Bankruptcy and Diligence etc. (Scotland) Act 2007
BD(S)A 2024	Bankruptcy and Diligence (Scotland) Act 2024
CCA 1974	Consumer Credit Act 1974
CCA 2006	Consumer Credit Act 2006
COA 1979	Charging Orders Act 1979
CFR(S)A 1970	Conveyancing and Feudal Reform (Scotland) Act 1970
CMOPA 2008	Child Maintenance and Other Payments Act 2008

Appendix 4: Abbreviations used in the notes

CP(S)A 1995	Criminal Procedure (Scotland) Act 1995
CSA 1991	Child Support Act 1991
D(S)A 1987	Debtors (Scotland) Act 1987
DAA(S)A 2002	Debt Arrangement and Attachment (Scotland) Act 2002
H(S)A 1988	Housing (Scotland) Act 1988
H(S)A 2001	Housing (Scotland) Act 2001
LGFA 1992	Local Government Finance Act 1992
PH(T)(S)A 2016	Private Housing (Tenancies) (Scotland) Act 2016
PL(S) Act 1973	Prescription and Limitation (Scotland) Act 1973
PSA 2018	Prescription (Scotland) Act 2018

Regulations and other statutory instruments

AoS(DAA(S)) 2002	Act of Sederunt (Debt Arrangement and Attachment (Scotland) Act 2002) 2002 SSI No.560
AoS(MASO) Rules	Act of Sederunt (Messengers-at-Arms and Sheriff Officers Rules) 1991 SSI No.1397
AoS(SCB) Rules	Act of Sederunt (Sheriff Court Bankruptcy Rules) 2016 SSI No.313
B(S) Regs	The Bankruptcy (Scotland) Regulations 2016 SSI No.397
B(CS)(S) Regs	The Bankruptcy (Certificate for Sequestration) (Scotland) Regulations 2010 SSI No.397
BF(S) Regs	The Bankruptcy Fees (Scotland) Regulations 2018 SSI No.127
CFT(S) Regs	The Common Financial Tool etc. (Scotland) Regulations 2014 SSI No.290
CS(C&E) Regs	The Child Support (Collection and Enforcement) Regulations 1992 No.1989
CS(MOC&NCR) Regs	The Child Support (Meaning of Child and New Calculation Rules) (Consequential and Miscellaneous Amendment) Regulations 2012 No.2785
CT(ED)(S)O	The Council Tax (Exempt Dwellings) (Scotland) Order 1997 SSI No.728
DaE(V)(S) Regs	The Diligence against Earnings (Variation) (Scotland) Regulations 2023 SSI No.27

Appendix 4: Abbreviations used in the notes

DAS(IFP)(S) Regs	The Debt Arrangement Scheme (Interest, Fees, Penalties and other charges) (Scotland) Regulations 2011 SSI No.238
DAS(S) Regs	The Debt Arrangement Scheme (Scotland) Regulations 2011 SSI No.141
F(DIS) Regs	Fines (Deductions from Income Support) Regulations 1992 No.2182
FTTSHPC(P) Regs	The First-tier Tribunal for Scotland Housing and Property Chamber (Procedure) Regulations 2017 SSI No.328
OCR	Act of Sederunt (Sheriff Court Ordinary Cause Rules) 1993 SSI No.1956
SPR	Act of Sederunt (Simple Procedure) 2016 SSI No.200
SS(C&P) Regs	The Social Security (Claims and Payments) Regulations 1987 No.1968
SS(OR) Regs	The Social Security (Overpayments and Recovery) Regulations 2013 No.384
Summary Cause Rules	Act of Sederunt (Summary Cause Rules) 2002 SSI No.132
UC,PIP,JSA&ESA(C&P) Regs	The Universal Credit, Personal Independence Payment, Jobseeker's Allowance and Employment and Support Allowance (Claims and Payments) Regulations 2013 No.380

Other information

CFT guidance	*Notes for Guidance – Common Financial Tool*
CONC	*Consumer Credit Sourcebook*
PERG	*Perimeter Guidance Manual*
MCOB	*Mortgages and Home Finance: conduct of business sourcebook*
SLC	Standard licence conditions for gas and electricity

Index

How to use this Index

Entries against the bold headings direct you to the general information on the subject, or where the subject is covered most fully. Sub-entries are listed alphabetically and direct you to specific aspects of the subject.

A
adjudication for debt 298
Adjudicator's Office 26
adoption payments
   statutory adoption pay 435
   statutory shared parental pay 436
adult disability payment 422
advice agencies
   accreditation 2
   Citizens Advice accreditation 5
alcohol
   capacity to make a contract 51
aliment 72
   enforcement 73
alternative dispute resolution 212
ancillary order 106
arrears notices
   regulated credit agreements 103
arrest warrant
   unpaid fines
      emergency action 47
assured tenants 241
attachment 271
   challenging an attachment 274
   enforcement 272
   forms 279
attendance allowance 423
auctions
   attached goods 274

B
bank arrestment 284
   protected minimum balance 286
   striking down a bank arrestment 291
   unduly harsh 290

bankruptcy 115, 186
   acquirenda 192
   assets 188, 192
   award by AiB 199
   bank accounts 188
   business debt 371
   child support 187
   complaints 196
   creditor petitions for bankruptcy 165
   criminal injuries compensation 188
   critical illness 188
   death of debtor 415
   discharge 195
   financial education course 192
   Full Administration Bankruptcy 156
   gratuitous alienation 191
   home 190
      rented 191
   income 187
   insurance policies 189
   interest on debts 193
   Minimal Asset Process 150
   pensions 187
   recall 193
   redundancy 187
   sale of vehicle 190
   statutory moratorium on diligence 199
   undervalue transactions 191
   unfair preference 191
bankruptcy restrictions order 193
banks
   bank arrestment 284
benefits
   deductions 419
   maximising income 62
   overpayments 419

prescription period 334
recovery of overpayments 303
treatment as income 120, 123
bereavement support payment 424
Best Start food 424
Best Start grants 424
budgeting advice 33
essential items 34
financial contributions from family members 35
budgeting loans 434
bursaries
treatment as income 121
business debt 346
bankruptcy 371
checklist 373
rent arrears 366
stages of debt advice 354
creating trust 355
financial statement 361
listing business income and expenditure 358
listing creditors 355
maximising income 360
minimising debts 355
non-priority debts 371
priority debts 362
types of small business 348
co-operative 354
franchise 354
limited company 352
limited liability partnership 354
partnership 350
sole trader 348
VAT arrears 367
Business Debt Arrangement Scheme 372
Business Debtline 348
business expenses 359

C

cable television
essential expenditure 35
cancellation rights
regulated credit agreement 100
capital repayment mortgage 251
carer support payment 425
carer's allowance 425

carers
carer support payment 425
carer's allowance 425
case recording 13
catalogues
prescription period 331
Certificate for Sequestration 197
Full Administration Bankruptcy 159
Minimal Asset Process bankruptcy 152
charities 64, 440
child benefit 426
child disability payment 426
child support payments 68
deductions from benefits 318
deductions from earnings order 308
enforcement 69, 70
priority debts 53
qualifying child 68
child tax credit 427
children
Best Start food 424
Best Start grants 424
child benefit 426
child disability payment 426
child tax credit 427
dependent children 119
disability living allowance 428
guardian's allowance 429
liability for debts 50
Scottish child payment 433
Civil Online 213
civil partnerships
bereavement support payment 424
cohabiting partners
bereavement support payment 424
co-operatives 354
codes of practice
creditors 33
fuel suppliers 73
coerced debt 406
common financial statement 58
Common Financial Tool 61, 116
expenditure 125
household income and expenditure 117
income 119
trigger figure categories 128
who can access the CFT 61

485

compensation for damages 441
conjoined arrestment order 281
consumer credit 92
    exempt agreements 95
    regulated agreements 94
Consumer Credit Act 1974 93
Consumer Credit Sourcebook 29
consumer protection
    regulatory bodies 25
contracts
    capacity to make a contract 382
    pre-contract information 97
    unfair relationship 101
cooling-off period
    regulated credit agreement 100
council tax 79
    arrears 85
        deductions from benefits 317
        prescription period 335
        summary warrant 230
    carers 82
    Common Financial Tool 127
    disability 83
    empty properties 84
    enforcement 86
    exempt properties 81
    liability 80
        joint and several liability 80
    priority debts 53
    severe mental impairment 83
    single person discount 82
    students 82, 462
    third-party deductions 86
    valuation band 85
council tax reduction scheme 84, 441
    part-time students 462
court fines 448
    alternatives to prosecution 449
    checklist 452
    deductions from benefits 317
    enforcement orders 450
    exempt from insolvency solutions 452
    fines issued after prosecution 450
    priority debts 53
    referred back to court 452
courts
    liaison groups 27
    monitoring local courts 27

    representation by debt advisers 21
    user groups 27
credit agreements
    not regulated 95
    regulated 94
credit authorisation 112
credit cards
    prescription period 331
    section 75 credit card protection 107
credit reference agencies 108
    accounts recorded as in default 110
    correcting information held 111
    information collected 108
    obtaining file details 110
credit repair companies 111
credit scoring 108
credit unions 36
creditors
    codes of practice 33
    collecting information 52
    consent required for a Debt Arrangement Scheme 137
    credit scoring 108
    creditor's petition 165
        application to the court 166
        checklist 169
        court hearing 167
        recall 167
    death of debtor 415
    Debt Arrangement Scheme 140
    debt collection
        dealing with harassment 28
    guidance on mental health issues 384
    harassment 28
    listing creditors 51
    monitoring practices 11
    negotiating with creditors 17
    refusal to deal with advisers 18
    statutory demand 168
    trust deed 173
criminal offences
    harassment 28
Crown Office and Procurator Fiscal Service 448
current maintenance arrestment 281

D

death
 bereavement support payment 424
 checklist 416
 dealing with an estate after death 414
 liability for debts 50, 412
 statutory parental bereavement pay 436

debt
 listing debts 52

debt advice 1
 administrative systems 12
 advice system 10
 business debt 346
 case files 13
 client authorisation 11
 client's best interests 7
 closing cases 14
 correspondence 13
 Debt and Mental Health Evidence Form 380
 financial statement 34
 good practice 2
 harassment 28
 initial interview 11, 39
 letter writing framework 20
 mental health 9, 375
 national standards 2
 prescription periods 336
 referrals 12, 48
 reviews 13
 stages of debt advice 11, 39
  business debt 354
  checking liability 49
  emergencies 45
  financial statement 57
  listing creditors 51
  maximising income 62, 418, 420
 Tackling Problem Debt Group 5
 triage interview 12

debt adviser
 attitudes to debt 8
 budgeting advice 33
 business debt 347
 client with mental health issues 9
 court representation 21
 creating trust 40
 dealing with harassment 28
 Debt Arrangement Scheme 131
 economic abuse 402
 emergencies 45
 hierarchy of debts following a death 415
 information from client 41
 interviewing 16
 involving the client 9
 knowledge of law of procedures 8
 letter writing 18
 mental health issues 378
 negotiating 17
 representing in sheriff court 23
 role and functions 131
 social policy work 8, 25
 student debt 454
 tools to support vulnerable clients 396
 vulnerable clients 390

Debt Arrangement Scheme 129
 administration process 140
 aliment arrears 73
 application process 133, 135, 137
 application rejected 138
 child support arrears 71
 completion 149
 composition 149
 DAS administrator 130
 death 415
 eligibility 134
 mortgage arrears 266
 private sector rent arrears 249
 procedure following approval of DAS 138
 revocation 146
 variation 141

debt collection
 breach of guidance 33
 Consumer Credit Sourcebook 29
 creditors' codes of practice 33
 harassment 28

debt management companies 1
debt packager referral fees 183
debt payment programme
 Debt Arrangement Scheme 129

Debtor Contribution Order 197
 Full Administration Bankruptcy 162
 Minimal Asset Process bankruptcy 155

Index

debts not covered by Consumer Credit Act – expenditure

debts not covered by Consumer Credit Act 95
deduction from earnings order
    child support payments 69, 308
    trust deed payments 177
deductions from benefits 313, 419
    amounts 315
    bankruptcy 318
    consent 318
    Debt Arrangement Scheme 319
    deductions from benefits order 452
    more than one deduction 314
    priority order of deductions 315
default notice
    regulated credit agreements 104
diligence 271
    adjudication for debt 298
    attachment 271
    bank arrestment 284
    court procedures 297
    earnings arrestment 281
    exceptional attachment 276
    inhibition in execution 295
    money attachment 292
    moratorium on diligence 134, 199
    non-diligence debt recovery 303
    on the dependence 297
    summary diligence 299
diligence stopper 322
direct earnings attachment 303
    rate of deductions 305
disability
    adult disability payment 422
    assistance funds 445
    attendance allowance 423
    child disability payment 426
    disability living allowance 428
    employment and support allowance 428
    industrial injuries benefits 432
    personal independence payment 433
discretionary housing payments 441
dismissal
    pay in lieu of notice 444
domestic abuse 399
drugs
    capacity to make a contract 51

E

earnings
    direct earnings attachment 303
    evidence of earnings 120
earnings arrestment 281, 451
    challenging an earnings arrestment 283
    schedule 282
economic abuse 399
    coerced debt 406
    definition 399
    identifying economic abuse 401
    role of adviser 402
emergency action
    fuel disconnection 46
    overview 48
    possession of home 47
    preventing goods being taken 46
employment and support allowance 428
    deductions from benefit 313
        maximum deductions 316
enforcement action
    commercial rent arrears 366
    enforcement orders 450
enforcement orders 450
equal pay 442
European Commission Consumer Credit Directive 2008 93
eviction
    Debt Arrangement Scheme 249
    enforcement by sheriff officers 343
    private residential tenancies 242
    private sector tenants 240, 248
    short-assured and assured tenancies
        assured tenancies 241
        grounds for eviction 241
        short-assured tenancies 241
    social housing 234
        notice of proceedings 235
        pre-action requirements 234
exceptional attachment 276
    challenging an exceptional attachment 276
    enforcement 277
    forms 279
executor 413
expenditure
    business expenses 359
    challenging expenditure 66

Common Financial Tool 125
contingency allowance 129
essential expenditure 126
luxury items 34, 129
reducing expenditure 65

F
faulty goods/services 50
financial abuse 393, 400
    Financial Abuse Code of Practice 410
financial capability 36, 392
Financial Conduct Authority 25
    consumer credit activities 112
    Consumer Credit Sourcebook 29
    credit authorisation 112
    debt collection guidance 29
    guidance for advisers 7
    guidance for lenders 254
    mental capacity 384
financial inclusion 36
Financial Ombudsman Service 26, 112
    mortgage arrears 268
Financial Services Compensation Scheme 113
financial statement 34
    business debt 361
    common financial statement 58
        accessing common financial statement 58
        completing common financial statement 58
        local and UK government creditors 60
        trigger figures 60
    standard financial statement 62
fines enforcement officers 450
First-tier Tribunal for Scotland (Housing and Property Chamber) 240
    appeals 248
    application to tribunal 243
    hearings 246
    lay representatives 244
    tribunal options 245
fiscal fines 449
fixed penalty notices 449
fixed-rate mortgage 251
food banks 442
franchises 354

free school meals 442
fuel charges 73
    arrears 75
        deductions from benefits 317
    backbilling 76
    Common Financial Tool 126
    disconnection
        emergency action 46
    estimated bills 75
    extra support 78
    liability
        electricity 74
        gas 74
    limitation period 76
    prepayment meters 77
    priority debts 53
    priority services register 78
    reducing expenditure 65
    smart meters 77
    support and advice 76, 78
    Warm Home Discount 76, 447
Full Administration Bankruptcy 156
    apparent insolvency 158
    application 159, 160
    checklist 164
    date of sequestration 164
    duration of bankruptcy 163
    fees 160
    included and excluded debts 160
    non-payment 164
    qualifying criteria 157
    Statement of Truth 162
    Statement of Undertaking 162
funeral support payment 429

G
gambling
    gambling-related vulnerability 389
guarantee payments 442
guardian's allowance 429

H
harassment 28
hardship funds
    trade unions 447
health benefits 429
Help to Save 443

Index

hire purchase agreements
- Common Financial Tool 127
- personal contract purchases 104
- preventing repossession 46
- voluntary termination 104

Homeowners' Support Fund 266

housekeeping costs
- listing expenditure 128

housing 234
- discretionary housing payment 441
- equity in the home 124
- housing benefit 430
- private rented sector 240
- social housing 234

housing benefit 430

I

income 62
- benefits 120, 123
- business 359
- calculating income 119
- Common Financial Tool 119

income support 431
- deductions from benefit 313
- maximum deductions 316

income tax
- allowances 63, 446
- arrears 369
- summary warrant 230
- rebate 63, 446
- reliefs 446
- self-employment 363

indemnity insurance 252
industrial diseases/accidents 432
industrial injuries benefits 432
inhibition 295
- checklist 296

insolvency
- creditor's petition 165
- Full Administration Bankruptcy 158
- Minimal Asset Process 150
- private sector rent arrears 249

insurance
- surrender value of policies 124

interest-only mortgage 251
interviewing skills 16, 379

J

jobseeker's allowance 432
- deductions from benefit 313
- maximum deductions 316

joint and several liability
- council tax 80

L

landlords
- landlord hypothec 366

lay representation 22
- techniques for sheriff court representation 23
- time to pay directions 324
- time to pay orders 327

lay-offs
- guarantee payments 442

leases
- business equipment 367
- business premises 366

legally competent 382
letter writing 18
liability for debts 49
- acknowledgement of debt 50
- capacity to make a contract 50
- children and young people 50
- co-operatives 354
- death 50, 412
- electricity charges 74
- faulty goods/services 50
- franchises 354
- gas charges 74
- joint and several liability 49
- limited liability partnerships 354
- sole trader 348
- undue influence 51
- unfair relationship 101

liability order
- child support payments 70

limitation periods 330
- fuel charges 76

limited company 352
limited liability partnerships 354
loans
- prescription period 331

local authority
- councillors 26

long negative prescription 333
low income
 health benefits 430
lump sums
 trade unions 447
luxury items 34

M
maintenance payments 72
 enforcement 73
 priority debts 53
 treatment as income 123
 treatment of contributions 123
marriage
 bereavement support payment 424
maternity allowance 433
maternity benefits
 maternity allowance 433
 statutory maternity pay 435
 statutory shared parental pay 436
MATRICS project 6
maximising income 62, 418
 benefits and tax credits 62, 420
 businesses 360
 charities 64, 440
 child maintenance 64, 440
 compensation for damages 64, 441
 council tax reduction 64, 441
 disability/illness assistance funds 445
 discretionary housing payment 441
 equal pay 442
 food banks 65, 442
 free school lunches 442
 guarantee payments 442
 income tax
  allowances 63, 446
  rebate 63, 446
  reliefs 446
 minimum wage 444
 notice pay 444
 pensions 65, 444
 redundancy payments 445
 school clothing 445
 school transport 445
 Scottish Welfare Fund 443
 social work 445
 trade unions 64, 447
 war pensions 444
 Warm Home Discount 447

McKenzie friend 22
media
 social policy work 28
Member of Parliament 26
Member of the Scottish Parliament 26
mental capacity 389
 adults with incapacity 383
 FCA guidance 384
mental health 375
 advising clients 9, 378
 capacity to make a contract 51
 conditions 376
 Debt and Mental Health Evidence Form 380
 guidance for creditors 384
 interview techniques 379
 sensitive personal data 380
messengers-at-arms 340
meters
 fuel
  prepayment meters 77
  smart meters 77
Minimal Asset Process bankruptcy 150
 application 153, 154
 date of sequestration 156
 duration of bankruptcy 156
 fees 153
 included and excluded debts 153
 qualifying criteria 152
 Statement of Truth 155
 Statement of Undertaking 155
minimising debts
 business debt 355
minimum wage 444
mobile phones
 essential expenditure 35
money attachment 292
 checklist 295
money claims in the sheriff court 208
 ordinary cause procedure 220
 simple procedure 208
MoneyHelper 36
Mortgage Charter 255, 267
mortgage interest loans 252, 443
mortgages 250
 arrears 263
 capital repayment mortgages 251
 capitalising arrears 265
 changing to cheaper mortgage 253

Index
mortgages – pensions

checklist 268
complaints 268
consumer protection 258
Debt Arrangement Scheme 266
fixed-rate mortgages 251
Homeowners' Support Fund 266
indemnity guarantee 252
insolvency 266
interest-only mortgages 251, 263
    FCA guidance 257
loans for mortgage interest 252
mortgage prisoners 253
payment holiday 265
post-pandemic support 254
priority debts 53, 250
reduced payments 265
regulated contracts 253
repossession process 260
shared ownership mortgages 251
Sharia-compliant mortgages 252
shortfall on sale 267
    indemnity insurance 252
    prescription period 335
standard security 250
standard variable rate mortgages 251
tailored support 254
time order 267
tracker mortgages 251
voluntary surrender 266
Mortgages and Home Finance: conduct of business sourcebook 258

N
national insurance contributions
    self-employment 363
negotiation 17
non-dependants
    contribution to budget 35, 118
non-priority debts 53, 56
    business debt 371
    freezing interest 56
    general approach 56
    pro-rata payments 57
    token payments 56
notice
    pay in lieu of notice 444

O
occupational pension 444
Ofcom 25
Ofgem 25
Ofwat 25
older people
    age-related vulnerability 389
Ombudsman Services: Energy 27
Ombudsmen 26
ordinary cause procedure 220
    appeals 228
    decisions 226
    fees 221
    going to court 225
    initial writ 221
    lay representation 224
    options hearing 225
    post decree 228
    raising an action 220
    serving an initial writ 222
    time to pay order 229
overdrafts
    prescription period 331
    student debt 463
overpayments
    benefits 419
        prescription period 333, 334
    Scottish benefits
        prescription period 331

P
partnerships 350
    limited liability partnerships 354
paternity payments
    statutory paternity pay 436
    statutory shared parental pay 436
pay in lieu of notice 444
    treatment as income 122
payday loans
    prescription period 331
pension credit 433
    deductions from benefit 313
        maximum deductions 316
pensions
    occupational pensions 444
    private pensions 444
    state retirement pension 434
    treatment as income 121
    treatment of contributions 121

Index
personal independence payment – self-employment

personal independence payment 433
personal injury claims 441
possession proceedings
   mortgage arrears 260
   private sector tenants 240
      notice of proceedings 242
      notice to quit 242
      section 11 notice 242
   social housing 234
      decree for possession 238
      notice of proceedings 235
prescription periods 330
   20-year prescription period 333
   benefit overpayments 334
   council tax arrears 335
   court decree/judgment 335
   debt advice 336
   five-year prescription period 331
   mortgage shortfall 335
   student loans 335
priority debts 53
   business debt 362
   deciding on priorities 55
   definition 53
   mortgage arrears 250
   negotiations 55
   sanctions for non-payment 54
private residential tenancies 242
   notice to leave 243
private sector tenants 240
   eviction and possession orders 240
protected minimum balance 286

R
redundancy 445
   treatment as income 122
regulated credit agreements 94
   arrears notices 103
   cancellation 100
      distance contracts 101
   credit card protection 107
   default notices 104
   early settlement 108
   exempt agreements 95
   information that must be in the agreement 99
   non-prescribed terms 99

   pre-contract information 97
   prescribed terms 99
   section 75 credit card protection 107
   time orders 105
   unfair relationship 101
   withdrawal from agreement 100
regulatory bodies
   Financial Conduct Authority 25
   Ofcom 25
   Ofgem 25
   Ofwat 25
rent
   arrears
      commercial properties 366
      deductions from benefits 317
      emergency action 47
      pre-action protocol 241, 243
      prescription period 331
      priority debts 53
      private sector housing 240
      social housing sector 234
   discretionary housing payment 441
representation in court 21
retirement
   pension credit 433
   state retirement pension 434

S
safeguarding 395
   adults with incapacity 383
satellite television
   essential expenditure 35
Scottish child payment 433
Scottish Public Services Ombudsman 26
Scottish Welfare Fund 443
self-employment
   business debt 346
   Business Debt Arrangement Scheme 373
   business debt solutions 372
   checklist 373
   Common Financial Tool 120
   financial statement 361
   national insurance contributions 364
   tax arrears 363, 369
   tax reliefs 446
   VAT 365

Index
sequestration – student financial support

sequestration
  Common Financial Tool 117
  date of sequestration
    Full Administration Bankruptcy 164
    Minimal Asses Process 156
  sequestration petition 174
shared ownership mortgages 251
Sharia-compliant mortgages 252
sheriff courts
  court personnel 21
  court procedure 23
  ordinary cause 220
  representation by debt advisers 21
  simple procedure 208
  summary warrant 230
  user groups 27
sheriff officers 341
  complaints 344
  emergency action 46
  exceptional attachment 343
  identification 342
  powers 341
    enforce debts from other parts of UK 344
    entry 342
    eviction 343
    removing goods for sale 343
short negative prescription 331
short-assured tenancies 241
sickness
  employment and support allowance 428
  industrial injuries benefits 432
  statutory sick pay 437
simple procedure 208
  alternative dispute resolution 212
  appeals 217
  changes to simple procedure rules and forms 218
  Civil Online 213
  claim form 211
  decision 216
  fees 211
  filing and serving documents 210
  going to court 216
  lay representation 216
  orders 214
  pause and restart 215
  procedures 213
  provisional measures 297
  provisional orders 209
  raising an action 209
  timetable 210
social fund 434
social housing
  decree for possession 238
  eviction for rent arrears 234
  rent arrears 234
  summary cause process 236
social policy 8, 25
sole trader 348
solicitors
  complaints 27
standard security 250
standard variable rate mortgages 251
state retirement pension 434
statutory adoption pay 435
statutory demand
  response 168
statutory maternity pay 435
statutory moratorium
  application 200
  moratorium on diligence 168, 199
  period of moratorium 201
  ready reckoner 202
  summary warrant 232
statutory parental bereavement pay 436
statutory paternity pay 436
statutory shared parental pay 436
statutory sick pay 437
store cards
  prescription period 331
student debt 454
  advising students 454
  bankruptcy 153
  bursaries 458
  housing costs 461
  overdrafts 463
  tuition fees 455
student financial support
  bursaries 458
    care-experienced students' bursary 460
    childcare fund 460
    dependants' grant 460
    disabled students' allowance 459
    estranged students' bursary 459

higher education discretionary fund 461
independent students' bursary 459
lone parents' grant 461
paramedic, nursing and midwifery student bursaries 461
summer accommodation grant 460
young students' bursary 459
housing costs 461
student loans 455
student loans 455
amount 456
cancellation 457
credit rating 458
non-payment of repayment 458
prescription period 335
refund of overpaid student loan 458
repayment 456
suicidal ideation 392
summary cause process
social housing summonses 236
summary diligence 299
checklist 301
summary sheriff 208
summary warrant 230
court process 231
dealing with a summary warrant 231
Debt Arrangement Scheme 232
pre-court procedures 230
prescription period 333
recovery process 231
statutory moratorium 232
time to pay order 232
Surviving Economic Abuse 403

T
Tackling Problem Debt Group 5
telephones
essential expenditure 35
listing expenditure 128
third-party payments
deductions from benefits 313
trust deeds 178
time order 105
advantages 106
disadvantages 106

time to pay directions 321
application 323
bankruptcy 324
checklist 324
interest 324
time to pay orders 229, 325
application 326
checklist 329
court hearing 326
interest 328
tracker mortgage 251
trade associations 25
transport costs
listing expenditure 128
trust deeds 169
appointing a trustee 180
checklist 186
complaints 186
contents 180
deductions from earnings 177
duration of trust deed 175
family home 178
fees 171
how to take on a trust deed 171
included and excluded debts 171
non-payment 177
non-performing trust deeds 181
procedures 172
protected trust deeds 172, 174
protocol 183
registration 172
regular contributions 176
third-party payments 178
trustee refuses to discharge debtor 184
unprotected trust deeds 175
who can sign a trust deed 170
trustee in trust deed 180
tuition fees 455
TV licence
priority debts 53

U
undue influence
coerced debt 409
unduly harsh 290
unemployment
jobseeker's allowance 432
unfair relationships 101
coerced debts 408

495

Index
universal credit – young people

universal credit 437
    deductions from benefit 313
        maximum deductions 315
    students 461
unregulated credit agreements
    unfair relationship 101

V
VAT
    arrears 367
    self-employment 363
vehicles
    essential expenditure 35
    seizure of vehicle order 451
    valuation of a vehicle 124
vulnerable people 387
    advising vulnerable clients 390, 395
    creditors' policies 391
    defining vulnerability 387
    financial capability 392
    fuel bills 78
    special category data 390
    suicidal ideation 392

W
war pensions 444
Warm Home Discount 76, 447
water charges 87
    business debt 89
    complaints 89
    deductions from benefits 88, 318
    disconnection 89
    Priority Services Register 88
    summary warrant 89
    Water Direct scheme 318
winter fuel payments 434
work capability assessment 428, 439
working tax credit 439

Y
young people
    child benefit 426
    child tax credit 427